THE ROMANOV
ROYAL MARTYRS
WHAT SILENCE COULD NOT CONCEAL

AUTHORED BY
Saint John the Forerunner Monastery of Mesa Potamos, Cyprus.

RESEARCH COLLEAGUES
George Hawkins, BA, Dip. Tchg.: Romanov researcher and translator, New Zealand.
Helen Azar, MS, MLIS: Biochemist, historical researcher and Romanovs writer, Australia.
Helen Rappaport, BA Hons, D. Litt.: Writer, historian and Russianist, UK.
Nicholas B. A. Nicholson: Russian Arts Specialist, Romanov historian and author, USA.
Olga Shirnina, PhD: Translator, historical researcher, pictures colorist, Russia.
Paul Gilbert: Independent researcher on the life and reign of Nicholas II, Canada.
Pyotr Multatul, PhD: Author, journalist and historian, professor at the Moscow State Institute for Culture and Arts, Russia.
Rob Moshein: Administrator of Alexander Palace Time Machine website and Romanov researcher, USA.
Sophie Law, MA (Oxon): Russian Arts Specialist, Romanov researcher and author, UK.

TRANSLATION FROM THE ORIGINAL GREEK TEXT
Reverend George Lardas.

PRIMARY SOURCES TRANSLATIONS
Russian sources: Helen Azar, George Hawkins, Sophie Law, Rev. George Lardas.
French sources: Rob Moshein.

REDACTION OF TEXTS AND EDITING
Reverend Ignatius Green, M.Div., M.Th., Editor at St Vladimir's Seminary Press.

COVER DESIGN AND COLORIZATION OF BLACK & WHITE PHOTOGRAPHS
Olga Shirnina.

UNIFORM EXPERTS FOR COLORIZATION OF PHOTOGRAPHS
Andrey Malov-Gra: Historian, author, military costume expert.
Vladimir Vladimirovich Glazkov: Military historian and military costume expert.

PICTURES EDITING: Charalambos Iakovou, A&C Photokinisi Ltd, Cyprus.
PAGE LAYOUT: Maria Papaefstathiou.
IMAGE PROCESSING & PRODUCTION MANAGEMENT: Nikos Glykeas.
PUBLICATION COORDINATION: St John the Forerunner Monastery of Mesa Potamos.

Copyright © St John the Forerunner Monastery of Mesa Potamos, Cyprus 2020.
Second edition, ISBN: 978-9963-9517-7-2

EDITORIAL PRODUCTION
Stamoulis Publications Llc.
Averoff 2, Athens 104 33, Greece. Tel.: (+30) 210 5238305, Fax: (+30) 210 5238959.
E-mail: info@stamoulis.gr, Website: www.stamoulis.gr

Address all correspondence to: St John the Forerunner Monastery of Mesa Potamos,
P.O. Box 56873, 3310 Limassol, Cyprus. Email: mesapotamos@cytanet.com.cy

THE ROMANOV
ROYAL MARTYRS
WHAT SILENCE COULD NOT CONCEAL

MESA POTAMOS PUBLICATIONS
2019

PUBLICATION PHOTOGRAPHS

The present edition includes photographs from the Russian State Archives (ГА РФ), with special permission of the Archive, as well as numerous photographs from private collections to which the collectors granted the Monastery access. Photographs from the ГА РФ are specially marked with a superscription. Mesa Potamos Monastery thanks ГА РФ for kindly giving their necessary permission for the publication of these photographs.

CONTENTS

AUTHOR'S NOTE 11
TRANSLATOR'S NOTE 13
PROLOGUE 15
INTRODUCTION 17

PART I: In the Path of Love

CHAPTER 1 – LOVE WITHOUT BOUNDS

Nicholas Alexandrovich Romanov: The Early Years 23
Crown Prince 30
Brush With Death 35
Alix of Hesse: A Sorrowful Princess 39
'We Love Each Other' 45
Blessing from Above 48

CHAPTER 2 – AT THE HEIGHT OF GLORY

A New Life Begins through Death 59
Coronation: The Royal Sacrament 66
Portent of Death 76
Princesses in Heart 78
Portrait of a Tsar 92
The Love of God 99
The Orthodox Tsar, Patron of the Church 104

CHAPTER 3 – THE BEGINNING OF SORROWS

The War With Japan and Bloody Sunday 117
The Revolution of 1905 125
Peter Arkadievitch Stolypin 133
Tsarevich Alexis 134
Spala: At the Whiff of Death 143
Culmination of a Drama 146
Elisabeth Feodorovna: Revealing the Depths of a Noble Heart 153
A Brief Glimmer 169

CONTENTS

CHAPTER 4 – MARCH TO THE END

World War: The Great Heart of Russia Beats 171
The Revelation of a Magnificent Soul............................179
Angels of Mercy...183
'I Will Perish, But I Will Save Russia' 191
'We Will All Pray for You' 197
The Eve of a Nightmare 206
An Orthodox View 208
'In the New Year May the Clouds Disperse'......................210
'The Czar Himself Must Be Removed' 214
A Treasonous Countdown: The Myth of the "Bread Revolution" 221

PART II: In the Path of Blood

CHAPTER 5 – CAPTIVITY

The Palace Prison 247
Passion Week 251
Spiritual Respite...255
Kerensky and Nicholas: A Foreseen Encounter 257
Unwanted unto Death...263
An Historical Parenthesis.......................................271
Lenin: The Fateful Return 272
Unknown Destination 274
A Family in Exile...279
Forgotten by the World..284
Bolshevik Revolution 292
Royal Heart in Grace..294
Unexpected Developments 296
A Mysterious Journey..303

CHAPTER 6 – THE CHAPTER OF BLOOD

The House of Special Purpose....................................309
The Second Departure from Tobolsk...............................323
The New Inmates of Ekaterinburg 325
Faithful unto Death...327
The New Reality 329
Counterpoints 337

CONTENTS

Another Historical Parenthesis 342
The Game of Escape 343
A Final Countdown. 347
The Agonizing Wait 355
Eternal Present Continuous. 356
Martyrdom after Death 365
The Hour of Revelation 371
'Them That Honour Me I Will Honor' 375

PART III: In the Words of the Saints

Saint John of Kronstadt 379
Saint Macarius of Moscow 380
Saint Anatole of Optina 381
Saint Nektary of Optina 381
Saint Tikhon, Patriarch of Moscow. 382
Saint John Maximovitch 388

EPILOGUE. 393
APPENDIX: Russia's Czarina 399
ACKNOWLEDGMENTS 407
PHOTO-INSERT: Eternally Living Past 411
NOTES 469
BIBLIOGRAPHY 499

AUTHOR'S NOTE

In the work the reader will come across an abundance of quotes from the diaries and correspondence of the Royal Martyrs. Much of this material was originally written by the members of the Royal family in the English language, such as is the case of the correspondence between Nicholas and Alexandra and the letters from Grand Duchess Elisabeth to Nicholas included herein. We have not made any changes to the content of these texts, but have only corrected all spelling errors and edited the punctuation so as to render the reading of these texts easier. However, having left the texts in their original form, it is quite possible that in some points the reader may find it difficult to grasp the exact meaning of a phrase, since the English language was not the native one for any of the Royal Martyrs. Nevertheless, we trust that this very element helps in retaining the freshness and immediacy of the writing style of each member of the Royal family.

Finally, just as with every historical work which covers this particular period in the history of Russia, so likewise in this work we must address the known problem of the calendar change. In Russia the use of the New Calendar was officially adopted on 14 February 1918, while most of the rest of the world had already adopted it earlier. However, the members of the family of the Royal Martyrs continued to use the Old Calendar in entries to their diaries and in correspondence until the end of their lives. In some instances, they wrote both calendars dates. In the present work, to better chronicle the flow of events recorded here, we have observed the following principle: From the beginning of the events of the First World War and after, the New Calendar is used because world historical events are known by those dates. However, where excerpts from the diaries and correspondence of the Royal Martyrs are cited, both dates are recorded. A few isolated exceptions are indicated either in the text or in the notes.

TRANSLATOR'S NOTE

The present translation of this work from the Greek generally renders the Christian (given) names of royal, aristocratic, official and ecclesiastical persons by their commonly used English equivalents, or if such is lacking, according to the rules of transliteration from ancient classical history. Thus, Nicholas and Alexandra rather than Nikolai and Aleksandra, Theophan rather than Feofan. All other Russian names are transliterated, including patronymics and surnames, but not necessarily consistently, in line with common usage. Titles are capitalized when attached to names but are generally lower case in other circumstances.

All references to the Deity, both by name and by pronoun, are capitalized, as are also the names of holy days, divine services and other sacred references, generally according to common usage among Orthodox Christians in English.

Citations from the Scripture are from the Authorised (King James) Version, except where they differ from the Septuagint Greek Old Testament. Citations from the Psalms are from the Psalter According to the Seventy, an Orthodox translation. All liturgical texts are in British spelling to agree with the citations from Scripture.

However, all quotations (everything within quotation marks) from English sources are given according to their original in spelling and punctuation, and do not necessarily conform to the above-mentioned points of spelling, style and punctuation. The Translator begs indulgence for certain inconsistencies in the above points.

PROLOGUE

ELDER EPHRAIM
ABBOT OF VATOPEDI MONASTERY
OF MOUNT ATHOS

The Orthodox world has had a difficult and often martyric history. Centuries-long oppression and severe persecution have troubled and continue to trouble its communal life, testing its faith and driving it to the limits of its endurance. And so the Russian people have lived through a recent "Babylonian captivity" during the twentieth century, enduring a reign of tyranny and fierce persecution for seventy years.

Setting aside all human imperfections and weaknesses, we discern in the life of the Orthodox faithful who have confronted these difficult conditions two characteristic traits: an eschatological mindset and a forgiving spirit. Furthermore, these also characterize all the holy Martyrs of the Church as their proper traits.

An eschatological frame of mind does not imply passivity or indifference to daily life. On the contrary, it implies, rather, activity and care for its proper use. It also implies an awareness of God's paternal providence, not only for His welcome gifts, but also for those that are unpleasant. Characteristic of this is the letter that Empress Alexandra sent during her period of exile in Tobolsk: "The way of the cross first—then joy and gladness…. The more we suffer here the fairer it will be on that other shore where so many dear ones await us…. How can one ask more? We simply give thanks to God for every day safely ended."

A forgiving spirit manifests love and humility. The self-centered man never forgives because he has no love in his heart. Egoism does not leave room in the heart of a man to be able to forgive his neighbor. Even more certainly can he not forgive his enemy. But this is true Christian love, the love that forgives even one's enemies. This selfless love inspires the forgiving spirit of the Orthodox faithful.

In one of Olga Romanov's notebooks, which was found after her terrible execution, was a handwritten prayer that said, among other things, "Grant us Thy patience, Lord, in these our woeful days, the mob's wrath to endure, the torturer's ire; Thy unction to forgive our neighbors' persecution, and mild, like Thee, to bear a bloodstained Cross. ... And when the hour comes to pass the last dread gate, breathe strength in us to pray, 'Father, forgive them.'"

We view as praiseworthy and God-pleasing the initiative of the Monastery of St John the Forerunner in Mesa Potamos to publish this present book on the Romanov Holy Royal Martyrs. We pray that the readers of this book may be edified and inspired by the virtues of these seven Holy Royal Martyrs of Russia.

Archimandrite Ephraim

INTRODUCTION

With great joy and feelings of deep emotion, the Holy Monastery of St John the Forerunner of Mesa Potamos, in Cyprus, presents to the reading public a work which is the fruit of a long-term study. It would not be bold to say that this project retains a uniquely significant feature, which accords to it a great honour and distinction. This is the fact that besides being simply a book written by the personal efforts and abilities of a single author, this work was produced through the contributions of many world-renowned and distinguished scholars. All these historical researchers, who have devoted a considerable part of their lives to the study of the life and martyrdom of the Romanov Royal Martyrs, have contributed to this project in various ways, such as the translation of texts from primary sources, the compiling of archival documents, the offering of historical advice, the sharing of information and material and many more.

Although an abundance of books has been written about Russia's last royal family, the present work anticipates that it will offer to its readers a new revelation and a fresh experience of the events described herein. The effort for the attainment of this objective is summarized in a two-fold approach.

The first side of this aim focused on creating a work that could inspire the readers, by presenting the lives of the Royal Martyrs through a different prism, the prism of their spiritual grandeur and the purity of their noble souls. In the pages of the book, the eye of the reader's mind will be apprised of the portraits of the Royal Martyrs' psyche, depicted with the liveliest colours: the colours of their very own words from the personal writings of the family and of those who lived very close to them. The result is a psychographic biography, which aims in presenting the deeper essence of the characters of the royal family in an inspiring way.

The second side of the project's aim was to bring to light a multitude of unknown and unrevealed facts, aspects and elements of history, which evince that many truths in regard to the life and martyrdom of the Royal Martyrs remain silenced or distorted to this day. This part of the project presents unvarnished factually sourced events, deriving all its material stringently from primary sources –as it is the case with the entire work–

which allow no grounds for questioning their legitimacy, gravity and validity. Thus, many major historical events, such as the 1905 revolution and Bloody Sunday, Russia's involvement in World War I, the February coup d'état of 1917 and the events relating to Nicholas' II abdication, are set in their true proportions and are presented through a proper prospective. Readers may be surprised by the facts surrounding these historical events, because up to now, these events have generally been presented in an inaccurate light.

The study for the authoring of the book began in July 2017 and the book was initially released in the Greek language, in February 2018, in the framework of the 100th anniversary from the Royal Martyrs' martyrdom. The book was, and still remains, the first and only biography of the Royal Martyrs published in the Greek language and the readers have welcomed the publication with immense love and enthusiasm.

We hope that the English edition of the book will receive the same warm welcome and will succeed in both aspects of its aim: to inspire the readers to follow the path of love and forgiveness in which the Royal Martyrs walked; and reveal to them *What Silence Could Not Conceal.*

We have a Tsar of righteous and pious life. God has sent a heavy cross of sufferings to him as to His chosen one and beloved child, ... If there is no repentance in the Russian people, ... God will remove from it the pious Tsar and send a scourge in the person of impure, cruel, self-called rulers, who will drench the whole land in blood and tears.

Saint John of Kronstadt, 1905.

PART I
In the Path of Love

CHAPTER I

LOVE WITHOUT BOUNDS

NICHOLAS ALEXANDROVICH ROMANOV
THE EARLY YEARS

Since 1330 the Ipatiev Monastery has dominated the banks of the River Kostroma and the Russian city of the same name. On 24 March, 1613, nearly three hundred years after its founding, a delegation of the Zemsky Sobor[1] arrived at the monastery unexpectedly. Their visit was to seal the history of Russia for the next three hundred years. The delegates from Moscow had arrived to announce to the sixteen-year-old exile Michael Feodorovich Romanov, who was staying at the monastery, that he had been unanimously chosen as the new Tsar of the Russian Empire.

The mother of the young Michael refused to accept this decision. Russia was still in the fifteenth year of its Time of Troubles, which followed the death of Tsar Ivan IV the Terrible. The Empire was in complete anarchy, soaked with the blood of the armies of contenders for the throne. The election of Michael, grandson of the brother of Tsaritsa Anastasia, wife of Ivan the Terrible, was the only hope for a definitive end to that terrible period. At last, the decision of the Sobor prevailed and on 22 July of 1613 the young Michael Feodorovich Romanov was enthroned as Tsar of Russia. That day marked the end of the Time of Troubles and the beginning of the Romanov Dynasty.

The first Tsar of the Romanov Dynasty was summoned to his great calling while he was at the Ipatiev Monastery. Three hundred years later the last Tsar of that dynasty, Nicholas II Romanov would yield his last breath in a house with the same name, the Ipatiev House.

Nicholas Alexandrovich Romanov was born on 6 May 1868.[2] On that day the Orthodox Church honors the memory of Saint Job the Much-

The family of Tsar Alexander III.

Suffering. Since every detail of the life of man is an event set in the framework of God's providence, so also the day of Nicholas' birth was a sign of the terrible trials that he was to experience. Nevertheless, as a veritable new Job, Nicholas would exhibit a faith comparable to that of the great saint of the Old Testament. The fearful billows of temptations that would beset this chosen servant of God would serve to show the greatness of his holiness.

Nicholas' father wrote in his diary on that day: "6 May, Monday. The birth of our son Nicholas. Minnie [Maria Feodorovna] woke me just after four saying that she was starting to have strong pains which were stopping her from sleeping; however, she slept intermittently until 8 o'clock.... Minnie had already begun to suffer quite badly, and even cried out from time to time. At about 12:30 my wife went to the bedroom and lay down on the couch where everything was already prepared. The pains were getting more and more intense, and Minnie was really suffering. Papa returned and helped me support my darling throughout. At last, at 3:30, the final moment came, and at once all the pain was over. God has sent us a son whom we have called Nicholas. What joy, it's impossible to imagine; I rushed to embrace my darling, who had cheered up straightaway and was terribly happy. I cried like a child, and my heart felt so light and glad."[3]

Nicholas with his brother George, 1878.

The family of Tsar Alexander III.

Nicholas' father was the second son of Emperor Alexander II Nikolaevich, the Grand Duke Alexander Alexandrovich. The first-born and heir to the throne was Grand Duke Nicholas, who in the summer of 1864 was engaged to Princess Dagmar, daughter of King Christian IX of Denmark. However, on 24 April 1865, before his marriage to Dagmar, Nicholas died of spinal meningitis. Thus, Alexander became heir to the throne of Russia, and one year later, in the spring of 1866, he made a proposal of marriage to Dagmar, the betrothed of his late brother. The wedding took place on 9 November 1866, and after her conversion from Lutheranism to Orthodoxy, Dagmar took the name Maria Feodorovna.

Alexander had four sons with Maria, and two daughters. After the eldest, Nicholas, was born Alexander (1869), who died of meningitis at the age of ten months. Then came George (1871), Ksenia (1875), Michael (1878) and Olga (1882). Maria Feodorovna was a tender and affectionate woman. She embraced her new faith, Orthodoxy, with great zeal and, together with her husband, took care to pass on their love for the Church to their children as well.

Nicholas' favorite companion in his early childhood years was George, his younger brother by three years. Having a keen sense of humor, George was able to make Nicholas laugh with his jokes. Much later, when Nicholas came to the throne of Russia, he was often heard to laugh in his office. The reason was that he was reading his brother George's jokes, which Nicholas had written down as a child on slips of paper and made into an entire collection. In this way he would call to mind the memory of his

At Gatchina Palace.

beloved brother, whom he had lost sooner than he may have wished. In his boyhood years George was diagnosed with tuberculosis and was sent to live in isolation on the sun-drenched mountains of the Caucuses. Finally, at 27 years of age George died.

The royal family resided most of the time at the Gatchina Palace near Saint Petersburg in the city of the same name. Although that palace had nine hundred rooms, Nicholas and his siblings were not allowed by their father to maintain more than one personal room, nor to use sought-after modern amenities. Instead, they were raised with Spartan discipline and simplicity. They slept on simple camp cots with hard pillows, took baths in cold water in the morning, and had oats for breakfast. Their midday meal was rich, but usually they left the table hungry. This was because they were served last after the multitude of their guests. As a result, before they had finished eating, their father would rise from the table, and so they would have to rise also. Only when they dined alone were they able to eat to satiety.

Most of all God's creatures, Nicholas loved birds. When he heard them singing, he would become so absorbed in their song that his friends would often comment on it. Once, when a small sparrow fell from its nest, little Nicholas said, "It is necessary to pray for the little sparrows; May our dear God not take it, He already has enough sparrows."[4]

From a small child Nicholas showed great love for the services of the Church, which made a deep impression on him. So great was his admiration for the liturgical life, that after the Divine Liturgy "when they were alone he and his friends used to play priests and deacons. Nicholas, however, was also deeply moved and impressed by the narration of the events of the Passion and Resurrection [of the Lord]."[5]

He also showed great interest in learning. "Since he hadn't yet learnt to read, he would continually ask his mother to read to him, and as she did so he would reverently repeat the words after her. ... He only agreed to write in his exercise book after his mother showed him a whole pile stacked up in reserve. He had an unusual respect for paper and wrote his lines with the utmost care, breathing heavily and sometimes even sweating from the exertion."[6]

Nicholas' education was according to the usual custom for members of royal families. "A twelve-year period of study was planned for the young Grand Duke, eight of which were to cover the school syllabus, and the final four university studies. The school syllabus was extremely onerous, and the great deal of time was spent on practical subjects: the tsarevich studied mineralogy, botany, and zoology, as well as of the basics of anatomy and physiology. The university course combined the disciplines of the politics and economics departments of The Faculty of Jurisprudence. The sheer number of subjects to be studied meant that Nicholas' education had to be extended by a year. His teachers were all famous professors."[7] Of all the subjects he was taught, history was closest to his heart. He also greatly loved literature and he was particularly a linguist. He spoke French and German, and his fluency in English was so extraordinary that an Oxford professor could have taken him for an Englishman. His knowledge of languages gave him the ability to read with great interest many works of foreign classic literature. His unusually powerful memory was one of his exceptional characteristics.

Nicholas' schooling was centered on the principle of classic Russian triad: Tsar, Church, and People. Deeply rooted within his being was faith in the divine mission of the Tsar. The Tsar was the anointed elect servant of God who was called to set himself forth as an example of the keeping of the divine commandments, to preserve Orthodoxy intact in his realm, and to take care for the spiritual and material welfare of his subjects. This divine view of monarchy, which according to the age-old belief and concept of authority, clergy, and people, constituted the only means of survival for Russia and had no room for any proposal of the representation of the people in government. Any concession in this matter on the part of the Tsar meant a failure to observe his duties before God and to his divine calling.

An important personality of that time, Constantine Pobedonostsev, was a contributing factor in the inculcation of this concept in the depth of Nicholas' being. Pobedonostsev, who served as Ober-Procurator[8] of the Synod of the Church of Russia until 1905, was personal advisor to three Tsars of Russia,

CHAPTER I

Tsar Alexander II.

Alexander II, Alexander III and finally Nicholas. He was also the main tutor of the latter two. Pobedonostsev was a philosopher of Conservatism, and he dedicated his entire life to polemics against the ideology of the French Revolution. He rejected any movement towards progressivism, liberalism, constitutional government, and popular sovereignty. His faith in absolute monarchy as a God-given institution convinced him that the changes that were taking place in Western Europe could never successfully be applied to Russia. He also endeavored to pass these convictions on to the young heir, Nicholas, setting forth Peter the Great as the ideal model of a ruler. Although Nicholas accepted the divine aspect of the role of the Sovereign and firmly believed in the triad, Tsar, Church, and People, nevertheless he could not identify with Pobedonostsev's view of Peter the Great. This became evident in many occasions. Once, when A. Mossolov, head of the Court Chancellery, happened to speak with great admiration of Peter the Great, hearing him Nicholas characteristically noted, "I recognize my ancestor's great merits, but I should be lacking in sincerity if I were to echo your enthusiasm. ... He is the ancestor who appeals to me least of all. He had too much admiration for European 'culture.' He stamped out Russian habits, the good customs of his sires, the usages bequeathed by the nation, on too many occasions."[9] On the contrary, of all his ancestors Nicholas most admired Tsar Alexis who was known in history chiefly for his kindness of character, for which he received the epithet "the Most Peaceful,"[10] but also for his steadfast adherence to Orthodox ecclesiastical tradition and worship.

Although Pobedonostsev failed to impart to Nicholas his extreme ideas on methods of exercising authority, he was nevertheless able to contribute to rendering him extremely conservative in regard to any demands of movements that aimed to radically reform the monarchical government. For Nicholas the most dramatic evidence of mortal dangers that lurked within those groups and organizations was the heinous murder of his grandfather, Tsar Alexander II. Alexander II was the most liberal of all the tsars of the nineteenth century and was known as the "Liberator" due to his historic abolition of serfdom in Russia. It was a most tragic irony that his murder was committed mere hours after he had approved the establishment of a national body of representatives that would have operated as an advisory organ on matters of legislation.

The assassination took place on 1 March, 1881. Just as the carriage of the Tsar was passing via the Catherine Canal and over the Pevchesky Bridge, in Saint Petersburg, a member of the terrorist organization People's Will[11] detonated a bomb under his carriage. The explosion shattered the carriage, killed one of the six Cossacks who were accompanying the tsar and seriously wounded the driver and people on the sidewalk. The tsar himself did not suffer any harm. He then approached the wounded to see their condition and asked politely about the terrorist who had already been captured. At that moment a second terrorist appeared shouting, "It is too early to thank God!"[12] and he threw a second bomb at the feet of the Tsar.

This time the terrorists achieved their goal. The Tsar's legs were shattered, and his stomach was torn open and his face was heavily wounded. Still alive, Alexander whispered, "Home to the palace, to die there."[13] When they arrived at the palace, they laid the Tsar, still conscious, in his bed and the devastated members of the royal family began to arrive. On that tragic day Nicholas wrote in his diary, in which he recorded all the events of his daily life with laconic simplicity:

"1st of March 1881. We were having breakfast in the Anichkov Palace, my brother and I, when a frightened servant ran in and said: 'An accident has happened to the Emperor!' The Crown Prince[14] gave command to take the Grand Duke (namely myself) to the Winter Palace: 'One must not lose time.' General Danilov and we ran down, got into a carriage and rushed along Nevsky [Prospect] to the Winter Palace. When we were going up the staircase, I saw that all those who met us had pale faces and that there were big red spots on the carpet—when they had carried my grandfather up the staircase, blood from the terrible wounds he had suffered from the explosion had poured out. My parents were already in the study. My uncle and aunt were standing near the window. Nobody said a word. My grandfather was lying on the narrow camp bed on which he always slept. He was covered with the military greatcoat that served as his dressing-gown. His face was mortally pale, it was covered with small wounds. My father led me up to the bed: 'Papa,' he said, raising his voice, 'your sun ray is here.' I saw a fluttering of his eyelids. The light blue eyes of my grandfather opened. He tried to smile. He moved his finger, but could not raise his hand and say what he wanted, but he undoubtedly recognised me. Protopresbyter Bazhenov came up to him and gave him Communion for the last time, we fell on our knees, and the Emperor quietly died. Thus was it pleasing to the Lord."[15]

Submission to the will of God was the distinguishing characteristic of Nicholas' personality. His faith in the Divine wisdom that directs events gave him that supernatural calm that never abandoned him in all the unbelievably tragic events in his life.

CROWN PRINCE

On proclaiming his accession to the throne, Nicholas' father declared that he would govern Russia "with faith in the power and right of autocracy."[16] In fact, in the thirteen years of the reign of his father Nicholas saw Russia governed on the principles of the ancient ideals of Orthodox Russian monarchy. Alexander III Alexandrovich was a strong man and proved to be one of the most important tsars of Russia in the nineteenth century, even though the period of his reign was short. He was extremely conservative, and he revoked certain of the liberal reforms of his father, among which was the approval of a proposed constitution. He led a pacifist foreign policy and did not involve Russia in any war during his reign. Due to this he was called "the Peacemaker."

In his domestic sphere, Tsar Alexander adhered to strict, traditional Russian principles. His personal office was not grand but rather small and comfortable, with little furniture, as were also the rest of the rooms of the palace. The simplicity that characterized the palace reflected the character of a man who did not wish to live according to the typical autocratic manner of monarchs. When he was at home, Alexander's favorite clothing was a military tunic that he wore until it was frayed.

Family life at the palace was very warm and ran on a prescribed schedule that Alexander required to be followed with military precision. The members of the family were closely tied to each other and absolutely enjoyed familial companionship. In the winter they enjoyed cutting wood together and shoveling snow from walkways and yards and making snow forts. In the summertime their entertainment consisted of horseback riding, hiking, and planting trees. Their favorite sport was tennis. During this period of his life Nicholas wrote in his diary "We worked in the garden. Cleared three trees that had fallen on top of one another. Then made a huge bonfire. Mama came to look at our bonfire, it was so inviting."[17]

The Tsar inculcated in his children absolute respect towards his person. Thus, Alexander took pleasure that his family was able to exemplify for their subjects the highest of ethical principles and faithful adherence to Orthodox ideals. Nicholas' respect and trust in his father was such that later, when he himself was on the throne, whenever he had to deal with some serious matter he would ask himself, "What would father do in this instance, how would he have acted in this case, or if I were father how should I act?"[18]

At thirteen years of age, immediately after the death of his grandfather and his father's ascent to the throne, Nicholas was officially made Tsarevich,[19] that is, the heir to the throne of Russia. Nicholas' exceptional virtues from his earliest years of age were politeness, affability, and affection. His characteristic shy, tender, and somewhat sad smile always made an impression on all. He tried to see only the good side of people and was ready to show love to all.

As Crown Prince, after the completion of his education, Nicholas had in effect only one serious obligation: to await his turn to take up the kingdom with all discretion. In 1890 when Nicholas was twenty-two years old, his father was only forty-five. Judging from his strong personal constitution and unshakable good health and strength, Alexander believed that he would remain in his position as Autocrat for another twenty or perhaps thirty years. For this reason, he did not hasten to prepare Nicholas to assume this dreadful burden this early. Furthermore, he considered that at that age Nicholas could not measure up to the demands of so difficult and

Tsar Alexander III.

demanding an office. Thus, the presence of Nicholas at the morning sessions of the Imperial Council was, for the time being, simply out of convention.

Nicholas usually spent his afternoons ice-skating with his sister Ksenia and his aunt Elisabeth, wife of Grand Duke Serge Alexandrovich, brother of his father. In the evenings he liked to attend performances of operas, theater, and ballet. However, all these entertainments completely ceased during the period of Great Lent. During these holy days he remained immured with his family at home. His only, infrequent, outings then were an all-day hunt in the woods with his father and his companions.

Nicholas' greatest love, however, was the military life. "It was traditional for the emperor to be above all a military man, and for this reason Nicholas' military studies were modelled on the course of the General Staff Academy. Theoretical knowledge was bolstered by practical experience: the tsarevich attended two summer camps with the Guards regiments in order to experience military service at first hand."[20] The army and its glorious history fascinated him to the end of his life. He enjoyed no other title as much as that of colonel, which his father had bestowed on him. When he turned eighteen, he gave him command of a squadron of the Royal Cavalry with which he was stationed at Krasnoe Selo, at the great camp outside of Saint Petersburg where the Royal

Tsarevich Nicholas Alexandrovich, 1885.

Guard performed their military exercises in the summer. He himself was stationed in a small private cabin with a bedroom, an office, a dining room, and a balcony with a view on a small garden, where he lived a happy and carefree life as a simple young Russian officer. He participated fully in the simple daily life of the soldiers, and his modesty and moderation especially endeared him to his fellow officers. He wrote to his mother of this:

"I am now happier than I can say to have joined the army and every day I become more and more used to the camp life. Each day we drill twice—there is either target practice in the morning and battalion drill in the evening or the other way round.... We have lunch at 12 o'clock and dine at 8, with siesta and tea in between. The dinners are very merry; they feed us well. ... We get up fairly early in the morning, today we began target practice at 6 am. It's very pleasant for me because I'm used to getting up early."[21]

Empress Maria was concerned that the young Tsarevich might lose his sense of the importance of his person in all this enjoyment, and wished to remind him that he should always present himself as an example to his subordinates, writing, "Never forget that everyone's eyes are turned on you now, waiting to see what your own first independent steps in life will be. Always be polite and courteous with everybody, see that you will get along

CHAPTER I

Nicholas with his mother Empress Maria.

with all your comrades without discrimination, although without too much familiarity or intimacy, and never listen to flatterers. ... I miss you terribly, my dear Nicky, everywhere and every moment of the day. God bless and protect you. I kiss you lovingly, and I know your kind heart and your faith in Almighty God will always help you to be the joy and consolation of your parents."[22]

In contrast with the military austerity of Tsar Alexander III, Empress Maria was a very mild soul and strove to maintain a balance between the absolutism of her husband and the simple everyday needs of her children. Precisely for this reason, whenever the children wanted anything, they would come to their mother and she in turn, knowing how to approach Alexander, transmitted their requests to their father. Not finding especial pleasure in the absolute seclusion with which her husband surrounded his family, Maria especially preferred spending the greater part of the day with her children in their play room and playing with them. Thus, from his very earliest years Nicholas was closely tied to his mother. This bond of theirs would remain especially close to the end.

The role of empress was what Maria held as most precious in her life. Her interest in the well-being of her subjects and her sense of duty before the state was truly genuine and unique. She also loved the pomp and participated with especial pleasure in royal and imperial receptions. She was a social and gregarious person, which was greatly appreciated by the aristocratic circles of Saint Petersburg; and so, the empress easily gained favor with those in her milieu.

This conception, however, which Maria had regarding the image she should project as empress, which was the usual case of every tsarina in Russia, would prove contrary to the humble and modest personality of Nicholas. Recognizing these traits in her son's character early on, Maria was concerned about his future. However, Nicholas' kind nature could not by any means be a detriment to his personality. On the contrary, just as history itself has proved, Nicholas' path was after the type of Christ. Nicholas bore the weight of responsibility and of the unreasonable moods and actions of his people, and in the end his stewardship was sealed with his sacrifice, which came about due to the general corruption.

BRUSH WITH DEATH

On 17 October, 1888, Nicholas experienced a brush with death for the first time. The family was travelling in the royal train. All sat together in the dining car when suddenly near Kharkov, two loud bangs were heard, and the train derailed. Nicholas wrote, "A fateful day for us all. We might all have been killed, but by the Lord's will we were not. During breakfast our train jumped the rails. The dining car and coach were demolished, but we emerged from it all unscathed. However, 20 people were killed and 16 injured."[23]

The family was rescued by God's providence through the superhuman strength of the mighty Alexander. The roof of the car in which the family rode collapsed and under usual circumstances would have crushed all those inside. However, as a veritable Atlas, Alexander was able to hold up the whole roof of the car on his shoulders until all the members of the family were able to get out unharmed.

Only two years passed after Nicholas' first encounter with mortal danger when his life was once again directly threatened. In 1890 his father sent him on a grand tour to the countries of the Far East. The purpose of this trip was not merely a vacation. Even from the time of Peter the Great, these tours were meant to be an important part of the education of members of the Russian royal house, in order to prepare them to better execute their state duties. This training was through the royals' contact with various foreign cultures.

Cairo, 1890.

Nicholas' tour began on 23 October, 1890. The final destination of the tour, before returning to Saint Petersburg, was Vladivostok, where Nicholas was to lay the cornerstone at the inauguration ceremony for the construction of the Trans-Siberian Railroad. After a church service at the Gatchina Palace, the Crown Prince departed with his brother George, accompanied by a small retinue. Their first stop was Trieste in Italy, where they arrived by way of Vienna. Then they visited Greece where Nicholas' godmother, Queen Olga Constantinovna, and her husband, George I, King of Greece, received them. There, Prince George, the son of the King of Greece, joined the entourage. Then the tour continued through Egypt, the Indies, Sri Lanka, Thailand, and Hong Kong. After Hong Kong, on 15 April, 1891, they arrived at Nagasaki in Japan. Meanwhile, George, Nicholas' brother, became gravely ill when the company was in India, and had to return to Russia.

Two weeks later, on 29 April, an unforeseen and inexplicable incident took place. That day, after departing from Kyoto, Nicholas and his companions visited Lake Biwa, one of the twenty oldest lakes in the world, which is near the city of Otsu. As soon as they set off for their return, Tsuda Sanzo, a member of the Japanese police escort provided to Nicholas by the Japanese authorities, attempted to assassinate the young Russian Crown Prince.

Nicholas wrote in his diary, "Woke up to a marvelous day whose end I

Nicholas in a jinrikisha in Nagasaki, Japan.

would not have seen had I not been saved by the Lord God's great mercy. We set out from Kyoto in a jinrikisha for the small town of Otsu, where we went to the house of the little round governor. In his house, which was utterly European, he had set up a bazaar where each of us ruined ourselves on some knickknack. This was where Georgie bought his bamboo cane, which was to do me such a great service an hour later. After lunch we prepared to make the return trip, and Georgie and I were glad we would be able to take a rest in Kyoto before evening. We rode out in our jinrikishas and turned left down a narrow street crowded to either side. At that point I received a strong blow to the right side of my head, above my ear. Turned and saw the loathsome scowl of a policeman, who was waving his saber over me in both hands a second time."[24]

With lightning speed, the Greek Prince George blocked the second blow of the sword with his bamboo cane, rescuing Nicholas from certain death. However, the first blow of the sword opened a large nine centimeter [four and a half inch] gash on Nicholas' head, which would occasionally give him severe headaches for the rest of his life. Sanzo managed to flee, but two Japanese rickshaw drivers were able to immobilize him.

Nicholas continued in his diary, "Had to reassure everyone and stay on my feet as long as possible. Rambakh [the doctor] did the first bandage and, most important, stanched the blood. The people on the street were touching: most of them got down on their knees and raised their arms in a sign of regret."[25]

In a letter to his mother he related all that had happened in detail:

> My Dearest Darling Mama,
> I am writing you these lines so that you hear directly from me about the unfortunate incident that took place in Japan, the very country that interested me more than any other and which, after seeing it, I liked so much. Having spent a couple of pleasant days in Kyoto, we set off on the morning of 29 April in our rickshaws for the town of Otsu. We visited the temple and had lunch with the governor, and were just getting ready for our return to Kyoto when it happened: we had not gone two hundred paces when suddenly a Japanese policeman rushed into the middle of the street and, wielding a sabre with both hands, struck me from behind on the right-hand side of my head. I cried out in Russian: 'What's the matter with you?,' and jumped out of the rickshaw. Turning round, I saw that he was coming at me again with his sword raised, so I ran as fast as I could down the street, stemming the wound to my head with my hand. I tried to hide in the crowd, but they immediately ran off, and I had to take my heels again to escape the pursuing policeman. In the end I stopped and turned round to see dear Georgie about ten paces from me, with the policeman, whom he had knocked to the ground with one blow of his cane, lying at his feet. Had Georgie not been in the rickshaw behind me, dearest Mama, perhaps I would never have seen you again! But God willed otherwise! When that monster fell, he was pounced upon by two rickshaw drivers; one of them used his sabre to seize him by the neck and drag him bound to the nearest house. I was bandaged up and taken back to the governor's house. I was very touched by the Japanese, who knelt in the street as we passed and look terribly sad. We returned to Kyoto by train, where I spent another two days. I have received a thousand telegrams from various Japanese expressing their regret. The emperor himself, and all the princes, came; I felt sorry for them, so stricken were they.[26]

The Prime Minister of Japan feared that this incident would result in a Russian cause for war against his country. The military strength of Japan at that time was no match for that of Russia, and so the Japanese Prime Minister, in order to avoid the possibility of conflict, urged the Emperor Meiji to visit Nicholas immediately. In fact, the emperor of Japan travelled hastily during the night so as to arrive early in the morning at Kyoto, where Nicholas lay. Later, he expressed his regret publicly for the country's breach of hospitality before so important a state visitor. Indeed, the interior and foreign ministers, accepting responsibility for failing to assure his safety, resigned their offices.

Nicholas' visit was no small event. It was the most important visit to Japan after the visit of the British prince ten years earlier, in 1881. Hence the reception and hospitality of Nicholas was with all state honors and care. Finally, the apologetic stance of Japan over the event led the Russian government to officially express satisfaction for the friendly intentions of the Japanese. Nicholas himself wrote a few days later in his diary, "1 May. Tokyo. I am not so very angry at the good Japanese for the repulsive act of one fanatic. As before, their model order and cleanliness is a pleasure, and I must confess I keep on watching... whom I see on the street from afar."[27]

The motives of the attempted assassination on the part of Tsuda Sanzo were never ascertained. He was finally sentenced to life imprisonment, but only a few months later, in September of 1891, he died in prison from some illness.

After this incident, Tsar Alexander commanded his son to cut short his tour and to hasten his return. Thus, after attending the ceremony inaugurating work on the railroad in Vladivostok, where he arrived on 11 May, Nicholas set off on his journey to Saint Petersburg, where he arrived on 4 August after a nine month's absence. On the way home he made stops at various cities of the Russian Empire. One of these was at Tobolsk, where he was received at the Governor's house with hospitality. He would return to this very house again much later, in 1917, under terribly different circumstances, as a prisoner.

ALIX OF HESSE
A SORROWFUL PRINCESS

Apart from its educational aspect, Nicholas' tour of the East had another purpose. His father hoped that the pleasant experience of his tour would help sway Nicholas' thought and heart away from the German-English Princess of Hesse, Alix.

Princess Alix was born on 6 June, 1872 in the medieval city of Darmstadt, the capital of the Grand Duchy of Hesse, which was a state of the German Empire. Her parents were the Grand Duke of Hesse, Louis IV, and Princess Alice of the United Kingdom, daughter of Queen Victoria. Louis and Alice had seven children, Victoria (1863), the future Grand Duchess of Russia and Venerable Martyr Elisabeth (1864), Irene (1866), Ernst (1868), Friedrich (1870), Alix (1872) and Marie (1874). Friedrich had hemophilia, which was called the "royal sickness," since in the nineteenth and twentieth centuries it appeared mainly in the offspring of the royal houses of Europe. Little Friedrich died at the age of three years as a result of a blow, before Alix was one year old.

When Alix was born, her two older sisters, Victoria and Elisabeth had already begun their schooling and the greater part of their time was given

CHAPTER I

to lessons and study. Irene was in the early period of her studies and so for this reason her time in the common nursery was limited. Thus, Alix passed the first years of her childhood with Ernst and Marie. Ernst especially loved his little sister and tried all means to amuse her with the various games that he could come up with. For this reason, right from the beginning, her brother was the person Alix most admired and until the end of her life she always kept in close touch with him.

The palace of the Grand Duke, Alix's father, was in the center of the town, surrounded by a lovely garden, the site having originally been that of the botanical gardens. Her mother had filled the interior of the palace with keepsakes from her native England. The rooms of the palace were large and airy, but very simply furnished. The same simplicity characterized their meals, which consisted mainly of baked apples and rice puddings. Their tutor, Mrs. Orchard, was also an Englishwoman of strict moral principles and she personified the ideal governess: logical and modest, she inculcated in the children obedience, and despite her gentleness, did not avoid imposing punishment whenever she thought necessary. Mrs. Orchard kept a strict daily schedule of activities for the children. Alix later applied the same routine to her own family, which Mrs. Orchard, who accompanied Alix to Russia, heartily endorsed.

Their mother's room was also on the same floor as the nursery. There the girls brought their toys and played, while their mother read and wrote. Their toys were very simple. However, Alix did not display a special interest in dolls, which she considered exceedingly lifeless! She preferred pets, who returned her caresses, and she especially loved group activities.

In her early years Princess Alix was a happy child, active and always laughing. In the summers Grand Duke Louis took his family to a hunting lodge in the country. There Alix passed her mornings in the sun-drenched yard, going up and down the exterior stone stairs of the house and trying to catch with her hands the goldfish that swam in the fountain in the yard. For her cheerful and bright character her mother called her "Sunny."

In the winter Princess Alice used to take the children with her to hospitals and various philanthropic institutions, which operated under her personal sponsorship and supervision. In this way the children learned from their earliest years to take pleasure in bringing joy to their fellow man. When she was still very little, Alix often brought flowers to the patients on behalf of her mother.

The family of Grand Duke Louis IV of Hesse. Alix is held by her mother.

Alix, the sorrowful princess.

These happy days for Alix and for the family would come to a dramatic end. In November of 1878, diphtheria struck the palace in Darmstadt. Alix was six years old at the time. Louis and all the children contracted the disease. The only ones who escaped infection were the children's mother and Elisabeth, who at that time had been visiting her paternal grandparents. Queen Victoria sent her personal physician from England to help the German doctors in their work.

Although several nurses were sent to the palace, Princess Alice did not cease for a moment to go from one sick child to another. Alix later remembered her mother coming to her whenever she called her in the middle of the night to comfort and reassure her. In spite of this, Alix's four-year-old sister, Marie—with whom she was inseparable and whom she loved much—finally died, while the remaining children barely managed to escape the clutches of death. The worst blow had not yet come. Princess Alice, exhausted and consumed with her attempts to care for the children, and grieving the loss of her child, finally fell ill herself. In little less than a week, on 14 December, she yielded up her soul. She was only thirty-five years old.

The Grand Duke did everything he could to fill the void that the untimely death of his wife created in the life of his children. He was a kind and good-hearted man whom the children practically worshipped. Naturally his attention particularly turned to Alix who after the death of Marie was now the youngest child of the family.

Despite her father's care, the death of her beloved sister and of her mother was decisive for Alix, who had already begun to become estranged from her surroundings. The first months after her mother's death laid the foundations for the cultivation of a seriousness in her character rare for her age. She was already completely alone in the nursery. Her beloved brother Ernst, now ten years old, had also begun his schooling, and the greater part of his time was passed in his studies. Many years later, Alix remembered those unspeakably sorrowful months, which she sat alone with Mrs. Orchard in the nursery trying to play with new toys that were unfamiliar to her, because the old toys were burned because they were tainted with diphtheria. When she looked up to find a little consolation from her nanny, she saw that she was teary-eyed. Poor Mrs. Orchard deeply felt the loss of her beloved Princess Alice.

A shell of aloofness then began to conceal the feelings of little Alix, and she rarely smiled. Unfamiliar places and persons brought her difficulty, and she only felt comfortable in her own warm family surroundings. Within this environment the now introverted Alix would transform, and again become the happy child whom everyone knew. But those warm family moments were already an infrequent occurrence, because the older daughters of Louis, Victoria and Elisabeth, attempting to replace their mother, were often absent with their father on various social duties.

After the death of Alice, Queen Victoria surrounded the family with special love and care. She cared for Louis as for her very own son and

CHAPTER I

Queen Victoria with her granddaughters, princesses of Hesse, holding Alix by the hand, 1879.

Grand Duke Louis with his children. Alix is the first on the left.

---

often invited him to England with the children, to spend their vacations there. Now as the littlest child in the family, Alix was the favorite of Queen Victoria, who looked out with special care for the upbringing of her granddaughter. The children's teachers and governesses in Darmstadt had to send special reports to the Queen of England on the children's progress. Subsequently they received detailed instructions from her on how to conduct their work. Moreover, Alix remained in England for a long time under the direct supervision of her grandmother. Under such guardianship and education, Alix, as well as her brothers and sisters, were brought up with English moral principles. Thus, as Alix matured, she came to be in all regards an English noblewoman.

One other person who took an important part in the formation of Alix's personality in her youth was Miss Margaret Jackson, one of her teachers.

Maggie, as Alix later fondly called her, was a cultivated woman with liberal views, who quickly drew the keen admiration of the older daughters of the Grand Duke's household. Margaret's aim was not only to transmit knowledge to her pupils, but to develop their moral principles, and to broaden their views on life. Having a particular interest in current events and social issues of the time, she discussed these topics with her royal pupils, stimulating them with deep intellectual questions.

Alix turned out to be an exceptional student. She devoted herself to study with all the diligence and strictness that characterized her from childhood. She always had a keen sense of duty and, as her teachers attested, she was ready to sacrifice her every personal pleasure in order to fulfill any duty she had. By the age of fifteen she had already excelled in the subjects of history, geography, and English and German literature. Her abilities on the piano approached perfection, but she did not like playing in front of company. Occasionally, when Queen Victoria asked her to play the piano for guests at Windsor Castle, Alix obeyed, but her reddened face revealed the discomfort she experienced.

The spring of 1888 became a significant point in Alix's life. Having completed her sixteenth year, in accordance with the expectations of Lutheran doctrine, Alix prepared for her confirmation. This was a serious event in the life of every pious Lutheran. Preparation began long before with a broad and detailed catechesis in Protestant doctrine by prominent theologians and clerics.

When she was still alive, Princess Alice entrusted the catechesis of Alix and her siblings to the theologian, Doctor Schell. He was a very cultured man, who quickly became a significant influence on Alix's religious education. Through his teaching, Doctor Schell implanted in Alix's heart the desire to live Christian truth in all its fulness, which became the most important aspect of her character throughout her entire life.

From this time on, Alix began to cultivate a special care for her spiritual life. She made a strict examination of her conscience and analyzed the motives of her every deed and thought, trying to identify her weaknesses and to work on their correction. She sought by every means to guard this deep spiritual work from the view of all who surrounded her. She believed that her relationship with God was an absolutely personal matter, into which no one had the right to intrude.

'WE LOVE EACH OTHER'

In 1884 at the age of twelve Princess Alix visited Russia for the first time in order to attend the marriage of her sister Elisabeth to Grand Duke Serge, brother of Tsar Alexander III. Because of her young age, Alix was

CHAPTER I

The princesses of Hesse.
From left: Irene, Victoria, Elisabeth and Alix, 1885.

---

not able to attend the various balls that followed the wedding service in Saint Petersburg. However, she did especially enjoy the few days that her family spent at the Peterhof Palace, where she first met the Crown Prince of Russia and his siblings.

When Nicholas first saw Alix, he sensed that their union was the will of God. Alix had the same feelings. In fact, in remembrance of this their first meeting, they carved their names on one of the windows of the royal estate at Peterhof. Nicholas wrote in his diary revealingly, "Alix and I wrote our names on the rear window of the Italian house (we love each other)."[28] However, five years would pass before their next encounter.

The winter of 1889, now seventeen years old, Princess Alix visited Russia for the second time to see her sister Elisabeth. During this time Nicholas often came to the palace of Serge and Elisabeth to see Alix, but neither of the two openly expressed their feelings. In fact, Alix so restrained herself that at first, she herself did not recognize the depths of her feelings. Only when she returned to Darmstadt did she understand that her heart remained behind in Russia, close to Nicholas.

During her stay in Russia Alix took part in many recreational activities in Saint Petersburg, such as formal balls and opera and ballet performances. There, along with her siblings Ernst and Elisabeth, and Nicholas and his siblings, George and Ksenia, and other young friends, Alix felt completely at ease. Her radiant smile and bright eyes testified how happy she was, even though her natural shyness and bashfulness did not allow her to socialize freely with persons unknown to her.

Alix remained in Saint Petersburg through the early part of Great Lent. The first week of Lent was an especially austere time in Russia. No one went to places of entertainment in those days. The theaters were closed, and everyone was obliged to go to church for services. The spirit of Great and Holy Lent captured young Alix from then on, and the spiritual quality of those quiet days of the Fast was deeply etched into her soul.

Nicholas' meeting with Alix in 1889 was pivotal for him. He was now entirely convinced that his heart belonged to Alix unconditionally. He could think of no one else as his future wife. However, Nicholas' father was not in agreement with this desire of his son. The reasons were purely political. Tsar Alexander was seeking to strengthen Russia's alliance with France. And so, he hoped that Nicholas would take to wife Princess Hélène of Orleans, daughter of Prince Phillipe, Count of Paris and heir to the throne of France. Furthermore, Alexander considered England to be a perpetual bastion of liberalism and was concerned that Alix's English upbringing would ignite the hopes of the liberal party in Russia.

The prospect of marriage to the French princess came to nothing, because apart from Nicholas' refusal, Hélène's father would not accept the conversion of his daughter to Orthodoxy, which was expected of the consort of the heir to the tsar of Russia. Surprisingly, despite his anti-German sentiments, Alexander then tried to betroth Nicholas to Princess Margaret of Prussia, sister of the German Emperor, Kaiser Wilhelm II. Nicholas however was even more unbudging and opposed to this suggestion.

Coming to a deadlock, father and son sat down to discuss this topic exhaustively. In this conversation Alexander stated to Nicholas in no uncertain terms that he must put out of his mind any possible marriage with Alix. Humble and obedient, Nicholas did not wish to oppose the iron will of his powerful father. However, even though he agreed to forget Alix, he in turn stated categorically that he would not agree to either of his father's two proposals. Thus, Nicholas chose a third path, to remain quiet without complaint and without human hope. He placed all his hope on God alone.

The following summer of 1890, Alix, with her father and her brother Ernst and her sister Victoria, again visited Elisabeth and Serge in Russia at their country estate in Ilyinskoe. This time, however, Nicholas was not permitted to see her. He wrote in pain, "20 August, 1890. O Lord, how I want to go to Ilyinskoe... otherwise if I do not see her now I shall have to wait a whole year, and that will be hard."²⁹ However, Nicholas' great faith in the will of God remained unshakable. One year later, on 21 December, 1891, he would write in his diary:

> In the evening I sat with Mama and Aprak [Princess A.A. Obolenskaya, lady-in-waiting to Empress Maria Feodorovna] discussing the family life of the young people of society today; the conversation struck a most sensitive chord within me, touching as it did on that dream and hope that I live by from day to day. Already a year and a half has passed since I spoke to Papa about it at Peterhof, and since then nothing has changed either for better or worse! My dream is one day to marry Alix H[esse]. I have loved her for a long time, but all the more deeply and strongly since the winter of 1889 when she spent six weeks in St. Petersburg! For a long time I resisted my feelings, trying to deceive myself about the impossibility of fulfilling my most cherished dream. But since this winter Eddy³⁰ has either withdrawn or been turned down, the only obstacle or gulf between us is the question of religion! This is the only barrier; I am almost convinced that our feelings are mutual! Everything is dependent on the will of God. Trusting in His mercy, I look to the future calmly and with humility.³¹

Immediately after that summer of 1890, Nicholas was sent on his tour of the East with the hope that his feelings for Alix would slowly fade away.

BLESSING FROM ABOVE

Alix's father was a quintessential true soldier. In 1866 in the Austria-Prussian War and in the Franco-Prussian War of 1870 he displayed notable military abilities and his soldiers, with whom he always kept in close contact, loved and revered him deeply. He undertook his duties as leader of the Duchy of Darmstadt with great seriousness and displayed notable interest in the broader political situation outside his small dukedom. He greeted the idea of a Greater Germany with pleasure, even though his country, Hesse, lost significant territory in the war against Prussia. Furthermore, the Grand Duke loved his bride's homeland, England, and its British institutions. His ties with the family of his dear departed wife remained close and cordial to the end of his life.

At the beginning of 1892, Louis developed minor cardiac problems, which were not considered serious. But on the fourth of March, as he was eating with his family, he suffered a heart attack, and although he had a strong constitution, on 13 March, he succumbed at last without ever having recovered consciousness.

Those final two years Alix remained at home almost constantly, only going to England once a year for her regular visit. The death of her father, with whom she lived closely in those latest years, because all her sisters had already married and had left the house, was a new, deep blow to her sensitive soul. Day and night those last days of her father's earthly life, she remained at his side, hoping for even a brief recovery so that she could hear some last words of his, but in vain.

The sudden death of her father surpassed Alix's endurance. She was on the brink of collapse, and so her brother, who was now her only support, felt compelled to take her with him to England in August, so that she might find herself again. There her cousins surrounded her with special love and care and helped her to recover her strength. As for her grandmother, Queen Victoria, she hoped to persuade Alix to marry in England so as to have her near her always. During her stay there, Alix saw many princes who wished to marry her, but she remained faithful to her feelings for Nicholas.

Just as after their first meeting in 1884, so now, Nicholas and Alix did not meet at all for five more years. They kept a correspondence, however, and exchanged small gifts by mail. Nicholas found consolation in Alix's sister Elisabeth, who was pained by these young ones' inability to finally come together. She wrote about this to her grandmother, Queen Victoria, "all is in God's hands... alas, the world is so spiteful, and not knowing how long and deep this affection on both sides has been, the spiteful tongues will call it ambition. What fools, as if to mount this throne was enviable; only love, pure and intense can give strength to such a serious step—will it ever be, I wonder? ...I like the boy, his parents lead a model family life, all heart and religion which gives them strength in the difficult moments of life and brings them nearer to God."[32]

Nicholas' trust, however, in Divine will, did not remain unanswered. On the contrary, what was humanly impossible became reality. It all began to change when it became clear that the mighty Tsar Alexander III was nearing the end of his life at the beginning of 1894. Six years earlier, when he upheld the roof of the railroad car with supernatural strength, saving the lives of his family, his entire nation applauded. But not, however, his body. A simple bruising was the price he paid for his self-sacrifice in 1888, but this trivial wound developed little by little into a mortal enemy, nephritis.

In anticipation of Alexander's imminent death, it was necessary to hasten Nicholas' marriage, otherwise the throne of Russia would remain vacant indefinitely. Thus, that which the logic of politics did not favor, found favor from the necessity of circumstances. For Nicholas matters were perfectly clear. God had spoken. The sanction that he awaited from heaven was given, and Alexander could only yield. Thus, he gave permission for his son to make a proposal of marriage to Alix.

However, the obstacles to a favorable outcome of this matter did not end here. Apart from the impediment of the refusal of Nicholas' parents, another obstacle turned out to be more serious. For the wedding to take place, as future empress of Russia, Alix would be obliged to convert to the Orthodox Faith. The matter, however, of Alix's conversion from Lutheranism to Orthodoxy was also exceedingly critical for her.

From her childhood years Alix had immersed herself in Protestant theology with great zeal and dedication. As with every side of her life, here too Alix did not approach her religion frivolously. On the contrary, her faith was the most important part of her life. To simply reject the faith that she had sworn in her sixteenth year to keep inviolate in her oath of confirmation would be an affront to God Himself. At the same time, the fact that her love for Nicholas was so strong and her sense that their union was in accordance with the will of God created a terrible dilemma in her soul. In fact, she experienced a crisis of conscience and emotion.

That Nicholas would one day become one of the most powerful sovereigns in the world did not influence Alix at all. She did not nurse any interest in titles and kingdoms. Already in 1889, she had rejected a proposal of marriage from Prince Albert, Crown Prince of England. Not even Queen Victoria, who greatly desired to see her beloved granddaughter on the British throne, was able to convince her to marry him. The queen wrote to a friend, "I fear all hope of Alicky's marrying Eddy is at an end. She has written to tell him how it pains her to pain him, but that she cannot marry him, much as she likes him as a Cousin, that she knows she would not be happy with him and that he would not be happy with her and that he must not think of her. ... It is a real sorrow to us... but... she says—that if she is forced she will do it—but that she would be unhappy and he too. This shows great strength of character as all her family and all of us wish it, and she refuses the greatest position there is."[33]

How seriously Alix took God's blessing in her life is clearly seen in the letter that she sent to Nicholas in November 1893. In this letter Alix completely rejects the possibility of violating her conscience and declares that she preferred to be wounded in her own feelings rather than to sin against God. This letter, which was essentially a rejection of Nicholas, was the following:

> 8 November, 1893—Darmstadt.
> Dearest Nicky,
> I send you my very best thanks for your dear letter, and enclose the photograph you wished to have and which Ella will forward to you.
> I believe it must have been a stronger will than ours which ordained that we should not meet at Coburg, for like this it gives me the chance to write to you all my innermost feelings which perhaps on the spur of the moment I might not have said, so that you may have misunderstood me.

You know what my feelings are as Ella has told them to you already, but I feel it my duty to tell them to you myself. I thought everything for a long time, and I only beg you not to think that I take it lightly for it grieves me terribly and makes me very unhappy.

I have tried to look at it in every light that is possible, but I always return to one thing. I cannot do it against my conscience. You, dear Nicky, who have also such a strong belief will understand me that I think it is a sin to change my belief, and I should be miserable all the days of my life, knowing that I had done a wrongful thing.

I am certain that you would not wish me to change against my conviction. What happiness can come from a marriage which begins without the real blessing of God? For I feel it a sin to change that belief in which I have been brought up and which I love. I should never find my peace of mind again, and like that I should never be your real companion who should help you on in life; for there always should be something between us two, in my not having the real conviction of the belief I had taken, and in the regret for the one I had left.

It would be acting a lie to you, your Religion and to God. This is my feeling of right and wrong, and one's innermost religious convictions and one's peace of conscience toward God before all one's earthly wishes. As all these years have not made it possible for me to change my resolution in acting thus, I feel that now is the moment to tell you again that I can never change my confession.

I am certain that you will understand this clearly and see as I do, that we are only torturing ourselves, about something impossible and it would not be a kindness to let you go on having vain hopes, which will never be realized.

And now Goodbye my darling Nicky, and may God bless and protect you.

Ever your loving Alix.[34]

This letter devastated Nicholas. Although he knew from the beginning the seriousness with which Alix confronted this topic, he believed that it could finally be overcome. For a month after he received this letter, Nicholas was in a charged emotional state. At last, on 17 December he was able to compose his reply. In his letter his great faith in the will of God again appears, which even now kept his hopes alive. He wrote the following:

17 December, 1893—Gatchina.
My dearest Alix,
Please excuse my not having answered your letter sooner, but you may well imagine what a blow it proved to me.

I could not write to you all these days on account of the sad state of mind I was in. Now that my restlessness has passed I feel more calm and am able to answer your letter quietly. Let me thank you first of all for the frank and open way in which you spoke to me in that letter! There is nothing worse in the world than things misunderstood and not brought to the point.

I knew from the beginning what an obstacle there rose between us and I felt so deeply for you all these years, knowing perfectly the great difficulties you would have had to overcome! But still it is so awfully hard, when you have cherished a dream for many a year and think—now you are near to its being realized—then suddenly the curtain is drawn and—you see only an empty space and feel oh! so lonely and so beaten down!!

I cannot deny the reasons you give me, dear Alix; but I have got one which is also true: you hardly know the depth of our religion. If you only could have learnt it with somebody, who knows it, and could have read books, where you might see the likeness and difference of the two—perhaps then! it would not have troubled you in the same way as it does now!

Your living quite alone without anyone's help in such a matter, is also a sad circumstance in the barrier that apparently stands between us! It is too sad for words to know that that barrier is—religion!

Don't you think, dearest, that the five years, since we know each other, have passed in vain and with no result? Certainly not—for me at least. And how am I to change my feelings after waiting and wishing for so long, even now after that sad letter you sent me? I trust in God's mercy; maybe it is His will that we both, but you especially should suffer long—maybe after helping us through all these miseries and trials—He will yet guide my darling along the path that I daily pray for!

Oh! do not say 'no' directly, my dearest Alix, do not ruin my life already! Do you think there can exist any happiness in the whole world without you! After having involuntarily! kept me waiting and hoping, can this end in such a way?

Oh! do not get angry with me if I am beginning to say silly things, though I promised in this letter to be calm! Your heart is too kind not to understand what tortures I am going through now.

But I have spoken enough and must end this epistle of mine. Thank you so much for your charming photo.

Let me wish, dearest Alix, that the coming Year may bring you peace, happiness, comfort, and the fulfilment of your wishes. God bless you and protect you!

Ever your loving and devoted Nicky.[35]

In April of 1894, the wedding of Alix's brother Ernst took place in Coburg. Overlooking that great obstacle, Nicholas decided to use the opportunity to propose to Alix. Among Nicholas' companions who would follow him to Coburg was the spiritual father of the Royal Family, as well as their tutor,

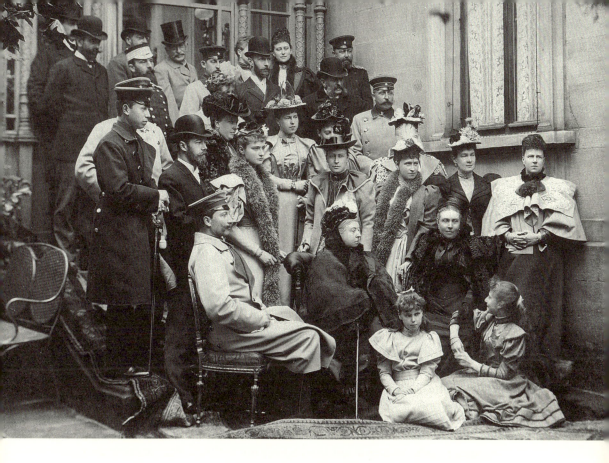

On the day of Nicholas and Alix's engagement. Queen Victoria is in the center with Kaiser Wilhelm II on her left.

Catherine Schneider, who taught Alix's sister Elisabeth Russian. If all went well, the priest would catechize Alix in the Orthodox Faith and the tutor would give her the first lessons in Russian.

Being impatient, Nicholas made the long-desired marriage proposal to Alix the day after he arrived in Coburg. From his diary: "5th of April [1894]. Tuesday. God! What a day! After coffee around 10 o'clock we came to aunt Ella [and we went] to Ernie's and Alix's rooms. She was remarkably prettier, but looked extremely sad. They left us alone and then we began the conversation, for which I have been longing so long and of which I was also very afraid. We spoke until 12 o'clock, but without any success, [because] she still opposes to changing her religion. The poor thing cried so much."[36] In a letter to his mother he described the event: "I don't know how to begin this letter. I want to see you so much, but my thoughts are somehow quite confused. This is how, with God's merciful help, my quest which seemed to me so desperate found its fulfilment. The day after I came here I had a long and very difficult talk with Alix, in which I tried to explain to her that there was no other way for her than to give her consent, and that she simply could not withhold it. She cried the whole time, and only whispered now and then, 'No, I cannot!' Still I went on, repeating and insisting on what I had said before. And though this talk went on for two hours it came to nothing."[37]

Queen Victoria arrived from England for the wedding of her grandson Ernst, and she tried to calm Alix, explaining to her that conversion to the Orthodox Faith did not constitute an affront to God. However, a more important influence on the sorrowing princess came from her sister, Elisabeth. Elisabeth was not obliged to convert to Orthodoxy to marry Grand Duke Serge. She herself, however, being a deeply religious soul, found in Orthodoxy the fulness of Christian truth. Speaking then to her sister about the sublimity of the Orthodox Faith, she soothed her soul and dispelled her uneasiness.

From Nicholas' diary the day after Ernst's wedding: "8th of April. Friday. A wonderful, unforgettable day of my life—the day of my engagement to my dear, beloved Alix. After 10 o'clock she came to Aunt Miechen, and after talking with her we came to an understanding. God! What a mountain fell off my shoulders.... I was like in a dream all day, not quite aware of what actually happened to me!"[38] In a letter to his mother he wrote: "We were left alone, and with her very first words she consented! The Almighty only knows what happened to me then. I cried like a child and she did too; but her expression had changed; her face was lit by a quiet content. No, dear Mama, I can't tell you how happy I am and how sad at the same time that I am not with you and can't take you and dearest Papa to my heart at this moment. The whole world is changed for me: nature, mankind, everything; and all seem to be good and lovable and happy. I couldn't even write, my hands trembled so, and indeed I hadn't a second to myself. ... I had to answer hundreds of telegrams, though what I really wanted all the time was to be sitting alone in a quiet corner with my dear fiancée. She is quite changed. She is gay and amusing and talkative and tender. I can't thank God enough for His mercy."[39]

His mother's reply was full of enthusiasm. Among other things she wrote, "Words cannot express with what delight and great joy I received this happy news! I almost felt faint, I was so overjoyed! But how sad not to be with you my beloved Nicky at this great moment in your life! Not to be able to kiss you and bless you from the depths of my soul! May God shower you both with his blessings and grant you every possible happiness on this earth; this is my most fervent and ardent prayer for you my Nicky. I was so happy, and shed tears of joy and emotion and ran to announce this happy news to Papa first of all, then to Ksenia and Sandro and there were nothing but shouts of joy and real jubilation!"[40]

The Emperor also wrote to his son to congratulate him. His letter was at the same time moving, and also full of wisdom:

On the day of the engagement.

Formal picture of the engagement.

14 April, 1894—Gatchina.

My dear sweet Nicky,

You can imagine the feeling of joy and gratitude towards the Lord with which we learnt of your engagement! I have to admit that I did not believe the possibility of such an outcome and was sure your attempt would fail completely, but the Lord guided you, gave you strength and blessed you, many thanks to Him for His mercy. If only you had seen the happiness and rejoicing with which everyone greeted the news: we immediately started to receive a mass of telegrams, and are still being overwhelmed by them.

I am sure that you are doubly happy, and everything that happened, although forgotten, will surely have been useful in showing that not everything is so easy, particularly such an enormous step, which will decide your whole future and your ensuing family life.

I cannot imagine you as a fiancé, how strange and unusual! How sad it was for Mama and I not to be with you at such a time, not to embrace you, not to talk to you or know anything, just to wait for letters with the details.

Please tell your dear fiancée from me, how much I thank her for at last consenting, and how I wish her to flourish for the joy, comfort, and peace she has given us by deciding to agree to be your wife!

I embrace and congratulate you, my dear sweet Nicky; we are happy for your happiness, and may the Lord bless your future life, as he has blessed it from the beginning![41]

Alix herself was elated with the result. As soon as she left the room where she gave her consent for the marriage, she ran next door to the room of her cousin, Princess Marie Louise of England and embracing her told her with great joy that she would marry Nicholas. Later she wrote of her feelings, "I dreamt that I was loved, I woke and found it true, and thanked God on my knees for it. True love is the gift which God has given—daily stronger, deeper, fuller, purer."[42]

The quality and depth of the love with which Alix embraced Nicholas pricked his conscience on one sensitive point. In his youth, during the years of his disappointment that his parents rejected the possibility of marrying Alix, Nicholas succumbed to one temptation. For a long time, his cousins attempted to persuade him to be involved with a performer of the Royal Ballet, Mathilde Kschessinskaya, who nursed strong feelings for the young prince. This relation, certainly, could not have any serious result whatsoever, because every member of the royal house was obliged to marry only with persons who also belonged to a royal family. However, in the capital of the Russian Empire, the corruption of the upper class had reached such a degree as to contemplate daily relations between members of the aristocracy and artists as a presupposition of "normal" aristocratic conduct. Almost all the princes had mistresses without considering this at all an impropriety, but rather an advantage.

Nicholas could not bring himself to agree with this mentality. A deeply cultivated soul and having true fear of God, he wished to preserve his purity for the bride whom Divine Providence would grant him. The warfare was, however, difficult. At the same time, even though she knew that an affair with Nicholas had no future, the undoubtedly genuine feelings of this girl affected the sensitive soul of Nicholas, who indeed started to feel emotionally attracted to her. He managed to resist the temptation for a long time, but finally he yielded.

Now, shortly before his marriage with Alix, he felt the necessity to reveal his fall to his betrothed, so that he would not enter into his marriage with this burden. Alix's reaction was truly magnanimous. Despite her young age, she was then only twenty-two years old, she faced this event with the manner and dignity of a perfectly cultivated soul and personality. Her reply, which she recorded in Nicholas' diary, was:

> My own boysy dear, never changing, always true. Have confidence and faith in y[our] girly dear, who loves you more deeply and devotedly than she can ever say. Words are too poor to express my love and admiration and respect—what is past, is past, and will never return, and we can look back on it with calm—we all are tempted in this world, and when we are young we cannot always fight and hold our own against the temptation, but as long as we repent and come back to the good and on to the straight path, God forgives us. "If we confess our sins, He is faithful and just to forgive us our sins."[43] God pardons those who confess their faults. Forgive my writing so much, but I want you to be quite sure of my love for you and that I love you even more since you told me that little story; your confidence in me touched me, oh, so deeply, and I pray to God that I may always show myself worthy of it. God bless you, beloved Ники [Nicky]![44]

The betrothed couple spent a few days in Coburg and subsequently made a one-day visit to Darmstadt, and from there Nicholas departed for Russia. Soon after Alix left for England, where at the insistence of the Queen, her grandmother, she had long-lasting conversations with the Anglican bishop of Ripon, Doctor Boyd Carpenter about the topic of conversion to Orthodoxy. Bishop Carpenter, with whom Alix carried a correspondence to the end of her life, helped make her passage to Orthodoxy as best he could. Subsequently Alix underwent treatment for her chronic sciatica, while Father Yanishev arrived in England from Russia to catechize Alix in the Orthodox Faith. Catherine Schneider also came to England to begin Alix's instruction in the Russian language. Father Yanishev later confessed that he had never before heard the theological questions that Alix posed, not even from distinguished theologians. Such was the depth of her thought that the priest often encountered significant difficulties in giving her the desired answers!

After Alix's course of therapy, Nicholas arrived in England, where he stayed to be near his beloved. Then they passed perhaps the most beautiful moments in their lives. Carefree, without any important obligations, they freely reveled in the joy of their companionship, going for long walks in nature and conversing for endless hours by the side of a lake. They would remember these days with nostalgia for the rest of their lives, for very soon they would be suddenly immersed in the most unexpected developments.

CHAPTER 2

AT THE HEIGHT OF GLORY

A NEW LIFE BEGINS THROUGH DEATH

On returning to Russia, Nicholas found his family in a state of alarm over the health of his father. Despite all advice of physicians, the Tsar insisted on not taking his problem seriously. At last, however, his condition worsened to the degree that he himself, the one-time robust autocrat, understood that his case was serious. So, obeying the advice of physicians, he moved to the Livadia Palace in Crimea where the sunny weather and clean sea air at first seemed to promote an improvement of his health. But after a few days, his condition began to worsen again, and left him bedridden. They then called for Father John of Kronstadt, who made haste to come to their assistance and to pray with the royal family for the restoration of the tsar's health. Father John, who was later glorified as a saint of the Orthodox Church, was closely tied to the royal family and his spiritual counsels and admonitions were a rule of life for them. Nicholas described those days in his diary:

"At 10:30 [am], a large part of the family went on foot to the church of Oreanda for the liturgy, which was served by Fr John. He [Fr John] pronounces the prayers very sharply, nearly loud—he read a prayer for Father, which made a strong impression on me."[1]

The emperor's condition continued to worsen. At the beginning of October Nicholas summoned Alix to come to Crimea as quickly as possible. While she was on her way, Alix sent a message asking to hasten the process of her Rite of Conversion to Orthodoxy. On the way to Livadia she met her sister Elisabeth who accompanied her to her destination. At last, they arrived at the station at Simferopol on 10 October, where Nicholas waited to convey her to the palace. In his diary Nicholas wrote:

CHAPTER 2

"10th of October. Monday... [M]y beloved Alix arrived from Simferopol with Ella. ... After breakfast, I sat with Alix in the carriage and the two of us went to Livadia. My God! What joy to meet her at home [in my country] and to have her close to me—half of the worries and sorrows seemed to have fled from my shoulders. At every station the Tatars received us with bread and salt. ... Our carriage was full of flowers and vine leaves."[2]

At the Palace, the Emperor awaited the young couple sitting in an armchair in his bedchamber. He was clothed in his whole regalia, saying that only thus was it proper for the tsar of Russia to receive the future empress of his country. Kneeling before Alexander, Alix received his blessing. "What a joy it was to my father when she [Alix] came," recalled Grand Duchess Olga Alexandrovna, Nicholas' sister. "I remember that he kept her for a long time in his room."[3] Not many days would pass, however, before the worst came to pass.

"18th of October. Tuesday. A difficult, sad day! Dear Papa did not sleep at all and in the morning he felt bad, so that they woke us up and called us upstairs. What kind of ordeal is this? ...All our aspiration and our hope are in the Merciful God: may His holy will be done!"[4]

At last, on 20 October, the Emperor's condition had significantly deteriorated. The end drew nearer from moment to moment. Saint John was at the Tsar's side and had laid his hands on his head. At one point, the saint asked the tsar whether his pains were intolerable. Alexander replied, "On the contrary, I experience great relief when I feel your hands on my head." The saint then said to him, "You are one of the just. The Russian people love you, and they love you because they know who you are and what you are."[5] After a few moments, the tsar departed for the heavens.

"20th of October. Thursday. My God, my God, what a day! The Lord called [to Himself] our adored, dear, much-beloved Papa. My head is spinning, I don't want to believe it—this terrible reality seems so implausible. We spent the entire morning near him! His breathing was difficult and it was required to give him oxygen to inhale. Around half past 3 [pm] he received holy Communion; soon light seizures began and soon came the end. Fr John [of Kronstadt] remained on his bedside for more than an hour and held his head. It was the death of a saint! Lord, help us in these difficult days!"[6]

Olga Alexandrovna described the scene: "We all rose as quietly as we could, crossed the room, and kissed my father's forehead and hand. Then we kissed my mother. It seemed as though the fog outside had entered the room. All of us turned to Nicky and kissed his hand for the first time."[7]

Shortly before he gave up his soul to the Lord, Alexander called Nicholas to himself and entrusted him with his final testament. Among other things, he told him the following:

> You shall have to take from my shoulders the heavy burden of national authority and bear it to the grave, as I and our ancestors

Nicholas with his sister Olga.

have done. I give to you the kingdom entrusted to me by God. I received it thirteen years ago from my bleeding father. ... From the height of the throne your grandfather carried out many important reforms, directed to the good of the Russian people. As a reward for this, he received a bomb and death from Russian revolutionaries. ... On that tragic day the question stood before me: which path was I to follow? Was it the one toward which I was being urged by so-called progressive society, infected with the liberal ideas of the West, or was it the one recommended by my own convictions, by my highest, sacred duty as sovereign, by my own conscience? I chose my path. The liberals called it reactionary. I was interested only in the good of my people and the greatness of Russia. I strove to give it internal and external peace, that the state might freely and calmly develop, becoming strong, rich and prosperous in an orderly way. Autocracy has created Russia's historical individuality. If autocracy falls, God forbid, Russia will collapse with it. The fall of the time-honored Russian government will inaugurate an era of civil strife and bloody internecine wars. I adjure you to love everything that serves the good, the honor, and the dignity of Russia. Guard autocracy, remembering at the same time that you bear the responsibility for the fate of your subjects before the throne of the Most High. May faith in God and in the sanctity of your royal duty be the foundation of your life. Be firm and courageous, and never show any weakness. Listen to everyone— there is nothing shameful in that— but hearken only to yourself and to your own conscience. In foreign policy, preserve an independent position. Remember—Russia has no friends. They fear our vastness. Avoid war. In domestic policy, first and foremost protect the Church. She has often saved Russia in times of misfortune. Strengthen the family, for it is the foundation of any state.[8]

Things were difficult, however. Alexander's sudden death brought Nicholas face to face with a hard reality: the lack of necessary preparation to take up his tremendous duties. His sister Olga remembers one of those first days after the repose of her father. She had gone out onto the balcony when Nicholas approached her, embraced her, and wept: "He was in despair. He kept saying that he did not know what would become of us all, that he was wholly unfit to reign. ... He had intelligence, he had faith and courage— and he was wholly ignorant about governmental matters. Nicky had been trained as a soldier. He should have been taught statesmanship, and he was not. It was my father's fault. He would not even have Nicky sit in Council of State until 1893. I can't tell you why. The mistake was there. I know my father disliked the mere idea of state matters encroaching on our family life—but after all, Nicky was his heir. And what a ghastly price was later paid for the mistake. Of course, my father, who had always enjoyed an athlete's health, could not have foreseen such an early end to his life. But the mistake was there."[9]

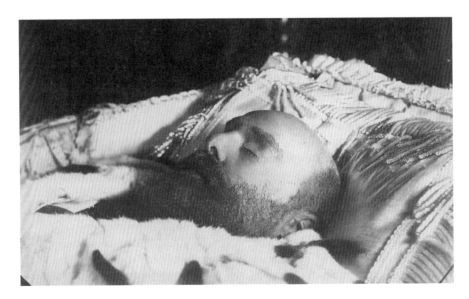

Alexander III on his death bed.

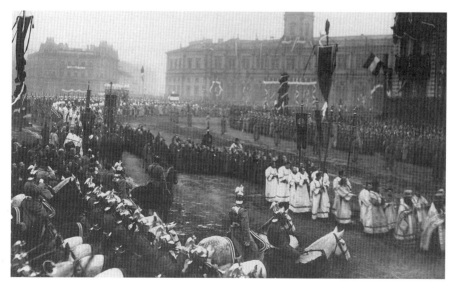

From the funeral of Alexander III.

CHAPTER 2

From Nicholas' diary: "21st of October. Friday. Even in our deep sorrow the Lord gives us peaceful and bright joy: at 10 o'clock [am] in the presence of only the family, my sweet, dear Alix was anointed [with holy Chrism and entered the Orthodox Church], and after the liturgy we both received holy Communion along with Mama and Ella. Alix read her replies and the prayers remarkably well and clearly! After breakfast we had a panikhida [memorial service], and at 9 o'clock in the evening—another one. The expression on the face of dear Papa is beautiful, smiling, as if he wants to laugh!"[10]

After Alix received the Holy Chrism, Nicholas issued his first royal decree. In it he made note of his fiancée's entrance into Orthodoxy and her new name and title. The former Princess Alix of Hesse was now the Orthodox Grand Duchess Alexandra Feodorovna.

The funeral of the Emperor was celebrated in the Cathedral of the Apostles Peter and Paul. For this tragic event, one year of mourning was proclaimed, during which protocol forbade the celebration of the young monarchs' marriage. However, one week later (14 November) was the birthday of the widowed Queen Mother. Therefore, that day was set for the celebration of the marriage, because the double joy of the day permitted the setting aside of mourning. Later, in a letter to one of her sisters, Alexandra related characteristically, "Such was my entry into Russia.... Our marriage seemed to me to be a mere continuation of the masses for the dead, with this difference, that I now wore a white dress instead of a black."[11]

From Nicholas' diary: "14th of November. Monday. The day of my wedding! ...At 10 past twelve began the procession to the cathedral, from which I returned a married man! ...We mounted with Alix on a carriage adorned with Russian harness, which was driven by a coachman. We proceeded to the Cathedral of the Mother of God of Kazan. There was a huge public in the streets—we were barely able to go through!"[12] The cannons of the Peter and Paul Fortress announced the beginning of the Sacrament. The Queen Mother accompanied her daughter-in-law who went on ahead, and Nicholas followed wearing the military uniform of the Hussars. Nicholas ascended the platform first and then Alexandra. Each holding a lit candle, they stood before Archpriest John Yanishev, the confessor of the Royal Family and rector of the palace, and the Rite of Matrimony began. After the blessing of the rings, the pair knelt and gave the vows of Matrimony. At the completion of the Rite of Matrimony, a general peal of bells sounded over the entire city of Saint Petersburg, with celebratory fireworks from the Peter and Paul Fortress.

On account of mourning, no honeymoon followed. The royal couple returned immediately to the Anichkov Palace, first passing by the Cathedral Church of the Mother of God of Kazan to venerate the Wonderworking Icon of the Mother of God. In the years that followed, Alexandra often went to that church with some of her ladies in waiting. She customarily knelt in the shadow of a pillar and prayed without being recognized by those present.

No one was able to guess who that woman was who just before she knelt had very discreetly taken a candle and lit it before the Icon of the Theotokos.

Returning to the palace, the newlyweds encountered a sea of people along the way cheering and acclaiming them with great enthusiasm. At the palace, the Queen Mother waited for them with the traditional Russian bread and salt. In the evening they remained in the house replying only to telegrams of congratulations. Two weeks later, while the couple were enjoying a few relaxing days in Tsarskoe Selo, Alexandra noted in Nicholas' diary:

> Ever more and more, stronger and deeper my love and devotion grows and my longing for you. Never can I thank God enough for the treasure He has given me for my very own—and to be called yours, sweety, what happiness can be greater. Never shall I forget this place, already dear to me on account of the remembrances of [18]89, and now—our first quiet time together. God bless you my beloved little husband, I cover y[our] sweet face with kisses.
>
> Never did I believe there could be such utter happiness in this world, such a feeling of unity between two mortal beings. I love you—those three words have my life in them.[13] No more separations! At last united, bound for life; and when this life is ended we meet again in the other world to remain together for all eternity. Yours, yours, my душки [darling].[14]

In a letter to one of her sisters she wrote, "If only I could find words to tell you of my happiness—daily it grows more and more and my love greater. Never can I thank God enough for having given me such a treasure. He is too good, and dear, and loving and kind."[15]

Elisabeth wrote to Queen Victoria, "It does our hearts good to know Nicky and Alix at last happy and I am sure God will bless this union in which [there are] such deep feelings of religion."[16]

Nicholas and Alexandra preserved in a wonderful way with the same intensity all their lives the experience of the perfection of this love, which was given to that good couple for the purity of their feelings and the spiritual understanding of their relationship. Years later, Symeon Fabritsky, an aide-de-camp to Nicholas, wrote: "It would have been hard to find a better family man and husband, or a man who loved his wife more. On those infrequent occasions when he had to speak with ladies, the Emperor always seemed shy, embarrassed, and ill-at-ease."[17]

After the unprecedented historical storms that they passed through in the course of their lives, the unfaltering love between them—which later would also characterize the relationship with their children—in combination with their absolute trust in the will of God, worked as an steadfast anchor protecting them from the manifold harrowing blows of their ordeals.

CHAPTER 2

CORONATION
THE ROYAL SACRAMENT

Although protocol prescribed a suspension of mourning at the death of the tsar for the marriage of the new royal pair, the great event of Coronation had to await the completion of the prescribed period of mourning. The preparations for this historic event were set in motion in the fall of 1895. The fourteenth of May of 1896 was designated the day for the expected event, which, as for all coronations of tsars of Russia, would take place in the Cathedral of the Dormition of the Theotokos (Uspensky Sobor) in the Kremlin of Moscow.

In the hope that they would see the royal couple close up, and in the even more remote hope that they would be able to receive their blessing, throngs of people began to arrive in Moscow from every corner of Russia even before the beginning of May. Batiushka and Matushka,[18] as the people called the imperial couple, did not merely hold the position of rulers of the Russian Empire in the consciousness of the people.

The Orthodox rulers of Russia, just like those in the Byzantine period, in their capacity of autocratic authority, were the anointed of God. They were the divinely appointed protectors of Orthodoxy, who were endowed with divine power and blessing. Orthodox autocracy does not consist a system of absolute, uncontrolled power. Rather, it is based on the anointing of the Church and on the faith of the people. If it betrays either, by disobeying the Church, or by trampling on the people's faith, it loses its legitimacy.[19] It is therefore limited, not absolute, and must not be confused with the system of absolutist monarchy that we see, for example, in the French King Louis XIV, or the English King Henry VIII, who felt limited by nothing and no one on earth.

The spiritual dimension of the work and person of the Orthodox autocrat is also clearly set forth in the Rite of Coronation, which was a Sacrament of the Church with a very distinct order of service. The culmination of the Rite of the Anointing and Crowning of a Monarch was his entry into the Holy Sanctuary through the Royal Doors, where he communed according to the order of the priesthood, that is, by himself taking the Body and Blood of the Lord each separately. In this manner the Church underscored the spiritual dimension of the capacity of the monarch, likening it to the sacred and pastoral ministry by which the monarch takes up responsibility not only for the material, but also for the spiritual well being and advancement of his subjects.

The most famous decorators were deployed in preparing Moscow for the Coronation. The result of their work was as expected. From the very beginning of May, Moscow was resplendent with all the ancient, Orthodox Byzantine majesty, awash in the glory of royal Christian tradition. It was now ready to receive from God the chosen father of the Russian nation. According to tradition, he was not to enter Moscow until the day of the inauguration of the official ceremonies for his coronation.

Nicholas' entry into Moscow was set for the ninth of May. In anticipation of that day Nicholas and Alexandra were conveyed to the Petrovsky Palace a few kilometers outside of Moscow. There they remained inside in fasting and prayer that God should bless them and give them strength to accomplish the divine mission for which He Himself chose and appointed them. From the beginning, Grand Duke Serge, Elisabeth's husband, had already undertaken Alexandra's due preparation, so that at the coming of that holy hour, she would be able to be endued to her depths with the Sacrament of Coronation, and to understand the great and solemn spiritual dimensions of her divine calling and ministry.

The roar of nine cannon shots from the Kremlin proclaimed the historic entrance of the imperial procession into Moscow. An innumerable series of cavalry and infantry of the palace guard stretched along the length of the road where the royal procession passed. Every church along the processional route sounded their festal peals, vying with patriotic paeans. Along with these, tens of thousands of cheers of acclamation resounded in the streets of Moscow from the celebration of the pious and Christ-loving throngs that gathered, which witnessed that their hearts resounded as living chimes of jubilation. From every point where the pair passed, the crowds blessed them piously with the sign of the Cross.

Behind the multitude of cavalry, all the military ranks of the palace followed the tsar on horseback and then all the grand dukes of the Romanov dynasty. Representatives of foreign royal houses followed, and then the carriage of the widowed Queen Mother and then followed Alexandra's carriage. Finally, Alexandra's carriage was followed by those of the grand duchesses of the Romanovs.

Before the Kremlin walls the procession halted, and Nicholas prayed with Alexandra before an ancient copy of the Portaitissa Icon of the Mother of God that was sent to Russia from the Iveron Monastery on Mount Athos in 1648. After their entrance into the Kremlin, the royal pair worshipped at the Cathedral of the Dormition, at the Church of the Archangel where the mausoleum of the Tsars was, and at the private chapel of the Tsars, the Church of the Annunciation of the Theotokos. At last, they arrived at the Great Palace of the Kremlin where they would remain until the day of the coronation. From Nicholas' diary:

"10th of May. Friday. ... We began with Alix to fast and to prepare for receiving Communion. 13th of May. Monday. ... We made our confession.... May the Merciful God help us, may He strengthen us tomorrow and he bless us with a peaceful working life!!!"[20]

Five days after their official entrance into Moscow, at 10:30 in the morning of 14 May, Nicholas and Alexandra, under an imperial canopy,

CHAPTER 2

The entrance in the cathedral for the coronation.

went again in procession to the Assumption Cathedral. The great hour had arrived. Peals of bells greeted history once again. Before the gates of the Church, the hierarchy received the monarchs, and the Metropolitan of Moscow had them kiss the Cross and the Gospel. Then he sprinkled them with holy water, and they entered the church to perform the Sacrament. The service would begin with the Rite of Coronation and continue with the Divine Liturgy, during which the Anointing of the King was to be performed.

The service, which lasted nearly five hours, began immediately upon the entrance of the monarchs into the church, with the choir singing Psalm 100: Of mercy and judgement will I sing unto Thee, O Lord; I will chant and have understanding in a blameless path. At that point the monarchs venerated the icons. Subsequently Nicholas was called to recite the Creed and then he approached the Royal Doors. There he knelt and the Metropolitan of Moscow placed his hand on the head of the new monarch, and read the Prayer of Coronation of a King:

> O Lord our God, King of kings, and Lord of lords, who through Samuel the prophet didst choose thy servant David, and didst anoint

Nicholas receiving the crown to carry out his crowning by himself.

him to be king over thy people Israel; hear now the supplication of us though unworthy, and look forth from thy holy dwelling place, and vouchsafe to anoint with the oil of gladness thy faithful servant Nicholas, whom thou hast been pleased to establish as king over thy holy people, which thou hast made thine own by the precious blood of thine Only-begotten Son. Clothe him with power from on high; set on his head a crown of precious stones; bestow on him length of days; set in his right hand a sceptre of salvation; stablish him upon the throne of righteousness; defend him with the panoply of thy Holy Spirit; strengthen his arm; subject to him all the barbarous nations; sow in his heart the fear of Thee, and feeling for his subjects; preserve him in the blameless faith; make him manifest as the sure guardian of the doctrines of thy Holy Catholic Church; that he may judge thy people in righteousness, and thy poor in judgement, and save the sons of those in want; and may be an heir of thy heavenly kingdom. For thine is the might, and thine is the kingdom and the power. Amen.[21]

Then the Metropolitan gave him the crown. As ever, in accordance with the Byzantine liturgical practice, the emperor had to carry out his crowning by himself, which act manifested the direct assumption of power from God Himself. With reverence and deep compunction, Nicholas received the crown from the hands of the Metropolitan, and with hands trembling from unspeakable emotion, he set it upon his head as the hierarch offered

CHAPTER 2

Nicholas crowning Alexandra.   Nicholas kissing Alexandra.

the appointed prayer. Then the hierarch gave the royal scepter into his right hand and the orb into his left, pronouncing the appropriate prayer.

Nicholas, now crowned Emperor of All Russias, sat on his throne and called Alexandra to approach. She in her turn wore the imperial mantle and knelt before the Tsar, who took the crown from off his head and placed it on the brow of Alexandra and put it back on. Then he took up a smaller crown and crowned Alexandra Empress. Raising her up he kissed her and guided her to the middle of the church where they ascended the thrones that had been placed upon a platform before the Royal Doors. Beside them, on a third throne, sat the widowed Queen Mother. Subsequently, the choir chanted the polychronion (Many Years) of the imperial couple, accompanied by the ringing of bells and one hundred and one congratulatory gunshots outside the church. Next, Nicholas knelt and read the following prayer:

> *O Lord God of our fathers, and King of Kings, Who created all things by Thy word, and by Thy wisdom hast made man, that he should walk uprightly and rule righteously over Thy world; Thou hast chosen me as Tsar and judge over Thy people. I acknowledge Thine unsearchable purpose towards me, and bow in thankfulness before Thy Majesty. Do Thou, my Lord and Governor, fit me for the work to which Thou has sent me; teach me and guide me in this great service. May there be with me the wisdom which belongs to Thy throne; send it from Thy Holy Heaven, that I may know what is well-pleasing in Thy sight, and what is right according to Thy commandment. May*

Nicholas praying on his knees.

---

my heart be in Thine hand, to accomplish all that is to the profit of the people committed to my charge, and to Thy glory, that so in the day of Thy Judgment I may give Thee account of my stewardship without blame; through the grace and mercy of Thy Son, Who was once crucified for us, to Whom be all honor and glory with Thee and the Holy Spirit, the Giver of Life, for ever and ever. Amen.[22]

As soon as Nicholas rose up, the entire congregation, including the hierarchs, Empress Alexandra, and Queen Mother Maria, knelt before him, thus showing their submission before him, while at the same time the choir sang the doxology.

At this point the Rite of Coronation was complete, and the Divine Liturgy began. Before Holy Communion was given, while the Communion Hymn was being chanted, the Metropolitan of Moscow called Nicholas and Alexandra before the Royal Doors and there he anointed them with the Holy Chrism. Nicholas received the seal of the Chrism on his forehead, his eyes, his nose, his mouth, his ears, his breast and his hands. Then he stood before the Icon of Christ, while the hierarch anointed Alexandra only upon her forehead. Alexandra then stood before the Icon of the Theotokos. A new peal of bells and another hundred and one rifle shots followed.

Before receiving Holy Communion, Nicholas read the Oath of Coronation, according to which he was bound to preserve inviolate the imperial constitution and to govern with righteousness. Subsequently the Emperor entered the Sanctuary through the Royal Doors where he received Holy Communion according to the priestly order along with the hierarchs and

Official entry into Moscow, 9 May, 1896.
Nicholas enters into the Red Square through the Resurrection (Iberian) Gate.

From the official entry into Moscow.

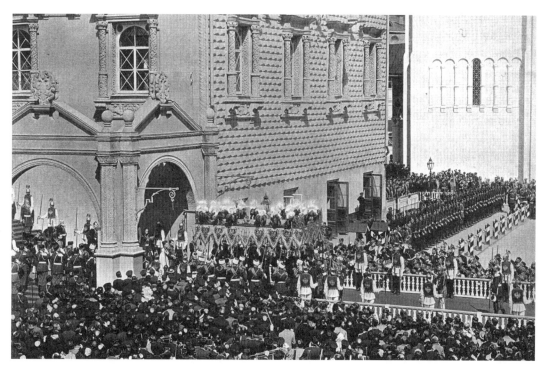

Nicholas and Alexandra at the gate of the Grand Kremlin Palace,
ready for the procession to the Assumption Cathedral for the Coronation.

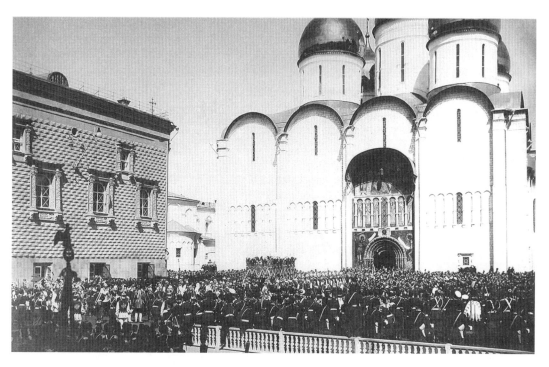

Entry into the Assumption Cathedral.

From the procession back to the Grand Kremlin Palace after the coronation.

Above: From the procession back to the Grand Kremlin Palace after the coronation.
Below: Nicholas and Alexandra at the top of the Red Staircase
of the Grand Kremlin bowing to the people.

the concelebrating priests. At the end of the Liturgy the new monarchs returned festively to the Great Palace in the Kremlin.

That evening Nicholas wrote in his diary, "14th of May. Tuesday. … The weather has been, fortunately, marvelous; the Red Porch represented a radiant view. Everything that took place in the Uspenski Cathedral, although it seems like a real dream, it will not be forgotten throughout a lifetime!!! …At 4 o'clock everything ended quite well; with [my] soul full of gratitude to God, I rested perfectly well afterwards."[23]

Some years later, in a letter to his mother, Nicholas would write, "In the sight of my Maker I have to carry the burden of a terrible responsibility, and at all times, therefore, be ready to render an account to Him of my actions. I must always keep firmly to my convictions and follow the dictates of my conscience."[24] In an interview, he also revealed this following wonderful principle, something that one encounters only in the lives of great saints, "I never prepare what I am going to say in audience, but, praying to the Lord God, I speak what comes into my mind."[25] These two principles show the manner in which he walked and served as anointed king before the Lord until his last breath.

PORTENT OF DEATH

Four days after the coronation, the new tsar organized an outdoor reception for the public in the suburbs of Moscow, in the Khodynka district. At the reception refreshments would be served, and a commemorative cup would be given to those attending. Crowds began to gather at the open-air venue of the reception beginning the night before. By morning the gathered crowd reached half a million. A fateful rumor then began to spread, that there would not be enough of the commemorative gifts and refreshments for everyone present. The crowd then began to shove toward the place where the gifts were, and due to the panic caused by the uncontrollable rush of the crowd, many people fell into the ditches in the field where the reception was organized. The result was tragic. More than a thousand people lost their lives by being trampled, and as many again were hurt. The reception had not yet even begun.

The full magnitude of the tragedy was not apparent at first. At the beginning of the reception, the official guests, and the crowd of people that were present, did not know what exactly had just happened. The authorities were careful to clean up the area promptly to avoid scandal. The imperial couple were informed of the event hours later.

Nicholas wrote, "18th of May. Saturday. Up until this point, by the grace of God, everything had run smoothly, but today, a great evil occurred.

The crowd which had spent the night on Khodynka field, waiting for the distribution of lunch and the Coronation cups, thronged against the stands and then there was a ghastly crush and consequently, terribly, about 1300 people were crushed!! I learned of this at 10:30 o'clock, before Vannovsky's report; this news has had the most revolting effect on me. At 12.30 PM we had breakfast and then Alix and I went to Khodynka to attend this saddest of 'national holidays.'"[26]

Nicholas and Alexandra spent the rest of the day visiting the wounded in the hospitals. Only then did they realize the enormity of the tragedy; this fact completely shattered them. They immediately decided to cancel all the remaining celebrations, but they encountered strong opposition from the grand dukes, brothers of the late Tsar Alexander III. Both they and the broader aristocratic class insisted that it was completely impossible to cancel or postpone the reception that the French ambassador had organized in honor of the royal couple. That might have badly affected the alliance that Alexander III had signed only two years earlier with France. The personal feelings of the royal couple were held of no account. The official duties had to be fulfilled and the diplomatic interests of the empire could not be spoiled! Nicholas yielded with terrible pain.

On the evening of the reception, the physical condition of the couple was apparent to all. Alexandra's eyes were completely red with shed tears. The couple's participation was completely mechanical, and it was very clear that their thoughts were on the suffering of the victims of this terrible calamity. Baroness Buxhoeveden wrote, "Both he and the Empress wanted to cancel the French Ambassador's ball, arranged for the very night. They were told this was impossible, the French Government having made the most extravagant preparations for the ball. (Beautiful tapestries and plate had been sent expressly and at great expense from the *Garde-meuble National* in Paris.) The Emperor had to give in and go. The Empress had to control her tears, but it was with a face of utter misery that she attended the Marquis de Montebello's wonderful entertainment. She behaved like an automaton, and all her thoughts were with the dead and dying."[27]

The sovereigns showed their participation in the drama of those people in action. Beyond the daily visitation at the hospitals in the following days, Nicholas also took thought for the unfortunate victims who lost their lives in the incident. Disregarding the usual custom of burying the dead of a mass catastrophe in a common grave, he gave a decree that all the dead of Khodynka be buried individually, taking upon himself the expenses of each burial. Furthermore, again from his own personal purse, he gave one thousand rubles to each family that mourned a casualty of the accident.

Nevertheless, the enemies of the monarchy found opportunity to undermine the new Tsar right from the beginning. They circulated rumors among the people that while thousands of poor people were suffering in their sickbeds because of their desire to see and to bless the couple for their coronation, the tsar and his consort drank and feasted with complete disregard at the balls of the aristocracy. It was then that the epithet "Bloody Nicholas" was first heard. Grand Duke Serge, who was the governor of Moscow, was considered chiefly responsible for the lack of the necessary safety measures that led to the tragedy. Thus, the already existing hatred for his person by the anti-monarchists now found new material to undermine his authority. He, too, received the ironic title, "Prince of Khodynka."

PRINCESSES IN HEART

Nicholas and Alexandra were par excellence people with intense love for the institution of family. Their dream and deep desire was to found a blessed family, which would have its foundation soundly built upon a base of close inner ties. Unassuming people and with love for the simple joys of life, they hoped that they would be able to build their life far from the noise of the capital and aristocratic manners. That could become a reality within the framework of a loving family that would operate as one microcosm, apart from the glittering but hard aristocratic surroundings.

God blessed their desire abundantly, granting them five wonderful children, all of them admirable for their exceptional manner and innocence, who loved their parents with all their being. These were Olga (1895), Tatiana (1897), Maria (1899) and Anastasia (1901), and the Tsarevich Alexis (1904). After the birth of Olga, the three-member family moved from the Anichkov Palace in Saint Petersburg to the Alexander Palace in Tsarskoe Selo, which was in the suburbs of the capital.

The Alexander Palace was somewhat simpler in comparison with the other palaces of the royal family. Alexandra remaining faithful to the English family model, took care to furnish and design the space where she would live with her family as simply and austerely as possible. Thus, she avoided the usual luxuries of palaces and simply created a comfortable home based on the practical necessities of family life.

Tsarskoe Selo was essentially a village, as its very name implied, which means "Royal Village." Here in the quiet of the suburbs Nicholas and Alexandra were much more comfortable and at home, and they could devote their available time to the upbringing of their children. The children were brought up with the very same Spartan methods as Nicholas and his siblings. They slept on hard camp cots without pillows, unless they were ill. Likewise, every morning, they began their day with a cold bath to toughen them up. The four girls, growing up apart from the rest of the world by reason of their royal identity, cultivated very close and warm ties among themselves. In order to make their close tie obvious to those around them, they chose a common name that they used as a signature: OTMA. This name was nothing other than the initials of their names in order of their

The Royal children. From left:
Maria, Olga and Alexis, Anastasia, Tatiana.

age. Thus, whenever they gave gifts or sent letters, they always signed them with this common name.

Their royal station did not have any special significance for the girls. They worked along with the servants, made their own beds, and cleaned their own rooms. Although such activities may seem simple, they were never encountered within the framework of other families in royal circles, they were furthermore unheard of and considered improper! Very often the girls also visited their servants in their own quarters and played with their children. Furthermore, when they had to address them for some matter, they never made it as a command, but with great politeness and humility.

CHAPTER 2

OTMA: Olga, Tatiana, Maria and Anastasia, 1906.

They would say, for example, "If you wouldn't mind, Mother would like to see you."

On the other hand, the palace service staff were not expected to address the girls with the usual royal forms of address, but by their name and patronymic according to the traditional Russian manner, Olga Nikolaevna, Tatiana Nikolaevna, and so on. When, however, they were in public places, the servants addressed the girls with the expected forms of address, something which brought them discomfort. Once, at a meeting with some committee of which Tatiana was honorary chairman, one of Alexandra's ladies in waiting, Baroness Sophia Buxhoeveden, who was very closely tied to the family, addressed Tatiana saying, "May it please Your Imperial Highness…." Tatiana looked at her with surprise, and when the baroness sat down beside her, Tatiana gave her a firm kick under the table and whispered, "Are you crazy to address me like that?"[28]

Something similar also happened with Maria at a meeting. Tatiana referred to the incident in one of her letters, "Yesterday I was in town, had a [committee] meeting at the Winter Palace. [It] was so tiring. Maria was also with me. Since it was her first time at my meeting, Neydgart decided to give her a few words of welcome. So he and the others all got up and bowed to her. She almost crawled under the table in horror."[29]

Not having any friends, the girls showed interest and love to all the members of the countless staff of the palaces. They knew the names of all the staff, as well as those of their spouses and children. They shared their letters with them, they looked at family photographs, and for all of them they prepared small gifts. For them this was a significant sacrifice because they received a small sum every month from their parents for pocket money, which instead of using for personal gratification, they preferred to spend to make others happy.

One of their favorites was their teacher Peter Vasilievich Petrov, who taught them Russian. "Petrov was already an elderly man, very gentle, and very good-hearted. He held the Tsar's children in affection and they, in turn, were attached to him as if to a kindly relative. Often, when they were alone with him, the Grand Duchesses used to play with him, shouting, laughing, pushing him, and generally hauling him about without mercy. It was Tatiana Nicholaievna, graceful and agile as a gazelle, who would always give the signal on these occasions and direct the games. She was, at that time, a very pale little girl. One day, Petrov asked Olga Nicholaievna to name a white object for him.

'My blouse,' replied the Grand Duchess.

'And a black object?'

'My slate pencil.'

'And a green one?'

'My sister Tatiana.'

"That really was the tint of her complexion. Petrov faithfully preserved the first notebooks of his pupils, just as, later on, he was to preserve the first alphabet traced by the Heir Alexis Nicholaievitch."[30]

Their only outings away from home were when their young aunt, the Grand Duchess Olga, their father's sister, came to take them with her. There they met other children their own age, and their joy was indescribable. "I wanted them to have a little free fun," the Grand Duchess said many years later. "I discussed it with Nicky and Alicky, and they knew they could trust their children to me. ... Intoxicating drinks, of course, were never served—even for the grown-ups in the party. In those days gaiety did not depend on vodka or cocktails. I remember the girls enjoyed every minute of it—especially my dear god-daughter. Why, I can still hear her laughter rippling all over the room. Dancing, music, games—she threw herself wholeheartedly into them all."[31]

The four girls, despite their tight bonds, had quite different personalities. As they grew up, their individual characteristics grew ever more apparent. Olga, the firstborn, was born a few months before the coronation of the imperial couple, on 3 November 1895, at Anichkov Palace, where they had first settled. Nicholas wrote that day, "3rd of November [1895]. Friday. A day I shall never forget, and one during which I endured a great deal! By one in the morning my sweet Alix began to suffer pains which prevented her from sleeping. All day she lay in bed in acute pain—poor darling! I couldn't look at

CHAPTER 2

Olga Alexandrovna with her god-daughter Anastasia. Next to them: Olga and Maria.

her unconcerned. Dear Mama arrived from Gatchina around 2 o'clock [pm]; the three of us—for she had Ella with her—stayed with Alix ceaselessly. At exactly 9 o'clock [pm] we heard a child's cry and we all breathed a sigh of relief! God gave us a daughter and with prayer we have called her Olga!"[32]

From her childhood years Olga was characterized by a compassionate heart, and a disposition to help others. She was an emotional and sensitive person, something that can even be seen in her diaries, in which she tended to write more of her personal feelings and thoughts than the others. She even devised a special code that she used to keep anyone who may read her diary from knowing what she wrote. But another element of her character when she was a child was utter candor, which often led her to comical results. Once, when she was still very young, she was supposed to sit still for some time, so that an artist could sketch her portrait. When she lost her temper, she said to the artist, "You are a very ugly man, and I don't like you a bit!"[33]

In 1901, when she was five years old, Olga became very sick with typhoid fever and was in danger of losing her life, but after five weeks she recovered completely. However, three years later, at the age of eight, Olga experienced the death of someone dear to her for the first time. Her cousin Elisabeth, also eight years old, the daughter of her mother's brother, Ernst, died of the same disease that she herself had suffered earlier. Then they explained to Olga that God had taken the soul of her little cousin close to Himself, and that later He would take also her body. Elisabeth died in November of 1903. One month later, on Christmas morning, Olga awoke early and asked whether

Olga with her father.

God had taken Elisabeth's body the previous night. When her nanny, Mrs. Eagar, replied, "Oh no, dear, not yet." She was greatly disappointed, and said, "I thought He would have sent for her to keep Christmas with Him."[34]

Olga had a special fondness for her father, and for this reason always wore on her neck a small icon of Saint Nicholas. On walks with him and during their common summer activities, she found opportunities to open her heart. Olga stood out with her special intellectual gifts. She was the most studious of the sisters, and the most cultivated. One time, while reading in her history lesson about some tragic event, she expressed satisfaction that she did not live in the old times, because the men of her time were better in contrast to the barbaric men of the past. How tragically wrong this conviction of the innocent girl would prove.

During one of their visits to Darmstadt, Nicholas with Alexandra took the children to a toy store where he told them that they could choose whichever toy they liked. Olga, when she looked at the toys, chose the smallest she could find, saying very politely, "Thank you very much." In vain the proprietors enticed her with more impressive toys. She replied, "Thank you, but I won't take it." When her nanny asked her why she would not take something better, she replied, "But the beautiful toys belong to some other little girls, I am sure; and think how sad they would be if they came home and found we had taken them while they were out."[35]

Two years younger than Olga, Tatiana was born on 29 May, 1897 at Peterhof Palace in Saint Petersburg. Nicholas wrote, "29th of May [1897]. Thursday. A second sweet and happy day for our family: at 10:40 in the morning, the Lord blessed us with a daughter—Tatiana. All night poor Alix labored, never resting, and at 8 o'clock went down to the bedroom of Grandma. Thank God, this time everything went quickly and completely without complication, and I didn't feel morally drained. Within an hour the little one had been bathed and Yanishev recited the prayers. Mama and Ksenia came and we breakfasted with them. At 4 o'clock there was a moleben. ... She is very taken with our older daughter."[36]

Olga, along with Tatiana, were "The Big Pair," in contrast with their two younger sisters, who were "The Little Pair." In 1901, when Olga was already recovering from typhoid fever, Tatiana was permitted to see her for five minutes. Tatiana then stood next to her sister's bed and conversed with her in a most amiable manner. Mrs. Eagar was astonished at the formal tone with which Tatiana spoke to her sister but did not comment. When she left the room, Tatiana exclaimed, "You told me you were bringing me to see Olga and I have not seen her." Mrs. Eagar replied with astonishment that the little girl in the bed was indeed Olga, her sister. Tatiana cried with great grief. "That little pale thin child is my dear sister Olga! Oh no, no! I cannot believe it!"[37] She wept bitterly at the change, and it was difficult to persuade her that Olga would soon be herself again.

Tatiana did not display the intellectual gifts and spontaneity of Olga, but she was a practical person, and had the gift of leadership. Her sisters called her "the Governess" and when they wanted some favor from their parents, they would send her as their representative. She was especially close to her

Olga and Tatiana: "The Big Pair".

mother and of all her sisters, she had inherited her character to the highest degree, and because of this she knew precisely what pleased her. Alexandra herself confirmed this. In a letter to Nicholas she wrote that of all the girls Tatiana was the one who best "grasped" her personal convictions.[38]

One comical incident of Tatiana's childhood years shows her adaptability: One morning while they were taking a walk in the garden with Mrs. Eagar their governess, one of the emperor's collie dogs, wanting to play, jumped on her back and threw her down. The child was frightened and cried very bitterly. Reassuringly her governess said, "She did not wish to hurt you; she only wanted to say 'good-morning' to you." Tatiana said to her, "Was that all? I don't think she is very polite; she could have said it to my face, and not to my back!"[39]

More than anything else, Tatiana liked most to study spiritual books, and she was especially noted for the self-examination to which she subjected herself. At one point, on Forgiveness Sunday 1916, she wrote to her mother, "My dear Mama, I only wanted to ask your forgiveness and dear Papa's, for all I have done to you, my dears, for all the worries that I caused. I pray for God to make me better. May the Lord bless the two angels whom I love so much. Forgive me again."[40]

On 14 June, 1899, a third daughter was born to the royal couple, Maria. Maria was the angel of the family. As Mrs. Eagar so characteristically writes, Maria "was born good, I often think, with the very smallest trace of original sin possible."[41] She was so noted for her goodness that everyone was astonished at an unexpected event that happened once. Mrs. Eagar remembers, "When she was a very little child, she was one day with her sister in the Empress' boudoir, where the Emperor and Empress were at tea. The Empress had tiny vanilla-flavoured wafers called *biblichen*, of which the children were particularly fond, but they were not allowed to ask for anything from the teatable. The Empress sent for me, and when I went down little Marie was standing in the middle of the room, her eyes drowned in tears and something was swallowed hastily. 'Dere! I've eaten it all up,' said she, 'you tant det it now.' I was properly shocked, and suggested bed at once as a suitable punishment. The Empress said, 'Very well, take her,' but the Emperor intervened, and begged that she might be allowed to remain, saying, 'I was always afraid of the wings growing, and I am glad to see she is only a human child.'"[42]

Her elder sisters at first somewhat took advantage of Maria's good nature. Once when she wanted to take part in one of their games, in order to be rid of her they ordered her to leave their room and told her to play the role of their footman! Maria did go out, but in a little while she returned with an armload of toys saying, "I won't be a *footman*, I'll be the kind, good aunt, who brings presents."[43] Olga and Tatiana admitted that they had been mean to poor little Marie, and from that hour they no longer excluded their little sister from their games.

Another time all four of the girls were ill with whooping cough, and they coughed a great deal. Mrs. Eagar told them that they were to be most

Tatiana with her mother.

careful not to cough on anyone, or that person might take the disease from them. One day as little Anastasia, then still an infant, was coughing and choking away, Maria came to her and putting her face close to her said, "Baby, darling, cough on me." Greatly amazed, Mrs. Eagar asked her what she meant, and Maria said, "I am so sorry to see my dear little sister so ill, and I thought if I could take it from her she would be better."[44]

Maria was probably the most social of all the sisters, and her diaries reveal that she did not have much patience for diary keeping, but found it tedious because she preferred real conversation. Her entries were short and her handwriting often a bit sloppy. She would also skip many entries, especially when she was younger. She did better when she got older but clearly never grew to like it. Her letters, on the other hand, were very descriptive and upbeat, using a light and conversational style; she was an excellent storyteller.

CHAPTER 2

The tease, the lively and enjoyably stubborn Anastasia, was born in Peterhof on 18 June 1901. Anastasia was the *enfant terrible* of the royal family, and she held the record of punishments among her sisters. She had the gift of cutting the most genial gaffes. She also had the special gift of mime, which always made her the focal point of the small plays that were put on and presented at home for the family. Even though she was very good in French and English, she was not at all good at mathematics and encountered serious difficulty in spelling.

Anastasia's farces were endless. Her godmother, Olga Alexandrovna, later said about her, "My favorite God-daughter she was indeed! I liked her fearlessness. She never whimpered or cried, even when hurt. She was a fearful tomboy."[45] She climbed trees, she set obstacles for the servants, and at official functions she would sometimes melt chocolate inside the pockets of her white dresses, and then put her white gloved hands inside to reveal the contents to all! All this, while not bringing especial joy to her parents, would always make everyone burst into laughter. Despite her vivacity, she had an astonishing sense of fairness. Her greatest joy was to run about assisting her mother, for this Alexandra called her "my legs."

The girls' relationship with their parents was especially warm. There was an ease among them that was enviable, and even though they revered their parents in an exemplary manner the girls felt them to be true friends with whom they were happy to pass unending hours. Nicholas and Alexandra, who liked to tease the girls at every opportunity and to laugh, felt the very same thing. Nicholas, indeed, said characteristically that "sometimes he forgot he was their father, as he enjoyed everything so much with them that he felt more like an elder brother to them."[46]

When they were yet children, Alexandra displayed genuine interest in all their childish interests and took part in their games with sincere enthusiasm. Later when they grew up, their games were replaced with embroidery, an activity that the girls took part in together with their mother nearly every evening. The entries in their diaries end nearly every day with the phrase, "We worked with mamá," since the evenings were the time when as they were gathered in the parlor; they embroidered as Nicholas read various works of classical literature for them.

Alexandra's letters reveal a sincerely caring person, and the notes to her children show that she was a very involved and loving mother. One can even say that she was far ahead of her time in her parenting style. For example, she directly supervised at least some of her children's studies, and would ask them to write back to her in different languages as a learning exercise, to which she would respond with her corrections and feedback, always encouraging and praising them. The letters and notes her children wrote to her make it very clear how much they adored their "Mama," how much they worried about her health, and how close each of them was to her.

Baroness Sophie Buxhoeveden wrote: "The empress really brought up her daughters herself, and she did so extremely well. It would be difficult

Tatiana embroidering.

On the Imperial yacht "Standart", where the family had their most pleasant moments.

to imagine more enchanting, pure, and intelligent girls. She only exercised her authority when absolutely necessary, and this never disturbed the atmosphere of complete trust which existed between her and her daughters. She understood the exuberance of youth and never restrained them when they played games and had fun. She also liked to be present at their lessons, where she would discuss the direction and content of their studies."[47]

PORTRAIT OF A TSAR

Although he may have wished to devote most of his time to his beloved family, Nicholas had to adjust very quickly to his unaccustomed reality. Taking up the duties of the tsar of the Russian Empire, Nicholas substantially shouldered the responsibility of governing one-sixth of the world. He was, however, but a young man twenty-six years of age when he found himself in this position. Apart from his youth and his sudden assumption of these high duties, which found him unprepared for this work, he had to deal with yet another more difficult reality: the attempts on the part of persons in his close circle to assert themselves over him and to influence his work. In addition to this problem, there were also the mounting slanders of the enemies of the monarchy, who strove to persuade the people that the young emperor was unsuitable and unfit for his work.

Nicholas thus found that he had to confront, right from the beginning, an unprecedented hard reality: the conflict between royal, aristocratic, administrative, liberal, and anti-monarchist factions. All of them sought their own personal interests. Nicholas, a man imbued with genuine patriotism, deeply believing, and nurtured on strict moral principles, quickly understood that he would be able to trust almost no one to support him in his exceedingly demanding and complicated work. The upper layers of society had already become corrupt to the degree that they could not be reconciled to the personality traits of the young tsar. In the past, it was nothing other than the despotism of the previous tsars that restrained these conflicted ambitious factions. In Nicholas' case matters were different.

Nicholas was not, as various historians wished to portray him, too meek and mild to hold this position. Those nearest to him preserved a few instances in which the young emperor's powerful personality became apparent. Anna Vyrubova, the closest friend of the royal couple relates the following: Nicholas "had qualities of leadership with very limited opportunities to exercise those qualities. In his own domain he was 'every inch an Emperor.' The whole Court, from the Grand Dukes down to the last petty official and intriguing maid of honor, recognized this and stood in real awe of their Sovereign. I have a keen recollection of an episode at dinner in which a certain young Grand Duke ventured to utter an ill-founded grievance against a distinguished general who had dared to rebuke his Highness in public. The Emperor instantly recognized this as a mere display of temper and egoism, and his contempt and indignation knew no bounds. He literally turned white with anger, and the unfortunate young Grand Duke trembled before him like an offending servant. Afterwards the still indignant Emperor said to me: 'He may thank God that the Empress and you were present. Otherwise I could not have held myself in hand.'"[48]

The undoubtedly exemplary meekness of Nicholas, his impressive self-control and his calm, remarked by all, was the result of long-standing and arduous inner work. As he himself had said, he did not at all admire the approach of Peter the Great, who was the incarnation of despotism and tyranny to an absolute degree. He preferred not to impose, but to inspire his subordinates with good example, sacrificing himself for the well-being of his people, rather than sacrifice others. His characteristic method of governance was absolutely his personal choice, and not evidence of weakness.

Alexandra once remarked to her close friend Lily Dehn on this topic with some bitterness, "He is accused of weakness. He is the strongest—not the weakest. I assure you, Lili, that it cost the Emperor a tremendous effort to subdue the attacks of rage to which the Romanoffs are subject. He has learnt the hard lesson of self-control, only to be called weak; people forget that the greatest conqueror is he who conquers himself.... I wonder they don't accuse him of being too good: that, at least, would be true!"[49]

Aide-de-Camp S. Fabritsky also notes: "Emperor Nicholas II had an even-tempered and tranquil disposition. He was also a man of rare steadiness and refinement, all of which made him seem weak to those who did not know him well. In the midst of the gravest moments of his reign and the infinitely painful times when his wife or children were ill, His Majesty always remained cool, with a seemingly perfect internal equilibrium, and many observers interpreted this as heartlessness. ...

The Emperor's compassion and sense of justice were extraordinary. In all his decisions he was always impelled by a desire not to injure anyone, even accidentally, and thus almost never acted rashly or in haste. This, however, engendered rumors to the effect that he was an indecisive man who disliked resolute people."[50]

Nicholas's peaceable intentions were manifest on the world stage and left his stamp on the pages of world history. In August 1898, he directed an appeal for the disarmament of nations, and collaboration between them for promoting world peace. In his letter to all the governments of the world, he proposed a convocation of an international congress for the investigation of this matter.

Because of his proposal, Nicholas was characterized as a tsar who would remain known in history as "Nicholas the Peacemaker." In fact, in May of the following year, on the day of the tsar's birthday, 6/18 May, 1899, the historic First Hague Conference convened, in which twenty nations of Europe, along with America, Mexico, Japan, China, Siam (present day Thailand), and Persia participated.

Here follows an address from citizens of America to Tsar Nicholas II, regarding his convention of the peace conference at the Hague. The address was signed by a total of 4,665 American citizens from 50 different towns of the United States:

> To His Imperial Majesty Nicholas II, Czar of All the Russias.
>
> We, the undersigned, sovereign citizens of the United States of America, without regard to race, creed, or political affinity, desire to express our hearty sympathy with the Czar's noble effort for the cause of God and humanity. Appreciating the difficulties which confront him at home and abroad, we admire the high moral courage with which he dares to face them, in the faith which, in all ages, has removed mountains. We think no more fitting place can be found from which to start an American crusade, than this city of Philadelphia (Brotherly Love) in this State of Pennsylvania, whose founder, in 1693, published an appeal for arbitration to the nations of Europe, while war was raging among them, and practically gave them an illustrious example of what a colony can be whose chief defenses are arbitration and justice extended to all men. Here, from the cradle of liberty, where later we proclaimed that not only ourselves, but all the world, had a right to 'life, liberty and the pursuit of happiness' we stretch forth the helping hand to Russia, our friend, when she 'bringeth good tidings, when she publisheth peace.' The Czar of Russia, Nicholas II, has called a Conference of all those nations which sent representatives to St. Petersburg, to meet at the Hague, May 18th, 1899, to consider a plan to promote 'Arbitration and Gradual Disarmament.' We desire to send him the enclosed address of sympathy, and invite all who will unite with us to add their signatures.[51]

Europeans were amazed by Nicholas' initiative for this historical conference. This astonishment was due to their conception of Russia as a semi-barbaric autocracy, and as such, so refined and so great an idea could not possibly arise from within her. However, this caricature was in complete opposition to the diverse flowering that the Russian Empire now experienced during this first period of Nicholas' reign. Literature, philosophy, painting, music, and all the arts in general, showed such notable progress in the last decade of the nineteenth century and the beginning of the twentieth, that this period remains known in history as the "Silver Age" of Russia and the "Russian Renaissance."

Under the leadership of Nicholas II, Russia made vast strides in economic development. The emperor altered the passport system introduced by Peter the Great and thus facilitated the free movement of people, including travel abroad. The poll tax was abolished and a voluntary program of health insurance was introduced, under which, for payment of one ruble a year, a person was entitled to free hospital care. Notably, during Nicholas's reign, the parity of the ruble was vastly increased. In 1897, a law was enacted to limit working hours, so that night work was forbidden for women and minors under seventeen years of age; this at a time when the majority of countries in the West had almost no labor legislation at all. As William Taft, president of the United States, commented in 1913, "the Russian Emperor has enacted labor legislation which not a single democratic state could boast of."[52]

Nicholas worked mainly alone, with rare diligence and meticulousness. "To this characterization of Emperor Nicholas II," writes S. Fabritsky, "–and in opposition to the rumors and gossip about him being almost stunted in his development– I would add the impression of one of my relatives, Y.T. Sudeikin, a Senator and university professor who, like so many of our intelligentsia, held political convictions that inclined quite a bit to the left. Before his appointment as senator, he had spent a long time directing the chancellery of the Governor General of Lithuania, Adjutant-General Trotsky. The executive authorities of every province, region and territory in the Russian Empire were each required to compile an annual report for His Majesty's personal perusal, and Sudeikin fulfilled this task on behalf of the Governor General. These reports were then returned with the Emperor's comments and resolutions.

My kinsman confessed to me that, after reading the returned reports and familiarizing himself with the Emperor's notes, he had asked himself more than once whether he could have expressed his thoughts, given instructions, made comments, or expressed approval in such clear, plain, precise, and concise language. In the majority of instances, as he himself admitted, the Emperor's knowledge and ability had amazed him, especially since he knew that His Majesty wrote all his notes in the privacy of his study, without any kind of assistance."[53]

It is true that Nicholas did not even have a personal secretary. Above his desk there was a large calendar, where he entered the scheduled appointments for every day. Whenever important documents were delivered to him, he read them, signed them, and put them in envelopes to return to the proper addresses. When he was asked why he was so regular in keeping such order in his workspace, "the Emperor often said that he wanted to be able to go into his study in the dark and put his hand at once on any object he knew to be there."[54]

For the governance of his country, but also of his family, Nicholas drew his inspiration from Russian history and tradition. He took care to act as a genuine Russian even down to the last detail. When he worked in his study, he wore a simple peasant shirt. Even though he spoke French, English, and German fluently, that is, the languages that were used in the upper levels of society, Nicholas preferred to speak to his children in Russian. He even required his ministers, who always used French, to report to him in Russian.

Alongside the governance of the Empire, Nicholas, now as head of the House of Romanov, became administrator of vast royal properties. His annual expenditures reached 24 million rubles, an amount that would now be equivalent to about 10 million Euros. But, paradoxically, the personal purse of the Tsar was usually empty! From this amount he had to maintain seven palaces. These palaces had a staff of twenty-five thousand, whom the Tsar supported entirely: food, clothing, salary, and gifts on all holidays. Three theaters in Saint Petersburg, two in Moscow, the Imperial Academy of Fine Arts, and the Imperial Ballet, with all their personnel, received financial support exclusively from the personal expenditures of the tsar. Moreover, all the members of the vast house of Romanov received a huge annual subsidy from the tsar. Countless hospitals, orphanages, and institutions for the blind, as well as innumerable extraordinary petitions for economic aid from every corner of the empire, were based on the personal contributions of the tsar. The result was that before the end of the year, sometimes even before the beginning of autumn, Nicholas found himself in the difficult position of having empty pockets!

Fabritsky testifies to "Emperor Nicholas II's extraordinary lack of concern about luxury and comfort, his modest approach to food and drink, and his complete indifference to money. His Majesty gave his entire income to the Russian people, either in the form of financial support when appeals were made to him, funds for the education of children, or the improvement of his personal estates, transforming wastelands into fertile expanses. On himself, his family, his table, he spent the bare minimum, making economies everywhere, ceasing to give balls, gala dinners, etc."[55]

Compassion and forgiveness were also among the precious adornments of Nicholas' kind soul. Russia's history does not recall any example of such magnanimity among the preceding tsars. Criminals and rebels received repeated pardons from the Emperor. The examples are numerous. One such incident, related by Alexander Spiridovitch, took place in the room of the Peterhof palace set aside for receiving petitions, in the presence of Major-General Orlov.[56]

> It was about midnight. Orlov was getting ready to go to bed, when his attention was drawn to a noise in the antechamber, a feminine voice which betrayed a profound emotion. He went toward the entrance, and there he found himself in the presence of a pale woman who was extraordinarily upset, and begging to be let in to see the aide-de-camp. Orlov asked her to come in.
>
> "I am coming to you with an entreaty," began the woman, but her words were cut off by a violent nervous spasm. Sobs stifled her. With the help of a few drops of valerian (a medication which was always available there) and a glass of cool water, Orlov managed to

calm the unknown woman and get her to control herself. Hesitantly, finding the words with difficulty, she told him the following story:

"I am betrothed to a student. He has tuberculosis. Once he got into the revolutionary party, he could not extricate himself from it, and, against his will, became part of a terrorist circle. Once he learned what its goal was, he wanted to get out of it, but they kept him there by force. His organization ended up under arrest, my fiancé among the other plotters, and locked down. But he is innocent. He was dragged into it against his will. He has just been judged by a military court and condemned to hang. He is to be executed tomorrow. I beg you to tell the Emperor about it and implore his pardon, so that my fiancé can die a natural death, for he is so sick that he does not have long to live."

The woman was in a pitifully overwrought state. In vain Orlov told her that the hour was too late to make an approach to the Emperor, that the execution might well not take place the following day, and that the matter could wait until morning: the woman kept pleading, sobbing and dragging herself after him on her knees.

So Orlov had a troika hitched and went to Alexandria. When he had awakened the valet de chambre, he told him to announce him to the Emperor; but the man advised him not to disturb the Sovereign before morning. Orlov insisted, and the valet de chambre went off to announce him. Very shaken, and not knowing what turn the entire business might take, Orlov waited. ... Suddenly, the Emperor appeared in his pyjamas. "What is going on?" he asked quietly. Orlov told him everything he knew and handed him the woman's request. The Emperor read it through, and said in a singularly calm voice: "I thank you very much for having acted as you did. When one can save a man's life, one must not hesitate. Thank God, neither you nor I will have anything on our consciences. Wait."

He withdrew and returned after a few minutes to hand Orlov one telegram addressed to the Minister of Justice and another to the commander of the Peter and Paul fortress: "Defer the execution of a certain man. Await orders. Nicholas."

"Run," added the Emperor, "to the Court telegraph, hand in these telegrams and telephone the minister and commander as well, to inform them that telegrams are on their way and that they must take steps."

Orlov, left, overcome with emotion. He had himself driven to the telegraph. Once he had expedited the telegrams, he hastened back to the guard room. In the woman's presence, he telephoned the commander of the fortress. Hearing the conversation, the woman cried out and fainted. Once she recovered her senses, she again fell to her knees and poured out her thanks for the grace granted her fiancé by the Tsar. Then, beside herself with joy, she left for Petersburg.

CHAPTER 2

One year passed. Orlov had no idea what had become of the pardoned man, when he received a letter with the Yalta (Crimea) postmark. It was from the woman whom he had met under the tragic circumstances which I have just described. After reminding him of that terrible night, she told him that her fiancé had been granted a full pardon, and that a few days after his reprieve, at the order of the Empress he had been examined by the Court physician and then, at Her Majesty's expense, sent for treatment in the Crimea. She added that he was in fact completely recovered, and that they were married. She requested that Orlov tell the Emperor all about it, and to thank him once again for having saved her husband's life, and for making them both happy. "Whatever happens, we are ready to sacrifice our lives for the Emperor," she concluded.

Orlov hastened to give this letter to the Emperor. "You see, you did right to follow your inspiration. You have made two people happy," the latter told him.

"Sire, I only did my duty. As for happiness, it is Your Majesty who is the author of that," replied Orlov.[57]

Amalia Coudert, the American miniaturist known for her portraits of prominent figures of the late nineteenth century, recorded another such incident: "I had never heard that the Tsar was in the habit of driving out entirely unattended; but now I heard that he had always done so whenever he liked, which was frequently, and a Russian lady whom I had reason to believe spoke the truth told me a little story of one of the Tsar's drives when he chanced to be entirely alone. This well-authenticated story stated that the Tsar thus caught sight of a party of students who were being marched through the street on their way to Siberia, and, so the story went, at once ordered the release of the students. Afterward, the lady told me in a whisper, the police marched their prisoners on streets through which the Tsar did not drive."[58]

Nicholas' dislike towards extreme police measures and reinforced security was manifested in various occasions. Once, "during his visit to the newly built Fort Inoniemi,[59] the Emperor, coming ashore and seeing the construction workers segregated behind some kind of specially erected rope cordon, immediately ordered its destruction so that they could move about freely. This measure did not impact the orderliness of the visit, but it touched the workers greatly.

"A very similar thing happened during the Poltava celebrations, when the Emperor, on his way to an evening prayer service in the chapel at the grave site, spotted some kind of barracks along the road. It turned out that these had been specially built for the peasant representatives gathered from throughout Russia, who were, at that moment, being temporarily detained within them. Despite the entreaties of the Governor, His Majesty insisted on entering the barracks and spent more than two hours among the peasants, talking with them, asking about their needs, and all without any security whatsoever."⁶⁰

In every action and decision, Nicholas always had his beloved spouse as his help and support, who once being completely devoted to her father and brother, had now given herself with all her powers to be a rock and support to her husband. Alexandra was truly an ideal model of a spouse. She always displayed unstinted and lively interest every time Nicholas sought her counsel in any matter, without ever showing him even the smallest trace of boredom or unease. She believed unshakably that the role of the wife was the management of family matters and the upbringing of children. In political matters she never displayed any interest, and never intruded in them, unless Nicholas sought her opinion, something that rarely occurred, or to be precise, hardly ever. As Buxhoeveden writes, "She [Alexandra] did not think that politics were a woman's sphere. The woman's duty was to make the home, and she made a real home for her husband and children."⁶¹

THE LOVE OF GOD

Lili Dehn, one of the imperial family's closest friends, recorded her impressions of her first encounter with the emperor, "His kind eyes, and his smile, struck me at once, he seemed to move in an aura of goodwill, and his peculiar fascinating charm of manner has been admitted even by his enemies."⁶²

This was Lili's first impression of Nicholas, which agrees almost completely with all similar remembrances of those that knew the emperor. But later when Lili became attached to the family, and could penetrate more deeply into their lives, she wrote, "Nicholas II seemed as if he saw into the tragic future, but he also seemed to see the Heaven that lies beyond this earth. He was 'God's good man.' I can give no higher praise, render him no more fitting homage."⁶³

This was the greatest secret of Nicholas and of his entire family: their tie with God. Few appreciated this important dimension of their lives, and even today few know about it. But there are more who, even if they know about it, are not able to understand its depth. This happens with all spiritual people. Their lives constitute a mystery hidden from the eyes of many.

The most important element of the family's spiritual life, which reveals their sound relationship with God, was their participation in the mystical and liturgical life of the Church. Their supreme office and power did not prevent them, as is often the case, from regarding themselves as humble members of the Church, and from understanding that only by Divine institutions could they become truly worthy as men of God. Alexandra

CHAPTER 2

Alexis' bedroom. Nicholas and Alexandra's bedroom.

---

always "stood from beginning to end at every church service, not allowing herself to become distracted, and praying fervently the whole time. When her health no longer permitted her to stand, she sat through services, but was very attentive."[64] She also loved to pray in the church at times when there were few people about and she could stand there unrecognized.[65]

Nicholas and Alexandra took care to transmit their faith and practice to their children as well, from their earliest childhood years. Mrs. Eagar, the governess, remembered: "The little Grand Duchesses went to church regularly from the time they were babies.... The little Grand Duchess Olga made her first confession in Moscow, during Lent, 1903 [i.e., when she was seven years old], and she received a gift from the children of Moscow, of an icon of the Virgin Mary."[66]

For Nicholas and Alexandra, Christian education was the primary goal of the formation and upbringing of their children. Alexandra once wrote about her children to the Anglican bishop and family counsellor of her childhood years, Dr William Boyd Carpenter, "May God help us to give them a good and sound education and make them above all good little Christian soldiers fighting for our Saviour."[67]

One had only to enter the children's rooms to perceive their spiritual state. Instead of the usual items one encounters in children's and adolescents' rooms, the royal children had beside their beds New Testaments, prayer books, crosses, and candles. As for the walls, hardly any point remained uncovered by the numerous icons that hung above them.

From very early on, Alexandra took care to implant in her children's souls a love for prayer. Nearly every day she took them with her to some church to light their little candles and to pray quietly in a corner. Every evening she went to their rooms to pray with them, and when she herself was not in good health—something that happened often—she used to send them written notes from her room containing spiritual counsel and encouragement to prayer. She wrote for example to Tatiana:

"24 January, 1909. My darling Tatiana, Very tender kisses and thanks for your dear letter. That's a dear you pray for old Mama perhaps God may make her better, but sometimes He sends illness for the good of one's soul … A good hug from your loving old Mama. God bless you."[68] "24 March, 1910. Yes, dear, you must show a good example to the little ones and not always turn round and look about in Church. … Kisses and blessings from your loving old Mama."[69] Likewise she also wrote to Maria, "10 February, 1910. Sweet little Marie, your tiny letter touched me very much. Certainly, you can hang the ring up at the icon. I shall keep it for you and then we can think over when and how to do it. Sleep well. God bless you. Try always to love Him above all and to be a good, patient little girl and try never to be disobedient. I kiss you very tenderly. Your own Mama."[70]

The girls wrote the same kind of notes to their mother, and afterward this resulted in the preservation of valuable reflections of their spiritual world. For example, once, when she sent something to her mother during one of her bouts of ill-health, Tatiana wrote, "Would you not want to try to put this piece of fur to your cheek? Olga… gave it to me when I too was suffering from headaches. It is from the grave of [saint] Semyon Verkhotursky.[71] Try it, maybe it will help you. If not, then return it to me tomorrow. I hope that the Lord will help you, and all will be well with you. May God bless you. 1000 kisses from your very own daughter, Tatiana."[72]

Another time, after some small misunderstanding between them, Tatiana wrote to her mother, "I was such a fool today! When you called me several times to come to you (while Anya was here in the afternoon), I wanted to come so awfully much. But then I felt that if I go, I will howl, and I didn't want to be such an idiot in front of Anya, but I so wanted to go to you and be caressed. And then I never thanked you as I wanted to for the nice drive. I was so pleased, but by some stupid idea of mine, I did not want to show that I was pleased. When you asked me if I wanted to drive, I said I did not know. It was not true—because I wanted to but I was afraid you would be tired of driving. I was so happy in the morning, that it was simply the devil that got into me and made me so beastly nasty. Please forgive me, my own precious Mama sweet. God bless you, my angel. I kiss you 1,000 times and still more, as much as I love you. Good night, deary, from your own loving—very very much more than I can say in the world." Alexandra replied as follows, "Thanks for your little note, sweet child. I completely understood your mood, when you said that you just don't care—I often feel the same; cannot bother [anyone], and while I do want something, do everything in order not to get it—such a silly humanity. I saw that you were close to tears, and was certain that you would have started crying in response to affection. I am very glad that we had such a nice walk. Sleep peacefully. Affectionate kiss from your Mama."⁷³

These examples are evidence of the deep spiritual work that the members of this blessed family mystically expended on their souls. Also, it becomes obvious that Nicholas and Alexandra's personal example and prayers succeeded in imparting to the souls of their children true piety and faith in God.

It is known that the love that bound Nicholas with Alexandra to the end of their lives was unusually powerful. However, as Lili Dehn writes, "Her [Alexandra's] love of God and her belief in His mercy came before her love of her husband and her children."⁷⁴ Right next to her bed there was a small door that led to a small, dim chapel, lit only by lamps that hung before the icons. Inside the chapel there was a small lectern on which were placed the Holy Scripture and an icon of the Saviour.

There Alexandra would remain for hours praying and studying the word of God. Her thirst for prayer was such that often although she had prayed for hours, when she went to rest, she felt the need to rise again and return to her private chapel. This was also the reason why she made sure to have the door to it right next to her bed.

Alexandra studied every day. She loved the ascetic and spiritual works of the Fathers, and especially the *Ladder* of Saint John the Sinaite.⁷⁵ As for the Holy Scripture, as Lili Dehn relates, "she knew the Bible from cover to cover."⁷⁶ However for her and for the rest of the family, their greatest love was the liturgical life. Church attendance every Sunday, beginning with Vespers on Saturday, and on all the great feasts, was inviolable. Furthermore, on all family anniversaries and on all their name days and birthdays, they always celebrated the Divine Liturgy. Also, for the duration of Great Lent, every Wednesday and Friday, the Divine Liturgy of the Presanctified Gifts was served at the palace.⁷⁷ The culmination, however, of the devotional majesty at the palace was Holy Week and Pascha. During this week, two services were served daily. In the morning was the service of the Hours, and in the evening Matins. But the most moving moments took place from Holy Thursday onward.

On Holy Thursday the imperial family received Holy Communion. Shortly before Holy Communion, Nicholas and Alexandra stood in the middle of the church and turning towards the congregation, made deep bows asking forgiveness of those present. Afterward they piously venerated the icons with a prostration before each of them, and then received Communion. On this day, also, the Empress, with sincere compunction and humility, personally asked forgiveness of all present in the palace, offering her hand as a sign of reconciliation. This event always astonished those who saw it for the first time.

The Vigil of Pascha began at 11:00 PM and lasted three hours and more. The display of lights was astonishing. All the chandeliers and all the candles

Nicholas and Alexandra.

in the church scattered the light of the Resurrection everywhere, which the congregation, with their lit candles, later brought to all corners of the palace. On the morning of Easter Sunday, the imperial couple greeted all the staff of the palaces personally as follows: one by one all the men of the staff approached the emperor, taking his hand, and then they received from him the triple kiss of the Paschal greeting. Then they greeted him with "Christ is risen!" and the Emperor replied, "Indeed He is risen!" At last the grand duchesses, the daughters of the emperor, gave to each one a commemorative egg as a gift. In the same manner, all the women of the staff simultaneously greeted the empress.

The same rite of greeting was repeated on Monday of Pascha at the Winter Palace. The difference was that this time all the imperial guard came forth for the greeting, around five thousand soldiers, who having received the Paschal greeting from the emperor kissed the hand of Alexandra and they brought her a red egg, receiving in return a commemorative porcelain egg.

From a ceremony for laying the cornerstone of a new church.

THE ORTHODOX TSAR, PATRON OF THE CHURCH

The emperor rose between 7 and 8 o'clock in the morning and he started each and every day with prayer.[78] He was a man of true and strong faith in God and "nothing could shake his belief in the Lord or his conviction that not a single hair falls from one's head unless it is the will of the Most High God. During the direst moments of his life… he never lost his faith in God and His Providence. It gave him the strength to hold up beneath grief and horror. And even during the most brilliant periods of his reign he turned to the Lord with fervent prayers and fasted three times a year."[79]

"In the person of the Emperor Nicholas II the believers had the best and most worthy representative of the Church, truly 'The Most Pious' as he was referred to in church services. He was a true patron of the Church, and a solicitor of all her blessings."[80] The deep religiosity and piety, both of the emperor and of his consort, which was the core and absolute center of their life, was of benefit to the Church of Russia. In contrast with his predecessors and forbears, the reformer Tsars Peter the Great and Catherine the Great, Nicholas was a champion of Byzantine tradition and an opponent of every influence of the Western type. Although Tsar Peter and Catherine received the title "Great" for building up the Russian State based on Western

At the Feodorovsky Cathedral.

prototypes, Nicholas ought to be called Great for the restoration of Russia's inherent Orthodox character.

During the reign of Nicholas, "By the outbreak of revolution in 1917… [the Church] had between 115 and 125 million adherents (about 70 per cent of the population), around 120,000 priests, deacons and other clergy, 130 bishops, 78,000 churches [up by 10,000], 1,253 monasteries [up by 250], 57 seminaries and four ecclesiastical academies."[81] In 1901, the Tsar decreed that every military unit having its own clergy should have its own church in the form of a separate building. In many instances he took care to be present in person at the service to mark the beginning of the construction of a church and set the cornerstone. Furthermore, he visited many churches and monasteries in all parts of the country and he himself undertook the expenditures for innumerable icons to be made in accordance with the Byzantine and ancient Russian style. Traditional church arts were encouraged, and old churches were renovated.

The Russian autocracy of the seventeenth century sets forth one of the most balanced examples of symphony between Church and State in history. Regardless of the fact that the autocrats were supreme in the secular sphere, they did not attempt to dictate to the Church or modify her role as the conscience of the nation. In the eighteenth century, however, Peter the Great disturbed the balance by trying to subject the Church to his own will, introducing the western theory of Divine Right absolutism into the government of the country, together with many other innovations.

Gradually, in the nineteenth century, from the time of Paul I to Nicholas II, the balance began to be restored. In 1901 Tsar Nicholas removed from the "Basic Laws" the phrase designating the Tsar as "Supreme Judge" of the Church, and then, during the period between 1904 and 1906, he worked closely with the Church for the convening of a Council [Sobor], the first since the seventeenth century, with the intention of electing a Patriarch and a patriarchal administration to realize the Church's administrative independence. The fact that the Sobor was never convened in Tsar Nicholas' reign was the result of the continuing atmosphere of revolutionary violence. Nevertheless, the Local Russian Council of 1917–18 may be rightly regarded as a fruit of the Tsar's reign, even if was convened after his abdication.

The Emperor stressed the importance of educating the peasant children within the framework of church and parish and, as a result, the number of parish schools—which were more popular among the peasants than the state Zemstvo schools—grew to 37,000. Moreover, Christian literature flourished; excellent books were published, such as *Soul-Profiting Reading, Soul-Profiting Converser, The Wanderer, The Rudder, The Russian Monk, The Trinity Leaflets*, and the ever-popular *Russian Pilgrim*. The Russian people were surrounded by spiritual nourishment as never before.

Nicholas gained yet another title. He was the tsar who pushed forward and approved the greatest number of canonizations of saints in the history of Russia. Among those glorified during his reign were: St Theodosius of Chernigov (1896), St Isidore of Yuriev (1897), St Seraphim of Sarov (1903), St Euphrosyne of Polotsk (1909), St Anna of Kashin (1910), St Joasaph of Belgorod (1911), St Hermogenes of Moscow (1913), St Pitirim of Tambov (1914), St John Maximovitch of Tobolsk (1916), and St Paul of Tobolsk (1917).

Unfortunately, it must be noted that on this point Nicholas often encountered difficulties on the part of the Synod of the Russian Church. In certain circumstances, despite the general lay recognition of the sanctity of some holy person, the synod opposed the official act of canonization of the given saint. There are at least two known instances of these. One related to the canonization of Saint John of Tobolsk, the ancestor of the well-known contemporary Saint, John Maximovitch of Shanghai and San Francisco (1898–1966), which Nicholas labored to promote.

The second canonization that Nicholas attempted to promote, but met with great difficulty before he finally succeeded, was of one of the most beloved saints of the Russian Church, Seraphim of Sarov, whom the tsar and his family especially honored. Nicholas kept a portrait of the saint in his study and long before his canonization, expressed his certainty of his sanctity. He characteristically said, "As concerns the sanctity and miraculousness of the venerable Seraphim, I am already so convinced of this that no one will ever shake my conviction. I have unconquerable proof of it."[82] As for Alexandra, she had placed all her hopes in the saint that she would give birth to a boy, an heir to the Russian throne.

Saint Seraphim himself had prophetically foretold the event of his own glorification to Nicholas Motovilov,[83] his well-known spiritual child who authored his famous *Conversation*[84] with the saint about the acquisition of the Holy Spirit. In fact, when mentioning the translation of his "flesh" (he did not use the term "relics" for his remains) the saint connected this event with the visit of a Tsar Nicholas, of his Consort Alexandra Feodorovna and of a widowed Queen Mother Maria Feodorovna. Speaking of that tsar, the saint said, "He will be Christian to his very depths."

It is clear from the entries in Motovilov's personal diary, his correspondence, and his other notes, that he himself expected, and also labored for the glorification of Saint Seraphim during the reign of Nicholas I, whose spouse was Alexandra Feodorovna, and the widowed Queen Mother was Maria Feodorovna. However, Motovilov's efforts bore no fruit, and he himself was very disappointed because he considered that the relevant prophecy of the saint remained unfulfilled. Neither he himself, nor anyone else, could imagine that fifty years later, precisely the same names that the saint mentioned in his prophecy would appear on the throne of Russia: Tsar Nicholas II, Tsaritsa Alexandra Feodorovna, and the widowed Queen Mother Maria Feodorovna!

Nicholas Motovilov reposed in 1879, but his wife Helena Ivanovna Miliukova, who was much younger than her husband, lived until the glorification of Saint Seraphim in 1903. Then the following words of the saint came true, "The Tsar will come to us with his entire family. What joy there will be and Pascha will be sung in the summer."[85]

The celebratory services were set in motion from the beginning of July. Daily, after the morning service, thousands of worshippers who had arrived from every corner of the empire for the great event withdrew for a little while into shelters. On 17 July, however, learning of the imminent arrival of the royal family in the nearby city of Arzamas, the worshippers remained for the great reception. Their number reached nearly half a million. Like two living walls along the length of the two sides of the road, the crowds of faithful turned their gaze to the forest of Sarov from whence the royal procession would come. At six in the evening a triple peal of all the monastery bells began, and soon the first carriage appeared carrying the Emperor Nicholas with his wife. Then followed the carriage of the widowed Queen Mother Maria, and finally the carriages of the grand dukes and duchesses of the House of Romanov.

Descending from their carriages, Nicholas and Alexandra walked the final piece of the route to the monastery on foot, along with the thousands of worshippers. At the monastery gates the metropolitan received them and, after a welcoming speech, they entered the church where the Doxology was sung. Later they departed to private accommodations that were specially prepared for the royal couple. During their stay in Sarov, Alexandra bathed

CHAPTER 2

Meeting the Royal Family in Diveyevo Convent.

At the Abbess' quarters in Diveyevo.

in the miraculous spring of Saint Seraphim with deep faith and hope for the birth of the much-desired heir to the throne.

The following day, at the morning Divine Liturgy, the royal couple received Holy Communion and attended the Rite of Glorification of Saint Seraphim, with the reading of the prayers for the sanctification of his icons. In the afternoon, the service of Great Vespers and Matins (the All-Night Vigil) was served in which Saint Seraphim was officially honored as a saint for the first time. Afterward, the metropolitan with the clergy and the royal family knelt in the middle of the church before the holy relics, whereupon the tsar with five other grand dukes raised the reliquary on their shoulders and exited the church for the Lity of the relics. During the litany many miraculous cures took place, from the blind receiving their sight even to the raising of paralytics. When the litany was completed and the procession with the reliquary returned to the church, the relics of the saint were placed in a new, magnificent reliquary, an offering of the tsar and his family.

Returning from Sarov, the royal family visited the women's convent of Diveyevo to meet Venerable Paraskeva (Pasha), a fool for Christ's sake.[86] Venerable Paraskeva had the custom of making her prophecies known using dolls! Knowing the imperial couple's desire for the birth of an heir, two days before their visit she took the likeness of a small boy, made a fluffy little crib of scarves and laid the baby inside of it. Afterward she said, "Quiet! Quiet! He is sleeping..."

Paraskeva's novices, as soon as they learnt that the tsar would come, wanted to tidy up her cell a bit because it was terribly messy. Venerable Paraskeva, however, did not permit them. Just as they were trying to change her mind, there was a knock at the door. It was the royal couple. "Everyone left so that they could be alone, but the Royal couple could not understand what the blessed one was saying, and soon the Emperor came out and said, 'Would the oldest please come in?'"[87]

Archimandrite Seraphim Chichagov[88] also followed in with the cell attendant. Parasceva Ivanovna opened the cupboard. She "took out a new tablecloth, spread it on the table and began to place some gifts on it: a piece of linen canvas she had made herself (she spun thread), a partial lump of sugar, colored eggs, and some more pieces of sugar. She tied all of this up tightly in several knots, even having to sit down from the exertion, then gave the bundle to the Tsar. 'Tsar, carry it yourself,' she said. Then, stretching out her hand, she said, 'And give us some money—we need to build a hut (the new cathedral).' The Emperor had no money with him, so he immediately sent for some. They brought it, and he gave her a purse full of gold. This purse was given to the Abbess right away."[89]

In the course of the discussion, at one point she told him: 'Your Highness, come down from the throne yourself.'"[90] Finally, "they said good-bye and kissed each others' hands. ... When the Tsar left, he said that Parasceva Ivanovna was the only true slave of God. Everywhere he was received like a Tsar, but she alone received him as a simple man."[91]

From that time a close relationship began between the emperor with Venerable Paraskeva. Repeatedly Nicholas sent his representatives to Diveyevo to bring him the counsels and admonitions of the venerable one. "Before her death [in August of 1915] she was always making prostrations before the Tsar's portrait. When she no longer had the strength, her cell attendants lifted her up and let her down. 'Mamashenka, why are you praying to the Tsar?' 'Sillies! He will be higher than all other Tsars... I don't know, maybe a monk-saint, maybe a martyr.'"[92] A little before her repose, the venerable one "took down the portrait of the Tsar and kissed his feet with the words, 'My dear one is already near the end.'"[93]

Leaving Venerable Paraskeva, they went to meet Elena Ivanovna, the wife of blessed Nicholas Motovilov. The tsar knew that Elena preserved a letter that Saint Seraphim himself wrote shortly before his repose in 1833. He gave the letter to Motovilov with the instruction that it be given to the tsar when he visited Diveyevo. He told him: "You will not live that long, but your wife will live to the time when the Royal Family will come to Diveyevo, and the Tsar will come to see her. Let her give it to him."[94] After the death of Motovilov, his wife Elena kept the letter to be delivered to the tsar.

When he had heard Elena's explanation, "the Tsar received the letter, he placed it

Venerable Paraskeva (Pasha) of Diveyevo.

The people greet the Imperial family in Sarov Monastery. Above, Nicholas in the center with his mother on his right and Alexandra on his left.

Above: Alexandra, on the right, with her sister Elisabeth walking through the Sarov forest to St Seraphim's spring. Below: Alexandra departing after bathing in St Seraphim's spring with the prayer of conceiving a long-awaited heir to the throne.

Above: At the chapel over the grave of St Seraphim. Below and on the right page: Nicholas with other Grand Dukes carrying the relics of St Seraphim.

reverently in his breast pocket, saying that he would read it later. Elena Ivanovna became quite lively and spoke with him for one and a half to two hours."[95] Later, when he was in the abbess' quarters, which was yielded for his stay, Nicholas read the letter. He began to weep bitterly. His companions, perceiving that the content of the letter was obviously quite distressing, attempted to comfort him saying that even the greatest saints could make mistakes. The tsar, however, continued to grieve inconsolably. The content of the letter remains unknown to this day. One can easily suppose that the saint prepared Nicholas for his coming sorrows.

Dr. A. P. Timofievich, who visited Sarov and Diveyevo in 1926, also relates that Professor Ivan Andreyev wrote the following about a visit of his in Diveyevo in a brochure he published in 1946, in Munich, entitled "St Seraphim of Sarov": "We also met an eldress who told us that in 1903, at the uncovering of St Seraphim's relics, she handed to His Majesty Tsar Nicholas II a letter from St Seraphim, addressed to the fourth Tsar who would come here. The letter had been preserved at Sarov Monastery during the course of four successive reigns. The emperor was profoundly shaken when he read the letter. No one is acquainted with its contents. The nun's story deeply struck me, for never before had I heard about this fact.

"If I expound in some other writing on the communication of this letter to the Emperor, the very fact of this letter's existence and its being made known to me at least are not subject to any doubt, as well as the very idea of this incredible event itself, which is being carefully preserved in the Diveyevo Chronicles. As is known, St Seraphim accurately predicted the arrival of the Royal Family for the celebration, that is, not only the Tsar himself, but his family, and in the summertime: 'The Tsar will come to us with his entire family. What joy there will be and Pascha will be sung in the summer.'

"Further in the Diveyevo Chronicles the following is recounted: 'Before his repose, St. Seraphim handed to N. A. Motovilov a letter with instructions to hand it to the Tsar who would visit Sarov. After Motovilov's death, the letter was preserved by his faithful spouse Elena lvanovna. When Tsar Nicholas II came from Sarov in 1903 to visit Diveyevo, he was met by the Diveyevo nuns, standing in long lines on both sides of the road leading to Sarov, with the marvelous Eldress Elena lvanovna at the head, who handed the letter from St. Seraphim to the Tsar on a plate. After their visit to Sarov and to Blessed Paraskeva (Pasha), everyone noticed that the Tsar left highly upset.' This startling fact has yet to be revealed in all its fullness—this is something for the future, but undoubtedly, its significance in the historical fate of Russia is great."[96]

Already in 1854, N. A. Motovilov contacted Count V. F. Adlerberg, Minister of the Imperial Court of Tsar Nicholas I, asking permission to inform the emperor of the prophecies of St Seraphim of Sarov. The saint himself asked Motovilov to bring them to the attention of the emperor after his death. Motovilov received permission from the court, and sent the emperor several notes in which he revealed the prophecies of Saint Seraphim. In 1905 Empress Alexandra Feodorovna ordered that copies of the prophecies be made for her. The document survives to this day:

"They will wait for a time of great hardship to afflict the Russian land, and on an agreed day, at the agreed hour, they will raise up a general rebellion all over the Russian land, and, since many soldiers will join in their evil-doing, there will be no one to stop them, and at first much innocent blood will be spilt, it will run in rivers over the Russian land, and they will kill many of your brother nobles and priests, as well as merchants who support the emperor."[97]

Soon after the opening of St Seraphim relics a metochion[98] of the Diveyevo convent was opened in Peterhof. A sister remembers, "the Empress often visited our metochion with her daughters. [Sister] Matrosha, who had been transferred there in 1913, told me the following. The summer after she arrived, the Empress visited the metochion eleven times. She would come with one of the daughters, but never with the heir. The sisters asked her about this once, but she answered he was unable. Sometimes she would order a Liturgy without bells. At times she would bring some of her retinue. The sisters would always accompany her out, crowding around. ... On Pascha she would send each sister a beautiful porcelain egg."[99]

Saint Seraphim's answer to the sorrowing Alexandra was immediate: the following year the much-desired heir to the Russian throne was born. The joy that this event brought was almost heavenly. However, in the heaven of this joy there had already appeared black, threatening clouds with fatal intent. Perhaps one may say rather than the storm had already begun.

CHAPTER 3

THE BEGINNING OF SORROWS

THE WAR WITH JAPAN AND BLOODY SUNDAY

"We need a little victorious war to stem the tide of revolution."[1] This declaration was made by Plehve, Russia's Secretary of State, to one of his trusted higher aides. The document was found in his archives after his murder. The desire of the emperors of Japan and Russia to dominate Korea and Manchuria gave occasion for this, his "little" war. The Russian generals were boasting that they could annihilate the Japanese simply by throwing their caps at them.

They had persuaded Nicholas that taking territory in Manchuria would not be grounds for Japan to go to war against them. Russian interests in the East must be secure by all means. But when Nicholas understood the great danger of likely war with Japan, he instructed his prime minister, Sergius Witte, to compose a proposal to assuage Russo-Japanese relations. At the Ministerial Assembly on New Year's Day 1904, Nicholas noted the military superiority of Russia, but requested that all attempts be made to keep peace. Replying to the German warmonger, Kaiser Wilhelm, who pushed Nicholas toward war with Japan—in order to serve German interests—Nicholas wrote, "I am still in good hopes about a calm and peaceful understanding."[2]

It was, however, already too late. Those that urged Russia towards war had already succeeded. Japan did not allow Russia to make the first move, as all had thought. On 26 January, they suddenly hit the anchored Russian fleet in Port Arthur, before war against Russia was even declared. "May the Lord help us!"[3] wrote Nicholas in his diary.

The following morning, a tremendous crowd set forth in the streets of Saint Petersburg shouting patriotic slogans. One large parade of students proceeded to the Winter Palace singing hymns. Nicholas greeted them from the window. He wrote of this in his diary, "27th of January. Tuesday... At 4 o'clock there was a move to the Cathedral through the overflowing halls for the moleben. On the way back there were deafening shouts of "Hurrah!" Overall, everywhere there were heartening demonstrations of a unanimous rise in spirit and indignation towards the impudence of the Japanese."[4]

Despite this, these crowds did not please Nicholas; this war troubled him. And he was not wrong. The telegrams that soon began to arrive from the Orient, as he wrote in his diary, did not at all bring hope: "29th of January. Thursday. Today the only news was sad: the mine transport 'Yenisei' on the Talienvansky road ran into a floating mine and was blown up, and they all died—Captain Stepanov, 3 officers and 92 sailors. Terrible event!"[5] "31st of January. Saturday. ... In the evening I received unpleasant news of another tragedy: the cruiser 'Boyarin' overran our underwater mine and sank. All were saved except for 9 firemen. Painful and hard!"[6] However, Nicholas had set his hope on God. Daily he inspected the troops in Saint Petersburg and distributed icons of Saint Seraphim of Sarov to the soldiers departing to the Far East. As he himself reported, "4th of February. Wednesday... The carts stood behind the convoy. I blessed the battalion with St Seraphim's icon and took my leave."[7]

On its front page, the newspaper *The San Francisco Call,* in an article entitled "Czar to appeal for the remains of Russian saint to turn the fortunes of his Manchurian legions: Reposes His Faith in the Powers of St. Serafim", wrote the following: "…when the Russian army in Manchuria was in an unusually dangerous position he [the Emperor] spent two hours every day praying in the chapel of his palace for divine intervention to protect Russia from further humiliation at the hands of Japan. The Czar also telegraphed to Father John of Kronstadt asking the priest to compose special prayers for the victory of the Russian army. At the same time the Czar telegraphed to the Archbishop of Moscow to compose special prayers for the same purpose."[8]

Nicholas' desire was to assume supreme command of the troops himself, and to go with them to the front. His powerful uncles, however, and the council of ministers expressed an intense opposition to Nicholas' desire. They insisted that his presence at the front and his consequent absence from the capital could only yield negative consequences. Nicholas was forced to yield. He wrote in a letter to his mother, "My conscience is often very troubled by my staying here instead of sharing the dangers and privations of the Army. I asked Uncle Alexei yesterday what he thought about it: he thinks my presence with the Army *in this war* is not necessary—still, to stay behind in times like these is very upsetting to me."[9]

The Empress, for her part, had cancelled all her community activities and converted the enormous reception chambers of the Winter Palace into workshops. There, girls of all classes labored making clothes and bandages for the soldiers at the front. Alexandra visited the workshops every day and often participated in their work herself.

THE BEGINNING OF SORROWS

Nicholas blessing his troops with the icon of the Saviour.

The subsequent defeats of the Russian Army in the war gave occasion to the revolutionary factions to rekindle the political dissatisfaction throughout the whole country. During the war, repeated strikes—which had already begun at the end of 1904, with the purpose of changing the monarchical form of government, and the general instability that they caused—convinced Nicholas that he must institute some measure of reforms. The result was the manifesto of 12 December of 1904, which promised the extension of the jurisdiction of the Zemstvos, as the local governing bodies were called, insurance for agricultural workers, emancipation of various ethnic groups in Russia, and the abolition of censorship. However, the prospect of a legislative body of representatives of the people, which was the main demand of the liberals, was lacking from the manifesto. Then an event followed that became known to history as Bloody Sunday.

CHAPTER 3

Georgi Gapon.

Bloody Sunday, which took place on Sunday 9 January 1905, constitutes, even today, one of the most misrepresented events in the history of Russia. The commonly known and widespread narrative goes as follows: At dawn on 9 January, a crowd of workers that were unemployed began to gather with their families in six different points of Saint Petersburg. Holding icons, church banners, and portraits of the tsar, chanting hymns and patriotic songs, they set forth in a peaceful march with the Winter Palace as their goal. There they intended to personally present to the tsar a petition for the improvement of working conditions. Unemployment in all the land at that time had already reached its peak. The inspiration and organizer of the entire event was the charismatic speaker, Father George Gapon, president of the Assembly of Factory and Mill Workers of Saint Petersburg. For a long time Gapon had been rousing the workers with his sermons at factories to assert their rights militantly. At last his labors bore fruit and thus the march of 9 January was organized.

A large police and military force had been prepared to deter the crowds that would make up the march. The exact number of demonstrators has never been known. Estimates vary from 3,000 up to 50,000! When the march began, security forces had gathered at various points in the city; they instructed the demonstrators to disperse, but without result. At some point the security forces opened fire on the unarmed multitude, so that many were killed, and even more were wounded. The number of dead also remains unknown to this day. Eyewitness accounts vary from 40 up to 1,000 dead. The result of this tragic event was general indignation against the tsar. Nicholas was not Batiushka to his people any more, but their murderer. Many people, revulsed by the frightful behavior of their autocrat, declared "We have no tsar any more."

The things that took place on Bloody Sunday have been accepted in history as an undeniable fact for nearly an entire century. However, as with so many other events in this period of unrest in Russia, Bloody Sunday itself constitutes one of the most falsified chapters of history. From the beginning, more than any other event, Bloody Sunday has been set forth as the banner of Communist propaganda. Lenin even undertook the production of a film that depicted the "crime of Bloody Nicholas." Unfortunately, the period of Bolshevik dictatorship succeeded in etching what it desired in the consciousness of the people. But what exactly took place on Bloody Sunday, and what exactly was Nicholas' responsibility for the entire event?

First of all, it must be known that Father George Gapon was not the good and kindly father of the downtrodden workers that "history" portrays, but rather he played a curious, double game: he was an agent of the Okhrana, namely, of the Secret Police, while at the same time cooperating with the Socialist Revolutionary Party. Thus, Gapon's dark role and the true motives of all his actions are not at all easy to discern.

At first Gapon presented himself as a champion of the tsarist constitution, and so the Okrhana indicated that it wished to utilize his charismatic influence on the masses of workers with a view to safeguarding the monarchical constitution in Russia. Later, however, Gapon appeared to reconsider his ideology and then began to cooperate with the extreme left, which in turn wished to use Gapon for the promotion of its own revolutionary ideas among the workers.

When Gapon officially announced the organization of the march, which he scheduled for the ninth of January, the police warned him that such a thing would constitute an illegal demonstration, for the dispersal of which, if necessary, force would be used. Furthermore, they informed him that the tsar would not be at the Winter Palace at that time, thus it would be impossible to accomplish the demonstrators' purpose of handing over their demands to Nicholas in person.

On Saturday, 8 January, the Ministry of War in cooperation with the Ministry of the Interior placed the police and military forces necessary to confront the demonstrators in the capital. That evening an extraordinary meeting, attended by the Governor of Saint Petersburg, was called to consider which measures of public safety should be taken. After the end of the meeting the Minister of the Interior visited the emperor at Tsarskoe Selo in order to inform him that everything was under control, and that the impending march would not be able to cause any trouble.

Why did Nicholas not remain in the Winter Palace to receive the demands of the workers? The reason was the fear of yet another attempt on his life. These fears were absolutely justified, and their ground for this was not theoretical. A frightening event had taken place only a few days earlier during the Blessing of the Waters on the day of Epiphany. Some of the rifles fired during the celebratory greeting of the Feast were not loaded with blanks, as intended, but—quite strangely—contained live ammunition. The bullets wounded several of the bystanders and broke many windows in the neighborhood. Some of them passed directly over the head of the emperor. The crowd and the police began to run aimlessly in all directions causing great confusion and panic. However, Nicholas did not move one step from his place. Later at the palace, discussing the event with his sister Olga, he said "he had heard the shell whizz over his head. 'I knew that somebody was trying to kill me [he said]. I just crossed myself. What else could I do?' It was typical of Nicky, added the Grand Duchess. He did not know what fear meant."[10]

In the end, Gapon did not comply with the police's instructions. The march took place as planned. Perhaps Gapon did not believe that the authorities would disperse his "peaceful" march? He himself answered this question later when he admitted that he knew full well that the authorities would not permit the protest to take place under any circumstances, because—very simply—it would not have been peaceful. The chief of the Special Corps of the tsar's secret personal guard, and afterward historian, Alexander Spiridovitch, wrote of this, "Nobody had the idea then at the time [9 January 1905] that Gapon had played the role of traitor. It was some long time later that Gapon admitted that he had known, in inciting the workers to go before the Tsar with their petition, that the authorities would never permit the demonstration; he also knew that they would bring in the troops against the workers, and all the same, he still urged them to demonstrate and in fact insisted they do so."[11]

A great number of workers were members of the Socialist Revolutionary Party, and even though the party did not officially take part in the demonstration, many of their members participated in the march. A multitude of witnesses relate that many of the demonstrators were armed; they broke windows, they looted stores, they burned vehicles and even broke into houses! Thus, the shots of the security forces were not in cold blood, but in reply to the repeated provocations of the demonstrators.[12]

A highly confidential note by the head of the Petersburg Security Department L. N. Kremenetsky to the Director of the Police Department A. A. Lopukhin, on the preparation of workers for the demonstration of 8 January, reports the following:

> Top secret
>
> According to the information obtained for tomorrow, at the initiative of Father Gapon, the revolutionary organizations of the capital also intend to use the march of the striking workers to the Palace Square to produce an anti-government demonstration.
>
> For this purpose, flags with criminal inscriptions are made today, and these flags will be hidden until the police act against the march of the workers; then, taking advantage of the confusion, the flag bearers will take out the flags to create an impression that the workers marched under the flags of revolutionary organizations.
>
> Then the socialist revolutionaries intend to take advantage of the disorder in order to plunder the weapon shops along Bolshaya Konyushennaya [Большая Конюшенная] Street and Liteyny Avenue [литейный проспект].
>
> Today, during a meeting of workers in the Narva Department, some agitator from the Socialist Revolutionary Party, apparently a student of St Petersburg University, Valerian Pavlov Karetnikov, came to agitate there, but was beaten up by workers.
>
> In one of the departments of the assembly in the city district, the same fate befell the members of the local social democratic organization, Alexander Kharik and Yulia Zhilevich, who are well-

known to the police department (Note of the Branch on 3 January, No. 6).

Reporting on your excellency, I add that the possible measures for the removal of flags have been taken.

Lieutenant Colonel Kremenetsky
January 21/8, 1905.[13]

As for the fact that some of the demonstrators held icons, church banners, and portraits of the tsar, that can also be explained. A certain portion of the workers did not realize what was about to happen. They believed Gapon's fraudulent promises and did not know that the tsar was absent from the palace that day. These were the first to be surprised by the violent behavior of the other demonstrators. They indeed had peaceful intentions and believed that they would meet the tsar to hand over to him their humble petition. They also did not know that the content of the petition almost did not have anything to do with them at all.

A few days before the march Gapon met with Pinhas Rutenberg, a member of the Socialist Revolutionary Party, from whom he was inseparable during the days of preparation for the march. At midnight of the eighth going into the ninth of January, Rutenberg, with Gapon present, composed the petition on behalf of the workers who would hand it to the Tsar—certainly not personally, since they knew that the tsar would be absent. In no way was the content of this document a simple request to improve the working conditions of the workers, but a provocative political manifesto that demanded in a threatening tone the immediate devolvement of the absolute monarchy of Russia into a constitutional monarchy with a democratic constitution and the promulgation of significant reforms of a socialist character.

Rutenberg's meddling in the preparations for the march of 9 January constituted the active, however covert, participation of the revolutionary party in this demonstration. Rutenberg did not limit himself only to composing the document that they would submit to the tsar. Spiridovitch writes of this, "The [Socialist-Revolutionary] party as such had not taken part in the Gapon movement, however certain of its members had made a common cause with him. Thus, also many of the workers who were members of the party were also found among the crowds filling the streets. Rutenberg, a member of the party, had gotten to know Gapon some days before the 9th of January, and was almost never separated from him during those days. It was in fact Rutenberg who had chosen the route the marchers would follow, including Gapon himself, and it was also Rutenberg who came up with the suggestion that, in case the troops began to fire, to erect barricades, to seize the arms depots and to clear the streets, at all costs, to the Palace."[14] From this evidence it is manifest that he was essentially preparing for military action.

CHAPTER 3

What in the end was the purpose of the march that Gapon organized? Spiridovitch gives the answer to that, "His genuine intention was to prove to the workers, in light of the measures which were to be taken against them, that the Tsar was not really protecting them and that the workers could never really hope to have any assistance coming from either the Tsar or his ministers."[15] Foreseeing, then, what would follow, Gapon wished to demonstrate to all the Russian people that the tsar was not the father of the nation, but its murderer. And in order to best achieve his goal, he undertook all necessary measures so that the blood of workers would be spilled.

At the end of January, Gapon fled to Switzerland, where with the help of his friend Rutenberg he met with Plekhanov and Lenin. On 7 February, he called from Geneva upon the workers in Russia to rise up in arms against the sovereign, to whom he sent a threatening and aggressive letter in which he wrote the following, "Nicholas Romanov, formerly Tsar and at present soul-murderer of the Russian empire. The innocent blood of workers, their wives and children lies forever between you and the Russian people. ... May all the blood which must be spilled [in the forthcoming revolution] fall upon you, you Hangman!"[16] At the end of this letter Gapon informed the emperor that copies of his letter had been sent to all the branches of the terrorist revolutionary movement in Russia.

Simeon Rappaport, a member of the Revolutionary Party, recounts a meeting he had with Gapon. When he asked if he had any ties with Zubatov, the chief of the Secret Police, Gapon replied, "Never! Never! Right from the beginning, from the very first minute, I led them by the nose. Otherwise nothing could ever have been done! ...My entire plan was based on this."[17]

It is necessary, however, to mention yet another very important and very dark fact regarding the events that eventually led to the fall of the emperor. It has been asserted, but not proven, that some members of the Okhrana did not look on Nicholas II favorably, but wished for and acted to replace him. The curious tolerance of the double game that Gapon played, which fact the police knew, justifies the suspicion that the incident of Bloody Sunday was impelled by members of the Okhrana itself. One might ask, to which of the two "friends" was Gapon truly faithful, to the Okhrana or to the Revolutionary Party?

One thing is certain, when he returned to Russia the following year, Gapon wished to persuade his trusted friend Rutenberg to become a double agent, too. In other words, Gapon, after the events of Bloody Sunday, continued to work for the Okhrana! He had, however, overlooked Rutenberg's viciousness. On 26 March of 1916 he was found hanged in a house outside of Saint Petersburg, where he had been called to a meeting with Rutenberg. According to the latter, Gapon was condemned by a tribunal of comrades.[18]

The answer to the question that was first posed—what was Nicholas' responsibility for the events of Bloody Sunday—is clear: absolutely none. Based on information from his ministers, he believed that the march would not cause any significant disturbances in the capital. Surprised after these events, he wrote that evening in his diary about that fateful day, "9th of January. Sunday. A hard day! In Petersburg there was serious unrest due to the workers' wish to reach the Winter Palace. The troops had to shoot in different parts of the city and there were many killed and wounded. Lord, how painful and hard!"[19]

A few days later, on 14 January 1905, Alexandra wrote to her sister Victoria, "You understand the crisis we are going through! It is a time full of trials indeed. My poor Nicky's cross is a heavy one to bear, all the more as he has nobody on whom he can thoroughly rely and who can be a real help to him. He has had so many bitter disappointments, but through it all he remains brave and full of faith in God's mercy. He tries so hard, works with such perseverance, but the lack of what I call 'real' men is great. ... On my knees I pray to God to give me wisdom to help him in his heavy task. ... The Minister of the Interior is doing the greatest harm—he proclaims grand things without having prepared them. ... Reforms can only be made gently with the greatest care and forethought. ... All these disorders are thanks to his unpardonable folly and he won't believe what Nicky tells him, does not agree with his point of view.

"Things are in a bad state and it's abominably unpatriotic at the time when we are plunged into war to break forth with revolutionary ideas. The poor workmen, who had been utterly misled, had to suffer, and the organisers have hidden as usual behind them. Don't believe all the horrors the foreign papers say. They make one's hair stand on end—foul exaggeration. Yes, the troops, alas, were obliged to fire. Repeatedly the crowd was told to retreat and that Nicky was not in town (as we are living here [i.e., at Tsarskoe Selo] this winter) and that one would be forced to shoot, but they would not heed and so blood was shed. ... The Petition had only two questions concerning the workmen and all the rest was atrocious: separation of the Church from the Government, etc., etc. Had a small deputation brought, calmly, a real petition for the workmen's good, all would have been otherwise. Many of the workmen were in despair, when they heard later what the petition contained, and begged to work again under the protection of the troops."[20]

THE REVOLUTION OF 1905

The fourth of February of 1905 was marked by one of the most important political assassinations of that period. From a distance of four feet a revolutionary, Ivan Kalyayev, threw a bomb into the passing carriage of Grand Duke Sergius Alexandrovich, Military Governor of Moscow and husband of Elisabeth, sister of Alexandra. The bomb literally dissolved the body of the victim.

Soon after that, Nicholas' fears at last came true. The first major war of the twentieth century, which lasted nearly two years, found the Japanese gloriously triumphant in a series of great successes against Russia. Their victory was sealed with the complete destruction of Russia's Baltic fleet in the Battle of Tsushima, which took place on the anniversary of Nicholas and Alexandra's coronation, on 14 May, 1905. The entire Baltic fleet journeyed for six months before it arrived at Japan, where it was almost completely destroyed in a single day. From then on, the imperial couple did not celebrate the anniversary of their coronation, but dedicated it to prayer for the unjust loss of the Russian naval forces. At last, on 5 September, 1905, with the intervention of the American President Roosevelt, the Treaty of Portsmouth was signed, putting an end to the Russo-Japanese War. The end of the war, however, did not constitute the end of difficulties. On the contrary, the great trials were just beginning.

The public outcry in Saint Petersburg for the unfortunate outcome of the war and the aftermath of Bloody Sunday very quickly spread to all of Russia. The political tensions led to a meeting in Moscow of representatives from the Zemstvos, the nobility and the municipal councils, who called for the convocation of a national representative body elected on a secret, equal, universal, and direct ballot. On June 6 a delegation from the meeting led by Prince Sergius Trubetskoj was received by the tsar, and on August 6 what became known as the "Bulygin Constitution" was published: a proposal for a consultative parliamentary body called the Duma.

The tsar was never opposed to consultative bodies. He welcomed every opportunity to learn more about the opinions and attitudes of his subjects. But he said, "I shall never in any circumstances agree to a representative form of government, for I consider it harmful for the people entrusted to me by God."[21] The "Bulygin Constitution" was far from being a representative form of government in the full western sense: its powers were limited, and "the inviolability of autocratic power" was retained. Nevertheless, it was seen as a major concession to the liberal opposition by the government.

On August 27 the government made another unexpected concession: university faculties were allowed to elect rectors and students to hold assemblies. Moreover, the police were told to keep out of the universities, making them in effect "no-go" areas. Soon, workers and other non-students joined the student meetings, and, as Richard Pipes writes, "academic work became impossible as institutions of higher learning turned into 'political clubs': non-conforming professors and students were subjected to intimidation and harassment…. In Witte's view, the university regulations of August 27 were a disaster: 'It was the first breach through which the Revolution, which had ripened underground, emerged into the open.'"[22]

At the end of September, a wave of strikes, economic in origin, but politicized by the Union of Unions and the radical students, hit Central

Russia. The striking industrial workers reached up to 50% in Russia, and in Poland (at that time part of the Russian Empire) 93.2%. Strikes also occurred in Finland, the Baltic shore, the Caucuses and in the Urals. By mid-October more than two million workers were on strike, and the railways were not operating in nearly all of Russia.

In Moscow, on October 16, the future hieromartyr Metropolitan Vladimir, delivered a speech in the Kremlin Dormition cathedral after the liturgy, which included the following words:

"The heart bleeds when you see what is happening around us.... It is no longer the Poles, or external enemies, but our own Russian people, who, having lost the fear of God, have trusted the rebels and are holding our first capital as it were in a siege. Even without this we have been having a hard time because of our sins: first harvest failures [in 1891, 1897, 1898, and 1901], then illnesses, then an unsuccessful war [the Russo-Japanese war of 1904-05], and now something unheard of is taking place in Rus: it is as if God has deprived Russian people of their minds. By order of underground revolutionaries, strikes have begun everywhere, in the factories, in the schools, on the railways. ... Oh if only our unfortunate workers knew who is ruling them, who is sending them trouble-maker-agitators, then they would have turned from them in horror as from poisonous snakes! You know these are the so-called social-democrats, these are the revolutionaries, who have long ago renounced God in their works. They have renounced Him, and yet it may be that they have never known the Christian faith. ... With satanic cunning they catch lightminded people in their nets, promising them paradise on earth, but they carefully hide from them their secret aims, their criminal dreams. Having deceived the unfortunate, they drag him to the most terrible crimes, as if for the sake of the common good, and, in fact they make him into an obedient slave. They try in every way to cast out of his soul, or at any rate to distort, the teaching of Christ.... The commandment of Christ orders us to lay down our souls for our friends, but they teach to destroy people who are completely innocent, to kill them only for the fact they do not agree with them, and do not embark on robbery, but simply want to work honorably and are ready to stand for the law, for the tsar, for the Church of God."[23]

Although Nicholas found himself in the center of this terrible storm, in his very depths he remained calm to such a degree that those around him marveled. Russia's Minister of Foreign Affairs, Alexander Izvolsky preserved a very significant incident that took place in one of his meetings with Nicholas. In the period when the disturbances were cresting, he met with Nicholas at the Peterhof Palace to give him his daily report. The naval base of Kronstadt lay very close by, which was under siege by mutineers. The gunshots of the battle were clearly audible in the palace. Izvolsky describes the scene:

"On the day when the mutiny [of the Kronstadt Fleet] reached its culminating point, I happened to be with the Emperor, making my weekly verbal report concerning the affairs of my department. It was at Peterhof, in the imperial villa, situated on the border of the Gulf of Finland, facing the island on which stands the fortress of Cronstadt, some fifteen kilometers distant. ... From the window could be distinguished in the distance the line of fortifications, and as I lay before the Emperor the different matters of interest we heard distinctly the cannonade, which seemed to grow louder from one minute to another.

"He listened attentively, and, as was his habit, asked questions now and then, showing his interest in the smallest detail of my report. Glance as I would in his direction, I could not detect the slightest trace of emotion in his countenance, although he knew well that it was his crown that was at stake at that moment, only a few leagues away. If the fortress remained in the hands of the mutineers, not only the situation of the capital would become very precarious, but his own fate and that of his family would be seriously menaced, for the cannon of Cronstadt could prevent any attempt at flight by sea.

"When my report was finished, the Emperor remained a few moments looking calmly out of the open window at the line of the horizon. For my part, I was oppressed by a profound emotion, and could not refrain, even at the risk of infringing the rules of etiquette, from expressing my surprise at seeing him so unmoved. The Emperor did not apparently resent my observation, for he turned to me with a look which has so often been described as of extraordinary gentleness, and replied in these few words, deeply engraven in my memory: 'If you see me so calm, it is because I have the firm, the absolute conviction that the fate of Russia, my own fate, and that of my family, is in the hands of God Who placed me where I am. Whatever happens, I will bow to His will, conscious of never having had a thought other than that of serving the country that He confided to me.'"[24]

The country was descending into anarchy. Both Witte and D. F. Trepov, the Governor-General of St. Petersburg, were in favor of the creation of a constitutional monarchy along the lines of the resolution of the Zemstvo Congress held in Moscow. In a letter to his mother, the tsar wrote: "During these terrible days I have been with Witte almost all the time; our conversations began first thing in the morning and continued until dark. I was faced with choosing between two courses of action: to appoint an energetic military man and crush this sedition with the utmost force, as a result of which there would be a respite of a few months before force would be required once more. ... The other way was to grant the population citizens' rights—freedom of speech, freedom of the press, the right of public assembly and unions, and the inviolability of the individual. Furthermore, every bill has to pass through the State Duma—this is in effect the granting of a constitution. Witte argues passionately for the latter course of action, saying that although it is not without risk, it is the only way at the present time."[25]

The tsar did not believe in the use of force to suppress the rebellion. Nevertheless, he did think of making the reliable and loyal Trepov a kind of military dictator. However, "to the question whether he [Trepov] could restore order in the capital without risking a massacre, he answered that 'he could give no such guarantee either now or in the future: sedition [крамола] has attained a level at which it is doubtful whether [bloodshed] could be avoided. All that remains is faith in the mercy of God.'"[26]

The tsar then decided to ask Grand Duke Nicholas Nikolaevich, his six foot six inch tall cousin and Military Governor of Saint Petersburg, to take control of the situation. The grand duke, hearing about the intentions of the tsar, said: "Do you see this firearm? I will now go to the Emperor and beg him to sign the manifesto and Witte's program. He will either do it, or I will blow my brains out with this very weapon!"[27]

The circumstance did not allow Nicholas any latitude. He understood that the slaughter that continued to increase due to the demands of the people naturally did not constitute a God-pleasing reality. It was necessary to put an end to this situation. The choices were not many: either he yielded to what the people wanted, or the violent conflict between opposing sides would continue without end.

Even though he believed firmly in the idea of monarchy, which he swore to preserve before God and man in the Rite of Coronation and in his Anointing, the tsar's main concern was not the granting of a constitution itself, but rather the fact that Russia was not ready for this transition yet. "'Russia,' he said, 'will not escape it. In this regard Europe is exerting too strong a pressure on Russia, and it is better to accord a constitution spontaneously and of our own free will than to be forced into it from abroad. But if the constitution is inevitable, once we have granted it, we risk finding ourselves on a slope and precipitating ourselves into the abyss.'"[28]

He characteristically said, "I am not holding on to autocracy for my own pleasure. I act in this spirit only because I am certain that this is necessary for Russia. If it were only for myself, I would with pleasure have turned away from all of this."[29] He believed that "Only that state which preserves the heritage of its past is strong and firm. We ourselves have sinned against this, and God is perhaps [now] punishing us."[30]

Finally, Nicholas yielded. On 17 October, 1905, after great internal division and difficulty, he signed the October Manifesto composed by Sergius Witte. This manifesto put a definitive end to the absolute monarchy of Russia, an event that added an important new page to Russia's age-old history. With the October Manifesto, the main demands of the liberal councils were met: securing basic political rights, permission to form political parties, extension of suffrage to a general election, and most important of all, establishment of the Duma as the central legislative body. In his Manifesto, which was entitled "On the Improvement of Order in the State," the tsar declared:

The disturbances and unrest in St. Petersburg, Moscow and in many other parts of our empire have filled our heart with great and profound sorrow. The welfare of the Russian sovereign and his people are inseparable and national sorrow is his too. The present disturbances could give rise to national instability and present a threat to the unity of our state. The oath that we took as tsar compels us to use all our strength, intelligence, and power to put a speedy end to this unrest, which is so dangerous for the state. The relevant authorities have been ordered to take measures to deal with direct outbreaks of disorder and violence and to protect people who only want to go about their daily business in peace. However, in view of the need to speedily implement earlier measures to pacify the country, we have decided that the work of the government must be unified. We have therefore ordered the government to take the following measures in fulfilment of our unbending will:

1. Fundamental civil freedoms will be granted to the population, including real personal inviolability, freedom of conscience, speech, assembly, and association.

2. Participation in the Duma will be granted to those classes of the population that are at present deprived of voting powers, insofar as is possible in the short period before the convocation of the Duma, and this will lead to the development of a universal franchise. There will be no delay to the Duma elect already been organized.

3. It is established as an unshakeable rule that no law can come into force without its approval by the State Duma, and representatives of the people will be given the opportunity to take real part in the supervision of the legality of government bodies. We call on all true sons of Russia to remember the homeland, to help put a stop to this unprecedented unrest and, together with this, to devote all their strength to the restoration of peace to their native land.[31]

Alexandra told Anna Vyrubova that, for the duration of the meeting of the Council of State in which Nicholas was to sign the manifesto, she remained in her own private room in agony that at any moment a child would be born in the Council Hall with great difficulty and danger. However, Alexandra added, both her own and of the emperor's prayers were that this radical reform would, at last, bring peace to tormented Russia.[32]

In fact, the Manifesto did succeed in bringing the general bloody disturbances in Russia to an end. The publication of the Manifesto called forth spontaneous demonstrations of support in all the great cities of Russia, and the strikes in Saint Petersburg as well as in other cities officially came to an end. The Russian liberals, satisfied with the October Manifesto, had already started preparing for the coming elections of the Duma. At the same time, however, the underground forces of radical socialism denounced the election and called on the people to armed uprising for the complete abolition of the monarchy. In November a new series of strikes, workers' uprisings, terrorist activities, and military mutinies began, but were quelled after hard struggles. At last in December 1905, all the uprisings stopped completely. The toll of the Revolution of 1905 numbered thousands of dead and wounded.

The 1905 revolution was indeed crushed, but nevertheless the revolutionary spirit remained alive and the country remained divided. And even after the revolution had been defeated, "between January 1908 and May 1910, 19,957 terrorist attacks and revolutionary robberies were recorded; 732 government officials and 3,052 private citizens were killed, and nearly another 4,000 wounded."[33]

The Duma opened on April 27, 1906. Spiridovitch writes that "whilst apparently keeping calm, he [Nicholas] was profoundly troubled to the core of his soul. His anxiety was for Russia, his worry for her outcome. Once they had arrived in Petersburg, Their Majesties traveled in a small steamboat to the Peter and Paul Fortress to pray before the tombs, and then set off for the Winter Palace. ...

A Solemn Office was celebrated before the icon of the Divine Saviour, which had been brought from the little house of Peter the Great. The Tsar prayed fervently, without regard to anything else; and the Tsaritsa Alexandra Feodorovna, visibly moved, followed his example. At the conclusion of the service, the Tsar climbed the steps of the Throne... and, having received the parchment from the hands of the Minister of the Court, looking a little pale, but in calm, assured voice, he delivered the speech from the throne:

'Care for the well-being of the country which Divine Providence has entrusted to me has caused me to decide to make an appeal to the legislative collaboration of the representatives of the people....' He read the whole speech in the same calm, firm voice, stressing certain words, and sometimes glancing at the members of the Duma. '...That my ardent desire be realised of seeing my people instructed....' And he finished with these words: '... worthily to justify the confidence of the Tsar and of the people. May God help me and you!'

Those in attendance listened to this speech with marked attention. It created a singular atmosphere in the room. Indeed, they shouted 'Hurrah!' but there was no joy in these acclamations. One was very well aware that there were two parties present, one of which seemed to say, 'Well! We have finally obtained what we wanted,' while the other seemed to be thinking, in its sullen silence, 'Don't gloat too soon!' The Emperor was perhaps the only one at that moment to think solely of the interests of Russia."[34]

CHAPTER 3

Duma Opening, 27 April, 1906.

PETER ARKADIEVITCH STOLYPIN

In April, 1906, Nicholas called Sergius Witte to resign and asked Peter Stolypin to become prime minister. Stolypin was the former governor of Saratov. At first, Stolypin refused the post, but the tsar insisted: "Let us make the sign of the Cross over ourselves and let us ask the Lord to help us both in this difficult, perhaps historic moment."[35]

Stolypin's chief reform was agricultural, giving the farmers what the abolition of serfdom did not give them in 1861—land. The distribution of land to farmers was the only way to reduce the danger of revolution. Stolypin's target was to convert communal Russia into a Russia of landholders, so that landholding might constitute the basis of national agriculture. In this manner, a significant part of the farmers would succeed in becoming small landholders, and thus result in a conservative middle class.

Stolypin attempted to provide a balance between the introduction of much needed land reforms and the suppression of the radicals. In October 1906, he introduced legislation that gave peasants more opportunity to acquire land. They also received more freedom in the selection of their representatives to the Zemstvos. By avoiding confrontation with peasant representatives in the Duma, he was able to secure the privileges attached to nobles in local government and reject the idea of confiscation.

Despite the fact that the complete success of this plan would take some time to reach completion, Stolypin's vision very quickly began to become reality. Before the First World War, Russia had succeeded in reaching all her economic goals. In 1913 the annual growth of agricultural production in Russia was first in the world, the annual growth in its industrial productivity was also first in the world, the population growth was first in Europe, and the annual national revenue was sixth in the world.

In this period, Lenin, while in exile in Switzerland, had reached the utter limits of complete discouragement. Convinced that the Russian scene was no longer at all appropriate to foment revolution, he circulated through the libraries of Europe woefully killing time. In 1909 Laura Marx, daughter of the noted philosopher and founder of Communism, Karl Marx, with her husband, Paul Lafargue—full of despondency at the failure to spread revolutionary communist ideals in Europe—killed themselves. Lenin, reaching nearly the same condition wrote, "If one cannot work for the Party any longer, one must be able to look truth in the face and die the way the Lafargues did."[36]

Peter Stolypin instituted a new court system that made it easier for the arrest and conviction of political revolutionaries. The revolutionaries were now determined to assassinate Stolypin and there were several attempts on his life. The most serious one took place on 25 August, 1906. Three assassins wearing military uniforms bombed a public reception Stolypin was holding at his home on Aptekarsky Island. Stolypin was only slightly injured, but twenty-eight others were killed. Stolypin's fifteen-year-old daughter had both legs broken and his three-year-old son also had injuries.

Apart from the socialist revolutionaries who hated him for the large number of death penalties that he imposed on terrorists, Stolypin had an open confrontation with the large landholders. The latter were fanatical enemies of Stolypin, who had taken their land to distribute it to poor farmers.

Everyone considered Stolypin's assassination inevitable. And they were right. On 1 September, 1911, as he was attending an opera performance in Kiev, a young man named Dmitri Bogrov approached him and shot him in the chest. The tsar was present with his two daughters, Olga and Tatiana. Before he fell down, Stolypin turned to the place where the sovereign sat and blessed him with the sign of the cross. Later it was revealed that the murderer was simultaneously a member of the revolutionary movement and an agent of the secret police, in other words, the invisible third enemy.[37] Thus the great dream for radical reforms in a climate of mutual cooperation had now definitively lost its great architect.

TSAREVICH ALEXIS

Amid this vortex of dramatic political disturbances, the birth of Alexis brought great consolation to the imperial couple, and at news of this the Russian people broke out into frenetic celebration. The brightness of the demonstrations in all of Russia was unique. From Nicholas' diary: "30th of July. Friday. An unforgettable great day for us, in which the mercy of God visited us so clearly. At 1.15 o'clock, Alix gave birth to a son, whom with prayer we called Aleksey. ... There are no words to be able to thank God sufficiently for the consolation that has been given us during this time of great difficulty!"[38] Alexis was born during the war of Russia with Japan.

One of the first telegrams of congratulations that the imperial couple received for the birth of the heir was from Saint John of Kronstadt himself. Nicholas and Alexandra's spiritual tie to Saint John remained ever very tight and strong. The saint had in fact taken part in the Sacraments of Marriage and of Coronation of the imperial couple, as well as in Olga's Baptism. Replying now to the congratulatory telegram of Saint John, Nicholas wrote the following: "The Empress and I thank you cordially, and we hope that you will assist at the baptism of our son. Nicholas."[39]

The invitation to Saint John to participate at the baptism of Alexis was not simply an act of mere cordiality. This is obvious from the following article, published in the *New York Times*, on August 27, 1904:

CZAR REWARDS FATHER JOHN
Latter Said Birth of Heir Would Follow Royal Visit to Saroff.

THE BEGINNING OF SORROWS

Alexandra with Alexis.

Nicholas with Alexis.

ST. PETERSBURG, Aug. 26.—The Emperor has telegraphed his and the Empress's thanks to the monks of the St. Seraphim Monastery in reply to their congratulations on the birth of an heir to the throne. His Majesty has also presented a magnificent diamond and sapphire pectoral cross to Father John of Cronstadt, upon whose advice the Emperor and Empress went to Saroff to canonize St. Seraphim, Father John predicting that they would be sure to have a son and heir.[40]

The ascription of Alexis' birth to the intercessions of St. Seraphim was also commented upon in another article in *The Washington Post*:

ST. SERAPHIM'S GIFT
The Three-year-old Heir to the Throne of the Czar.
… The existence of Alexis is the greatest of the innumerable miracles ascribed to the last saint canonized during the religious career of the late Mr. Pobiedonostseff. Kneeling side by side on the stone at Saroff, worn thin by the knees of St.Seraphim, Nicholas II and his consort had besought the spirit of the monk to grant them a son. Her majesty bathed in the spring at which Seraphim

had quenched his thirst. The bones of the saint where removed by a procession of gorgeously appareled clergy from a monastery near the miraculous spring to a new marble tomb wherein they are now permanently enshrined in the Uspensky Cathedral at Saroff. Vestments embroidered in gold and silver, worn by the Metropolitan of St. Petersburg and the seventeen bishops escorting the relics, were the gift of the Czar for this particular occasion. The aggregate weight of the votive candles consumed in the two days of ceremony was over eleven tons. ... Within a year from the day on which the Czar and Czarina helped to carry the cedar wood box of relies through crowds of kneeling clergy from the monastery to the cathedral, Alexis was born. Seraphim, on this occasion as appears from a narrative in the St. Petersburg Novoye Vremya, manifested himself in the forest at Saroff. He was surrounded by innumerable bears.[41]

Nicholas named his son Alexis in honor of his beloved ancestor, Tsar Alexis. Little Alexis was the first male child born heir to the throne during the reign of his father from the seventeenth century onward. He was a comely blonde boy with deep blue eyes. At his baptism almost all the members of his huge family were present. Among them was his aged great grandfather, King Christian IX of Denmark, already eighty-seven years old. The Baptism was performed by Father John Yanishev, the rector of the palace. The children's English nanny, Mrs. Eagar, relates that when the priest anointed Alexis with the Holy Chrism, the infant "raised his hand and extended his fingers as though pronouncing a blessing!"[42]

Even from infancy, Alexis appeared to be an especially happy child, full of liveliness and vigor. In the spring of 1905, before he had even completed his first year, Alexis was presented to the Royal Guard, the Preobrazhensky Regiment. When the soldiers greeted Alexis with a powerful, "Hurrah!" he broke out into happy laughter.

Nicholas and Alexandra had accepted that in the years of their governance it was difficult to enjoy a politically balanced Russia. They exerted all their labors and efforts to hand over to their son a better reality, a better Russia, a better tomorrow. Soon, however, they received the most powerful blow in their life. They discovered that for Alexis there might be no tomorrow.

From Nicholas' diary six weeks after the birth of Alexis, "8th of September. Wednesday. ... Alix and I were very concerned about the bleeding of little Alexei from his umbilical cord, which had lasted intermittently until the evening. I had to write to Korovin and the surgeon Fedorov; at about 7 o'clock they put on a bandage. ... 9th of September. Thursday. In the morning there was blood on the bandage again."[43]

The months passed and Alexis began to attempt to stand on his feet. When he tripped and fell, little bruises appeared on him. After a little time, the bruises became dark blue swellings. It was obvious that his body did not have the ability to stanch the flow of blood. His parents' worst fears had been confirmed: Alexis suffered from the "royal disease," hemophilia.

The hereditary affliction of hemophilia mainly affects males, and it is transmitted through the mother. Alexandra, a carrier of this affliction, had transmitted this dreadful disease to their only son in a time when the chances that the patient would succeed in passing through his childhood years alive were almost nonexistent. Alexandra had already encountered this fatal enemy in the past. One of her uncles, her brother, and two nephews had lost their lives because of this disease. Thus, she knew well that death would hover every moment over the head of her beloved child. The inability of science to treat Alexis opened the door to a tragic, painful chapter in the life of the royal family, but mainly for Alexandra. She believed that she was the cause of the drama that now began to unfold before them.

The most terrible episodes for Alexis' health happened when he was injured in the joints. Beyond the fact that they brought about long-lasting

Alexis bedridden, with his mother always by his side.

CHAPTER 3

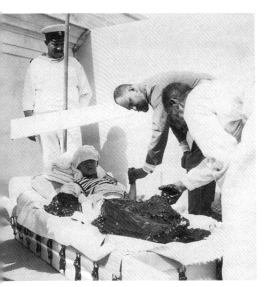
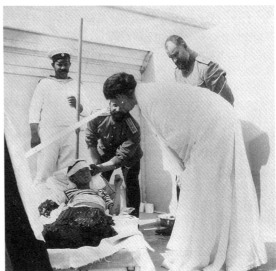

Alexis treated by Dr Botkin with mud bath therapy.
Alexandra always by his side.

disabilities, hemorrhages between the joints caused the patient unbelievable, unbearable pain. This occurred because the blood that entered into the narrow space of the joints, into the ankle, the knees, and the elbows pressed upon the nerves of that region. Often the trauma was so slight that it would pass unobserved. The following day, however, when Alexis woke up, he would say to his mother, "Mama, today I cannot walk" or "my elbow won't bend." As the internal bleeding continued, the pains became inhuman. Even though morphine was available, it could not be administered to hemophiliac patients because of its addictive properties with long-term use. In any case, the severity of the pains did not allow the patient to sleep. Thus, the only relief came when the patient, succumbing to the intensity of the pain, finally fainted. Traumas of this kind fixed Alexis to his bed for weeks. At last after every similar episode, subjection to long-term orthopedic therapy was necessary and afterwards baths in warm mud in order to avoid the possibility of permanent disability.

In these difficult and frightful hours, the only real weapon was prayer. Anna Vyrubova remembers, "This autumn [of 1909] was made sad also by one of the all too frequent illnesses of the unfortunate little Tsarevitch. ... We who could do nothing else for him took refuge in prayer and supplication in the little church near the palace. Mlle. Tutcheva, maid of honor to the young Grand Duchesses, read the psalms, while the Empress, the older girls, Olga and Tatiana, two of the Tsar's aides, and myself assisted in the singing."[44]

The problem of Alexis' health, however, did not end here for Nicholas and Alexandra. The family drama was twofold. Beside their inability to help their child in the hours of terrible pain, it was necessary by any possible means to assure that news of this terrible reality did not leak out from the palace. Under no circumstance must it become known that the future emperor of Russia suffered from an incurable disease that could at any moment deprive him of life. Despite all the family's efforts to keep Alexis' illness a secret, it was impossible for the people not to understand that something was not right with the tsarevich. As was natural, some of the frequent public appearances of the family occurred when Alexis was wounded. In those instances, the child appeared to be carried in the hands of a strong-armed Cossack of the Imperial Guard, making it obvious that the tsarevich suffered from some sickness. Thus, Nicholas' sister, Grand Duchess Olga Alexandrovna, was completely right when she said, "The birth of a son, which should have been the happiest event in the lives of Nicky and Alicky, became their heaviest cross."[45]

Grand Duchess Olga Alexandrovna.

CHAPTER 3

When Alexis was well, however, the whole life of the palace was transformed. Everything seemed bathed in a very sweet light. The young heir was undoubtedly the epicenter of the attention and love of the entire family. His sisters adored him. Within the family he was known by the pet name, "Little One," and "Baby." At first his parents' particularly indulgent treatment because of his ailment turned him into a rather spoiled child. For example, when people used to kiss his hand, Alexis "didn't miss the chance to boast about it and give himself airs in front of his sisters,"[46] which compelled his parents to stop this custom.

Alexei was an exceptionally lively child. In order to limit the opportunities for accidents, his parents assigned two sailors of the Imperial Navy to serve Alexis by turns as his personal assistants, seeing to it that they would protect him from dangerous activities. These sailors, Andrei Derevenko and Clementy Nagorny, were practically the child's shadow. Furthermore, he was forbidden to ride a bicycle or a horse, and in general any kind of play in which he could come to harm. Nevertheless, that did not keep Alexis from being a happy and a lively child. There are many charming stories about his childish gaffes and games. General Alexander Spiridovitch has preserved a few of them.

"The Tsarevitch then seemed like a child in perfect health, and he played with all the gaiety and vivacity of children his age. He loved to play on the sand with Derevenko. That year [1908], his favourite game was *tchekarda* (leapfrog). He had fun climbing up on the big, burly Derevenko, and crawling over his back by straddling him. He imagined that in so doing, he accomplished the leap. When he had 'jumped' enough, he would get down on all fours and say, 'All right, Derevenko, it's your turn to jump.' Derevenko, big and robust, would start off at a run and, barely touching the Tsarevitch with his hand, jumped effortlessly over the little body, which gave the child a lot of pleasure.

"In his little white sailor suit, with his invariable small velvet bag, which he wore as a bandolier and which contained his handkerchief, the Tsarevitch was a delightful child. Everybody wanted his photograph, but he never liked to let anybody take his picture, and every time he saw a camera pointed at him—which happened more than once a day—he would make a face. I nevertheless managed to surprise him with my box camera, without his noticing it, and snapped him when he was playing leapfrog and in his pose of 'All right, Derevenko, it's your turn to jump.'"[47]

One day, while the tsar was inspecting the *Asia* crew, "the Tsarevitch insisted upon doing as the sentinels did: standing at attention, rifle in hand. At Derevenko's request, they gave him a rifle, but it goes without saying that the Tsarevitch could not lift it and contented himself by holding it beside him, steadying it with his hand."[48]

Another charming incident took place as follows. Every morning, after his walk, the emperor would taste the usual fare of the escort, which was brought to him in his dressing-room. "Once he had conscientiously tasted

Pierre Gilliard giving a lesson to Olga.

all the 'proba,' the Tsar always thanked the man who had brought it. Later on, when the Tsarevitch was of an age to carry out the same duty, the Tsar, after having tasted it himself, would say to the under-officer of the Escort, 'And now, take the 'proba' to the Ataman' (the Tsarevitch was Ataman of all the Cossack troops). They would conduct the under-officer to the Tsarevitch, who would sit down with him at the table and apply himself to the duty of tasting, while chatting with the man, and asking him if he had any children, above all little girls. When the reply was in the affirmative, off he would go to his sisters' room, bringing back a doll intended for the officer's little daughter."[49]

Lively and playful as he was, Alexis was nevertheless a very gentle and sensitive boy. Once, during a visit to the villa of an admiral in Sevastopol, he was playing in "an artificial pond, stocked with live fish. The Tsarevitch fished for shells and seaweed, but when someone offered him a fishing net, he refused it, saying, 'No, we mustn't. We must let them live.'"[50]

As Alexis grew up, he became very affectionate, with simple manners and a humble disposition. One time a delegation of farmers visited him bringing gifts. His personal assistant required that they kneel before him. The boy blushed with shame and embarrassment. Later his tutor, Pierre Gilliard, who taught French to Nicholas' children, asked him whether he was pleased with what had happened. The child then replied that he was not at all pleased. Thus, when Gilliard saw to it that this did not happen again, Alexis felt great happiness that he had been delivered from this troubling ceremony.

CHAPTER 3

Pierre Gilliard with Alexis.

Beyond simply being Alexis' French teacher, Pierre Gilliard established close ties with him. All the upbringing and education of the young Tsarevich occupied him significantly, and making use of the trust the royal couple placed in him, he attempted to influence them positively in this matter. Thus, recognizing that the sailor guardians' close monitoring of Alexis did not help the child, he wished to bring this to his parents' attention. His opinion was that with this arrangement the child would not be able to cultivate self-control and the necessary self-confidence that he would need when he grew up. This was even more important given Alexis' calling as heir to the throne. Gilliard in fact persuaded his parents to allow the child more independence. This proved very important, because Alexis then began to overcome many of the weaknesses in his character.

As he grew, Alexis became more and more serious and reflective. His repeated personal encounter with death made him especially compassionate with the problems of other people. He tried in every way to relieve their hurts, and with impressive tenderness he consoled even the least servants of the palace when they passed through difficult times in their personal life.

Another worthy component of his character was a sense of gratitude, something that is very rare in children who learn early that they have whatever they may desire at their disposal. Baroness Buxhoeveden remembered with emotion the hours that she gave him English lessons, "It was pretty to see him when a lesson was over, getting up ceremoniously… and … giving me his hand, with an exact imitation of the Emperor's manner, and thanking me with his own particularly sweet smile: 'It is really nice of you, you know.' He felt he was under an obligation to me, as I was not one of his regular teachers."[51]

Fabritsky wrote: "I knew the Heir from the time he was in the cradle, and played the leading role in the choice of his sailor-nanny, Derevenko whom I assigned, in accordance with Imperial orders … I saw Alexis Nikolaevich reviewing the crew and playing with cabin boys on the yacht; I saw him receiving presentations, and I saw him in moments of childish mischief, etc. He always impressed everyone with his clear-sightedness, quick decision-making, loud voice, and resolute air, as well as his mildness, gentleness, kind-heartedness, and the attentiveness he showed to everyone and everything."[52]

Thus, this little child gave the best hopes for his distinction as a particularly cultivated and rounded personality. These qualities constituted valuable attributes of the character of the future emperor of Russia.

SPALA
AT THE WHIFF OF DEATH

Despite the great promises for a bright future given by the personality of this beautiful crown prince of Russia, his terrible disease never ceased to remind the family that death stood by to seize him at any moment. Alexis' most critical traumatic incident occurred at the beginning of September 1912. The family was then on the way to a hunting lodge in Spala, Poland, where they would stay for a few days. At some station on the route, Alexis was ready to go rowing in a nearby lake. Rowing was one of the few safe activities that he was allowed, in contrast with horseback riding and other such things. But while he leapt onto the boat, he fell and hit himself on the left thigh, so that by the time they reached Spala, a swelling had formed in the region.

The family doctor, Eugene Botkin, who was always with the family, kept Alexis in bed for a week until his pain and the swelling began to recede.

CHAPTER 3

Alexis was still in the period of recovery, when one day while he was in the carriage with his mother, he began to complain of an intense pain. When they had returned to the house, the child's condition had already progressed. On examining him, Doctor Botkin diagnosed a severe internal bleeding in the groin. That same evening the doctors from Saint Petersburg began to arrive one by one, only to add to the anxious persons in the house. No one was able to stop the hemorrhage and the child experienced dreadful, indescribable pains. The episode was without precedent.

From Nicholas' letter to his mother: "The days between the 6th and the 10th were the worst. The poor darling suffered intensely, the pain came in spasms and recurred every quarter of an hour. His high temperature made him delirious day and night; and he would sit up in bed and every movement brought the pain on again. He hardly slept at all, had not even the strength to cry, just moaned and kept repeating: 'Oh Lord have mercy upon me.'"[53] One of those days, when the problem was on the rise, Nicholas could not bear the sight of his son's terrible condition and stepping out of the house he broke into sobs.

Alexandra hardly ever left his side. She sat for hours beside her pallid child who groaned in pain, seeing his swollen body, the black circles under his eyes, hearing his painful voice beseeching her, "Mamma, help me!"[54] She kissed his head on the forehead and on the eyes, wishing if it were possible in that manner to assuage the pain, to impart a little life for that which was departing from him. Her tears ran ceaselessly, and she prayed constantly whispering that God would ease the suffering of her child, for which she herself felt responsible. Indeed which of the two sufferings was more severe? The mother's or the child's? In those days everyone observed that Alexandra's hair suddenly greyed.

Both parents were already certain that their child would leave them this time. Alexis himself began to hope that the end would not delay in coming. "When I am dead, it will not hurt any more, mamma, will it?"[55] he asked with whatever strength remained to him. "When I am dead, build me a little monument of stones in the wood."[56] The greater drama, however, had not unfolded in Alexis' room, but below, in the reception hall. Not wanting to publicize their son's condition, the parents had to behave as if nothing was happening before their visitors, who came every evening to the house. Gilliard witnessed this terrible double reality, himself not yet knowing exactly what was happening with Alexis:

"One evening after dinner the Grand-Duchesses Marie and Anastasie Nicolaievna gave two short scenes from the *Bourgeois Gentilhomme* in the dining-room before Their Majesties, the suite, and several guests. I was the prompter, concealed behind a screen which did duty for the wings. By craning my neck a little I could see the Czarina in the front row of the audience smiling and talking gaily to her neighbours.

"When the play was over I went out by the service door and found myself in the corridor opposite Alexis Nicolaievitch's room, from which a moaning sound came distinctly to my ears. I suddenly noticed the Czarina running up, holding her long and awkward train in her two hands. I shrank back against the wall, and she passed me without observing my presence. There was a distracted and terror-stricken look in her face. ...

"A few minutes later the Czarina came back. She had resumed the mask and forced herself to smile pleasantly at the guests who crowded round her. But I had noticed that the Czar, even while engaged in conversation, had taken up a position from which he could watch the door, and I caught the despairing glance which the Czarina threw him as she came in."[57]

Finally, when the doctors informed Nicholas that the uncontrolled hemorrhage could turn fatal at any moment, the emperor officially announced, without giving details as to the nature of the illness, that the life of the heir was in mortal danger. This news plunged all of Russia into national prayer. From huge metropolitan cathedrals down to the least little chapels in the remotest villages continual services were held for the recovery of the health of the tsarevich. Throngs of faithful remained in prayer day and night before the icon of the Mother of God of Kazan in the cathedral of Saint Petersburg.

At the hunting lodge in Spala there was no chapel, but at that time of Alexis' health crisis an outdoor emergency chapel was set up in a large tent. There Father Alexander Vasiliev held services daily. He greatly impressed the imperial couple and was from that time appointed Rector of the Feodorovsky Cathedral in Tsarskoe Selo; he also served as spiritual father to the family. Later after the outbreak of the second Revolution, he was executed by the Bolsheviks in 1918.

Nicholas wrote in his letter to his mother, "All the servants, the Cossacks, the soldiers, and all the rest of the people were wonderfully sympathetic. At the beginning of Alexei's illness they begged the priest Vassilieff of the Sisterhood of the Assumption, the children's chaplain, to hold a Te Deum in the open. They begged him to repeat it every day till he recovered. Polish peasants came in crowds and wept while he read the sermon to them. What piles of telegrams, letters, ikons with wishes for the darling's speedy recovery we received!"[58]

During his illness, little Alexis received Communion twice from the reverend Father Alexander. In one of her letters Alexandra later wrote, "It was a terrible time we went through, and to see his fearful suffering was heartrending—but he was of an angelical patience and never complained at being ill—he would only make the sign of the cross and beg God to help him, groaning and moaning from pain.... Twice we let him have that joy [of Holy Communion], and the poor thin little face with its big suffering eyes lit up with blessed happiness as the Priest approached him with the Sacrament."[59]

The first time Alexis received Communion was the evening that all signs indicated would be the last of his life. Father Alexander performed the Divine Liturgy and brought Holy Communion to the sick child's room with reverence. Afterwards, those present at the house were informed that all was accomplished, and notice was sent to Saint Petersburg to prepare the people for the impending death of the heir. Precisely on that evening, Alexandra asked her dear friend Anna Vyrobova to send a telegram to Rasputin in Siberia beseeching him to pray for her child. Rasputin's reply to Alexandra came immediately: "God has seen your tears and heard your prayers. Be anxious no longer. Your son will recover."[60] "The little one will not die. Do not allow the doctors to bother him too much."[61] The next day the hemorrhage stopped.

From Nicholas' letter to his mother, "On October 10th we decided to give him [Alexei] Holy Communion and his condition began to improve at once, temperature went down to 39.5 and 38.2 [Celsius degrees], the pain almost disappeared and he fell quietly into a sound sleep for the first time."[62]

Nicholas did not mention anything at all to his mother of Rasputin's involvement, perhaps because he knew her antipathy towards him. Others affirmed that the improvement came as a result of medical help, and others, such as Gilliard, did not wish to attempt any explanation at all for the unexpected healing. To Alexandra, however, matters were crystal clear. Salvation was the result of Rasputin's prayers.

CULMINATION OF A DRAMA

Alexandra, from the very first years of her reign with Nicholas failed to achieve the most important goal that she had set for herself with the ascent to the throne of Russia. Her desire to earn the love of her people came to shipwreck. If Divine Providence had disposed for Alexandra to marry Nicholas earlier and come to Russia as the wife of the heir to the throne, things would have probably been completely different. Empress Maria, the widowed Queen Mother, had the fortune to remain in this position, of being the wife of the heir, for fourteen years, which gave her time to make friends and gain supporters. Thus, her adjustment to her new homeland and her reception by the people came about gradually and smoothly. On the contrary, Alexandra found herself right from the beginning at the height of power, which, as with all rulers, inevitably cut her off and isolated her from the lower classes of people and from the simple social realities of Russia.

An even more important factor, which set the course of events in this matter, was the extreme contrast in manners between Alexandra and the aristocratic circles of the palace. Alexandra, a shy, modest, and taciturn person, did not find it easy to adjust to the high society of Saint Petersburg with its loose morals. As Fabritsky remembers, "Her Majesty's introversion was apparent in everything she did, but never more so than when she was attending celebratory or gala receptions. Outwardly she expressed this through a particular facial expression. On such occasions one got the impression that the Empress was enduring something painful. Thus, many people who didn't know her Majesty well formed the opinion that she was a cold and ungracious woman."[63] From her very first official public appearance after coronation in 1896, she gave the worst impression. Terrified, embarrassed in her unaccustomed surroundings, she gave the impression of a cold and proud person. As she herself confided later, from her shyness she felt that the shiny floor of the hall would swallow her up.

Growing up with the austere Victorian moral principles of Windsor, Alexandra was not prepared for all night parties and the illicit romantic relationships of Saint Petersburg. Scandalized by this reality, she took the catalog of foreseeable invitations to the palace and began to cross out names, excising without hesitation even the most distinguished of guests. The result, naturally, was then an increased antipathy towards her.

This chasm perhaps might have been mitigated by Alexandra's sister, Elisabeth, who had been in Russia for years and was much beloved in the circles of all classes in Russia. However, the appointment of her husband as Military Governor of Moscow kept her hopelessly far away from the capital and from her sister, without being able to contribute at all to the mitigation of the problem.

Moreover, the zeal with which Alexandra embraced Orthodoxy and the spiritual life constituted a caustic reproof to society. The empress, by nature particularly religious, gave herself over entirely to the faith and the ascetic practice of Orthodox tradition. She dedicated many hours to prayer, and she especially loved church services and the richness of the liturgical and mystical life. She studied patristic works with great thirst, she collected a multitude of icons and made frequent pilgrimage trips to various monasteries and churches. But to the aristocratic circles of the capital the empress' behavior was something completely irrational. Her mentions of holy elders and hermits, whom she met on her pilgrimages or of whom she read in works of patristic literature, were received by those around her as psychosis and hysterical behavior. They themselves, born Orthodox, had not shown any interest in the spiritual life beyond perfunctory church attendance.

The empress, "no longer finding satisfaction in her customary religious ambiance… began to frequent the Offices and Vespers in public churches, as if she sought to set herself on a common level, to blend in with the crowd … [but] the nasty gossip which had started among the common folk and in the Palace pantry had started to circulate in town; everybody soon knew that the Empress was in the grip of a strange kind of piety. What might have seemed rather natural on the part of a private individual, the desire to strip off one's personality and melt into the throng, could not but damage the prestige of the Imperial Family when coming from an Empress of Russia. That an Empress should want to 'go amongst the people'—that was what they refused to comprehend."[64]

Alexandra and Alexis.

Unfortunately for Alexandra, Nicholas' mother also shared these views of the upper levels of society. Then a certain distance began to appear between them, which later would come to the point that the queen mother would hold Alexandra responsible for all of Russia's misfortunes. Seeing how there was no longer a way to ameliorate this problem, Alexandra began to draw back from social life. And so, evil rumors about the cold German empress continued to grow. But those who knew her and those who lived close to her family surroundings, such as her close friends, tutors, and servants, knew the tsarina's precious quality. Their witness was all the same: Alexandra was a very sensitive soul, completely devoted to her maternal and spousal duties, who only sought affection from the people around her.

"Her kind-heartedness marked everything she did, but this was especially true of the way she treated others— her constant concern for all the humble people she encountered, who had fallen on hard times through illness, etc. The aid she provided was wide-ranging and included both financial and moral support. It's hard to imagine how many people Her Majesty helped with financial difficulties, how many children she provided with an education, and what a vast number of sick people she visited in various sanatoria. Many Russians came to see the Empress as a severe woman with a firm, stubborn character and enormous strength of will, unkind, humorless, hugely influential with her husband and directing his decisions at her own discretion. That view is completely mistaken. Her Majesty not only treated all those around her warmly, but actually spoiled them, thinking constantly of others and taking pains on their behalf."[65]

As for her love for Russia, it was great and genuine. After her coronation, she herself had written to one of her sisters that in that overwhelming moment of the Sacrament, she felt that she had married Russia and left behind her the little girl that grew up in Darmstadt; now she had become not just the empress, but also the mother of the Russian people. "Once she became Russian tsarina, she came to love Russia more than her original homeland. She was sensitive, compassionate, and responsive to the sorrow of others, and showed great persistence and inventiveness in setting up various charitable institutions. ... And yet, for all her qualities, she never inspired love in Russia as she should have. ... One is struck by the almost universal hostility towards the empress. Her Russian relatives, members of the Russian imperial family, almost without exception did not like her. ... High society, with very few exceptions, was hostile to her, and even within her retinue she had few supporters. ... She had many enemies and few friends."[66]

Alexis' terrible disease gave a new push isolating Alexandra from society. Recognizing that any human help was impossible, she now turned with all her strength of being toward God. Only Divine intervention, only a miracle would be able to resolve the tragedy of her child and of her family. She prayed for endless hours. However, her feeling of unworthiness never allowed her to believe that her prayers would be heard. Then the conviction was born inside her that only a man of God would be able to intercede

CHAPTER 3

Gregory Efimovich Rasputin.

with the heavenly Father for the healing of her child. And it was then that Gregory Rasputin appeared.

Gregory Efimovich Rasputin was born of peasant parents on 9 January, 1869, in the village of Pokrovskoe in Siberia. In 1887 he married and had seven children, of whom only three survived to adulthood. Ten years after his marriage, at the age of twenty-eight, Rasputin abandoned his village and went to the Monastery of Saint Nicholas in Verkhoturie, where he remained for some months. When at last he returned to his village he was greatly changed. He had become a vegetarian and prayed with great fervor. From then on, he also became a classic Russian pilgrim, travelling for long periods of time visiting monasteries and various other places of pilgrimage. Around that time, rumors of Rasputin as a miracle-worker also began to spread.

His wanderings led him at last to Saint Petersburg in 1904, where he became acquainted with Archimandrite Theophan, inspector of Saint Petersburg Theological Academy. Father Theophan was impressed by the spirituality of Rasputin, and introduced him to circles of high society, where his fame had already spread. Very soon Rasputin became the epicenter of a large party of the aristocracy with mystical and superstitious dispositions. At

Anna Vyrubova.   Alexandra and Vyrubova.

---

last, Grand Duchess Militsa Nikolaevna[67] succeeded in persuading Nicholas and Alexandra to meet Rasputin at her house. The meeting took place on 1 November 1905. Nicholas wrote in his diary, "1st of November [1905]. Tuesday. ... We drank tea with Militsa and Stanok [her husband]. We met a man of God, Grigory from the province of Tobolsk."[68]

This was the "man of God" whom Alexandra was expecting. She believed that Rasputin was the salvation of her child, sent from God. The healing of Alexis by Rasputin's prayers in 1912 in Spala was not the first. From 1904, when the family became acquainted with Rasputin until 1912 other similar phenomena had occurred, which convinced Alexandra of the power of the prayers and holiness of this *muzhik*.

In this conviction of hers, Alexandra found an important companion in Anna Vyrubova, who was the closest personal friend of the empress. Anna was a very simple person, with an unusually childish *naïveté*. After an unhappy marriage and the consequent bitterness which she experienced, Anna was tightly bound with Alexandra having as a common axis their deep religious faith and their great pain. Alexandra in her grievous isolation from society, found in Vyrubova the true friend whom her soul had always sought. Their friendship remained very strong and lasted until the end, even though it did undergo a certain crisis at one point. Hardly a single day passed that they did not meet. Vyrubova, who also believed in Rasputin as

Rasputin having tea with female admirers.

a true man of God and became one of his most fervent spiritual admirers, constituted Alexandra's main link with him.

Despite all of this, the mystery that surrounds this enigmatic figure remains quite unfathomable. How exactly Rasputin succeeded in "healing" Alexis is an inexplicable phenomenon. Many theories have been put forth with the passage of time. Many have testified to his hypnotic qualities from their own personal experience. Others have attributed the event to pure coincidence, asserting that when Rasputin would appear at the palace to pray for Alexis, the young tsarevich was already on the road to recovery from the current episode of his injury. Many spoke of a positive psychological impact on the young boy that contributed to his recovery, and others supported the idea that Rasputin's insistence in not allowing the doctors to experiment with the boy's health helped in shortening the recovery time of an injury. For Alexandra, however, only one thing was important: Rasputin's intervention always brought the much-desired result. Thus, there was nothing in the world that would have been able to change her mind that Rasputin was a living vessel of the divine grace.

Soon after his arrival at Saint Petersburg, however, rumors and reports started to circulate, stating that Rasputin began to lead an unprecedented prodigal life before the eyes of society. These reports spoke of drink and women, as well as various other obscene incidents. Nevertheless, when he was called to the palace, he always behaved in a most respectful manner, showing no signs of such an immoral side to his character.

Alexandra paid no heed to reports that were sent to the palace on the scandalous behavior of Rasputin. On the contrary, she considered that just as with every great saint, so also Rasputin had fallen victim to slander. Keeping in mind the general hostility towards her, she considered all accusations against Rasputin to be motivated by an intent to hurt her, which did indeed correspond with reality to a great degree.

For his part, Nicholas was somewhat skeptical of the holiness of Rasputin. Following the recommendations of his ministers, he gave instructions to the secret police, the Okhrana, to conduct investigations of his conduct outside the city. Studying the reports that appeared from the police, Nicholas was convinced that at least one of the circumstances that was reported of Rasuptin's debauchery with women could not but be false. The reason was simple: that specific day on which Rasputin was allegedly caught in a compromising situation, he was at the palace at Tsarskoe Selo. Thus, this realization was sufficient to make Nicholas distrustful of nearly all relevant reports of the Okhrana.

Nevertheless, the people of Saint Petersburg did believe all the stories of Rasputin's debauched life. At the same time, Alexandra's insistence, as well as the rest of the family's, on maintaining such close ties with Rasputin was occasion for terrible and scandalous rumors to circulate throughout all of Saint Petersburg society. For their own part, the people of the capital were not able to accept at all that the royal family did not know the real nature of this person, as they believed him to be. They considered it a given that Rasputin had carried over his commonly known debaucheries into the palace itself, and among the members of the royal family itself, defiling not only the empress, but also the girls with his carnal conquests. So great was the ignorance of these malicious people of the complete purity of these chaste souls. Thus, the chasm between the palace and the people grew ever greater and greater.

ELISABETH FEODOROVNA
REVEALING THE DEPTHS OF A NOBLE HEART

One of the most important people opposed to Rasputin and his conduct was Alexandra's sister Elisabeth. Four years after the death of her husband in 1909, Elisabeth definitively abandoned worldly things and embraced monastic life. She distributed all the valuable jewelry that her husband had given her into three parts: she gave one part to Dimitry and Maria, the children of Grand Duke Paul, the beloved brother of her husband, the second part to the royal couple, and she used the third part for philanthropic projects and for founding her convent, which would be devoted to ministering to the poor and suffering.

For a period of four years between 1905 and 1909, Elisabeth worked hard at her idea, studying various monastic rules through the centuries and preparing the petition that would be submitted to the Holy Synod for the establishment of her convent. During this time, the convent buildings were constructed along Great Ordynka street in Moscow, and on February 10, 1909, the convent began to operate according to a temporary monastic rule and Elisabeth, together with six other women who followed her in her vocation, were then living there.

The final founding tenets of the convent, which Elisabeth submitted to the holy synod for approval, were very particular to her vision for her religious institution and informed the way it would operate. Considering work to be the basis of all religious life and prayer to be its reward, the grand duchess wanted her nuns and the work of her convent to alleviate the suffering of the sick, poor and ill-educated. Consequently, on taking the veil, her sisters would not completely renounce all earthly life and contact with secular society. Elisabeth planned the operation of a hospital and a dental clinic incorporated into the convent, which would be fully supported by the sisters and the mother superior herself.

This rather unusual monastic institution envisioned by Elisabeth was not in absolute accordance with St Basil the Great's precepts for running an Orthodox monastery, and as a result it met a significant degree of opposition from some hierarchs and members of the holy synod. They considered it an innovation that did not align with traditional Orthodox monastic rules. However, Elisabeth did not trust only herself and her own judgement in suggesting this institution. She had discussed it with the holy elders of Optina and the Zosimov Hermitage, who gave her their blessing and full support.

As might be justifiably expected, this sudden change to Elisabeth's life worried Nicholas and Alexandra, as well as many others who knew her. They were afraid that her new way of life would test her strength and that she would not be able to bear the burden of the ascetic life she was leading. Further, Nicholas was somewhat concerned whether Elisabeth was under the appropriate spiritual guidance of experienced elders who could protect her from any unpleasant spiritual vicissitudes.

Elisabeth was very aware of the real dimensions of her decision and did her utmost to convey her feelings about the call she felt to her loved ones. In her letters to Nicholas, answering such worries, she was very reassuring and revealed much about the way she was now living:

> Moscow, 18 April 1909.
> Dearest Nicky,
>
> Thanks so very much for your long letter full of kind beautiful advice and in which I perfectly agree and understand only would

THE BEGINNING OF SORROWS

Alexandra with Elisabeth during the mourning period for the death of Grand Duke Serge.

like to answer and show you a little of my inner life so that you may know that part which rarely we speak about.

You mention the "spirit of delusion" into which, alas, one can fall and of which often with Serge we have talked about. He, with his large heart and tact, when I was protestant, never forced his religion upon me and found strength to bear up in the great grief of not seeing me in his faith, thanks to Father Ioann [of Kronstadt], who told him, "leave her alone, don't speak about our faith, she will come to it of herself"; and thank God it was so. Well, Serge, who knew his faith and lived in it as perfectly as a true Orthodox Christian can, brought me up and, thank God, warned me against this "spirit of delusion" you talk of. My nature is too calm to be carried away in that direction, but yet one must always be on one's guard as the devil slips in when we least expect.

Another question you mention, and which I must have not well explained, as you did not quite understand, [is] that I "rule myself, not under the influence of a priest." [What] I meant to say [is] that the priest did not influence me in taking up the life I am now leading, as when I had well thought it out, I spoke to him. One can't believe that I alone, without any outer influence decided this step, which to many seems an unbearable cross I have taken up and which I will either regret one day, throw over or break down under. I took it up not as a cross, but as a road full of light God showed me after Serge's death and which years and years before had begun in my soul. I can't tell you when it seems to me often that already as [a] child there was a longing to help those that suffer, above all those who have moral sufferings, and always more and more it grew in me. Only, being in a position where our duty was to receive, to see heaps of people, to give receptions, dinners, balls etc., it could not fill entirely my life, other duties having to go before. You can't agree to think "it is a great re-assortment in life" – only think, to me it was no "re-assorting"; it little by little grew and took form and many, many who followed all my life and know me well here, were not astonished [seeing me] taking it, [but they saw it] only as a continuation of what before had begun, and that is how I took it. I was taken aback when a whole battle broke out to prevent me, to frighten me about the difficulties, all [done] with great love and kindness, but with utter incomprehension of my character.

You find "all the same, you could do more good things in your former field." I can't say if you are right or I wrong, life and time will show, and certainly I am not worthy of the unboundless joy of

Saint Elisabeth Feodorovna.

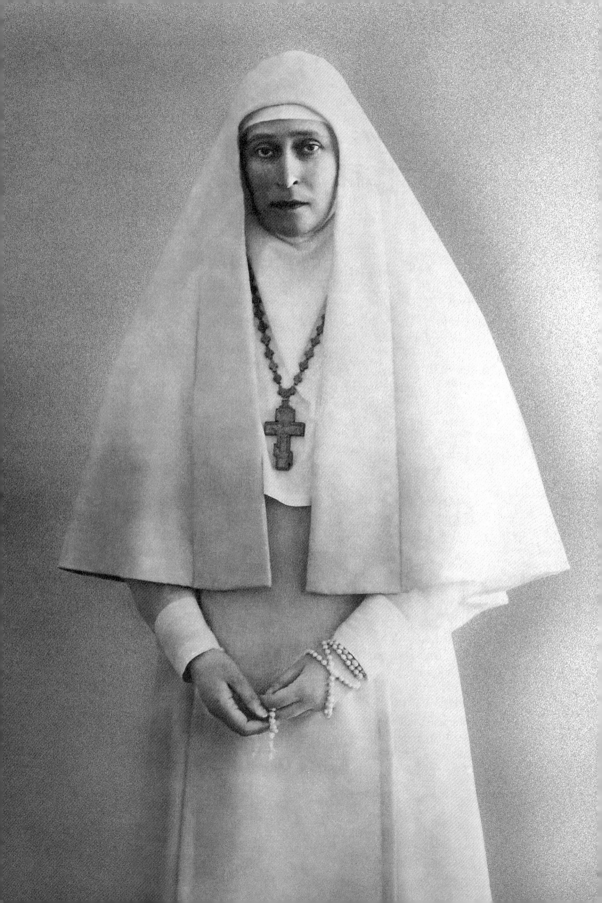

God letting me work this way, but I will try and He, who is all love, will forgive me my mistakes as He sees the wish I have of serving Him and His. In my life I had so much joy, in my sorrows so much unboundless comfort that I long to give a little of that to others. I could write pages and pages and yet it is difficult to put on paper all I feel – I long to thank every minute for all God gave me; I long to bring Him my feeble gratitude by serving Him and His suffering children – oh, this is not a new feeling, this is an old one which always was in me. God has been so kind to me.

Another question "It is necessary to be guided." How right and true! Until now I have unluckily not met the "experienced elder," but in spring I had before your letter already decided to go to him. He is at the Skete near St Serge Zosimov Hermitage. Alexei is his name and only comes out Saturday and Sunday to confess. Father Mitrophan goes to him as guide and advice and heaps of pilgrims etc. go there. He is wonderful and quite a Saint, but I fear, alas, will soon quite retire. Our priest, before entering my cloister, spoke with him and other elders, as always he was guided by holy elders and they all told him to take up this work with their blessing, as he being young feared. So, you see that God has blessed this work by a priest to whom as Orel from far one came to find consolation and strength, and here it is little by little beginning.

For myself, I find an immense and touching help in three of the Igumens; they consider me belonging to them, give me advice etc., which is a great help and, except that, there are the Metropolitans Triphon and Anastasi who are now my masters, whom I see and who have serious talks with me. I have also worldly workers whose advice I look for and please don't think I imagine that I can do and decide all alone. Every question I think and talk out and then, of course, being the master, decide trusting in God to guide me.

You both dears pray for me; even if you find I am mistaken, pray that once the step is taken God may guide me to do right. I have heard so much about your bishop Fr Theophan and long to know him and talk to him, ask him to pray for me please. I fear so you think I am proud and self-satisfied, that I internally puff myself up with satisfaction of creating something grand. Oh, I wish you knew me better. I know Alix imagines I allow people to call me a Saint – she said so to my Countess O. I, good gracious, what am I? No better and probably worse than others. If people may have said foolish exaggerated things, is it my fault? But they don't say it to my face. They know I hate flattery as a dangerous passion.

I can't help people loving me, but then you see I love them and they feel it. I try to do my best for them and people can be grateful, although one must never expect it. I don't think [for] one minute I have taken up a "podvig" [подвиг, spiritual feat]; it is a joy. I don't see my crosses nor feel them, because [of] the unboundless kindness of God I have always felt – I long to thank Him.

The few sisters I have are good girls and very religious, but all our work is founded and lives in religion. The priest guides them, we have three times a week admirable lectures to which outsiders ladies also come. Then at prayers in the morning he reads to them a text out of the New Testament and says a few words of guidance and I look after them, we talk. The meals they take without me except on feast days, Easter and our church feast. May be oftener we all take tea together, the priest and his wife too, and it ends by a talk about religion. Later we will have like in the convents a big dining hall and one will read the Saints lives, and like the head nun I will appear sometimes to assist and see if all is as I wish. There is a good deal of the convent in our life, which I find indispensable. We even have some novices recommended by their superiors, girls recommended by elders, and so that you see from all good sides we have sympathy and help.

Now, my old work I have not thrown over, committees and all my former work has remained. Those were my duties always and only since Serge's death receptions, dinners etc. have fallen away and will never rebegin. Some people I receive if there are reasons for it. Marie, my first visit, has been living in the Palace, had her meals with me in my house here and we have spent hours together when I was free. I try that others may find pleasure in my old home and [in] Moscow and a little rest, without my duty I have now taken up, suffering by my spending a few hours with them; travelling much about firstly costs and above all would not be right when you have "put your hand to the plough you must not look back."[69]

This moment my Kief regiment passed – I don't forget them, I have given a small capital in memory of Serge to help the bringing up of the present officers' daughters and at Xmas I send to them my Chernigorzi [from the Russian word for Montenegro] money for the soldiers' Xmas tree and amusement.

Forgive my imposing long letter, please read it with Alix and if [there is] anything else you want to know or where you find I am going wrong I will be so grateful for your advice or remarks. Forgive me both of you. I know and feel, alas, I worry you and perhaps you don't quite understand me; please forgive and be patient with me and forgive my mistakes, forgive my living differently than you would have wished, forgive that I can't often come to see you because of my duties here. Simply with your good hearts forgive and with your large Christian souls pray for me and my work.

Ever your loving old Sister and friend,
Ella.[70]

CHAPTER 3

Moscow April 1909
This letter and my tender love is to you both Dears.

Christ is Risen! Darling Nicky, ever so hearty thanks to you both for the lovely little image which hangs in my prayer room, where I put all the images I get since I am here in my new house. You are always such a dear brother and with interest told me you found our statutes good, that I want to tell you a little [of] how my life has arranged itself for the beginning, when every step must be thought out and one must go slowly with God's help forwards. I on purpose began Lent together with the few sisters who have entered so as to make our devotions together. Our first week passed full of prayer and peace and preparation in God and then the Holy Communion and after we began life. In a few words the day:

In the morning prayers together; one of the sisters read[s] in church at 7:30, at 8 o'clock, and [then] mass and those who are free assist, else they have to nurse the sick we have or sew etc. We have few sick as, according to the Dr's lectures, we take them so as to see in practice how to treat different cases and for the beginning only light ones were taken; now [we take] always more and more difficult [cases] and thank God the hospital, being airy and light and the sisters very loving at their work, our sick get on beautifully. At 12:30 luncheon the sisters together presided by [ill.] Sardeef, and I eat in my house alone – a thing I like and found better, as a certain distance must be kept in spite of living together. All Lent's Wednesday and Friday we eat Lent food, else they have meat, milk, eggs etc. As I, since years, don't eat meat –as you know– I continue my vegetarian regime, but those who are not accustomed must eat meat, especially if there is hard work.

I go into these details as my life at the cloister interests people and, not seeing our life, each has his little idea, often quite wrong, but imagination ruins and many think we live on bread and water and kasha [and we] are severer than a convent etc. [and they think] what a hard life – when it is only simple and healthy. We sleep all our eight hours, unless a person sits up longer than the rules – [we] have good beds and remarkably nice little rooms with bright chintz and summery furniture -my rooms are big, airy, light, cozy also summerlike – and all who see them are enchanted. My house is separate, then the hospital with house-church, then the Dr's house and soldiers [ill.] and then the priest's house = 4 houses. After luncheon, some go out to get fresh air then are occupied; tea at four and dinner at 7:30 and evening prayers in my prayer room at 8, to bed at 10.

Now for the lectures. Three times a week the priest, three times a week the Drs and between the sisters read or prepare. Until now of course they have only their sick practice in the hospital and I only send them into the homes of the poor to take information in different cases. You see, they must learn before. Our lectures with the priest are most interesting —quite exceptionally, so as he not only has his deep faith, but has read immensely— he begins from the Bible and will end by church history and all sharing the way how the sisters can after speak and help those in moral suffering.

You know the Fr Mitrophan; I had a good impression [of him] at Sarov. At Orel he was adored, here many come from far to our little church and find strength in his beautiful simple sermons and confession. He is large, nothing of the narrow-minded bigot, all founded on God's unboundless love and forgiveness —a true orthodox priest keeping strictly to our church— for our work [he is] God's blessing, as he has laid the foundation as it ought to be. So many he has brought back to faith, put on the right road, so many thank me for the great blessing they have received being able to come to him —no escalation— but you know me well enough that I love calm deep religion and would not choose a fanatic as priest in one way or the other.

Some kind hearted busybodies who love to potter about me are afraid I will exhaust myself in this life, end by breaking down my health, don't eat enough, don't sleep enough. Well dear, if you hear that, it is not true. I sleep my 8 hours, I eat with pleasure, I feel physically marvellously well and strong (a wee cold or rheumatic twinge or gout can't be prevented as our family all suffer from the latter). You know I have never had bright red cheeks and all deep feelings show themselves on my face, so that in church I often look pale because as you and Alix also love the service, know what deep joy a good service is.

I want you both and all, all to know I am as often said and written full of perfect peace and perfect peace is perfect happiness. My darling Serge rests in God with so many he loved who have gone to join him and God has given me on this earth a beautiful work to fulfil. Will I do it well or badly He only knows, but I will try my best and I put my hand in His and so with no fear whatever to the crosses and criticism this world may have in store; little by little my life has turned out this way. It is not a fantasy of the moment and no disappointment ever can come. I can be disappointed in myself, but then I also have no illusions and don't imagine I am different to others. I want to work for God and in God, for suffering mankind and in my old age, when my body can't anymore work, I hope God will let me then rest and pray for the work I began and then I will go out of the busy life and prepare for that great home. But I have health and energy and there is so, so much misery and Christ's steps as guide are amongst the suffering, in whom we help Him. All are kind, and wish to help, but many imagine I have taken a work more than I can do. Truly it is not so; I am physically and morally strong and profoundly, deeply religious, happy.

Forgive dears I did not come for Xmas and Easter, but the first steps are so so serious. Tell me you won't think I forget you as am hard hearted or selfish, if for birthdays I don't arrive. I think it will be nicer to have a time without feast days together. And one must not put one's hand to the plough and look back, don't you find so? Don't think anyone influences me. I am trying to find the way and of course will make mistakes.

People in their wish of doing good I have found out worry my poor priest that he must force me to eat when I do eat –and very well– that he must force me to travel etc. when [in reality] I am completely well and as strong as a horse. Since the operation I don't know what it is to have pain and my leg is astonishingly well and hardly swells from the long standing, when both feet swell as they got hot, but there is hardly a person who has not that. People don't see me in my life, don't see how completely calm, contented and profoundly grateful I am to God for all that. Instead of worrying about me they ought to thank God he found me worthy of such a consolation as the work I have, which gives me such complete entire satisfaction.

If you find a minute time to answer me, please do, and say if you understand all and perhaps a kind little word add in your English letter in Russian that I can read it to the priest, where you say you believe in him and are sure he will know how to help me if God wills difficult moments to come. You see, I look upon you and Alix as brother and sister, [whereas] he as his sovereign and master and I feel one has tormented him that you might be vexed by my conduct and think he influences me to cut myself off from you all and kill myself through an ascetic life and much work, whereas not one of these suppositions is true. He confesses me, guides me in the church and gives me an immense help and example through his pure simple life, so modest and high in its unboundless love for God and the orthodox church. Only to speak to him for a few minutes one sees he is modest, pure and a man of God and God's servant in our church. He has never been in contact with the high world, so that many strange weaknesses and the love of meddling in all etc. have only come to him now. A kind word of encouragement from you, his adored sovereign, will abolish all these crosses and truly he merits them. Forgive this long letter; it is for you both dears, as some time I have not seen you and you may like to know my present life. If there are any questions to write, then do.

God bless you both.
Your tenderly loving old sister,
Ella.[71]

THE BEGINNING OF SORROWS

The Tsar trusted Elisabeth's decision and early in 1910, by Imperial decree, he approved the petition. Soon after the formal establishment of the cloister Elisabeth began preparing herself for her monastic tonsure. In a letter she sent to Nicholas just two weeks before this, apart from expressing her deep spiritual joy for the approaching great event of her tonsure, Elisabeth expresses her grief about an argument that took place between them that came about as a result of their disagreement on the spiritual genuineness of a certain person. The person under discussion was Rasputin, who had already by that point appeared in the lives of the imperial family. Even from such an early stage, Elisabeth was deeply concerned about the true essence of Rasputin's spirituality:

> 26 March 1910
> Friday eve
> Archangel Gabriel
>
> God bless you for that kind look when I asked you pardon before going to confess. I saw your true soul in your eyes like of olden times and the other day they had lost that look and in my intense sorrow that was one of the deepest. One says that "eyes are the window of the soul" and I believe that.
> Oh dear, dear child – I may call you so, may I not? So long I know you and with Serge have prayed for you and now more than ever my prayers accompany you. Please, please forgive me now and forgive me the past (I of course never will forgive myself and there is hardly a confess I don't again repeat that why was I too rough then and when perhaps with profound gentle love I might have helped you really and not lost your confidence for ever). Perhaps if all that had been managed by me otherwise you would have seen the real truth and no more looked for helpers who, hidden from others, bring you their particular religion in seeming not to break you from the true Orthodox Church.
> *"Du choc des opinions jaillit la verité"* [From the clash of opinions springs the truth] and perhaps we all would have quietly talked and examined and come to the conclusion that we can be mistaken and that not all who seem holy are. Perhaps they are sincere, it may be so, although it seems otherwise, but let us say they are sincere, alas, the devil has caught them and the more we try to mount the more we take "spiritual struggles" upon ourselves the more the devil is at work, to blind us to the truth; the higher we mount, the oftener we fall, we must advance so slowly that we have the feeling of not advancing at all. "The house of the soul is patience; the food of the soul is humility." One must not look from above down, one must feel oneself the worst of the worse. It seemed to me often like false to try and acknowledge one is the worst of the worse, but that is what we must come to – with God's help all is possible.

Don't look upon my letter as a long epistle of preaching. I call it my confess to you. In two weeks my new life blessed in the church begins. I am as if bidding goodbye to the past, its faults and sins and with the hope of a higher goal and a newer existence. Pray for me deary. Oh, if you came and then spent the week of Lent and Easter. My taking of vows is ever more serious than if a young girl married. I am espousing Christ and His cause, I am giving all I can to Him and our neighbours, I am going deeper into our Orthodox Church and becoming like a missionary of Christian faith and charity and, oh dear, I am so, so unworthy of it all and I do so want blessing and prayers. Can you truly not come? Oh, Alix would not be tired and the happier brighter days of old would warm her heart and give health. You all love Moscow, so [ill.] bit care for me.

Your true friend Sister Ella.

[P.S.] 27 March – I am so happy to take the Holy communion living amongst you. May Christ envelop us all in His complete unboundless love.[72]

A few days before her monastic tonsure, Elisabeth wrote Nicholas a very moving letter, seeking his royal blessing for the labor that she was about to undertake:

Moscow 7 April 1910.
Dearest brother dear,

I ask your blessing, prayers and forgiveness before the solemn day I am approaching. May God help me to be worthy of this task which is one of deep joy and soul's peace for me. May my humble trials find acceptance in His sight. May you deary, as my earthly Sovereign, get a little help in your work which I will try to do with God's help by bringing comfort to your children. Please, please be convinced that however awkward or sinful my poor earthly life may go, I am a true subject of yours. The will is always full of good intentions and religious wishes, even if on the way I stumble and make endless mistakes.

Serge died with joy for you and his country. It was two days before that he said how willingly he would give his blood if thereby he could be of help. I hope God may give me strength that never one can say I was unworthy of having been in olden times guided by such a true noble husband and true Christian. With all my heart I kiss you and send my humble blessings and prayers.
Your true old friend,
Sister Ella.[73]

THE BEGINNING OF SORROWS

Elisabeth was given the monastic veil on April 15, 1910.[74] Countess Alexandra Olsoufieff wrote that Elisabeth's monastic tonsure "was a beautiful ceremony, which those who took part in it can never forget. She left the world where she had played a brilliant part, to go, as she said herself, 'into the greater world, the world of the poor and afflicted.' The Bishop, Thriphonius, who in the world had been Prince Turkenestanoff, presented her with the veil, saying these prophetic words: 'This veil will hide you from the world, and the world will be hidden from you, but it will be a witness to your good works, which will shine before God, and glorify the Lord.'"[75]

The name of the convent, of which Elisabeth became abbess— the Martha and Mary Convent of Mercy—reflected the inspiration Elisabeth drew upon in founding it. Sisters of Lazarus, St Martha served the Lord through helping mankind, while St Mary served through prayer and self-improvement; accordingly, Elisabeth's convent would combine charity, work, and prayer and, like the grand duchess herself, was to be the only one of its kind in Russia.

As mother superior, Elisabeth led an ascetic life. She arose at midnight to pray in her chapel or to go to the night services at Tchoudoff Kremlin, from where she would return in the morning hours without being observed. At night she also visited the hospital ward, frequently staying at the bedside of a patient in pain or fear, doing everything she could to soothe their anguish. Many attested to the healing power of her presence, and people—particularly those in need—flocked to her, drawn by the love she radiated for her fellow man.

Occupying only three rooms in the convent—a study, sitting room, and bedroom—Elisabeth denied herself all that had been plentiful in her previous life as a grand duchess. Her quarters were painted white and adorned only with icons, while her furniture was sparse and simple. She fasted rigorously and existed only on a diet of milk, eggs, vegetables, and bread, avoiding the consumption of any animal flesh, as she had done since the violent assassination of her beloved husband Serge. She wore only grey or white cotton dresses daily, wearing black with a veil on her trips out of the convent so as not to be recognized. All these observances of the ascetic life were no privation to her; instead she drew nourishment from her labor and prayerful life serving the Lord.

The day began at 6 am at the convent and the routine followed monastic practice. After common morning prayers in the hospital church, the grand duchess gave the sisters instructions for the working day. At midday, during the meal, one of the sisters read from the lives of saints; Vespers was at 5:00 PM followed by Matins, and at 9:00 PM evening prayers were read in the hospital church, after which the sisters received a blessing from their abbess and retired to their cells for the night.

Elisabeth achieved a super-human amount of work, seamlessly threading it into her day. She undertook the hardest tasks herself, never asking her sisters for help or expecting them to shoulder her workload in any way. Every day she had to examine countless petitions and letters from all corners of the country and she received many visitors from all backgrounds, to each of whom she gave her time and assiduous attention. In the hospital she assumed the most taxing and skilled roles, assisting at operations and surgical dressings as well as nursing, but also devoting precious hours to sitting at the bedside of those in need of spiritual succor. The grand duchess had not only trained her convent sisters in practical medicine, but also in the qualities needed to prepare the terminally ill for the passage to eternal life. For Elisabeth, death was not something to be mourned but an inevitability to be embraced, where possible, with love and courage. The deceased were passing into the Lord's heavenly kingdom where He would care for them, while those on earth continued to suffer and cry for help.

Far beyond the walls of the convent, Elisabeth sought out those in dire straits, ensuring that her charitable activity was providing relief where it was needed most. Determined not to ignore suffering in the outside world, the grand duchess insisted on visiting the Hitrov Market—a Moscow slum—being among the very first to do so in spite of warnings from the police, who told her that they were unable to assure her safety if she ventured into such places. There she visited hovels and persuaded parents to allow her to take their children and educate them; she also gathered orphans and placed them in hostels or boarding schools where they were well tended. Such was her good work in 'Hitrovka' that Elisabeth was adored by the vagrants, beggars, tramps, and criminals who lived there, referring to her as 'Sister Elisabeth' or 'Matushka' (Little Mother). In 1913, the grand duchess opened an orphanage at the convent, starting by taking in eighteen girls who were prepared for eventual entry into the convent if it were to be their calling. Not content with any limit to her ministry, Elisabeth also organized a Sunday School in the convent for girls with little or no literacy and for female factory workers. Her aim was to contribute to their education both pastorally and spiritually. In 1913, some seventy-five women attended these lessons.

In establishing the Martha and Mary Convent of Mercy and ensuring the wide reach of her good works, Elisabeth hoped that branches of the convent could, in time, be set up outside Moscow.

Though living in Moscow, Elisabeth received direct knowledge of the negative influence Rasputin's ties to the royal family had on the consciousness of the people. She wished on several occasions to inform Nicholas and Alexandra of this. However, her disposition towards Rasputin did not remain unnoticed and it disgruntled the circle of Rasputin's

Saint Elisabeth Feodorovna.

CHAPTER 3

supporters who tried to find a means of discrediting her to the royal couple. In a letter to Nicholas, she mentions an incident of the kind:

> May God bless and protect you dearest Nicky,
> Two weeks have passed and not a wee word you have sent me as a little token of old brotherly affection after having accused me of what I never did! Again, I assure you, you were led into error and if I last time wrote such a short letter, I did so not wishing to add from my part still more pain to yours, which the false explanations must have caused you, as alas! you believed it. Now to this false news an ignoble lie is being added.
> I know as a fact that Ania [Vyrubova] spreads the news of my taking an active part in the movement against G[rigory Rasputin] – (I know personally the people who heard it from her and I told them it is a lie) – she of course knows me little I see! And certainly I would not have written about their lies if your silence did not awaken in me fears that others are upholding in your erroneous ideas against me. Your accusations were so bitter and unlike you!! Especially after the loyal way I have always behaved to you. I always spoke openly to you against G[rigory]. From all sides of Russia in travelling and here people brought me their anguish, it is true, because I am your sister "you must open their eyes…" [they say to me]. All this I brought you as I found it my duty to do so and because I was full to bursting with fears for your welfare. It is not for the first time that out of the same source untruths against me have been said. Two years ago, it was G[rigory] whom unexpectedly little Felix met in Mme Salovine's salon. The first thing he said (apropos of Novosoleff's article in the paper) [was:] "You know well the G.D! it is nice what she is doing in writing horrid articles against me in the papers…" Felix of course denied it, knowing me too well as incapable of such an act and Mme Salovine, who does not know me, said "Gr[igory] Eph[imovich], never would the G.D. do such a thing!" I only mention all this as it is an important fact which corresponds now again with what is being said.[76]

When the evil rumors of Rasputin's ties with Alexandra began to swell ever greater, Elisabeth's pain and grief reached its climax. The great degree of her anguish was proportional to the vastness of her love for her sister and her brother-in-law. The misfortune was made even more intolerable by the fact that she could not influence them and draw their eyes to the danger she sensed lurking. This is apparent in another letter she wrote to Nicholas:

> Darling Nicky,
> My heart and soul ache too dreadfully that I cannot keep myself back from sending you a few lines. You must be suffering in anguish and poor darling Alix; tell her my prayers are near her with all the

strength of my soul. You know what I have suffered these years for you because of that poor soul [Rasputin], but always my prayers have been for him as well as you, that eternal light might clear up darkness and save from all evil, and more than ever in this moment with deep felt tears I cry to God: "Save, oh save, have pity on us all"; I don't form my prayer. His eternal love may it spread over the world, over [the] country, over [the] Church, our sovereign and his subjects. Both yours and Alix's dear hands I kiss tenderly in love and prayers. God be with you and yours.

Your old true subject and loving friend and sister,
Ella.
1 July 1914.[77]

A BRIEF GLIMMER

The spring of 1913 was marked by splendid country-wide celebrations for the Tercentenary of the Romanov dynasty. The celebrations began in February with an official hierarchical concelebration in the Cathedral of the Mother of God of Kazan in Saint Petersburg. Anna Vyrubova describes the following event from that day, "From my position I had a very good view of both the Emperor and the Tsarevitch, and I was puzzled to see them raise their heads and gaze long at the ceiling, but afterwards they told me that two doves had appeared and had floated for several minutes over their

From the Romanov Tercentenary celebrations, Moscow 1913.

heads. In the religious exaltation of the hour this appeared to the Emperor a symbol that the blessing of God, after three centuries, continued to rest on the House of Romanoff."[78]

In the middle of May, Nicholas visited Kostroma in the course of a great tour with his family and all the members of the House of Romanov. There they went to worship at the Ipatiev Monastery, where in 1613 the first tsar of the Romanov dynasty, Michael Feodorovich, was called to take power. Nicholas knelt before the Feodorovskaya Icon of the Mother of God, the protectress of the House of Romanov, and prayed for the stability of the Russian Empire.

The participation of the people in the celebrations of the Tercentenary of the Romanovs was stupendous. Crowds of people gathered in the provinces of the empire where the sovereigns visited. Innumerable ships were filled with people, and as they approached the ship which carried the sovereigns, they vied to see the persons of the royal family from as close as possible. Many went into the river and swam near the ship of the emperor so that they might cast even a brief glance on them as they passed by!

The conclusion of the anniversary celebrations took place in Moscow. On 25 May, Nicholas entered the city on foot among great acclamation. Priests processed before the emperor chanting, censing, and holding icons. Behind the emperor, the empress followed with Tsarevich Alexis in open carriages. The emperor finally entered the Cathedral of the Ascension in the Kremlin, where three hundred years earlier the coronation of Michael Romanov took place. The celebrations in Moscow lasted several days. Their conclusion also marked the beginning of the coming final chapter of the dynasty of the Romanovs.

CHAPTER 4

MARCH TO THE END

WORLD WAR
THE GREAT HEART OF RUSSIA BEATS

In Sarajevo on 28 June, 1914,[1] Gavrilo Princip, a Serb and a member of an organization that fought for the independence of Serbia from Austria-Hungary, assassinated the archduke and heir to the throne of the Austro-Hungarian Empire, Franz Ferdinand and his wife. The event of the assassination caused Austria-Hungary to undertake the neutralization of the Kingdom of Serbia's attempts to control the northern Balkans. At the same time, by doing so Austria-Hungary wished to establish their interests in the Balkans, with the goal of keeping Russia out of this region. Thus, on 23 July, 1914, on the pretext of the assassination, Austria-Hungary gave Serbia an ultimatum.

Serbia's view of the ultimatum is very clearly demonstrated by Regent Alexander's personal letter to Tsar Nicholas on July 24: "The demands in the Austro-Hungarian note humiliate Serbia quite unnecessarily and do not comply with the country's dignity as an independent state. ... We are willing to meet such Austro-Hungarian demands as are in accordance with the position of an independent state, as well as those that Your Majesty would advise us to observe. We shall ourselves rigorously punish all persons proved to have been involved in the assassination conspiracy. Certain demands cannot be met without altering our laws, and time is needed. The deadline given is too short."[2]

The arbitrary annexation of Bosnia and Herzegovina by Austria-Hungary earlier in 1908 was merely the first important step. Russia, being militarily weak at that time, did not react to this event. They had thought that the same would happen now. Russia, however, was not able to accept yet another similar humiliation. Furthermore, it was impossible to overlook the protection of its own interests in the Balkans. Finally, Russia considered that the common Orthodox Faith and Slavic kinship that tied it to Serbia was an important factor of great significance in the entire scenario. Moreover, Serbia had already applied to Russia for help.

On 25 July, Nicholas called an extraordinary council at Krasnoe Selo. The decision was to exert every effort to come to an honorable compromise with Austria-Hungary. Nicholas did not want war. Telegrams were flying from one capital to another. Ambassadors were meeting prime ministers and monarchs. Every country was focused only on solving its own problems and only Nicholas was doing everything in his power to avoid war. His known and declared peaceful intentions remained, as ever, constant.

In strictly military terms, there was good reason to postpone conflict until the so-called "Great Program" of armaments in Russia was completed in 1917–18. In more general terms, Russia already controlled almost one-sixth of the world's land surface. Its hitherto largely untapped potential was now beginning to be developed at great speed. It was by no means only Peter Stolypin who believed that, given twenty years of peace, Russia would be transformed in its wealth, stability, and power. Unfortunately for Russia, both the Germans and the Austrians were well aware of all these facts. Both in Berlin and Vienna it was widely believed that fear of revolution would stop Russia from responding decisively to the Austro-German challenge, but it was also felt that war now was much preferable to a conflict a decade hence.

The last week of July was a real agony for Nicholas. At last, despite Russia's proposals for direct talks between Saint Petersburg and Vienna, on 29 July, Austria-Hungary began a partial mobilization of the army. The next day they bombarded Belgrade.

At that time a telegram arrived from Rasputin who was at his village in Siberia. Rasputin advised to avoid war, because he "foresaw" that it would result in the destruction of the autocracy. According to Gilliard, "cunning and astute as he was, Rasputin never advised in political matters except with the most extreme caution. He always took the greatest care to be very well informed as to what was going on at Court and as to the private feelings of the Czar and his wife. As a rule, therefore, his prophecies only confirmed the secret wishes of the Czarina. In fact, it was almost impossible to doubt that it was she who inspired the 'inspired,' but as her desires were interpreted by Rasputin, they seemed in her eyes to have the sanction and authority of a revelation."[3] However, the content of this telegram angered Nicholas. He considered Rasputin's involvement in such a critical political issue to be completely inappropriate, and his displeasure was intense.[4]

At last, after Austria-Hungary's hostilities against Serbia, on 31 July, Nicholas commanded the mobilization of the entire armed forces of the Russian Empire with the view to deter the continuation of Austria-Hungary's assault on Serbia. "The emperor is sometimes accused," writes Lieven, "of 'caving in' to his generals in 1914 and thereby bringing on the descent into war. This is unfair. Nicholas was forced by the united pressure not just of the generals but also of the Foreign Ministry, the de facto head of the domestic government, and the spokesmen of the Duma and public opinion. In many ways, the surprise is that the emperor held out on his own for so long."[5]

That same day, 31 July, in the evening, the ambassador of Germany to Russia informed Russia's Ministry of State that his country had set a twelve hours deadline for Russia to cease the mobilization of her armies. Otherwise, Germany would also begin to mobilize her army. At last, on the evening of 1 August, the German ambassador handed his country's declaration of war against Russia to Russia's Minister of State. Trampling down every sense of kinship, the German Kaiser Wilhelm, Nicholas' third cousin and Alexandra's first cousin, had already been prepared for, and was expecting, conflict with Russia. Furthermore, two days later, on 3 August, he declared war on France, having already set sudden hostilities in motion against her the day before. Now that his gruesome dream had become reality, Kaiser Wilhelm declared his undoubted and quick victory with bloodthirsty boldness and self-assurance: he would "lunch in Paris and dine in St. Petersburg."[6]

A day earlier, on 30 July,[7] in the evening, Alexandra with the girls went to the metochion of the Holy Monastery of Diveyevo in Peterhof. Tatiana wrote in her diary, "[we] 4 with Mama rode to Podvoriye. Tomorrow is the feast of St. Seraphim."[8] There the women stayed at the Vigil in memory of Saint Seraphim and prayed fervently to the great saint for Russia. The next day, along with Alexandra, Nicholas visited the metochion to pray to the saint. One of the nuns of the metochion described the event, "The Empress and princesses had been at the Vigil the day before and at Liturgy that morning. The Liturgy ended and they [the nuns] had just conducted the guests out, when they began to call from the church, 'The Emperor is in the church.' He was wearing the guard uniform of a simple soldier, and the sister tending the church recognized him only because he walked in front of the Empress. The sisters jumped up, grabbed their ryassas and kamilavkas[9] and ran to the church. The Emperor stood before the icon of St. Seraphim. The priest also ran in. They began to sing, 'Save, O Lord, Thy people...' They say that when the sisters ran to the church, they saw the Emperor weeping greatly before the icon of St. Seraphim."[10]

In 1903, the day after the canonization of Saint Seraphim of Sarov, while Nicholas was visiting the Convent of Diveyevo, he received the letter that Saint Seraphim left for him a hundred years earlier. When he read the letter, Nicholas began to weep bitterly.[11] Now exactly eleven years later, on the anniversary of the canonization of Saint Seraphim (July 19/31), at the threshold of a war that would have inescapable worldwide and historical consequences and terrible catastrophes, and which he himself did not wish to become entangled in, Nicholas stood before the icon of Saint Seraphim and wept again. Is it then difficult for one to conclude that the content of the letter of Saint Seraphim, whatever it may have been, now resonated in Nicholas' soul?

Nicholas wrote in his diary that day, "We went with Alix to the metochion of Diveyevo. We took a walk with the children. At 6:30 PM we came to Vespers."[12] Pierre Gilliard was present at Vespers. Seeing Nicholas that evening left the deepest impressions in his memory, "The pouches which always appeared under his eyes when he was tired seemed to be markedly larger. He was now praying with all the fervour of his nature that God would avert the war which he felt was imminent and all but inevitable."

"His whole being seemed to go out in an expression of simple and confident faith. At his side was the Czarina, whose careworn face wore that look of suffering I had so often seen at her son's bedside [in the hours of his illness]. She too was praying fervently that night, as if she wished to banish an evil dream. ..."[13] At the exact same hour when Nicholas and Alexandra were with their daughters in church and praying, Russia's Minister of State was in his office receiving the declaration of war from Germany. It is quite noteworthy that the German ambassador accidentally delivered two versions of the note. One was in case of consent, to arrest the mobilization; the other, if Russia were to refuse. But regardless of the decision, according to both notes, Germany declared war on Russia![14]

Anastasia related to Gilliard what happened afterward. When they had returned from the service, it was nearly eight in the evening. Before they went down for supper, Nicholas went to his office to read the reports that had arrived in his absence. It was precisely at that moment that he received the declaration of war from Germany. Alexandra, uneasy that Nicholas delayed in coming down, asked Tatiana to go and see what was the matter. Then Nicholas appeared before them. Pale, with a trembling voice that betrayed his inward pain, which he tried in vain to hide, he announced to them the declaration of war. Alexandra and the four girls broke into sobs.

On 2 August, Nicholas was scheduled to attend an official meeting at the Winter Palace, where he was to proclaim to his people news of the war. When he went to say good bye to Alexis in the morning, the tsar was in still worse condition than the day before. Nevertheless, when he returned from the Winter Palace he was very different.

Here follow entries of Pierre Gilliard in his personal diary: "Monday, August 3rd.—The Czar came up to Alexis Nicolaievitch's room this morning. He was a changed man. Yesterday's ceremony resolved itself into an impressive manifestation. When he appeared on the balcony of the Winter Palace the enormous crowd which had collected on the square fell on their knees and sang the Russian National Anthem. The enthusiasm of his people has shown the Czar that this is unquestionably a national war."[15]

"Sunday, August 9th.—The Czar has had another long talk with me to-day. The Czar first spoke to me about the solemn session of the Duma on the previous day. He told me how tremendously pleased he had been with its resolute and dignified attitude and its fervent patriotism. ... 'The Duma was in every way worthy of the occasion. It expressed the real will of the nation, for the whole of Russia smarts under the insults heaped upon it by Germany. I have the greatest confidence in the future now. ... Speaking personally, I have done everything in my power to avert this war, and I am ready to make any concessions consistent with our dignity and national honour. You cannot imagine how glad I am that all the uncertainty is over, for I have never been through so terrible a time as the days preceding the outbreak of war. I am sure that there will now be a national uprising in Russia like that of the Great War[16] of 1812.'"[17]

"Monday, August 17th.—The arrival of Their Majesties at Moscow has been one of the most impressive and moving sights I have ever seen in my life. After the customary reception at the station we went in a long file of carriages towards the Kremlin. An enormous crowd had collected in the squares and in the streets, climbed on the roofs of the shops, into the branches of trees. They swarmed in the shop windows and filled the balconies and windows of the houses. While all the bells of the churches were ringing as if they would never stop, from those thousands of throats poured that wonderful Russian National Anthem, so overwhelming with its religious grandeur and pent emotion, in which the faith of a whole race is embodied:

"God save the Czar!

"Mighty and powerful, let him reign for our glory,

"For the confusion of our enemies, the Orthodox Czar.

"God save the Czar!"

"On the steps of the churches, through the great doorways of which one could see the light of the candles burning before the reliquaries, the priests in vestments, and holding their great crucifixes in both hands, blessed the Czar as he passed.

"The procession arrived at the Iberian Gate. [This is the gate by which the Czars always entered to go to the Kremlin when they visited Moscow. It leads from the city to the Red Square, which lies against the eastern wall of the Kremlin. The gate is named for the Iveron (or "Iberian") Icon of the Mother of God.] The Czar got out of his carriage and, in accordance with custom, entered the chapel to kiss the miraculous image of the Virgin of Iberia. He came out, walked a little way, and then stopped, high above the immense multitude. His face was grave and composed. He stood motionless to hear the voice of his people. He seemed to be in silent communion with them. Once again, he could hear the great heart of Russia beating. ...

"He then turned again towards the chapel, crossed himself, put on his cap, and slowly walked to his carriage, which disappeared under the old gate and went towards the Kremlin.

On the left: Nicholas and Alexandra at the balcony of the Winter Palace, after the official announcement of Germany's declaration of war against Russia.
On the right: Nicholas bowing to his people with the promise of fighting until the final victory.
Below: The people on their knees singing the Imperial Anthem "God Save the Tsar."

Nicholas inspecting his troops.

CHAPTER 4

"Tuesday, August 18th.—At eleven o'clock, when the Czar appeared at the top of the Red Staircase, the huge crowd in the square gave him a magnificent reception."[18]

From Nicholas' speech which he gave that day: "In this time of War which has appeared so suddenly and so against our wishes, I, my peace-loving people, in the tradition of our Sovereign Ancestors, seek to strengthen spiritual resolve through prayer at the holy sites of Moscow. Within the ancient walls of the Moscow Kremlin, on behalf of you, the inhabitants of Moscow, I welcome all the Russian people, faithful to me everywhere. ... From the heart of the Russian land I send my gallant and courageous troops to meet our foreign allies, who, in concert with Us have risen to bring the beginning of peace and truth! Warm greetings! God is with us!"[19]

Gilliard continues: "He came down slowly, with the Czarina on his arm, and at the head of a long procession slowly crossed the bridge connecting the palace with the Cathedral of the Assumption and entered the church amid a frantic outburst of cheering from the crowd. The Metropolitan Bishops of Kiev, St. Petersburg, and Moscow and the high dignitaries of the Orthodox clergy were present. When Mass was over, the members of the Imperial family in turn approached the holy relics and kissed them."

"Long after Their Majesties had returned to the palace the crowd continued to collect in the square in the hope of seeing them again. Even when we came out several hours later there were still hundreds of peasants outside the palace."

"Thursday, August 20th.—Popular enthusiasm is waxing from day to day. It seems as if the people of Moscow are so proud of having their Czar with them, and so anxious to keep him as long as possible, that they mean to hold him here by manifest proofs of their affection."

"Friday, August 21st.—Their Majesties, before returning to Tsarskoie-Selo, decided to visit the Troitsa Monastery, the most celebrated sanctuary in Russia after the world-famed *Laure* [Lavra] of Kiev. ... The Imperial family were present at a *Te Deum* and knelt before the relics of St. Sergius [of Radonezh], the founder of the monastery. The Archimandrite then handed the Czar an icon painted in a fragment of the coffin of the saint, one of the most revered in Russia. In olden times this image always accompanied the Czars on their campaigns. On the Czar's orders it is being sent to General Headquarters and placed in the 'field chapel' of the Commander-in-Chief of the Russian Armies."[20]

That was the final time that the last emperor of Russia would visit the Lavra of Saint Sergius of Radonezh. Nicholas wrote, "On the way there [to the Lavra] there was an eclipse of the sun."[21]

THE REVELATION OF A MAGNIFICENT SOUL

Wartime revealed the magnificence of Alexandra's soul and the real content of her heart. That very same evening, immediately after Germany's declaration of war, once she had recovered from the shock, the empress summoned Baroness Buxhoeveden and began to plan the organization of a hospital. Then she worked on scheduling trains to bring the wounded from the front. The network of hospitals and medical centers that the empress organized covered a vast expanse from Saint Petersburg through Moscow and as far as Kharkov and Odessa. The palace at Tsarskoe Selo became the center of operations, and its environs included eighty-five hospitals operating under Alexandra's aegis and direct oversight. More hospitals operated in nearly all the palaces of the royal family all over Russia.

In 1915 when the army's positions were somewhat stationary, Alexandra undertook to send mobile field chapels. The countries where the war was being waged were Roman Catholic and for this reason there were no Orthodox churches. Thus, the Empress sent priests with mobile chapels to hold services where the soldiers could receive Holy Communion. Thus many that were about to die were able to receive Communion before they yielded up their souls. Furthermore, she personally sent thousands of copies of the Holy Scripture and Psalters to nourish the souls of the soldiers.

Alexandra, however, did not confine her activities only to organization, scheduling, and the oversight of the hospitals. She had written to one of her sisters that she did not have any intention of being "a mere doll"[22] in her work. Overlooking her own weakened health, along with her two older daughters, Olga and Tatiana, and her friend Anna Vyrubova, after two months of classroom and practical nursing training, she joined the Red Cross nursing staff. As for the two younger sisters, Maria and Anastasia, because of their young age, were limited to daily visits to the hospitals and to sewing clothes for the soldiers.

As she characteristically said, Alexandra wanted her daughters to "realise the sadness underneath all this beauty,"[23] namely of the outward appearance that this present life presents.

The imperial family put much effort into this work, which was beyond the understanding of those who had not had similar experience. Every day, starting very early in the morning, the empress and her two older daughters would always go first to the Znamenie Church of the Mother of God[24] to pray, and then immediately after they began their work in the hospital in the wards, which received the wounded daily. These soldiers who had only received first aid in the trenches or in field hospitals at the front were in a wretched state—dirty, bloody, and in intense pain. The four women, along with the rest of the nurses, immediately began the procedures of washing and dressing amputated limbs, deformed faces, gouged eyes, and all sorts of terrible wounds.

CHAPTER 4

Later, when she had enough experience, Alexandra began work as a surgery nurse. There she removed soiled bandages from poorly dressed wounds, gave the surgeons their tools, and took the amputated limbs of the wounded from them, enduring with great bravery those frightful sights, the unbearable stenches, and the terrible agony for the life of those men. In most cases, it was already afternoon when they had the opportunity to take a much-needed meal while standing. Despite all that, they worked with great humility and tenderness, considering their work sacred before God.

The soldiers adored her. They always looked for when the empress would pass near them, and when she approached them, they reached out their hands to touch her. She would always stop and bend down near their pillow and share some few kind words to them. Those men's smiles then were truly an outpouring of deep thanks. Even those about to die smiled peacefully when she knelt by their bed as they whispered their last prayers before their departure from this world.

In one such instance, a young officer dying of his wounds, on hearing that the empress was on her way to visit the hospital where he was being treated, declared to his nurses that he was determined to live until Alexandra came. His great faith, in fact, unexpectedly kept him alive until the empress arrived, who, as soon as she was informed of this, hastened to his bedside. There she immediately knelt beside him and heard his last words and beheld his grateful smile before he expired.[25] Similar incidents often occurred late in the evening as well. After endless hours at surgery and in the hospital wards, Alexandra returned home in a state of complete fatigue. Then it she would receive a message from the hospital that someone about to die had asked for her and she immediately hastened back to the hospital.

Sometimes when an unfortunate soldier was told by the surgeons that he must suffer an amputation or undergo an operation that might be fatal, he turned in his bed calling out her name in anguished appeal. "Tsaritsa! Stand near me. Hold my hand that I may have courage."[26] And certainly Alexandra would always arrive immediately. With her hand below the head of the wounded, she spoke to him with words of consolation and encouragement, praying with him as the preparations proceeded for the operation. Afterward, she remained at the surgery helping the surgeons in their work. Tatiana relates one such circumstance in a letter to her father, "11 June, 1916: ...They brought to the infirmary this one old colonel of the 13th Belozersky Regiment, wounded in the chest, bleeding into the stomach, where there is a bullet, and another [wound] in the leg. Very serious condition. It seems they wanted to leave him in Kiev, but he asked to be brought here because he wanted to see Mama. So touching."[27]

When the emperor was inspecting the troops, Alexandra made rounds of the provincial hospitals with her four daughters. She wished to see with her own eyes what their needs were and to show personal interest in as many wounded as possible. In every city they visited, as soon as they disembarked from the train, they would go directly to the cathedral to worship and to pray to the local saints before they began their visits.

From Tatiana's diary in 1914:[28] "3 December [Moscow]: [On the] train. At 9 in the morning went to the Cathedral of the Assumption, where they had obednya [Liturgy] in the chapel of St. Dimitri the Great Martyr. Went to the Romanov hospital at the Pokrovsky convent. 4 December: At 9 o'clock arrived in Tula. Rode in carriages to the cathedral. Moleben.[29] Then to three infirmaries. Many wounded. At 11.30 left. Breakfast and lunch together. At 3 o'clock arrived in Orel. Also went to the cathedral, from there to a warehouse, then to 4 infirmaries. 5 December: At 9 o'clock arrived in Kursk. [Drove] in a motor to the cathedral and 3 infirmaries. Many wounded. Left at 11.30. Breakfast, tea and lunch on the train. Sat in my [car] with Ortino. At 4.20 arrived in Kharkov. Inspected Mama's empty hospital train, and there was a short moleben. After that again in motors to the cathedral. Unbelievable crowds. Went to Mama's warehouse and 3 infirmaries. An incredible number of people. At 7:15 [we] left. Arrived at 9 after dinner. In Belgorod [we] rode to the Cathedral in three carriages. Was wonderfully nice. Venerated the relics of St. Ioasaf."[30]

The entries in the diary continue with the same exact rhythms of this unbelievably compressed schedule. On occasion the empress and her daughters would see up to three thousand wounded soldiers in just one day. The joy that Alexandra saw in the faces of those men serbed as a driving force for her sickly nature. When, however, she returned to the train at the end of the day, she was so exhausted that she sank into the first seat that she found before her, unable even to go on to her own car.

The empress' mind worked constantly producing new ideas for the better management of her activities. The days seemed too few to achieve everything she had in mind. "My heart got so bad again," she wrote in her letters to Princess Louis in March 1915, "and it helps me when the heart is heavy and, knowing you bring happiness, how not go to the poor wounded? and forget yourself? … the wounded's grateful smiles are a recompense for every fatigue."[31]

However, as might be expected, Alexandra could not maintain this intense activity indefinitely. The continuous standing and hard physical labor seriously aggravated the heart problem that afflicted her from time to time. She suffered from continual pain and intense shortness of breath. She wrote to her beloved teacher, Miss Jackson, who was now in England, "my heart has been so bad again and such weakness—I utterly overtired myself. Nothing is more tiring than visiting heaps of hospitals and speaking by the hour to the poor wounded. So I have not been able to work in the hospital now, which is a great grief to me, as I love the work and find consolation in nursing the sick and binding up their wounds however terrible they may be."[32]

Furthermore, the problem with sciatica which tormented her from her youth grew much worse, and then appeared a terrible bout of neuralgia of

CHAPTER 4

Alexandra in her wheelchair.

the trigeminal nerve, which when inflamed caused her sharp pains. Hence, she was forced to reduce her workload, but she had no intention of giving it up. She did not wish to accept defeat because of her bodily infirmities. Therefore, when she visited the hospitals, very often she had to be carried from floor to floor. Later, it became necessary to use a wheelchair nearly all the time.

She wrote to her sister Victoria, "Don't think my ill health depresses me personally. I don't care, except to see my dear ones suffer on my account, and that I cannot fulfil my duties. But once God sends such a cross, it must be borne. … I have had so much, that, willingly, I give up any pleasures—they mean so little to me, and my family life is such an ideal one, that it is a recompense for anything I cannot take part in."[33]

ANGELS OF MERCY

When Alexandra's strength began to fail her, they decided to have Olga and Tatiana replace her in her duties. Tatiana undertook the presidency of the Committee on Refugees, in which she was responsible for the resettlement and care of the thousands of Russian refugees who arrived from the war zones of the empire. Every week Tatiana presided over meetings and regulated all the activities of the committee. Olga was responsible for the collection of revenues that would cover the needs of the families of the soldiers. They devoted the morning hours that remained after their service in the operating room to these obligations. In the afternoon they continued their rounds of visits to the hospitals of Saint Petersburg.

Their hospital work was a source of important experience for the young princesses, which they would never have gained under other circumstances. This encounter with the reality outside the palace showed them an entire world that they had not known. They conversed with their nursing colleagues, persons whom they would not have been able to know otherwise. They learned about their personal problems, their thoughts, and in general all that related to their lives. Thus, they studied in the school of life and acquired equipment that would later be valuable.

In the field of nursing, Tatiana was shown to be as gifted as her mother. Although she was only seventeen years old, she assisted at the more complicated surgical procedures with the abilities of an experienced nurse. Her diary in this period is full of her experiences while working at the hospital. From her diary of 1915:[34] "7 January: In the morning had lesson in Zakon Bozhiy [Закон Божий: Law of God]. At 10 o'clock we two [with Olga] went to 'Znamenie,' from there to our infirmary.... Went to the Big House for a craniotomy. Handled the instruments. 19 February: ...we went to the Big House for two surgeries. Removed a bullet from one [patient's] head. 23 February: ...Anisimov of the 27th Siberian Rifle Regiment had surgery, amputated his right foot. I assisted and held the hooks. His left leg was already amputated to the knee."[35]

The girls' work did not take place on an impersonal level. Even though throngs of wounded arrived daily at their hospital, the young duchesses met and connected personally with every one of them. They participated in their pain and agony and supported them with their pleasant company and consoling words.

The daughter of Doctor Botkin related the following: "Dr. Derevenko, a very demanding man towards the nurses, told me after the revolution that he rarely met such a calm, nimble and professional surgical nurse as Tatiana."[36] A professional nurse who worked with Tatiana in the operating room wrote likewise in her diary during this period: "The surgery was successful. After the first difficult cut, a river of incredibly smelly pus poured out. For the first time in my life I had the urge to vomit but Tatiana

Olga at a meeting of her committee.

Nikolaevna was fine, only when [patients] moaned pitifully, her little face twitched, and became crimson."[37]

Olga, however, was not able to bear the horror of this experience. Her sensitive soul suffered totally with those unfortunate youths. Thus after a few months of work in the operating rooms, exhausted by psychological pain, she had to withdraw from this work. She remained, however, responsible for the management of the hospital wings where she was assigned, and she continued to work on changing the bandages of the wounded and to perform all the necessary tasks in the recovery rooms of soldiers who were operated on.

Olga had an especially gifted mind. She had a flawless knowledge of the economic and political condition of Russia during the war and later during the revolution. Even from that period, she understood the increasing antipathy of the people towards her parents, and according to Dr Botkin's son, she sensed beforehand what soon awaited them. It was precisely this perception that frequently caused her intense trouble and uneasiness.

Maria and Anastasia, fifteen and thirteen years old respectively in 1914, were too young to be trained as nurses. However, they also had their own hospital in which they performed their own services. In their daily visits the little princesses used to read from various literary works to their wounded, helped them compose letters, played board games with them, and in general did whatever they could to strengthen the morale of the troops. Their experiences and impressions from these activities are preserved in letters that they sent to their father, who was at the front most of the time during the war.

Little Anastasia wrote on 15/28 October 1914: "My golden and good Papa Darling! ...Today I sat with our soldier and helped him read, and it was so pleasant for me. He learned to read and write with us." Further on

Alexis with Olga and Tatiana.

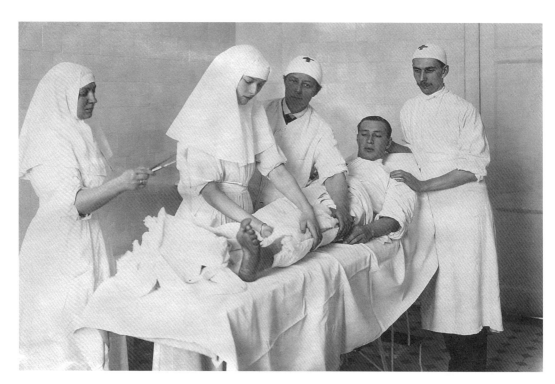
Tatiana treating a wounded leg.

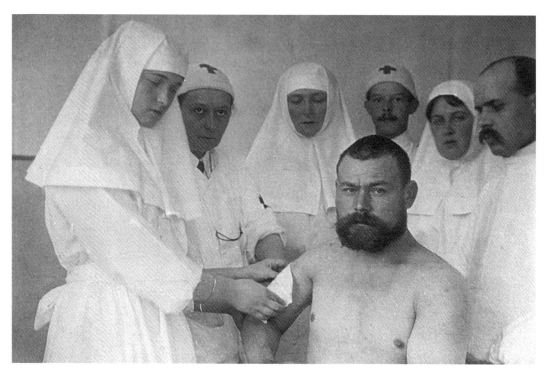
Olga treating a wounded arm.

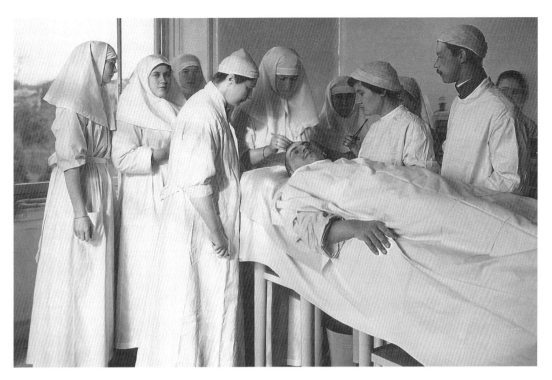
Alexandra treating a head wound. On the left: Tatiana, Vyrubova and Olga.

Alexandra, Olga and Tatiana with Red Cross uniforms. Maria and Anastasia are also present.

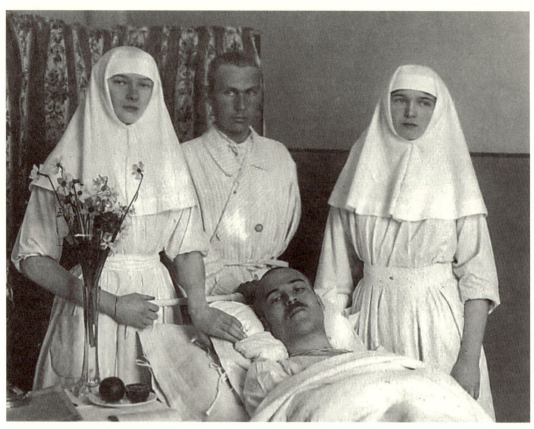

With wounded officers. Above: Olga and Tatiana. Below: Maria and Anastasia.

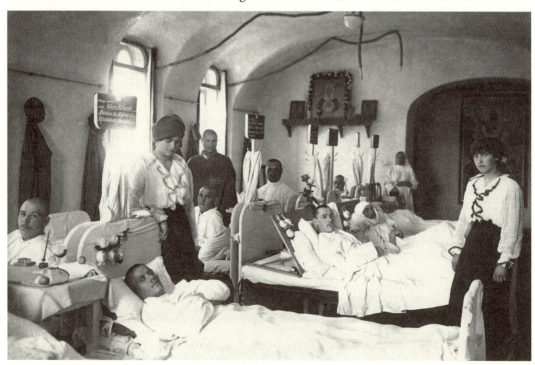

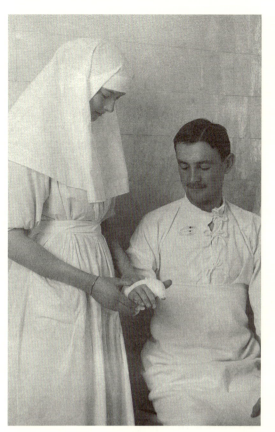 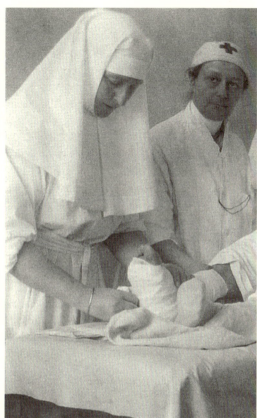

Tatiana on the left. Alexandra on the right and below.

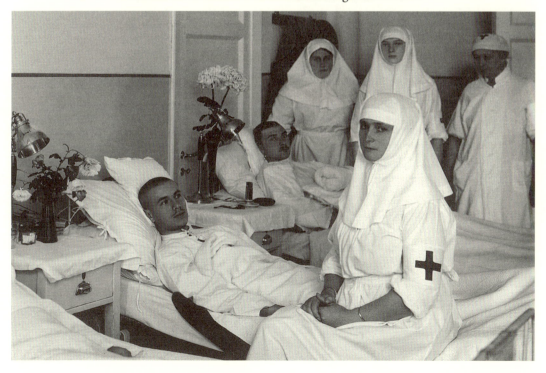

CHAPTER 4

in the letter it was clear how familiar the girls were with the fact of death from such a young age: "Two more died yesterday, we even sat with them earlier."[38] And in spite of the fact that they lived in the midst of the general terror of daily deaths and hideous wounds, thirteen year old Anastasia did not lose her lively disposition: "Sleep well and see me in your dreams. I kiss you 1000 times. Your loving daughter, 13-year-old God's Servant Nastasia ANRPZSG.[39] May God keep you."[40]

Even though they did not have nursing duties, the two younger girls' schedule was still very tiring and pressing. On 25 October/7 November 1914, Maria wrote to her father: "My dear Papa darling! I am terribly sorry that I did not have time to write to you. ... In the afternoon we went to 4 infirmaries in Pavlovsk with Mama and Aunt Mavra. ... Also today we went to the consecration of Svodny Regiment's infirmary. It is located in the building where the church used to be. A dining room was set up in that room, and moleben was held right there. ... After vsenoshnaya [всенощная: the All-Night Vigil] tonight we went to the infirmary."[41]

Even little Alexis often took part in the nursing activities of his sisters. On 30 November/13 December 1914, Tatiana wrote to her father: "Today we all five were at our infirmary and Aleksei was present at all dressings and during one of them [he] even held the tray where the pus dripped from the wound."[42]

Recapitulating this period in the lives of the girls and of their mother, the daughter of Doctor Botkin writes, "Indeed, during the entire war, the already modest life of the imperial family now passed [even more] monotonously, [filled] day-to-day with work. So passed the weekdays, the holidays only differed in that instead of a morning visit to the infirmary, Their Majesties and Their Highnesses went to Obednya [Liturgy] at Feodorovsky Cathedral."[43]

These young ladies made their debut in life through the gate of the hard reality of human drama. In contrast with other princesses of Europe, apart from the official celebration of their debuts into society when they turned sixteen years old, they had attended almost no dances up to then and certainly not afterward. Also, in contrast with their peers, they had no friends at all and no contact with the world. However, wartime revealed these pure beings as the most precious things that Russia had to offer in that period. Apart from their self-sacrificing love for the suffering, they took care to be the main human support to their parents in these critical and agonizing times of general turmoil. Their instructor, Gilliard, expressed with some dismay this characteristic observation, "If only the world had known what an example the Imperial family were setting with their tender and intimate association! But how few ever suspected it! For it was too indifferent to public opinion and avoided the public gaze."[44]

The malicious environment of high society, continually pouring oil on the flames of revolutionary attitudes, dogged Alexandra's every step, criticizing her every activity. Up until then they slandered the empress for the gulf that developed between her and high society, presenting it as the result of her supposed haughtiness. Now that Alexandra devoted her entire being to her people in practical ways and with unfathomable self-sacrifice, the slanders took on a new form. They asserted that it was completely unsuitable, completely improper and a great humiliation for the empress to wear a nurse's uniform and to work as a simple woman of the people in the hospitals! Thus, the words of the Lord came true, "We have piped unto you, and ye have not danced; we have mourned to you, and ye have not wept."[45] Alexandra was condemned regardless of her deeds and attitudes.

However, those that had the opportunity to know the Empress in this period of her work in the hospitals, saw the true light of her soul shine. They got to know her as she was in her close family surrounding, because the nurse's uniform gave her the ability to overcome her natural shyness and to manifest in practice her great maternal love towards her subjects.

In these times of crisis, the official recognition of her sacrifices by the Church gave Alexandra very great joy. The Holy Synod on 9 October, 1916 bestowed on the empress a gramota, an honorary award given in very rare cases when the offering on the part of some person is considered of tremendous significance. Alexandra's emotion was without description, because her recognition by the highest ecclesiastical authority was especially important in a time in which the basest rumors were circulating in church circles regarding her relationship to Rasputin.

'I WILL PERISH, BUT I WILL SAVE RUSSIA'

The burden of responsibility that Nicholas shouldered in the framework of this war was colossal. However, he displayed great stability and decisiveness in all his activities. He had given his entire being, soul and body, over to guiding Russia to victory. An invisible inward strength appeared to spring from within him, which was so apparent and impressive that anyone who encountered him during this time felt it intensely. Furthermore, these events brought him closer than ever to his people. The entire nation showed at every opportunity how much they valued his steady and dignified position in the world scene. All Russia to a man was at his side and the political passions seemed now to be lost in the past.

Nicholas did not follow the development of the war from his royal throne. He was constantly on the move, inspecting the Stavka [General Headquarters], the vast eastern front, the military hospitals, the factories, and in general every sector that contributed to the common national goal. Unfortunately, the first six months of the war did not have the expected result for Russia and her allies, England and France. The confidence that the war would be brief, and the victory of the Allies overwhelming was soon proven false. Everything now indicated that the battles would continue for a long time and their results would be inevitably grievous for both sides of the hostilities.

Russia's first few successes were followed by tremendous defeats. From May until October of 1915, the Russian army was in continual retreat, the so-called Russian Great Retreat. The enemy had already begun to invade Russian soil. This development shocked Nicholas, as it was entirely unforeseen. Bad leadership and inadequate transport resulted in enormous problems supplying the front with food and ammunition. The magnitude of this tragedy was depicted in the dramatic words of letters sent by many soldiers to their superiors. One wrote, "You know, sir, we have no weapon except the soldier's breast." And yet another, "This is not war, sir, it is slaughter."[46] In June, Nicholas dismissed the Minister of War, General Vladimir Sukhomlinov, who was considered responsible for criminal negligence in the task of supplying the troops. Sukhomlinov held Grand Duke Nicholas, Guchkov, and Polivanov, his successor as Minister of War, responsible for his downfall. It is, however, worthy of observation that later, after the Revolution, when he escaped to Germany he published his *Memoirs* in 1924, which he dedicated to his former friends in the army and to Kaiser Wilhelm II, who considered reciprocating by dedicating his own *Memoirs* to Sukhomlinov.

Russia's subsequent defeats, combined with the internal economic crisis that began to take on new dimensions, was the fuse for significant new political unrest. It was precisely then that Nicholas took the momentous decision to place himself at the head of the armies of his country. This was in fact his original intention, even from the beginning of the war, which, however, encountered opposition from his ministers, as was also the case in the time of the Russo-Japanese war. However, now that the Germans had begun to invade Russian territory, Nicholas considered it a crime to remain far from the front, where the battles for the defense of his homeland were waged.

The patriotism of the emperor was one of the most moving chapters of his personal history. When very soon after, he was compelled to abdicate the throne, he would characteristically say, "Just to think that, now I am Czar no longer, they won't even let me fight for my country!"[47] That was Nicholas, the man who loved his people and his country more than his own self. And this love was the result of the Divine Mystery that tied him spiritually to his subjects on the day of his Anointing and Coronation as father and protector of Russia and Orthodoxy.

Thus, in the most tragic and critical hours of the entire history of Russia, Nicholas instead of looking to shift responsibility elsewhere and attempting to keep his hands clean of soldiers' blood, was moved to do completely the opposite. It was a risky move. Since the times of Peter the Great not a single emperor dared to take command of the army. Many officials, and those close to the emperor, believed this to be a mistake. Taking command as head of the army, he in essence assumed the entire responsibility for the results of a war that was already nearly lost. To a man the government considered that with this action, Nicholas placed himself in greatest of danger, thereby giving his enemies the ability to heap upon him the entire responsibility for what were by now terrible failures. When the president of the Duma wished to point out to Nicholas that responsibility for the possible mistakes and failures of the operation that he assumed would be attributed to him personally, the emperor replied, "I will perish, but I will save Russia."[48]

On 4 September, not knowing all the opposing opinions of the ministers and of those around him, Nicholas departed for Stavka at Mogilev. A few days before his departure he wrote in his diary, "At 9:00 AM we went to Liturgy in the cave church and received Holy Communion. Such a great consolation in these difficult days!"[49] All his hope and faith were based on the power of God, as can be seen from his diary entry on the day of his departure, "May God bless this trip and my decision!"[50]

On 5 September, as Nicholas officially assumed the post of Commander-in-Chief of the Russian army, he issued the communique with the relevant order to his troops: "With unshakable faith in the goodness of God and firm confidence in final victory we shall accomplish our sacred duty in defending our Fatherland to the end, and we shall never let the soil of Russia be outraged."[51] Two days later, in his letter to Alexandra he wrote, "Thank God it is all over and here I am with this new heavy responsibility on my shoulders! But God's will be fulfilled—I feel so calm, a sort of feeling after the Holy Communion! The whole morning of that memorable day Aug 23 [5 Sep],[52] while coming here, I prayed much and read your first letter over and over again."[53]

Nicholas appointed General Alekseyev as his chief of staff, a notable military man who had already shown great abilities during the war. The weight of responsibility on both men at this critical period of the general advance of the German troops was incalculable. But the miracle was not long in coming. The military abilities of Alekseyev, the charismatic management of all the administrative and military matters by Nicholas, and the enthusiasm that his presence induced at the front strengthened the morale of the troops and their heroism reached its peak. Telegrams were flying to the front: "The emperor is with us! Not a step back!"

In an unprecedented short span of time, in just a few months, the situation changed completely. At the beginning of 1915, Russia's monthly manufacturing capacity could provide the army with only 15-30% of the necessary weapons and ammunition requirements. Of all allied countries, Russia's supply crisis was the most severe, because Russia was last to shift its manufacturing focus to military production. Such measures required substantial expenses and were deemed unnecessary at first. The much-expected weapons shipments from Europe did not come. Weapons ordered by Russia were manufactured but confiscated by the allies for their own needs. Furthermore, it was very problematic to deliver shipments to Russia. Europe was torn apart by front lines. The Baltic and Mediterranean Sea were engulfed in combat. Only two ports were left available for the allied ships: northernmost Arkhangelsk and remote Vladivostok.

Tsar Nicholas ordered to set up an emergency governmental body, the Special Council of Defense, which was made up of government officials, community spokesmen, and private entrepreneurs. Their task was to promptly mobilize the nation's war economy and military production. Machinery and equipment were bought instead of finished goods. Russia urgently built new arms factories and constructed a completely new ice-free port in the Barents Sea, Romanov-on-Murman, present day Murmansk. Russia was undergoing full-scale military-oriented industrialization. Within months, production of weapons and ammunition increased tenfold. In August of 1916, production of rifles was 1100% higher than in August of 1914. Canon (76 mm mountain gun) production from January 1916 until January 1917 increased by over 1000%, while that of 76 mm shells increased by 2000%. Gunpowder and explosives manufacture rose by 250–300%.[54]

The advance of the enemy was halted, the front line was stabilized, and significant successes against Austria followed. All these things came about already at the beginning of October 1915, sealing the end of the Russian retreat that had begun in May. Next year, on 4 June 1916, the Brusilov Offensive was launched, which constituted Russia's greatest success in the First World War, and one of the most formidable military offensives in history. In view of the launching of this great offensive, Nicholas commanded the wonder-working icon of the Mother of God of Vladimir to be brought from Moscow's Kremlin to Stavka in Mogilev. The Icon immediately arrived to bless the outcome of this great offensive. As Nicholas wrote to Tatiana, "Today the miraculous icon of Our Lady of Vladimir arrived from Moscow and at 5 o'cl. they will solemnly take [it] to our church."[55]

The Brusilov Offensive, which lasted until September 1916, succeeding in breaking the defensive line of the Austro-Germans, which required the Central Powers to transfer two divisions from France and another six from Italy to the Russian Front. As a result, the inevitable defeat of the Italians was avoided, the balance of the terrible battle of Verdun in France was shifted, and Romania entered the war on the side of the Allied Powers. These developments significantly determined the outcome of the War in favor of the Allies.

This bold and brilliantly executed plan will forever go down in history as the most famous strategic offensive of World War One. Already within the first weeks of the operation tens of thousands of prisoners were captured and by its final stages German and Austrian casualties amounted to 800,000 men. The Austrian army of the Eastern front was practically shattered. The Russians took back almost all of Western Ukraine. This was an unbelievable outcome for positional warfare. In the operation, Austria-Hungary and Germany lost over 1.5 million men, either killed, wounded, or missing. The Russian forces also captured an immense number of weapons. Casualties on the part of the Russian southwestern front amounted about 500,000 men.

The Russians were thrilled by the successful offensive. The Allies applauded the Russian troops as well. European newspapers printed countless praiseful articles about the Russian army. The emperor awarded General Brusilov with a diamond-clad St George's Weapon.

This is what Winston Churchill, the great statesman, testified about this magnificent moment in Russia's history: "Few episodes of the Great War are more impressive than the resuscitation, reequipment and renewed giant effort of Russia in 1916. It was the last glorious exertion of the Czar and the Russian people for victory before both were to sink into the abyss of ruin and horror. By the summer of 1916 Russia, who eighteen months before had been almost disarmed, who during 1915 had sustained an unbroken series of frightful defeats, had actually managed, by her own efforts and the resources of her Allies, to place in the field—organized, armed, and equipped—sixty Army Corps in place of the thirty-five with which she had begun the war. The Trans-Siberian Railway had been doubled over a distance of 6,000 kilometres, as far east as Lake Baikal. A new railway 1,400 kilometres long, built through the depth of winter at the cost of unnumbered lives, linked Petrograd with the perennially ice-free waters of the Murman coast. And by both these channels munitions from the rising factories of Britain, France, and Japan, or procured by British credit from the United States, were pouring into Russia in broadening streams. The domestic production of every form of war material had simultaneously been multiplied many fold."[56]

The truth was unambiguous: Nicholas had the blessing of God with him. His faith in God and love for his people became the invincible weapons that shattered his enemies, a fact to which history itself bears witness. A year later, he revealed his divine summons to take command of the Russian troops in a letter he sent to Alexandra, "My thoughts surround you particularly last evening and this morning, when you went to Holy Communion in our cozy underground church. It must be a year ago that we took it together during those hard days before my coming here! I remember so well that I was standing opposite our Saviour's big icon upstairs in the big church [when] an interior voice seemed to tell me to make up my mind and write about my decision [to assume personal command of my armies on the Western front] at once."[57]

The diary of Major-General John Hanbury-Williams, head of the British Military Mission at the Russian Stavka, contains a multitude of references to Nicholas' leadership abilities and integrity of his personality. On 14 January, 1916, he wrote regarding the great problem of supplying the Russian troops, "Had a long talk with [General] Alexeieff and Admiral Russin on munition matters, in which there appears to be some improvement, due no doubt to the energy with which the Emperor pursues this all-important question."[58]

On 14 November 1915, Hanbury relates concerning Nicholas' faithful adherence to the goals of the Allies and his patriotism, the following significant incident: "Count Fredericks… said that he had received a communication from Count Eulenburg, the Prussian Court Chamberlain… in which he said that the Kaiser [Wilhelm II] was so anxious to find some means of bringing the Russian Emperor and himself into the old standing of friendship again. It was regrettable that they should be at war, etc.; endeavouring, in fact, to induce Russia to come to terms with Germany.

"The communication, he said, had been laid before his Imperial master [Nicholas], and the end of the matter was that the Emperor said the letter could be thrown into the fire, and that any similar letters would be treated in the same way.

"'That,' said the Emperor, 'is my answer to any communications of the kind from the Kaiser.'"[59]

As for Nicholas' character, the British major-general recorded the following: "17th March 1916. The Emperor after an absence of some time returned to Headquarters yesterday. He is always so bright and cheerful that one cannot but be cheerful with him. It is a wonderful temperament for a man who must have such cares and anxieties on his mind, and I am sure is a good inspiration for others."[60] With some complaint he notes one further point: "He is so keen, if he were [only] well supported."[61]

In agreeance to this, Lieven writes: "[The Tsar] could not find a prime minister competent to do the job, who would obey his orders and pursue the line he required. Talented officials were no longer willing to simply assume public responsibility for executing the tsar's commands."[62]

Another significant historical fact must be mentioned here. Many have supported the idea that tsar Nicholas did not really consider the common Orthodox Faith and Slavic ethnic kinship that tied Russia to Serbia to be an important factor to get Russia into the war. Nevertheless, this is falsified by the historical facts themselves. In 1915, after being defeated by the Germans, the Serbian army was forced to retreat across the mountains to the Albanian coast. Tens of thousands began to die. Their allies looked upon them with indifference from their ships at anchor in the Adriatic. The tsar informed his allies that they must immediately evacuate the Serbs, otherwise he would consider the fall of the Serbs as an act of the greatest immorality.

On January 11, 1916, Nicholas sent a message to his Foreign Minister, Sergey D. Sazonov, urging him to put pressure on the Allies in every way, so as to offer help to the retreating Serbian army. To the complaints of the French representatives that it was too expensive and unprofitable to help the exhausted Serbs, who were unable to continue the war, Nicholas replied: "I will pay for all the expenses of the Serbs." On January 19, the Tsar went on to send letters to the French president R. Poincare and the English King George V, with a call to save the Serbian army at any cost. Indeed, Nicholas' call brought prompt action, and dozens of Italian, French, and English ships set about evacuating the dying army to Corfu, and from there, once they had recovered, to the new front that the Allies were forming in Thessalonica.[63]

In 2016, Serbian president Tomislav Nicolic said: "Serbia will never forget those who fought and died alongside its soldiers on the Macedonian Front. ... On the personal orders of Tsar Nicholas II 10,000 Russian soldiers joined the allies there, the best members of the Moscow Military District. Although everyone wanted them, they chose to fight as part of the Serbian Army. About 4,300 Russian soldiers died. All of them Serbia will never forget."[64]

As Saint Nikolai Velimirovich, Serbian Bishop of Zhicha, wrote: "Great is our debt to Russia. The debt of Serbia to Russia, for help to the Serbs in the war of 1914, is huge—many centuries will not be able to contain it for all following generations. This is the debt of love, which without thinking goes to its death, saving its neighbour. 'There is no greater love than this, that a man should lay down his life for his neighbour.' These are the words of Christ. The Russian tsar and the Russian people, having taken the decision to enter the war for the sake of the defence of Serbia, while being unprepared for it, knew that they were going to certain destruction. The love of the Russians for their Serbian brothers did not fear death, and did not retreat before it. Can we ever forget that the Russian tsar, in subjecting both his children and millions of his brothers to danger, went to his death for the sake of the Serbian people, for the sake of its salvation? Can we be silent before heaven and earth about the fact that our freedom and statehood were worth more to Russia than to us ourselves? The Russians in our days repeated the Kosovo tragedy. If the Russian Tsar Nicholas II had been striving for an earthly kingdom, a kingdom of petty personal calculations and egoism, he would be sitting to this day on his throne in Petrograd. But he chose the Heavenly Kingdom, the Kingdom of sacrifice in the name of the Lord, the Kingdom of Gospel spirituality, for which he laid down his own head, for which his children and millions of his subjects laid down their heads."[65]

'WE WILL ALL PRAY FOR YOU'

Nicholas' decision to assume command of his troops met complete agreement in Alexandra. The girls, already at a sufficiently mature age, understood in turn the necessity and seriousness of their father's decision. However, the separation of Alexandra as well as of their children from their father was rather difficult. A few days before Nicholas' departure, on 15/28 August 1915, Tatiana wrote in a note to her mother, "Mama, darling angel mine! I pray for you both dearies, the whole time, that God will help you now in this terrible time. I simply cannot tell you how awfully sorry I am for you, my beloved ones. I am so sorry I cannot help you in any way or be useful. In such moments I am sorry I am not a man. Bless you my own beloved one. Sleep well. I kiss you and dear Papa awfully much. Your own loving and loyal daughter, Tatiana."[66]

In her farewell letter to her father on 22 August/4 September 1915 Anastasia noted, "My dear and sweet Papa Darling. I wish you lots of well-

CHAPTER 4

being, and everything good and joyful, and that you are healthy and happy to everyone's joy. We will all pray for you here, for you to be able to bear everything easier. Be well, do not tire yourself out. God will help. Sleep well. May the Lord keep you. Your Loving daughter Nastenka."[67]

Anastasia's warm words and prayers show that she had deep understanding for her father's mission. However, she also knew something else. She knew that her father, under the unbearable weight of responsibilities and of the drama of the War, had need of rest occasionally, even if only for a few moments. And so in her letters, she also made sure to write a few "entertaining" lines to her father, such as these: "Ortipo and Joy asked to send big regards and to tell you that they miss you,"[68] "I just sneezed, you tell me 'Bless you,' I am very grateful to you for this."[69] Maria also wrote similar jests to her father: "I will finish writing now, or else your imperial eyes will start hurting from reading on this red paper."[70]

In 1915, after his father's assumption of his new duties and continual long-time absences from home, Alexis, now eleven years old, understood that he was now the man of the house. So, just like his sisters, he himself, due to the circumstances of his life, had to mature quickly. Thus, he undertook to care for his mother as best he could. In church and in her every social obligation, he was always found next to her—he took care to prepare the seat where she would sit, and afterwards helped her to get up. Also, when she would pray kneeling, Alexis would hold her and help her to bow down and then to rise up. Notably, in all this, his movements and conduct were exactly like those of the emperor. His father's example had already been deeply impressed on him. Soon, however, little Alexis would receive one more important experience in his life.

Nicholas never forgot the terrible difficulties that he encountered when he assumed command. Not only did he not forget them, but they wounded his kind soul deeply. He had endured the bitter experience of his father's neglect on this point, something that caused him to pass through fire and iron until he adjusted to the demands of his position, so that he himself wished to avoid the same mistake with Alexis. So, as soon as he took command of the army, he decided to take Alexis with him to Stavka, in order to introduce him to the duties and realities of his role as future emperor of Russia.

This constituted a terrible blow to Alexandra, who was never separated from Alexis for more than a few hours. Whenever she was away from him, she was in a continual state of intense agony, feeling the sword of Damocles hanging over the head of her child. However, for the love of country and for her husband, she stepped up to this greatest sacrifice of her life. She believed, and was proved right, that the presence of the tsarevich at the front would raise the morale of the troops. So, on 14 October, 1915 Nicholas took Alexis with him to Mogilev, along with his tutor and family friend, Pierre Gilliard.

Together they began a general inspection of the vast Eastern Front. That was the first time the Tsar himself came in immediate contact with the troops who had waged the great battles. The enthusiasm of the troops at the presence of the tsar was indescribable. After the official receptions, Nicholas mingled with the men, conversing with them on a personal level, asking them about their experiences and their activities. Alexis constantly stood at his father's side trying not to lose even a single word of his conversations with the troops, who had so many times personally confronted death. In their turn, the troops were impressed by the presence of the Tsarevich who was unusually tall for his age, perfectly cultivated, and especially friendly. However, what made the greatest impression on them all without exception was that Alexis wore the uniform of a simple soldier without decoration, something that did not set him above any member of the army. Nicholas' humility and his manner that he had cultivated in his children deeply moved all the members of the army.

Nicholas saw himself as equal of even the least of his soldiers who contended for the defense of his homeland. He acted not as tsar, but as a simple, true Russian soldier. One morning at one encampment they brought him breakfast. When he understood that there were soldiers who had not yet eaten anything, he himself refused to eat until he made sure that all the soldiers, without exception, had received their portion.

During his tours along the front, Nicholas also visited the wounded in the hospitals. He approached each wounded man separately and conversed with him very warmly and paternally. The feelings of the wounded soldiers were beyond description. In one instance a heavily wounded soldier gazed on the tsar with great astonishment. When he approached and bent down toward him, the soldier stretched out his hand to touch him, to assure himself that he was not dreaming, but that before him really stood his beloved sovereign and commander-in-chief.

On one of his visits to a hospital in Kiev, a very moving scene took place, demonstrating how Nicholas would not give way to low human passions. His sister Grand Duchess Olga Alexandrovna, who volunteered as a nurse at that hospital, recorded this incident, "We had a young… wounded deserter, court-martialed and condemned to death. Two soldiers were guarding him. All of us felt very troubled about him—he looked such a decent boy. The doctor spoke of him to Nicky who at once made for that corner of the ward. I followed him, and I could see the young man was petrified with fear. Nicky put his hand on the boy's shoulder and asked very quietly why he had deserted. The young man stammered that, having run out of ammunition, he had got frightened, turned, and run. We all waited, our breath held, and Nicky told him that he was free. The next moment the lad scrambled out of his bed, fell on the floor, his arms 'round Nicky's knees, and sobbed like a child. I believe all of us were in tears—even those very difficult nurses from Petrograd. And then there fell such a hush in the ward—all the men had their eyes on Nicky and what devotion there was in their look! Just for that moment, all the hard and disturbing elements had gone. … I have cherished the memory all down the years. I never saw Nicky again."[71]

CHAPTER 4

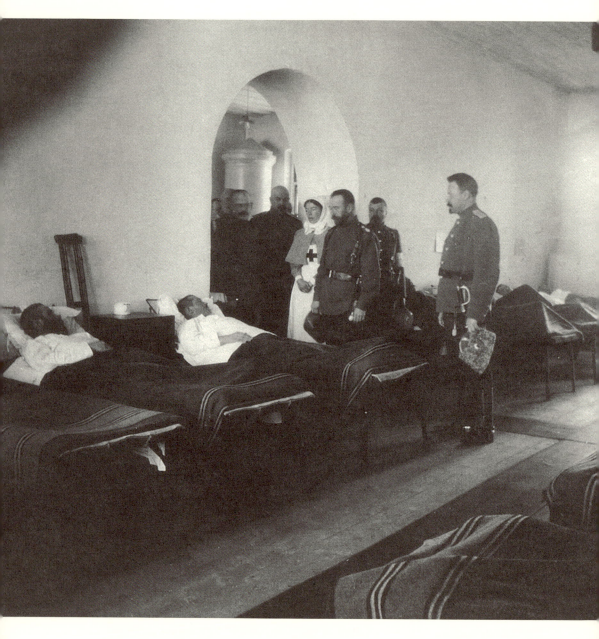

Nicholas visiting the hospital in Kiev,
where his sister Olga, standing next to him, served.

Alexandra also visited the headquarters from time to time with her four daughters. In such cases the family often visited monasteries of the region. Count Dimitry Sheremetev relates such a visit to the Monastery of Saint George in Sevastopol, where he was also present. Nicholas had visited this monastery with his family several times in the past because it was located relatively close to the Livadia Palace where the family withdrew every summer. This time, however, they did not inform the fathers of their impending visit. Their joy at the unexpected presence of the family was obviously great.

Count Sheremetev recounts, "We went into the church, and a moleben began. The harmonious voices of the monks immediately changed in mood: it was as if we had come into a quiet bay after a storm. Everything was so prayerful, penetrating and quiet…. Suddenly beyond the doors of the church, which were very small, there was an unusual sound, loud voices and a strange turmoil—in a word, something that did not correspond to the seriousness of the moment or the usual monastic order. His Majesty turned his head in surprise, knitted his brows in displeasure and sent to find out what had happened and from where this incomprehensible disturbance and whispering to each other was coming from. I went out of the church and learned the following from the monks who were standing there: in the rocks of the cliffs to the right and left there lived two schema-monks whom none of the monks had ever seen, and who were known to be alive only from the fact that the food that was placed for them on the narrow path in the rocks would be taken by some invisible hand by morning. …

"And then an improbable event took place that shook all the monks of the monastery: two elders in the clothing of schema-monks were quietly climbing the steep steps that led upwards from the direction of the sea. They could have known nothing about the arrival of his majesty, for neither the abbot nor the brothers themselves, nobody knew about the visit of his majesty, which had been decided on quite suddenly, at the last minute. That was what caused the disturbance among the brotherhood. I told his majesty about this and saw that this event made an impression on him, but he said nothing and the moleben continued.

"When the moleben had come to an end, his majesty and the empress kissed the Cross, then chatted for a while with the abbot and came out of the church onto the square…. There, at the point where the wooden staircase ended, stood the two old elders. One had a long white beard, while the other had a short beard. When his majesty came up to them, they both silently bowed to the earth before him. His majesty was clearly embarrassed, but he said nothing and slowly bowed to them." [72]

After the terrible events that followed in Russia, Count Sheremetev fled to that region where he had lived for some time. He wrote, "Now, after all that has happened, I wonder: did the schema-monks not foresee with their noetic eyes the destinies of Russia and the royal family, and did they not

From Alexis' visit at the G.H.Q. and the tour of the Eastern Front.

Above: From a visit of the girls at the G.H.Q. in Mogilev.

Below: From a visit of the girls to a village near the G.H.Q.

bow down to the feet of his majesty the Emperor Nicholas II as to the great sufferer of the Russian land?"[73]

During this visit to Sevastopol, the royal couple resisted their desire to visit their beloved Livadia Palace for a little while, even though the physicians recommended it to Alexandra for health reasons. The empress characteristically said that it was "too great a treat to indulge in during the war."[74]

Nicholas' tour with Alexis of the broad Eastern Front, from the Baltic to the Black Sea, was completed on 26 November, 1915 when they returned to Stavka in Mogilev. This inspection of the front turned out to be a great success. Everywhere the presence of the tsar called forth great enthusiasm, not only among the troops, but also among the peasants who thronged the train stations in order to see the sovereign. As for himself, he was equally impressed by this experience, because he saw with his eyes, and was assured of the patriotism and valor of his troops and their faithfulness to their sacred duty.

On 16 December after a cold, and because of repeated sneezing, Alexis began to bleed from the nose, and the hemorrhage became uncontrollable. His temperature began to rise dangerously, and episodes of loss of consciousness occurred, which necessitated his immediate return to Tsarskoe Selo. During his return, his condition worsened dangerously. When he arrived at Tsarskoe Selo, Rasputin was immediately called, who as soon as he arrived at the palace prayed and touched Alexis' face. Soon, the hemorrhage stopped. The personal physicians of the child attempted to explain that the danger had already passed earlier, but Alexandra was convinced that the recovery was yet again the result of Rasputin's prayers. Despite improvement in Alexis' condition, his return to Mogilev was not possible at the time, and so Nicholas returned to Stavka alone on 25 December.

THE EVE OF A NIGHTMARE

In this time of terrible world crisis and danger to the very integrity of Russia, while Nicholas was yet giving himself as a sheep to the slaughter, "the aristocracy of the Russian capital," writes Vyrubova, "was indulging in a reckless orgy of dancing, sports, dining, yes, and wining also in spite of the Emperor's edict against alcohol, spending enormous sums for gowns and jewels, and in every way ignoring the terrible fact that the world was on fire and that civilization was battling for its very life. In the palace the most frugal regime had been adopted. Meals were simple almost to parsimony, no money was spent except for absolute necessities, and the Empress and her daughters spent practically every waking hour working and praying for the soldiers."[75] Furthermore, "more than twenty million pounds sterling of the imperial family's private funds, which had been held in foreign banks, was spent on hospitals and aid for the wounded."[76]

"But society, when it was not otherwise amusing itself, was indulging in a new and madly exciting game of intrigue against the throne. To spread slanders about the Empress, to inflame the simple minds of workmen against the state was the most popular diversion of the aristocracy."[77] In this dishonorable and sinister game, a great ally was found: Germany.

At the end of 1916, Russia's military situation was in very good condition. The Russian command was optimistic about the future. They were building up military reserves, amassing weapons and ammunition. Campaign plans provided for the final defeat of Austria-Hungary, which was losing its power. The next target was Germany. It was time to win great victories.

The Germans were deprived of their great prize, which they believed they already held in their hands, and they began to understand that it was impossible to prevail against Russia with arms. The main and immovable obstacle to attaining their goal was clearly the person of the tsar. When he took command of the army, Nicholas put an end to the Germans' hopes of signing a cease-fire treaty with Russia. Such a treaty in the long preceding period of Russia's reversals would have contained exceedingly generous terms for Germany. Now Germany recognized that Nicholas would continue the war until his last breath. He was the constant mediating factor between the various factions of the empire, which after the unexpected positive developments of the war, were now united in the person of their monarch. There was now clearly only one solution for Germany: the neutralization of Nicholas.

What Germany was not able to accomplish with arms, she hoped to achieve by another method: propaganda and deception. Only by inner division could they hope to neutralize Russia. They began to put in motion their intense underground plots to erode the authority of the monarch and to bring about the downfall of the Tsar. Unfortunately, to achieve their goal, the German propaganda machine, which had strong support within Russia itself, found the Achilles' heel of their victim: Empress Alexandra.

An underground campaign of slander against Alexandra was put into operation. The plan had been drafted with great dexterity and it very quickly brought about significant results. Taking advantage of the empress' German origin, they began to disseminate rumors that she was betraying Russia. This method of undermining her found fertile ground in circles that would never had given credence to such theories earlier. There were no constraints to the slander. Gilliard was eyewitness to one such incident. Once at the home of some friends, he met a young officer who was a supporter of the sovereigns. With obvious displeasure this officer said that when he was in the hospital at the end of 1915, at the command of the empress, gifts and money were distributed to the German prisoners and wounded officers, while those that were sent by her did not even visit the Russian wounded! Gilliard, stunned by this incident, decided to investigate this, and found that the event had indeed happened in the hospital. However, it was not possible to ascertain which individual had presented the forged signatures by which he persuaded the authorities that he had an officially approved mission from the Empress. "Pure chance," said Gilliard, "had brought me into contact with one of the many provocations organised by German spies with German money."[78]

Alexandra's position became even more vulnerable because of her connection with Rasputin. For some time Rasputin had disappeared from life at the palace. Russia's dramatic setbacks in the war from May through September of 1915, which convinced Nicholas to assume command of the army, brought Rasputin back into the foreground. Before this period, Alexandra's involvement in political matters was sporadic and perfunctory. Now, however, with Nicholas' absence at the front, she was obligated to assume an important part of the responsibilities in this sector. It was then that Rasputin reappeared.

Alexandra believed that the word of Rasputin was the word of God. And during these critical moments, when she was called to play an important political role in Russia, in a few instances she trusted his opinion on important state matters, especially with regard to which person should be appointed in a certain significant position.

Alexandra, of course, had to receive Nicholas' approval for every important decision. In her letters to Nicholas during this period she repeatedly submitted the judgement of Rasputin for these matters as God-enlightened and as such insisted on the adoption of his recommendations. Nicholas, however, was not a man who yielded to any suggestions if he himself were not convinced of the rightness of the actions. In one of his letters to Alexandra about this matter he writes very characteristically: "Our Friend's [Rasputin's] ideas about men are sometimes queer, as you know—so one must be careful especially in nominations of high people."[79] It is certain, then, that under no circumstance did Nicholas yield to erroneous suggestions, except in those cases where he himself had a mistaken understanding of the facts.

AN ORTHODOX VIEW

The Orthodox Church has never claimed infallibility for any of her saints. On the contrary, sanctity, according to Orthodox doctrine, is a dynamic process, in the course of which those who struggle spiritually do fall repeatedly, only to rise to their feet time and again and continue their journey in repentance and humility. This humility is acquired through the very realization of their human weaknesses, which is then transformed into unfailing trust in God's will, a spiritual property of the most noble spirits, "which is in the sight of God of great price."[80] This is exactly what the Royal Martyrs Nicholas and Alexandra achieved in their own lives.

Nevertheless, this unique spiritual virtue that they had acquired was wrongfully viewed as blind religious fatalism by those unable to understand the true essence of the Orthodox faith. The Royal Martyrs surrendered themselves and their whole lives to the will of God, even unto death, in the most spiritually perfect degree and thus, regardless of their human errors, unavoidable for all created beings, they reached the level of the faith that overcomes death and renders its bearers living vessels of the grace of God in eternity—in a word: saints.

The unfortunate fact for the royal couple and for Russia, however, is that every decision in this period was doomed from the beginning by the general outcry which German propaganda called forth with the assistance of the revolutionary movement in Russia. The collapse of Russia now hung by a thread. It was simply a matter of time before it became reality. The enemies of the sovereign kept constant watch and struck relentlessly at every opportunity.

The human errors of Nicholas and Alexandra in any other epoch would not have had any consequence whatsoever, nor perhaps would they have been known to history. However, from the perspective of Russia's inescapable tragedy, they were used as material to slander them and to besmirch their names in the pettiest ways. In themselves and from the beginning, these slanders constituted the brightest crowns upon their heads, as Saint Seraphim of Sarov would soon reveal in a wondrous vision.

Furthermore, only three months before the royal family's great trial would begin, God desired to inform Alexandra of the impending path of martyrdom. She herself describes the fact in a letter to Nicholas on 12/25 December 1916, after her visit to Novgorod:

> Then [we went] to the Dessiatinni monastery,[81]—relics of St. Barbara are kept there. Sat a moment at the Abbess' room and then I asked to be taken to the eldress Maria Mikhailovna (Zhevakov told me about her) and we went to her on foot through the wet snow. She lay in bed in a small dark room, so they brought a candle for us to see each other. She is 107, wears irons (now they lay near her)—generally always works, goes about, sews for the convicts and soldiers without spectacles—never washes. And of course no smell, or feeling of dirt, scraggy grey hair standing out, a sweet fine, oval face with lovely young, shining eyes and sweet smile. She blessed us and kissed us. To you she sends the apple (please eat it)—said the war would soon be over [the following words are in Russian:]—'tell him that we are satisfied.' To me she said, 'and you the beautiful one—don't fear the

CHAPTER 4

heavy cross' (several times)—'for your coming to visit us, two churches will be built in Russia' (said it twice) 'don't forget us, come again.'[82]

As Alexandra entered the dark cell, the holy eldress said yet something more, which Alexandra did not hear, or did not understand, because the eldress spoke in a particularly old Russian dialect. Anna Vyrubova, however, and all that were present, heard it and were uneasy. The eldress said, then, "Here comes the martyred Empress, Alexandra Feodorovna."[83]

'IN THE NEW YEAR MAY THE CLOUDS DISPERSE'

German propaganda continually gained ground. Exploiting the tragedy of the war, the numberless deaths, the hardships, the fatigue, the economic crisis, and the increasing hunger, it frantically sowed the seeds of revolution. Erich Ludendorff, the German Deputy Chief of Staff, wrote, "How often had I not hoped for a revolution in Russia in order that our military burden might be alleviated! But my desire had been merely a castle in the air. [When it had finally come about] I felt as though a weight had been removed from my chest."[84] However, what the national "hero"—and later great collaborator of Hitler—"did not mention, and for good reason, was the untiring efforts Germany had made to produce this revolution which had broken out so unexpectedly."[85]

Pierre Gilliard wonders, "How is it that in Russia no one realised what everyone in Germany knew—that a revolution would inevitably deliver up the country to its enemies?" And he himself gives the answer: "The Germans were the only people in Europe who knew Russia. Their knowledge of it was fuller and more exact than that of the Russians themselves. ... They knew that with the fall of the Czar Russia would be at their mercy. They stopped at nothing to procure his fall. ... In the universal blindness which was the result of party passion, men did not realise that, in spite of all, a Czar pledged to the cause of victory was an immense moral asset for the Russian people. They did not see that a Czar who was what he was popularly supposed to be could alone lead the country to victory and save it from bondage to Germany."[86]

Despite Nicholas' inclination to cooperate with the Duma and to grant further freedoms, under the new pressures that occurred, he remained uncompromising. While the terrible war was in progress, he considered the time to be completely inappropriate and unsafe for reforms. But apart from the reality of the war, Nicholas hesitated to make liberal concessions at that time because the circumstances did not allow him to have a clear picture of the condition that prevailed in his country. He himself, commander-in-chief of the Russian troops, was constantly at the front, far from domestic developments. He considered that his presence among the troops was acutely more necessary for the salvation of his country in the present phase. As for the scale and seriousness of the domestic turmoil, he did not have precise information, either because his ministers intentionally hid them from him, or he himself did not trust the persons that dominated the political stage at that time. Inevitably, given these conditions, the general dissatisfaction took on dangerous dimensions.

Rumors of Rasputin's involvement in the country's political affairs constituted particularly inflammatory material for the pro-revolutionary flames that had already been ignited. At that time, while Rasputin was in his own country, Siberia, he made a great mistake in returning to the capital. This revived the slanderous chorus against Alexandra with fatal effect. Alexandra herself already understood that Rasputin's presence in the capital was very dangerous.

Lili Dehn remembers the characteristic words of the empress when they met on one of those days:

"'I know all, Lili,' she said. 'Why does Gregory stop in Petrograd? The Emperor doesn't wish it. I don't. And yet we can't possibly discard him—he's done no wrong. Oh, why won't he see his folly?'

'I'll do all in my power, Madame, to make him do so,' I replied. My heart overflowed with love for the Empress, she seemed so utterly broken, so tragically sad.

'I've already reproached Anna [Vyrubova] for not helping me in the matter.'"[87]

But certain others took matters into their own hands, whose deed caused great sorrow to the royal family. On 30 December, in hopes of giving a new turn of events and to secure the position of the sovereign, Grand Duke Demetrius Pavlovich and Prince Felix Yusupov assassinated Gregory Rasputin. This event evoked great enthusiasm in all of Saint Petersburg. All those who remained faithful to the tsar hoped that the end of Rasputin would also put an end to the storm that threatened to destroy the autocracy.

Shortly before the assassination, Elisabeth made her final and most serious attempt to persuade her sister and Nicholas to cut their ties with Rasputin. For this purpose, on 13 December she arrived from Moscow at Tsarskoe Selo. The conversation on this matter took place only between her and Alexandra, who sought from her sister not to trouble Nicholas with the matter of Rasputin in such a time so burdensome for him. However, Alexandra's stance regarding Rasputin remained as fixed as before. So the following day Elisabeth departed for Moscow without result.[88] This was the last time she would see Nicholas, Alexandra and the children. Her own martyrdom would follow one day after the martyric death of the family.[89]

When, at last, Elisabeth was informed of Rasputin's assassination, she wrote the following letter to Nicholas on 29 December, 1916/11 January 1917:

CHAPTER 4

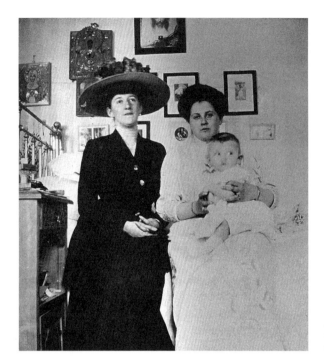

Lili Dehn
and Anna Vyrubova.

St Joan of Arc's † words[90]
"When I am vexed that faith is not readily placed in what I wish to say in God's name, I retire alone and pray to God. I complain to Him that those whom I address do not believe me more readily and my prayer ended. I hear a voice which says to me: 'Daughter of God! Go on! Go on! I will be thy Help: Go on!,' and when I hear this Voice, I have great joy. I would I could always hear it thus."

Reading these saintly words which uphold courage, I allow myself humbly to address a few words still in the old year to you dearest Nicky. I can't understand your silence, the silence you all my dear ones show me. When I wrote, truly, strongly, you with indulgence answered you received my letter. Maybe you found me too bold and so did not mention anything when I saw you, but I have never lied to you; perhaps have been at times rough, but always straightforward and it seems to me cowardly not to say what one knows and feels for fear of personal misunderstanding and suffering. I spoke with Alix all my fears, my anguish with which my heart was overwhelmed. Big waves seemed to be rushing over us all and in despair I flew to you. I love so truly to serve you that all classes from the lowest to the highest, even out at the war are at their wits' end. She [Alix] told me not to talk to you, as I had written, and I left with the feeling will we ever meet as now? What dreams may come to pass; what sufferings are in store.

[When I] Arrived here my interior anguish grew and I went to the beautiful night and morning service at St. Serge and near his relics prayed for all, all, that the black clouds might be lifted and you see clearly, and then I left for Saroff and Diveef [Sarov and Diveyevo Monasteries]. Ten days daily prayer, always for you all, for your army, country, ministers, for the sick at heart and body; and the name of that unhappy man [Rasputin] was on the list, that God might enlighten him. [When I] Arrived here, [I heard] the news Felix had killed him, my little Felix I knew as a child, who all his life feared to kill an animal, who did not wish to become military, so as never have the occasion to shed blood and I imagined what he must have gone through to do this act and how moved by patriotism he decided to save his Sovereign and country from what all were suffering. I telegraphed to Dimitri not knowing where the boy was, but got no answer and since then all is in a kind of silence. I don't want to know details; so many one says are mixed up. All have been sent off into different directions, thank God it was done so.

Crime remains crime, but this one, being of a special kind, can be counted as a duel and is considered a patriotic act and for those deeds the law I think is attenuating. Maybe nobody has had the courage to tell you how in the streets of the towns etc. people kissed like at Easter night, sang the [Imperial] hymn in the theaters etc., all moved by one feeling [that] 'at last the black wall between us and our Emperor is removed; at last we will see, hear, feel him as he is,' and a wave of pitying love for you moved all hearts. God grant you may know of this love and feel it and not miss this great moment as the storm is still and thunder rolls afar.

Oh, if you knew how all pray to God with tears of sorrow that God may enlighten you. Oh, Nicky dear, see the things as they are; oh, believe me feeble, little, humble, but true subject of yours that I am saying the truth. Oh, may Saint Seraphim go and tell you His holy words and guide you for the welfare of your country, Church and home. Your heart must be so heavy in spite of your deep faith in God, yet your heart must ache and maybe a doubt of the truth of the position knocks at the door of your brain; don't shut that door, open it deary and let bright wisdom from above enter for the welfare of all. ...

May in the new year 1917 the clouds be lifted, [may] the sun shine on Russia victorious in the interior and [in the] exterior bring a glorious peace to you our beloved Sovereign and all, all your subjects, of which I am one.

God bless you.
God help you.
Your faithful Sister Ella
Dec 29, 1916.[91]

CHAPTER 4

The hope that the death of Rasputin would alleviate the situation quickly proved false. The joy that was manifested was premature. The flame of revolution had already spread terribly. After the assassination of Rasputin, the police began to receive information of a threatened assassination attempt on Alexandra.

One day the Minister of the Interior, Alexander Protopopov called on the empress and recommended that she not receive anyone in audience because her life was in danger. At that moment Lili Dehn arrived and Alexandra informed her that Protopopov had warned her. Lili seeing the serenity with which Alexandra heard the news, exclaimed:

"'Oh, Madame, you don't seem afraid to die. I always dread death—I'm a horrible coward.' The Empress looked at me in astonishment.

'Surely, Lili, you are not really afraid to die?'

'Yes, Madame, I am.'

'I cannot understand anyone being afraid to die,' she said, quietly. 'I have always looked upon Death as such a friend, such a rest. You mustn't be afraid to die, Lili.'"[92]

'THE CZAR HIMSELF MUST BE REMOVED'

First week of March 1917. On the streets of Saint Petersburg, a general unease prevails. The transfer of capitals to the defense industry had its effect on the whole country's economy. Workers whose factories closed due to the lack of coal circulate on the streets, awaiting what might happen. Soldiers crowded in smoky barracks listen to the ceaseless speeches of the orators of revolution.

A few days earlier, 27 February, 1917, at a session of the Duma, Kerensky, the leader of the moderate socialists and a powerful speaker, called for ignoring not only the government but also the tsar: "To prevent a catastrophe, the Czar himself must be removed—by terrorist methods, if there is no other way. If you will not listen to the voice of warning now, you will find yourself face to face with facts —not warnings. Look up at the distant flashes that are lighting the skies of Russia!"[93]

Lenin, exiled in Switzerland, languished in the apartment of a shoemaker in Zurich. Ironically neither plans nor hopes for a revolution existed in that winter of 1917. Defeated, hopeless, speaking to a team of Swiss workers in January, he proclaimed with bitterness, "We older men may not live to see the decisive battles of the approaching revolution [in Europe]."[94]

For the past two months, Nicholas was at Tsarskoe Selo with his family. The general unease troubled him, but he could in no wise foresee what was about to come. Moreover, neither could the enthusiasts of revolution themselves imagine what stage the events could reach. Furthermore, that winter was very important for the allied powers, who were generally regrouping and reorganizing, especially the Russian armies, planning for a very great offensive in the coming spring.

Despite all this, Nicholas was hesitant to depart. He was planning to remain until things settled down somewhat in the capital. At last, however, he received an extremely urgent telegram from Alekseyev and had to leave, intending to return after eight days. Baroness Buxhoeveden was present when the emperor informed Alexandra about Alekseyev's telegram, saying, "General Alexeieff insists on my coming. I cannot really imagine what can have happened to make my presence at Headquarters so urgently necessary now. I shall have to go and see myself. I am determined to stay only a week at the utmost, for I must be here."[95] On 8 March, he departed for Stavka at Mogilev. Baroness Buxhoeveden rightly wondered, "Was it a plot?"[96] The answer was: yes, it was a plot.

By the end of 1916, rumors about a conspiracy led by Alexander Guchkov, one of the founders of the Progressive Bloc and Chairman of the Third Duma, began to reach the emperor. Russian historian, publicist, and politician Sergei P. Melgunov, wrote that the plan was to capture the imperial train on the road between Stavka and Tsarskoe Selo; announce both a coup and those who will lead the government, transferring the power to Alexei, under a regency of Grand Duke Michael Alexandrovich until his majority.[97] At the end of 1916, Prince Vladimir A. Obolensky asked Guchkov about the rumors of a forthcoming coup. Obolensky wrote, "Guchkov began to relate to me all the details of the conspiracy and to name its main participants.... I realized I had fallen into the very nest of the conspiracy. The Chairman of the Duma, Rodzianko, Guchkov and Alexeev were at the head of it. Others such as General Ruzsky and even A. A. Stolypin, brother of Peter Arkadievitch Stolypin, took part in it."[98]

In early 1917, N. N. Tikhanovich-Savitsky, a member of the Union of the Russian People from Astrakhan, obtained an audience with Empress Alexandra Feodorovna through Vyrubova, in which he assured her that he had irrefutable evidence of the "dangerous propaganda being conducted by the unions of Zemstvos and cities, with the help of Guchkov and Rodzianko and others, to overthrow the sovereign from the throne."[99]

While the tsar was certainly aware of the subversive activities of the opposition, he was not aware of the readiness of the military to support a coup against him. He understood that any repressive preventive actions against the opposition, without radical changes at the front, would cause such a wave of indignation that they could lead to serious upheavals, unacceptable during a time of war. Believing the army was loyal to him, the tsar thought a coup d'état impossible. Indeed, looking forward to victories in a spring offensive and a victorious 1917, it was believed this would change the balance of forces in the country and the opposition could be crushed effortlessly.

CHAPTER 4

The fact that the conspirators were in a hurry with the coup and understood that successful actions on the front would make it impossible, speak for themselves. Pavel Milyukov, the founder and leader of the Constitutional Democratic party, said that new successes at the front "would immediately stop all hints of discontent."[100] Tereshchenko and General Krymov[101] were in a hurry with a coup, saying that otherwise it would be too late. After the victory, they would inevitably have to answer for their criminal intentions and actions. Therefore, it was necessary for them to do everything to win over the generals to their side, and with it to accomplish a coup d'état.

Meanwhile, Nicholas was completely confident in the loyalty of the army, convinced that the Duma members' conspiratorial plans were doomed, as he, through the army, would be able to completely control the situation. This confidence of Nicholas was the reason for the apparent calm with which the emperor received news of various conspiracies. Unfortunately, the military elite had long been at one with the conspirators. Professor A. F. Smirnov writes: "In an alarming military situation, the Progressive Bloc and the forces behind it were determined to take over the administration of the country, displacing or removing the emperor. They were not interested in reforms, but in power."[102]

Thus, by the end of 1916, a conspiracy was organized against Nicholas II, the initiator of which was the Progressive Bloc and the upper bourgeoisie.

The events that broke out in Petrograd in February 1917 came as no surprise for the top generals, nor for the Ministry of the Interior. General Alekseyev and a number of generals at Stavka were actively involved in political intrigues in early 1916, when they began to be influenced by the liberal-public circles. But as General Denikin[103] wrote, connections between the Duma and the officers went back to the re-establishment of the fleet and reorganization of the army following the Russo-Japanese War.[104] Guchkov understood very well the need to have control over the army in order to achieve a successful coup, stating before World War I that the reason the 1905 revolution had failed was due to the fact the army was for the sovereign. Following the start of the war, communication between Duma members and the generals increased as Guchkov and others endeavored to win over the generals.

On February 14, 1916, Guchkov wrote a letter to Alekseyev, in which he asked to receive his assistant, A. I. Konovalov, in order to "make a report on all aspects of the activities of the Central Military Industrial Committee and get your instructions, which are important to the committee."[105] Thus Guchkov proposed the possibility of contact with Alekseyev, and Alekseyev accepted the bait. Now the conspirators could begin to quietly lead General Alekseyev to the actions they needed. The correspondence begins first between Alekseyev and Rodzianko, in which Alekseyev complains that everything is bad in the army, and then it continued between Alekseyev and Guchkov.

The empress found out about this correspondence and wrote to the Tsar in G.H.Q. on September 18, 1916: "Now a correspondence between Alekseyev and this brute Guchkov is going on and he [Guchkov] feeds him [Alekseyev] with vile things."[106] For the sovereign, this came as a complete surprise. He wrote in reply: "How do you know that Guchkov is in correspondence with Alekseyev? I never never heard about it before."[107] When summoned to the tsar, Alekseyev denied any such thing! Guchkov's main goal was to convince Alekseyev of the need for a "responsible ministry," without which the country would completely collapse, thereby drawing him into his conspiracy against the tsar. In his letters, Guchkov strongly denounced the head of the Imperial Government, B. V. Stürmer, and accused him of treason. The goal was to convince Alekseyev of the need to replace the "traitor" and "protégé of Rasputin" with a "progressive patriot."

Communication between Guchkov and Alekseyev did not stop while Alekseyev was in the Crimea. General Denikin wrote that Duma representatives came to Sevastopol to the sick Alekseyev, frankly stating that a coup was brewing and that they could not take into account what impression a revolution would produce at the front. They asked for advice. Alekseyev pointed out the inadmissibility of any kind of state upheaval during the war, and asked in the name of preserving the army not to take this step. The representatives left, promising to take measures to prevent a coup d'état being prepared.[108] However, if Alekseyev so categorically refused to conduct any talk of a coup, why then did he not immediately inform Nicholas about the imminent danger? Despite the fact that Ruzsky and Brusilov knew of the chief of staff's fluctuating nature, Alekseyev enjoyed great prestige among them. Agreeing to such a risky step as participating in a coup, directed against the tsar without Alekseyev's consent, even if silent, would mean putting themselves in an extremely delicate situation.

In January 1917, a meeting took place between Duma members, led by Rodzianko, and General Krymov, a confidant of Alekseyev. Rodzianko writes that the main purpose of this meeting was Krymov's request "to give him the opportunity, unofficially, to highlight to the Duma the catastrophic situation of the army." However, the conversation that led Krymov was not only about this. "The mood in the army is such that everyone will be glad to welcome news of a coup. A coup is inevitable and one feels it at the front. If you decide on this extreme measure, we will support you. Obviously, there are no other means. Everything has been tried both by you and by many others, but the harmful influence of his wife is stronger than honest words spoken to the tsar. There is no time to lose." Krymov fell silent, and for a few minutes everyone sat confused and dejected. Shingaryov,[109] a member of the Duma, was the first to break the silence: "The General is right—a coup is necessary.... But who will decide on it?" Noisy disputes arose. Brusilov's words were immediately quoted: "If I have to choose between the tsar and Russia, I will follow Russia."[110]

CHAPTER 4

The top brass of the army was pushing Rodzianko and the others to carry out a coup, assuring the latter that they could count on it. Tereshchenko himself speaks of the role of General Krymov: "I cannot fail to recall the last months before the revolution, when General Krymov turned out to be the only general who, out of great love for his homeland, was not afraid to join the ranks of that small group of people who decided to make a coup d'état. General Krymov repeatedly came to St Petersburg and tried to convince the doubters that he could not wait any longer. He and his friends were aware that if they did not take over the leadership of the palace coup, the masses would do it, and they understood perfectly well what consequences and what disastrous anarchy this could threaten."[111]

Another key player was General A. A. Manikovsky who had charge of many plants in Petrograd, including the largest and most revolutionary factory. Manikovsky was the head of the Main Artillery Directorate, and it is interesting to note that while there was a shortage of shells at the front, there were 30 million projectiles stockpiled in the warehouses. General Manikovsky was on good terms with the leaders of the military-industrial committees, in which the main role was played by the people of Guchkov. He was well aware of the mood among the workers and reported to the sovereign about it. Nicholas wrote to Alexandra on 5 November, 1916: "Yesterday I received that good general Manikovsky, the head of the artillery department and he told me many things concerning the workmen and the frightful propaganda among them with the heaps of money being distributed among them to make strikes and that on the other side no resistance is offered against this, the police does nothing and nobody seems to care what will happen! The ministers are as weak as usual—and that is the result."[112]

In this case, Nicholas was quite misled by Manikovsky. Knowing quite well who was distributing leaflets and calling for strikes, Manikovsky diverted the tsar's suspicions from the conspirators to the helplessness of the ministers. Another general, Mikhail D. Bonch-Bruyevich, was close not only with Guchkov, but his own brother Vladimir D. Bonch-Bruyevich had good contacts with the Bolshevik leadership and had been part of the revolutionary Bolshevik underground since the end of the nineteenth century.

The conspirators also approached Grand Duke Nicholas Nikolaevich with a proposal similar to the one that was given to Alekseyev. The grand duke, offended by his removal from commanding the army, helped in every way. In particular, he targeted the empress, a convenient target, who had been subjected to being called a "German" and a "spy," stories picked up by leftist and liberal deputies of the Duma, and also Rasputin being a "libertine," a "drunkard," and also a "spy." There was even the story about Rasputin asking to come to G.H.Q., with the Grand Duke's response being, "Come, and I will hang you." But had such an incident even happened?

People were ready to believe anything that was said, in particular that the empress was a staunch supporter of Germany.

Prince Lvov, through his representative Khatisov, proposed to the grand duke that he should take the Russian throne.[113] "On 9 December," writes Melgunov, "Lvov developed a plan for a palace coup in front of the assembly, in order to overthrow Nicholas II and replace the incapable monarch with the Grand Duke Nicholas Nikolaevich. The accession of Nicholas Nikolaevich was to be accompanied by the formation of a responsible ministry."[114] Melgunov writes: "Khatisov was authorized to enter into negotiations with Nicholas Nikolaevich and acquaint him with the project of a palace coup and find out how the grand duke would react to this project and whether it would be possible to count on his assistance. In case of agreement, Khatisov would have sent a conditional telegram: 'The hospital is open, come.' When I asked how the coup was actually supposed to be, Khatisov explained that Nicholas Nikolaevich had to establish himself in the Caucasus and declare himself ruler and tsar."[115]

The plot seems fanciful, in that even if the grand duke declared himself tsar in the Caucasus, the tsar at Stavka would order the arrest of the grand duke as a rebel. If some troops were loyal to the grand duke, then there would be civil war leading Russia towards military defeat, forcing the tsar to declare a dictatorship, arrest the opposition and dissolve the Duma. However, according to Khatisov, Lvov said that he had a statement from General Manikovsky that the army would support the coup. It was supposed to arrest the tsar and take him into exile, and imprison the empress in a convent. The coup would be carried out by guards under the command of the grand duke, with the ascension of Grand Duke Nicholas being a change of dynasty rather than a regency.[116]

The key was that the army would support the coup: these plots could only be realized if the tsar was unable to rely on the support of his army, that the army was under the control of generals supporting the coup.

Melgunov writes that in Tbilisi, at New Year 1917, Khatisov outlined Lvov's proposal to Grand Duke Nicholas, whose only objection was that it was not clear if the people's monarchist sentiments would be offended by the violent overthrow of the tsar, and how the army would react in the event that Nicholas II was overthrown. He asked for two days to think it over. After two days, meeting with Khatisov again, the grand duke refused to participate in the conspiracy, since the army was for the monarchy in the opinion of General Yanushkevich.[117]

However, later, when news reached the Caucasus about the February coup and the sovereign's abdication, Duke Sergei G. Leuchtenberg, stepson of Grand Duke Nikolai Nikolaevich, was urgently sent to Batum on a special destroyer for a meeting with Nicholas Nikolaevich. This mission was secret and so urgent that the commander of the destroyer was told to "burn the boilers, and deliver the grand duke at full speed to the Batum train."[118] Then it was rumored among the Baltic Fleet and some military units that the Black

Sea Fleet were to go to Batum and thence across the coast, to demonstrate in favor of Nicholas Nikolaevich, delivering him through Odessa to the Romanian front and declare him emperor, and the Duke Leichtenberg heir.[119]

Any such plans of the grand duke were not supported by Alekseyev and his associates, as any return of Nicholas Nikolaevich would have meant the return of his generals, such as Danilov and Yanushkevich, which was completely undesirable for Alekseyev's plans. For his part, Tsar Nicholas could not imagine that the generals he had worked with for two years, preparing strategic operations and victory, could betray him, and he had no idea of the extent of the communication between Guchkov's group and his generals. "In the middle of February," wrote the Interior Minister Protopopov, "the tsar, with displeasure, informed me that he had ordered V. I. Gurko[120] to send the Ulansky regiment and Cossacks to Petrograd, but Gurko did not send the indicated units, but commanded others, including sailors of the Guards crew (sailors who were considered revolutionary-minded)."[121]

In mid-February 1917, General-Adjutant Alekseyev hurriedly returned to General Headquarters, ostensibly to directly administer the preparations for the upcoming summer offensive, despite a summer offensive being at least three months away. Once in Mogilev, Alekseyev immediately began to insist that Nicholas return to Stavka. The sovereign left for headquarters not knowing exactly what it was that required his immediate attention, hoping to be able to return to Petrograd quickly. Empress Alexandra's friend, Lily Dehn, recalled: "One evening before dinner my aunt (who was always furious at the rumours current about the Empress) phoned me to come to her house at once. I found her in an excessively agitated condition. 'It's awful what people are saying, Lili,' she cried. 'And I must tell you—you must warn the Empress.' In somewhat calmer tones my aunt continued: 'Yesterday I was at the Kotzebue's. Many officers were present, and it was openly asserted that His Majesty will never return from G.H.Q.'"[122]

So, the adjutant generals set up a trap for the emperor. It remained only to lure him there. Colonel Mordvinov wrote: "On Tuesday, February 21, 1917, in the evening ... I heard from Count Fredericks, that according to the highest command, I was assigned to accompany the Sovereign on his journey to GHQ.... The departure of the imperial train from Tsarskoe Selo was scheduled at about three in the afternoon, Wednesday, 22 February. This notification was unexpected for me. The day before I had just returned from Tsarskoe Selo from my duty at the military-field office, and then there was still no talk about leaving. The internal political situation was particularly stormy and difficult in those days, which is why the sovereign spent all the Christmas holidays, all of January and most of February at Tsarskoe Selo and was slow to leave for GHQ."[123]

Vladimir Voeikov, the Commandant of the Guard at Tsarskoe Selo, testified: "At 5 o'clock there was cinema in the Round Hall of the Alexander Palace.... When the session ended, I escorted the sovereign into his office. Along the way, His Majesty addressed me with the words: 'Voeikov, I have decided to go to Stavka on Wednesday.' I knew that the tsar had had the intention to go, but I thought that this moment was not suitable for his departure, and therefore I asked why he had made the decision now, when everything was calm on the front, when, according to my information, there is little peace [in Petrograd] and his presence in Petrograd would be very important. The sovereign replied to this that the other day General Alekseyev returned from the Crimea, and wanted to see him and talk about some issues regarding the local situation."[124]

Voeikov asked Protopopov, Minister of the Interior, about the state of the capital and whether it was an appropriate time for the emperor to go to Stavka. He visited the palace on Tuesday and assured Voeikov that all was fine, but told those around him that he begged the empress to influence the emperor into not going. The emperor, on the other hand, confirmed to Voeikov that Protopopov had seen no reason to consider his departure as untimely, playing along, voluntarily or involuntarily, with those who at any cost wanted the emperor to leave Petersburg.

A TREASONOUS COUNTDOWN
THE MYTH OF THE "BREAD REVOLUTION"

One question arises. If the upheavals that occurred in the capital during February 1917 were nothing more than a spontaneous burst of discontent by the "hungry" people, how did the conspirators foresee it and get ready to take advantage of it? Why did they want the emperor to leave Petersburg at any cost at that very moment? The answer is: the demonstrations were not at all spontaneous, but very well organized indeed.

Regardless of Guchkov's assurances that he and his associates had abandoned riot organizations to carry out a coup, the truth was that both Guchkov and the Progressive Bloc not only did not abandon the organization of workers' speeches, but, on the contrary, pinned great hopes on them. However, Guchkov was not able to bring the workers to the streets himself. This assistance was rendered to him in the person of the so-called Working Group of the Central Military Industrial Committee.

Nevertheless, evidence points to Alexander Kerensky as being the key catalyst behind the February disturbances in St Petersburg. Kerensky was very familiar with the many different layers of revolutionary and opposition movements. As early as 1915, the Okhrana mentioned Kerensky as a main leader of the revolutionary underground, "recently beginning to play a dominant role"[125] as well as being a leader of the Socialist-Revolutionary Party. He also played a leading role in the Petrograd Bolshevik organizations. Kerensky was one of the loudest enemies of the monarchy and Nicholas II, and travelled across Russia meeting with revolutionaries, teaching that a "criminal and inept government cannot fight an external enemy,"[126] victory only being possible after the establishment of a Constituent Assembly.

In January 1917, Kerensky stated that, "We need a revolution, even if it means defeat at the front."[127] And, as it has already been mentioned, at the meeting of the State Duma on 14/27 February, 1917, he even declared the need to eliminate the tsar, without stopping at the use of terrorist acts of violence, if there was no other way. Kerensky envisioned the complete destruction of the monarchy, not a replacement of the autocracy with a constitutional monarchy. On this same day, the Bolsheviks called on the workers of St Petersburg to protest against the State Duma, the failure of which reassured the authorities that the opposition and revolutionaries were not capable of a powerful performance.

The following day, however, Kerensky began an aggressive campaign in the Duma, calling for the overthrow of the monarchy, signalling to the revolutionary forces that it is "now or never."[128] So the protagonist of the revolution at the start of the unrest in Petrograd was Kerensky rather than the Progressive Bloc. In this way, the workers and residents of St Petersburg did not go out with slogans of protecting the Duma or of revolution, but rather under the banner of hunger, with the revolutionary underground directed by Kerensky.

Using the slogan "bread" was a strong move by the conspirators, since marching with revolutionary slogans would have meant immediate dispersal by troops. However, it was a much more difficult matter to require troops to disperse "hungry" women and children asking for bread.

The Social Democrats ensured a supply of flour to the garrison soldiers to prevent their taking part in a suppression of the insurrection. Social Democrat B. V. Avilov recalled that in those eventful February days they had several thousand pounds of bread and scores of wagon-cars worth of flour.[129]

The Bolsheviks and Kerensky cooperated for the organisation of a strike by the Putilov Factory, which was to be the catalyst for the events in St Petersburg. On 22 February, a group of workers from the Putilov factory came to Kerensky letting him know a political movement was beginning at the factory, which would have far-reaching consequences.[130] On that same day, the Vyborg district Bolsheviks came out in support of the Putilovites and decided to organise a strike on the 23rd in the Narva and Vyborg districts, in solidarity with the Putilovites.

Historian S. V. Kholyaev writes that the Bolsheviks "at the very least initiated the outpouring of workers into the streets."[131] It should be noted that in February 1917, the Putilov factory was administered by the Chief Artillery Directorate General A. A. Manikovsky, who after the October Revolution joined the Red Army, making its connection with the Bolsheviks in February 1917 something that can be considered almost proved. At the same time, Manikovsky was in very close relations with Guchkov and Kerensky. This all, taken together, suggests joint actions on behalf of Kerensky and the Bolsheviks in the organization of the riots, carried out through an intermediary: General Manikovsky. In this way, Guchkov and Kerensky, in spite of their external difference, shared a general plan for a coup d'état, calling for the overthrow of the throne of Emperor Nicholas II.

Thursday 23 February/8 March. Nicholas is on his way to Stavka. Immediately after his departure, Alexis, Olga, Tatiana and Anna Vyrubova fall into bed with measles, a disease that was very dangerous in those days. The empress, dressed in her white nursing gown, hastens from one patient to another, looking after their care and nursing entirely by herself.

At the same time, in the center of St Petersburg there is a demonstration by women celebrating Women's Day. This procession is joined by factory workers: these are the Bolshevik-supported Putilov workers, whose strike had by now spread to many other factories, reaching a crowd of thirty thousand strikers in the streets. The key slogan is "Bread and Peace." There is more than enough bread in Petersburg, but it is white bread and it costs somewhat more than rye bread. Shipment of rye bread was delayed because of snow blockages on the railroads. There are long lines in front of shops that sell cheaper bread. Someone spreads a rumor about the introduction of "bread cards," which in fact was not planned. Suddenly, the long lines burst. They rush into the bakeries and seize by themselves as much bread as they want. Then follow demonstrations and marches of workers. One detachment of Cossacks from the security forces appear and calls for the crowds to disperse.

Friday 24 February/9 March. Nicholas, now in Mogilev, receives a telegram about some disturbances in the city the previous day, which, however, are not considered important. Hearing that the upheavals are "under control," Nicholas remains calm, not giving any instructions. But the number of demonstrators grows. The Cossacks appear again, but this time they do not warn. Instead they shout, "Don't be afraid, we will not hurt you!" The crowds celebrate. At the same time, provocateurs throw grenades at peaceful people and shout that it was the work of the police. Soldiers from reserve regiments are mutinying, policemen are killed in the streets, marauders are looting. Nicholas is informed that the upheaval in the streets is continuing. But still, the evaluation given is the same: it is nothing to worry about!

"In this last stay of the sovereign at Stavka, there was a lot of strange things going on: terrible things were happening in Petrograd, yet at GHQ there was a serene silence, calmer than usual. Any information that came to the sovereign went through the hands of Alekseyev. Now it is impossible to say to what extent Alekseyev was holding onto information, and to what degree this information from Petrograd was distorted. The fact is that until the 27th [March 12] the sovereign did not have a clear information about what was happening in Petrograd."[132]

CHAPTER 4

At Tsarskoe Selo, Alexandra continues to hurry from room to room caring for the patients. She knows nothing about the disturbances.

Saturday 25 February/10 March. The general strike organized by Kerensky and the Bolsheviks paralyzes all of St Petersburg. The crowds in the streets now appear with red banners and the "Bread and Peace" slogans change to, "Down with the German woman!"—the Empress; "Down with Protopopov!"—the incompetent Minister of the Interior; and, "Down with the War!" Protopopov, however, continues to evade properly informing Nicholas. He gives him the impression that it is just another of the usual disturbances of recent times.

At Tsarskoe Selo, Alexandra and the serving staff learn that in the city clashes came about between the demonstrators and the police. Protopopov informs her that everything is under control.

Sunday 26 February/11 March. In the morning Nicholas is in church for the Divine Liturgy. Suddenly, a terrible pain strikes him in the chest, which lasts fifteen minutes. He writes to Alexandra: "I could hardly stand and my forehead was covered with beads of sweat. I cannot understand what it was, as I had no heart beating, but it came and left me at once, when I knelt before the Virgin's image!"[133] The symptoms obviously reveal a coronary obstruction.

All this time, Rodzianko and the Progressive Bloc behind him, even though they were not the leading figures of the February events, understood well that they could come to power by taking advantage of the unrest caused by Kerensky. They were merely waiting for their chance to creep in. This chance was provided when on the evening of this day, 26 February/11 March, Kerensky's revolution was in danger of defeat. The reason for this outcome was that as soon as the slogans of "Bread and Peace" were replaced with those of "Down with the Autocracy!" the demonstrators did not find the expected support either in the army or among the people.

Indeed, significant chaos did occur in the streets of St Petersburg, mainly due to the authorities' lack of will and the fraternization between the workers and many of the soldiers. Nevertheless, the return of Nicholas to the capital with loyal troops would have easily restored order. It is, thus, quite obvious that from the point of view of the national structure of the Russian Empire, the disturbances in St Petersburg did not represent any great danger.

With Kerensky's coup under the threat of coming to a dead end, Rodzianko realizes that he now has the opportunity that he and the Progressive Bloc were waiting for, and so he reappears on the political scene. In the evening, he meets with Kerensky in the premises of the Duma.

Up to that point, Rodzianko's silencing of events and Protopopov's telegrams distorting them had one goal: to mislead the sovereign, to disorient him, and to enable the revolutionary process to adopt such a large scale that would allow the State Duma to begin blackmailing the tsar, demanding a responsible ministry. Notwithstanding this, Rodzianko's efforts and expectations would also come to a dead end if it were not for another determining factor: the induction in the conspiracy against the tsar of the generals and senior officers of the Supreme Command and the front commanders with their staff officers. This parameter, indeed, proved to be the main reason for the success of the coup. And so, the time now being appropriate, Rodzianko sends to the tsar the following exasperated telegram:

"Your most faithful servant reports to Your Majesty that popular uprisings, having begun in Petrograd, are taking on uncontrollable and threatening dimensions. ... State authority is totally paralyzed and utterly unable to reimpose order. Your Majesty, save Russia.... [T]he ferment has already spread to the army and threatens to grow if a decisive end cannot be put to anarchy and governmental disorder. Your Majesty, urgently summon a person in whom the whole country can have faith and entrust him with the formation of a government that all the people can trust."[134]

Colonel N. I. Artabalevsky[135] writes: "The shooters and all the other military officials decided and approved the slogan with which they opposed the old government: 'Tsar, new government, war to victory.' With this, we went to the State Duma. With difficulty we made our way into the Catherine Hall. Everything was jam-packed with the most disparate public. Rodzianko immediately came to us and delivered a short speech with a call to order, to which they answered: 'Hurray!' and a toast 'to the first citizen of Russia.' Having learned from me the slogan with which we came, he visibly brightened his face. I snuck into the room next to the one in which the Executive Committee of the State Duma was sitting. Then a member of the Duma approached me, tall with a black beard, exquisitely dressed. I could not find out who it was. He told me that Emperor Nicholas II would probably be forced to hand over the throne to his son, Tsesarevich Alexei, and for his juvenile caretaker to be Empress Alexandra Feodorovna, and the regent will be Grand Duke Mikhail Alexandrovich.

"At that moment, Milyukov intervened in the conversation. I did not think that he would make such a repulsive impression on me—a sly, two-faced fox. The eyes that ran around the pince-nez glasses did not inspire me with any confidence. Cunningly looking at me, then around, he was interested to find out from me about the attitude of the shooters towards Grand Duke Mikhail Alexandrovich. I answered him that I did not understand his question. If the sovereign finds it necessary to transfer the throne to another, then our duty is to serve the new sovereign. Miliukov did not answer this, and, smiling unpleasantly, withdrew from me."[136]

It is clear from these memoirs of Artabalevsky that the slogan with which the army took to the streets, "Tsar, new government, war to victory," was similar to the requirements of Rodzianko and the Duma. It was the external monarchism of the latter that deceived the troops, who believed that they were in favor of the tsar and the people against the traitors to the old government. But from the same passage one can see how the Duma opposition, in this case in the person of Milyukov, was ready to change the monarchist slogans that were used to deceive the army when they were no longer needed. Rodzianko, in this case, was used by conspirators in the dark. He overshadowed those oppositionists with a monarchist screen, who sought to overthrow the monarchy as such, and not specifically Nicholas II. With this "monarchism" Rodzianko mislead those who wished for the overthrow of Nicholas II and for a "responsible ministry," but who were against the overthrow of the monarchy. It is this deception that explains the fact that the Generals of the Stavka supported Rodzianko's betrayal of the tsar with such zeal: the preservation of the throne in exchange for a "responsible ministry."

Rodzianko's telegram reaches Nicholas, but it does not convince him. He does not trust Rodzianko's appraisal and instead of concessions he sends a telegram to General Khabalov, commander of the Petrograd Military District, with the following order: "I order an end to the riots in the capital tomorrow, which are unacceptable in this difficult time of war with Germany and Austria. NICHOLAS."[137] However, General Khabalov does not undertake the order of the emperor.

At Tsarskoe Selo, Gilliard is informed of the defection of a part of the guard to the demonstrators. Among them was also the elite Preobrazhensky Regiment. He informs Alexandra, who begins to perceive the imminence of the danger.

Monday 27 February/12 March. In the morning the government of the emperor stands under the sword of Damocles of creeping revolution. During the day there follows the mass defection of the army of the city to the uprising. This is the day in which Nicholas finally begins to realize the seriousness of the situation. At 10:25 AM he orders to allocate an infantry and cavalry brigade from the Northern and Western Fronts, and appoints General Ivanov as the head of the general-adjutants and commander-in-chief of the Petrograd Military District, replacing Lieutenant-General Sergei Khabalov.

Furthermore, the emperor decides to return to Tsarskoe Selo himself. General Alekseyev tries to persuade the tsar not to leave the headquarters, but Nicholas remains firm in his decision. The conspirators understand perfectly well that if the tsar returned to Petrograd, the revolution would be suppressed. At the instigation of Rodzianko, Grand Duke Mikhail Alexandrovich contacts the emperor through the telegraph and conveys to him a proposal to dismiss the current composition of the Council of Ministers and appoint Lvov as the chairman of the new council. At the end of the communication, the grand duke tries to convince the tsar not

MARCH TO THE END

to come to Tsarskoe Selo. The emperor refuses and begins to organize the suppression of the rebellion.[138]

At Tsarskoe Selo, Alexandra is informed of the mass defection of the army to the revolutionaries. She goes up to the room where the sick girls are and beckons her friend Lili Dehn to the next room. "'Lili,' she said, breathlessly, 'it is *very* bad. I have just seen Colonel Grotten, and General Resin, and they report that the Litovsky Regiment has mutinied, murdered the officers, and left barracks: the Volinsky Regiment has followed suit, I can't understand it. I'll never believe in the possibility of Revolution—why, only yesterday, everyone said it was impossible!'"[139]

By evening authority has passed to the Duma. Rodzianko, now president of the Provisional Committee of the State Duma, communicates with the palace and informs the aged Count Benckendorff, Grand Marshal of the Court, that the empress with her family were in danger. Their immediate departure from Tsarskoe Selo is urgent. Benckendorff prefers to communicate first with the tsar to receive his instructions before informing the empress of this. Nicholas instructs him to order a train for his family, but that Alexandra not be informed of the situation until the morning of the following day shortly before Nicholas' arrival.

Alexandra attempts to communicate with Nicholas by telephone, but without success. Nicholas at last informs her that he would be at Tsarskoe Selo at 6:00 in the morning of the 14th of March.

The emperor announces his immediate departure and asks Voeikov to make the preparations. Having fulfilled the order, Voeikov reports to the sovereign that he can go overnight by train, that everything is ready, and that the train could depart for Tsarskoe Selo in a few hours.

Voeikov recalls: "Then I went to General Alekseyev to let him know about the upcoming departure. I found him already in bed. As soon as I informed him about the tsar's decision to go to Tsarskoe Selo straight away, his sly face took on an even more cunning expression, and with a malicious smile, in a sweet voice, he asked me, 'Will there be a whole battalion ahead of the train to clear the way?' Although I never considered General Alekseyev an example of devotion to the tsar, I was stunned by both the essence and the tone of the answer given at such a moment. To my words: 'If you consider it dangerous to go, your direct duty is to tell me about it,' General Alekseyev answered: 'No, I don't know anything.' I asked him again: 'After what I have just heard from you, you must tell me clearly and definitely, do you consider it dangerous for the sovereign to go or not?'—to which General Alekseyev gave the answer that struck me: 'Why? Let the sovereign go... it's nothing.' After these words, I told General Alekseyev that he should go in person and find out the state of affairs from the sovereign. I thought ... he would not have the strength to deceive the tsar himself."[140]

But Voeikov was wrong. Alekseyev calmly watched the train take the emperor to a trap, from which the sovereign could not escape.

CHAPTER 4

Tuesday 28 February/13 March. At 1:00 AM, Nicholas boarded his train. At 2:10 AM he received General Ivanov on his train and gave him his instructions. He wrote in his diary: "I went to bed at 3:15, as I had a long talk with N. I. Ivanov, whom I am dispatching to Petrograd with troops to restore order.... We left Mogilev at 5 o'clock in the morning."[141]

The speakers of the Duma in Petrograd panic at the thought that the train would reach the capital and that they would be answerable for their deeds with all hope of seizing power collapsing. There is only one way out: to prevent the tsar from reaching the capital at any cost.

The task of preventing the tsar from entering Petrograd is entrusted to A. A. Bublikov,[142] who disseminates the false information that the railway track near Luga was cut off by revolutionary forces, and that the path to the capital was cut off. But Bublikov is only a performer. "The real organizers of the chase," writes Brachev, "or more correctly, the blocking of the royal train and its treacherous redirection to Pskov—directly into the hands of the conspirator N. V. Ruzsky—was done by a member of the Supreme Council of the Great East of the Peoples of Russia, N. V. Nekrasov.[143] ... The most striking thing in this story is the amazing synchronicity of the actions of Bublikov and the tsar's inner circle, which managed to change the initial course of his train and turn west to Pskov, where, allegedly, under the command of General Ruzsky, there still remained reliable parts of the Northern Front. Thus, as it turned out, the trap was cleverly arranged by the conspirators, since it was Ruzsky who was just one of the active participants in the coup d'état that was being prepared for April 1917. Of course, the tsar did not know anything of this, and in the evening of 1 March, 1917 his train arrived safely in Pskov."[144]

Meanwhile, Rodzianko, who until this day had considered himself the leader of the insurgents, is gradually being supplanted by more energetic and decisive figures who already demand the tsar's abdication. Rodzianko is in complete confusion and appeals to the military for help.

In the evening, Alekseyev sends to General Ivanov, who had been sent by the sovereign to Petrograd to suppress the insurrection, a telegram of a completely different content: "Private information says that complete peace came to Petrograd on February 28 [March 13]. The troops, having joined the Provisional Government as a whole, are being put in order. The Provisional Government, chaired by Rodzianko, sitting in the State Duma, invited commanders of military units to receive orders to maintain order. The appeal to the population, issued by the Provisional Government, speaks of the inviolability of the monarchical principle in Russia, the need for the grounds for the choice and appointment of the government. They are looking forward to the arrival of His Majesty at Tsarskoe, in order to present him everything stated and a request to accept this wish of the people. If this information is correct, then change your plans, negotiations will lead to peace, in order to avoid the shameful civil strife so desired by our enemy in order to preserve the institutions."[145]

Alekseyev's telegram was absolutely untrue. The city was in complete anarchy. The soldiers dispersed in the barracks, General Khabalov was completely alone in an isolated admiralty. All his actions not only led to nothing, but even more so, emphasized his complete helplessness. No one could read the state of siege declared in Petrograd, printed on posters, because there was no glue and they were scattered around the streets, where they were picked up by the wind and trampled by the crowd in the snow.

In the same evening of February 28/March 13, the generals decide to stop all resistance. The most amazing thing is that there is no one to resist. There are crowds of people, easily dispersed in the presence of troops, there is a helpless and untenable Interim Committee of the State Duma, waiting in fear for the outcome of events, which they had previously desired. But the Executive Committee of the Petrograd Soviet had already appeared, who arbitrarily occupied one of the wings of the Tauride Palace, and increasingly took power from Rodzianko. This committee demanded the overthrow of the monarchy. Therefore, Alekseyev's assertions about the "inviolability of the monarchical principle," which allegedly described the Provisional Government, also do not correspond to reality.

At Tsarskoe Selo, Benckendorff informs Alexandra of Rodzianko's recommendation about their immediate transport and of Nicholas' instructions to order a train for their departure and to meet him. But the task is now considered impossible. After communicating with the capital, the palace staff are informed that it is completely unlikely that the workers of the railway station would return to send the train for the royal family. Furthermore, Alexandra refuses the plan since it is impossible to transport her children, because they are sick. The children remain in bed with high fevers. She prefers to await Nicholas' return and depart together.

At 10:30 AM Alexandra calls Gilliard from Alexis' room and informs him that the capital is officially in the hands of the rebels. She informs him about the formation of a Provisional Government by the Duma, adding that "The Duma has shown itself equal to the occasion. I think it has realized the danger which is threatening the country, but I'm afraid it is too late. A Revolutionary-Socialist Committee has been formed which will not recognize the authority of the Provisional Government."[146] Afterward she informs him of the arrival of the tsar the following morning at six o'clock and of the immediate departure of the family from Tsarskoe Selo. She begs him to make the necessary preparations for Alexis' departure.

In the meanwhile, in Saint Petersburg, a crowd of deserted soldiers climbs on trucks and departs heading toward Tsarskoe Selo. The trucks' crews shout that they are going to capture the German woman and her son to take them to the capital. Alexandra runs to Lili, "Lili," she says, "they say that a hostile crowd of 300,000 persons is marching on the Palace. We shall not be, we *must* not be afraid. Everything is in the hands of God."[147]

CHAPTER 4

The Alexander Palace in Tsarskoe Selo is not completely undefended. There is a total force of 1,500 soldiers who were deployed there in the morning with instructions from Count Benckendorff. At last, at nine o'clock in the evening, a telephone call forewarns them that the rebels are near. Very soon a gunshot is heard. At less than five hundred yards distance from the palace, a gang had executed a guard on watch. The sound of the gunshots is heard approaching ever closer. Then Alexandra decides to go out to encourage the palace guard. Count Benckendorff and her daughter Maria follow her. From the window the staff see the empress in the middle of the deep and frozen night go from soldier to soldier, extending to each one a word of encouragement. When she returns inside, she is visibly glad for the soldiers' faithfulness. Benckendorff, an experienced and veteran military man, does not have the same opinion. He was not persuaded of the soldiers' devotion.

At last the gang of anarchist rebels, having heard rumors of a tremendous palace guard with machine guns, do not an assault on the palace. The gunshots, however, continue in the area through the entire night. The children know absolutely nothing yet. They are told that the gunshots come from military exercises. Anastasia seeing from the window the soldiers at the ready outside in the yard, calls out, "How astonished Papa will be!"[148]

Wednesday 1/14 March. At five in the morning Alexandra is already up, awaiting Nicholas' arrival at 6:00 AM. He is delayed, however, "Perhaps a snowstorm delays the train?" she thought. Anastasia, however, is troubled, "Lili, the train is *never* late. Oh, if Papa would only come quickly.... I'm beginning to feel ill."[149] At 8:00 AM Alexandra learns that the advance of tsar's train has come to a halt. She begins to send anxious telegrams. There is no reply, however.

Earlier, at 2:00 in the morning, about 150 kilometers [90 miles] north of the capital, the tsar's train stopped. An officer boarded and informed him that a little further on there were rebel soldiers with machine guns. The royal train then headed westward toward Pskov, where the Command of the Northern Troops under General Ruzsky was located. They arrived there at eight o'clock in the evening.

Nicholas was counting on Ruzsky, who commanded the troops of a huge front. If Ruzsky were loyal to his oath, the tsar would not only be completely safe, but also receive a powerful means to suppress the insurgency. "When the 'wandering train' approached Pskov," writes G. M. Katkov, "his passengers hoped that they were approaching a safe haven, and that the emperor's personal presence would produce a magical effect. The sovereign had the right to expect that the commander-in-chief of the Northern Front would first ask what his orders would be. However, something quite different happened."[150]

"Being the duty adjutant," writes Colonel A. A. Mordvinov, "I stood at the open door of the carriage platform and looked at the approaching platform. It

Count Paul Benckendorff.

was barely lit and completely deserted.... Somewhere in the middle of the platform there was probably a duty assistant to the station commander, and at the distant end was the silhouette of a guard soldier. The train stopped. A few minutes passed. An officer stepped onto the platform, looked at our train and disappeared. A few [more] minutes passed, and I finally saw General Ruzsky crossing the rails and heading in our direction. General Danilov and another two or three officers from his headquarters followed him a little way back."[151]

Having met with the emperor, General Ruzsky suggested that he should agree to the "Responsible Ministry." Nicholas was greatly surprised that instead of the expected support, he found in Ruzsky another opponent. Informing the tsar that the entire guard of St Petersburg and of Tsarskoe Selo with the more elite units of the tsar had defected to the revolution, General Ruzsky applied intense pressure on Nicholas, attempting to bring him to a dead end. The emperor decided then to call Rodzianko immediately and to offer what his opponents had always wanted, a Ministerial Council acceptable to the Duma, with a Prime Minister who would have full authority in domestic affairs.

In fact, General Ruzsky called Rodzianko and transmitted the emperor's proposal. In the middle of a storm of voices, which testified to the chaos that prevailed over the capital, Rodzianko replied to Ruzsky the following: "It is obvious that His Majesty and you have not taken what is happening here into account. One of the most terrible revolutions has begun, which it will not be so easy to overcome. ... The people's passions are so inflamed that it will hardly be possible to contain them; troops are completely demoralized—they not only disobey but murder their officers; hatred of Her Majesty the Empress has reached extremes. To avoid bloodshed, we were forced to imprison all the ministers, except for War and Navy, in the Peter and Paul Fortress. I very much fear that I will meet the same fate, because protests are directed against any whose demands are more moderate or limited. I consider it necessary to inform you that what you have proposed is already insufficient and that the dynastic question has been raised point-blank."[152] This communication by direct telegraph between Ruzsky and Rodzianko lasted for more than two hours.

A little later the Provisional Government was constituted, from which Rodzianko himself was excluded. The prominent figure from the beginning was Alexander Kerensky, now Minister of Justice. The Provisional Government decided that Nicholas must abdicate immediately in favor of his son, and that until he came of age, Michael Alexandrovich, Nicholas's brother, would be regent. Nicholas' abdication should be voluntary, so as by all means to avoid the use of force. Alekseyev was informed of this matter, and he undertook to collect the written opinion of all the generals who served at the various fronts. The following day Alekseyev had the replies, which he forwarded to Pskov, to the emperor.

Thursday 2 /15 March. General Ruzsky handed the generals' telegrams over to Nicholas. The replies were almost unanimous: Nicholas must abdicate. According to them, the situation on the front was out of control. The troops had progressed to revolutionary fever and only with great difficulty were the generals able to maintain any order. Even his very own cousin, Grand Duke Nicholas Nikolaevich, wrote to him: "A victorious conclusion to the war, which is so vital for the well-being and future of Russia, demands extraordinary measures. I, as a loyal subject, believe that by the bond and spirit of my oath of allegiance it is necessary to beg Your Imperial Majesty on my knees to save Russia and your heir, in the knowledge of your great love for Russia and for him. Make the sign of the cross and pass on your inheritance to him. There is no other way."[153] Nicholas was shaken. His face paled. He stood up, went to the window of the car, opened it and stuck out his head. In the car absolute quiet reigned. No one spoke, and most, recognizing how critical this moment was for all of Russian history, breathed with difficulty.

If Nicholas disregarded the condition of the political leaders in St Petersburg and of his generals, what could he accomplish afterwards? The army, and even his faithful personal guard had deserted. And even if he found faithful troops who would support him, the only option would be military confrontation with the rebels. That, in fact, essentially signified a civil war in the middle of the war with Germany, who would wholeheartedly rejoice in this development. Such a thing must not be permitted. It would mean handing over Russia to her enemies. Furthermore, such immediate and almost unanimous judgement from all the generals showed that his abdication had already been discussed in detail, and that they had already decided to demand it at the first opportunity.

When Nicholas visited Venerable Paraskeva of Diveyevo for the first time in 1903, the Venerable one among other things said to him: "Your Highness, come down from the throne yourself."[154]

Turning back to those present, Nicholas said:

"Are you sure—can you promise that my abdication will benefit Russia?"

"Your Majesty, it is the only thing to save Russia at the present crisis," they replied.[155]

Then he stated with a steady and clear voice:

"For the sake of the well-being, peace, and salvation of Russia, which I passionately love, I am prepared to abdicate from the throne in favor of my son. I ask you all to serve him truly and sincerely."[156]

As soon as he finished this sentence, he made the sign of the Cross. At 3:00 PM Nicholas signed the official document of his abdication and transfer of power to his son.

In the meanwhile, two representatives of the Provisional Government, Guchkov and Shulgin, were on the way to Pskov in order to be witnesses to Nicholas' abdication and to transmit the document to St Petersburg. Their arrival was expected late in the afternoon. Thus, there was a gap of six hours before their arrival, which gave Nicholas the opportunity to contemplate in quiet all that had happened so quickly.

His thoughts were concentrated on the hope that he and his family would be allowed to retreat to Livadia, and that Alexis would remain with them, at least until he completed his education. He then called Dr Feodorov, one of Alexis' and the family's personal physicians, and asked him, "Tell me frankly, Sergius Petrovitch. Is Alexis's malady incurable?" Dr Feodorov fully realizing the importance of what he was going to say answered, "Science teaches us, sire, that it is an incurable disease. Yet those who are afflicted with it sometimes reach an advanced old age. Still, Alexis Nicolaievitch is at the mercy of an accident."[157]

According to Dr Feodorov, Alexis would not ever be able to ride a horse and would always need to avoid any activity that would cause fatigue and exert pressure on his joints. Apart from his medical opinion, Dr Feodorov also indicated to Nicholas that after the fact of his abdication, the new government would never allow Alexis to leave Russia. Furthermore, even if the family remained in Russia, it was certain that other hands would undertake the upbringing of Alexis.

At nine o'clock in the evening, the representatives of the Provisional Government arrived. Nicholas received them with a handshake and asked them to be seated. One of them began to explain the reasons why his abdication was an imperative necessity. Nicholas interrupted him and said in a calm voice, "Through the morning, before your arrival and after Adjutant General Ruzsky's conversation with the Duma chairman over the direct line, I thought it over, and ... I was ready to abdicate from the throne in favor of my son. But now, having again thought the situation over, I have come to the conclusion that, in light of his illness, I should abdicate in my name and his name simultaneously, as I cannot be separated from him."[158] "The Emperor, speaking in a quiet voice, made no difficulty at all; but he communicated the all-important change which he had made in the order of succession, adding

CHAPTER 4

simply, 'You will understand a father's feelings.'"[159] Pronouncing the last sentence, Nicholas' voice dropped and almost extinguished.

The representatives then handed him the document of abdication to sign, which was composed by the Provisional Government. Nicholas took it and withdrew to his room. When he returned, he gave them a document with the text of the abdication that he had composed himself. The lordly courtesy and fervent patriotism that characterized every line of the text evoked wonder even from the enemies of the tsar. The document of abdication was as follows:

> In these days of great struggle with an external enemy who has tried to enslave our country for nearly three years, the Lord God saw fit to send down upon Russia a harsh new ordeal. The developing internal popular disturbances threaten to have a catastrophic effect upon the future conduct of the relentless war. The fate of Russia, the honor of our heroic army, the good of the people, the whole future of our dear fatherland demand that the war be brought to a victorious end no matter what. A cruel enemy is summoning his last strength, and the hour is near when our valiant army together with our renowned allies, can completely smash the enemy. During these decisive days for the life of Russia, we considered it a duty of conscience to facilitate our people's close unity and the rallying of all popular forces in order to achieve victory as quickly as possible, and, in agreement with the State Duma, we consider it to be for the good to abdicate from the Throne of the Russian State and to surrender supreme power. Not wishing to part with our beloved son, we name as our successor our Brother, our Grand Duke Mikhail Aleksandrovich, and bless his assumption to the Throne of the Russian State. We entrust our brother to conduct state affairs in complete and unshakeable unity with the representatives of the people in the legislative institutions according to principles they will determine, and on this to take an inviolable oath. In the name of our deeply beloved homeland, we call all faithful sons of the fatherland to fulfill their holy duty to this land in obedience to the tsar in this difficult moment of national trials and to help him, together with the representatives of the people, to lead the Russian State along the path of victory, prosperity, and glory. May the Lord God help Russia.
> Nicholas
> Town of Pskov
> 2 March (15:00) 1917[160]

Nicholas arose. Approaching him, Basil Shulgin, one of the representatives, full of commiseration for the drama of the fallen emperor, told him with especially manifest sorrow, "Oh, Your Majesty, if you had done all this earlier, even as late as the last summoning of the Duma, perhaps all that—" The Tsar looked at Shulgin in a curiously simple way and asked, "Do you think it might have been avoided?"[161]

That evening Nicholas wrote in his diary, "Ruzsky came over in the morning and read [the transcript of] his very long telephone conversation with Rodzianko. According to him, the situation in Petrograd is such that the Duma ministers are helpless to do anything since the soc.-dem [Social Democrat] party, in the form of the workers' committee, is fighting against them. They want my abdication. Ruzsky passed on this conversation to Stavka, and Alexeyev to all the military commanders. At 2:30 responses arrived from all. The bottom line is that in order to save Russia and keep the army at the front in tranquility, [I] must decide on this step. I agreed. They sent the draft of manifesto from Stavka. At one in the morning I left Pskov with a heavy feeling about all I had experienced. All around is treason and cowardice and deceit!"[162]

Long ago, in the 16th century, William Shakespeare wrote:

Not all the water in the rough rude sea
Can wash the balm off from an anointed king;
The breath of worldly men cannot depose
The deputy elected by the Lord.[163]

Nicholas was an anointed tsar, sealed by the grace of the Holy Spirit during the Sacrament of his Coronation. What God performs cannot be undone; therefore, Nicholas remained the anointed tsar to his martyric death.

As soon as the two representatives of the Provisional Government returned to St Petersburg, they asked them to give a speech to the workers at the railway station. Shulgin, believing that the abdication of Nicholas would be enough to please the crowd shouted with enthusiasm, "Long live Tsar Michael!" However, with terror he saw the anger of the crowd, and with great difficulty managed to flee their wrath. The Soviet of St Petersburg was likewise opposed to the continuation of the Romanov dynasty. A few hours later, Michael also abdicated the throne. After three hundred and fourteen years of rule, the dynasty of the Romanovs was now history.

At Tsarskoe Selo, already from the morning of the fifteenth, the clear-sighted military diagnosis of Count Benckendorff is proved correct. The entire palace guard deserts and abandons their post. Alexandra cannot believe it. All those soldiers had a nearly personal relationship with the family. They knew their families, their personal matters, they had lived with them for years!

To these problems are added the interruption of electricity and water. Every time they need to draw water, they must break the ice outside at the lake. The elevator no longer works, and Alexandra must be supported ascending the stairs, and when she reaches the top she is entirely winded. She is carried from room to room on a wheelchair along the dark passageways. "I must not give way. I keep on saying, '*I must not*'—it helps me,"[164] she confides to Lili. The children know nothing yet. She does not want to worry them.

While the three children who had first come down with measles show some improvement, Maria and Anastasia begin to show the first symptoms of having caught the disease. Because of their illness, all the children are losing some of their hair and must shave their heads. Alexandra feels the need to seek divine help more intensely at that moment. For this reason, she calls for the Znamenie icon of the Mother of God to be brought to the palace, and to sing a moleben for the condition of health of the children. Priest Athanasius Belyaev arrives at the palace accompanying the icon. He remembers characteristically:

"We passed a number of brightly lit rooms, and entered a large, dimly lit room, in which the sick children lay in their individual beds. The icon was placed on the table prepared for it. It was so dark in the room that I could barely make out who was present: the Empress, in the uniform of a Sister of Mercy, stood next to the Heir's bed. Near her stood other Sisters of Mercy and children's nurses. Several slender wax candles were lit before the icon. The moleben began…. Oh, what horrible and unexpected misfortune had befallen the Imperial Family! …Can one imagine the state in which the helpless Empress, a mother with five grievously ill children, found herself? Suppressing her womanly weakness and all of her human ills, she heroically, selflessly, devoted herself to caring for the sick. Placing all of her reliance on the Queen of Heaven, she decided that the first thing to be done was to pray before the Icon of Our Lady of the Sign; thus, she directed that the icon be brought to the sick children's quarters. On her knees, tearfully, the earthly queen implored the help and intercession of the Queen of Heaven. After venerating the icon and passing underneath it, she asked that the icon be taken to the children's beds, so that they might also venerate the miraculous icon. As I offered her the cross, I said, 'Take courage and be strong, Your Majesty; the dream may be frightening, but God is merciful. In all things, rely on His holy will. Believe, hope, and pray without ceasing.'"[165]

There are no tidings from Nicholas. Alexandra anxiously continues to send him telegrams. Instead of a reply from the Tsar, she receives the telegrams back with the notation in blue ink, "Address of person mentioned unknown!"[166]

Friday 3/16 March. Nicholas' final wish is to bid farewell to his beloved troops. Thus, in the morning he departs from Pskov to Mogilev. General Vladimir Voeikov recalled going to the Tsar's compartment as soon as they departed from Pskov: "My heart broke into pieces at the sight of such undeserved sufferings that had fallen to the lot of the noblest and kindest of tsars. He had only just endured the tragedy of abdicating from the throne for himself and his son, because of the treason and baseness of the people who had abdicated from him, although they had received only good from

The girls with their heads shaved, after their recovery from the measles.

him. He was torn away from his beloved family. All the misfortunes sent down upon him he bore with the humility of an ascetic. ... The image of the Tsar with his tear-blurred eyes in the half-lit compartment will never be erased from my memory to the end of my life."[167]

After arriving at the Headquarters, the leaders of the representatives of the allied powers, at the initiative of the British Major General Sir John Hanbury-Williams, ask Nicholas to accompany him to Tsarskoe Selo, and from there to take him abroad by way of Finland. But the emperor declines. He hopes that the situation will calm down so that they will allow them to remain in Russia.

In the afternoon as they return to the palace from the capital, the servants inform Alexandra that leaflets are being distributed announcing the abdication of the Tsar. She surely considers this to be lies of the revolutionaries. But these leaflets also arrive at the palace. The staff begin to mourn as they read about the abdication of Nicholas, as well as Michael, from the throne.

At 7:00 PM Grand Duke Paul, Nicholas' uncle, visits the palace. He asks to see Alexandra in private. Maria awaits with Lili Dehn in the adjoining room; they hear agitated voices. Afterward, writes Lili Dehn, "Hardly had the Grand Duchess left the study when the door opened and the Empress appeared. Her face was distorted with agony, her eyes were full of tears. She tottered rather than walked, and I rushed forward and supported her until she reached the writing-table between the windows. She leant heavily against it, and, taking my hands in hers, she said brokenly:

"'*Abdiqué!* [He has abdicated!]'

"I could not believe my ears. I waited for her next words. They were hardly audible. At last: '*Le pauvre... tout seul là bas ... et passé, ... oh, mon Dieu, par quoi il a passé! Et je ne puis pas être pres de lui pour le consoler.*' ['The poor thing ... all alone down there ... and it happened ... Oh, my God, why did it happen! And I could not be there with him to console him.']

"'*Madame, très chère Madame, il faut avoir du courage.*' ['My Lady, my very dear Lady, we must have courage.']

"She paid no attention to me, and kept on repeating, '*Mon Dieu, que c'est pénible. ... Tout seul là bas!*' ['My God, how painful ... All alone down there'] I put my arms around her and we walked slowly up and down the long room. At last, fearing for her reason, I cried: '*Mais Madame—au nom de Dieu—il vit!!*' ['But my Lady—in the name of God—he lives!!']

"'Yes, Lili,' she replied, as if new hope inspired her. 'Yes, he lives.'"[168]

Later in the evening, Count Benckendorff, Baroness Buxhoeveden, and other members of the staff came to see the empress and to assure her of their devotion. Buxhoeveden writes, "Count Benckendorff held her hand, tears running down his usually immobile face. The empress spoke to us in French ... '*C'est pour le mieux. C'est la volonté de Dieu. Dieu donne que cela sauve la Russie. C'est la seule chose qui signifie.* [It is for the best. It is the will of God. God permits this so that Russia may be saved. That is the only thing that matters.]' Before we shut the door we could see her sinking into her chair by the table, sobbing bitterly, covering her face with her hands."[169]

While the terrible unease of Alexandra for the Emperor reached its culmination, the health of the girls began to worsen dangerously. Tatiana suffered from ear infections, which caused her terrible pain and she lost, temporarily, nearly all her hearing. Anastasia also had abscesses in her ears. Maria took her turn, who until now was her mother's greatest support. Even in the first stages of her illness, she hoped that she would be able to avoid staying in bed. She intended to endure until her father returned and she begged Baroness Buxhoeveden not to trouble her mother when she also developed a fever. At last, however, her exhausted nature betrayed her very badly. Along with the measles she suffered double pneumonia and reached the gates of death. In her feverish delirium and nightmares, she saw terrible soldiers who came to kill her mother and she shouted in terror, "Crowds of people... dreadful people... they're coming to kill Mamma!! Why are they doing these things?"[170] A few days later, deeply troubled by Anastasia and Maria who continued to remain bedridden from the disease, Alexis wrote the following message, "Dear, gentle, beloved Anastasia. I will strongly pray for you and Maria. With God all will pass. Stay firm and pray! I firmly kiss you and Mashka. May God be with you, Your Alexei."[171]

Saturday 4/17 March. As soon as he arrived at Stavka, Nicholas obtained permission to telephone his wife. An aged servant trembling from his enthusiasm, announced to Alexandra stuttering, "The Emperor is on the telephone!"[172] Alexandra looked at him thinking he had lost his mind. A few moments later, realizing what he said to her, she jumped up like a young girl and ran to the telephone. Nicholas understood that the telephone line was being monitored, and for this reason asked, "You know?"[173] Alexandra answered affirmatively. Then they spoke about the health of their children.

The following day, on 18 March, the new Minister of War, Alexander Guchkov, along with General Kornilov came to inspect the palace at Tsarskoe Selo. Guchkov was the second representative sent with Shulgin to receive the abdication of Nicholas in Pskov. They arrived at the palace at eleven o'clock in the evening, a fact that raised suspicion that they had come to arrest the empress. Alexandra, expecting the arrival of the government emissaries, had called Grand Duke Paul to come immediately.

Along with the representatives of the Provisional Government, twenty members of the revolutionary committee of the Tsarskoe Selo Soviet also arrived. These men, for the most part workers and soldiers, began to surround the palace cursing and mistreating the staff. As it turned out, the visit did indeed take place for the purpose of inspection. When Guchkov asked Alexandra whether she needed anything, she asked only to be assured that the hospitals of Tsarskoe Selo, which she had directed up to now, had the necessary supplies. She also asked them to be sure to observe order around the palace for the sake of the children's safety. Guchkov assured her that they would take care of both matters. Grand Duke Paul later said to his wife that he had never seen Alexandra more calm and dignified.

Nicholas remained in Mogilev for five days. There, General Alekseyev organized in his honor a farewell ceremony. Addressing the gathered troops, Nicholas thanked them for their faithful devotion and exhorted them to overcome every hostile feeling so that they might guide the Russian army to victory. His humility moved all those present, who broke out into loud cheers. Most of them wept openly. Krymov's words that "everyone in the army would be glad to welcome the news of the coup"[174] turned out to be a lie. General Denikin wrote: "The troops were stunned – it is difficult to define with another word the first impression that the manifestos made. No joy, no sorrow. Silent, concentrated silence. ... and tears flowed down the cheeks of the old soldiers. ... There was no resentment personally against the Sovereign nor against the Royal Family. On the contrary, everyone was interested in their fate and feared for it."[175]

The second day after Nicholas' departure to Mogilev, his mother arrived from Kiev to see him. She was unbelievably crushed, practically in despair. She wept constantly for the entire three days of her stay there. Despite Nicholas' assurances that everything would be fine, she wept again as inconsolably when they parted. This meeting, as it turned out later, was their last.

At the same time, rumors began to spread in Saint Petersburg that Nicholas had returned to Stavka in order to lead the army against the revolution. Meanwhile, the newspapers daily published shameful slanders about the empress' relationship with Rasputin, and accusations of treason. The general outcry and increasing hatred of the family in this way took on dangerous dimensions. In order to protect the family from the maddened mob of revolutionaries, the Provisional Government decided to put them under guard, at first keeping them under house arrest in Tsarskoe Selo.

CHAPTER 4

On the morning of 21 March, General Kornilov arrived at the palace at Tsarskoe Selo and informed Alexandra that the purpose of his arrival was her arrest. On hearing this, Alexandra looked at him icily. Kornilov, however, explained to her that this decision was taken simply, and only, to protect the family from the uncontrolled madness of the Soviet and of the soldiers of the revolution. He further assured her that as soon as the health of the children permitted, the government would provide them with transportation to Murmansk where a British yacht would convey them to England. Alexandra began to weep in relief.

General Kornilov later informed the serving staff of the palace of the arrest of the family that as many as wished to leave were free to do so, but they would not be allowed to come back later. At 2 o'clock in the afternoon a new guard arrived and at 4 o'clock all the doors except the main entrance and the kitchen door were sealed. The prisoners were informed that from then on, they would be under complete obedience to the commandant of the palace, Admiral Kotzebue. Count Benckendorff wrote, "The soldiers of the new Guard were horrible to look at; untidy, noisy, quarrelling with everybody; the officers, who were afraid of them, had the greatest difficulty in preventing them from roaming about the Palace and entering every room. ... There were many quarrels between them and the household staff, whom they reproached for wearing livery and for the attentions they paid to the royal family."[176]

Once Baroness Buxhoeveden was awakened in the middle of the night by the noise made by a soldier gathering various gold and silver ornaments from her table. Lili Dehn was surprised at Alexandra's reply when, disgusted with the rude behavior of the soldiers, she expressed her displeasure to the empress:

"I can't bear Russia," she cried; "I hate it."

"Don't dare say such things, Lili," said the Empress. "You hurt me. ... If you love me, don't ever say you hate Russia. The people are not to blame; they don't understand what they are doing."[177]

Immediately after Kornilov's departure, the empress summoned Gilliard, "The Czar is coming back to-morrow. Alexis must be told everything. Will you do it? I am going to tell the girls myself."[178]

The girls displayed the same bravery as their mother. Not once did they think about anything else but how to help their parents. Although they were still ill when Alexandra told them about the terrible events, they managed to keep control over their feelings without showing their mother their pain. Tatiana's hearing was still sufficiently weak and she was not able to understand exactly what her mother was saying. Thus, her sisters had to write down what had happened.

As to how Alexis took the news, Gilliard relates, "I went to Alexis Nicolaievitch and told him that the Czar would be returning from Mohileff next morning and would never go back there again.

'Why?'

'Your father does not want to be Commander-in-Chief any more.' He was greatly moved at this, as he was very fond of going to G.H.Q. After a moment or two I added:

'You know your father does not want to be Czar any more, Alexis Nicolaievitch.' He looked at me in astonishment, trying to read in my face what had happened.

'What! Why?'

'He is very tired and has had a lot of trouble lately.'

'Oh yes! Mother told me they stopped his train when he wanted to come here. But won't papa be Czar again afterwards?' I then told him that the Czar had abdicated in favour of the Grand Duke Michael, who had also renounced the throne.

'But who's going to be Czar, then?'

'I don't know. Perhaps nobody now. ...' Not a word about himself. Not a single allusion to his rights as the Heir. He was very red and agitated. There was a silence, and then he said:

'But if there isn't a Czar, who's going to govern Russia?'"[179]

Earlier that same morning, Nicholas was arrested in Mogilev and the following day he would return to Tsarskoe Selo accompanied by four deputies. Alone in his office before his departure he composed his last official decree to the Russian troops. This text, just as the document of his abdication, is pervaded with Nicholas' genuine and intense feelings of patriotism, of his faith in the will of God, and his love for his people and troops.

The Provisional Government was afraid that this text might arouse the wonder and admiration of the troops for Nicholas, something that could perhaps lead to extreme displays of support for him. Guchkov, therefore, sent a special telegram addressed to Alekseyev, strictly forbidding the transferring of this address to the troops. Thus, the soldiers never saw it.

> Fervently beloved troops, I address you for the last time. After my abdication from Russia's throne on behalf of myself and my son, power has been transferred to the Provisional Government established at the initiative of the State Duma. May God help it lead Russia on the path of glory and prosperity. May God also help you, valiant troops, defend our homeland from the evil enemy. During the course of the past two and a half years you have constantly borne the burden of military service, much blood has been spilled, much effort has been expended, and the hour is near when Russia, tied to its valiant allies by a single common striving toward victory, will smash the last efforts of the opponent. This unprecedented war must be brought to a complete victory.
>
> Whoever thinks now of peace, whoever wishes it, is a turncoat to the fatherland, a traitor. I know that every honest fighting man believes this. Fulfill your duty, valiantly defend our great homeland,

obey the Provisional Government, heed your superiors, remember that any weakening of military order only plays into the hands of the enemy.

I firmly believe that boundless love for your great homeland has not gone out in your hearts. May the Lord God bless you, and may the Martyred Victor, St George, lead you to victory.

Nicholas
8 March, 1917
Headquarters
Signed: Chief of Staff, General Alekseev.[180]

Later Nicholas related an incident that took place during his departure, which moved him very much: "When I got into the train, I noticed five or six schoolgirls who were standing on the platform trying to attract my attention. I went to the window, and, when they saw me, they began to cry, and made signs for me to write something for them. So I signed my name on a piece of paper, and sent it to the children. But they still lingered on the platform, and, as it was bitterly cold, I tried to make them understand that they had better go home. However, when my train left, two hours later, they were still there. They blessed me, poor children," said the emperor, greatly moved by the recollection. "I hope their pure blessing will bring us happiness."[181]

In 1909 at a meeting between Nicholas and the then Prime Minister Peter Arkadievitch Stolypin, the following characteristic dialog transpired:

"'Peter Arkadievitch, I succeed in nothing I undertake, I've no luck at all. And anyhow the human will is so impotent!' Stolypin, a courageous and resolute character, protested vigorously. The Tsar then asked him:

'Have you ever read the Lives of the Saints?'

'Yes, some of it at any rate. If I remember rightly there are quite twenty volumes of it.'

'And do you know on what day my birthday falls?'

'How could I forget it? It is May 6.'

'What Saint's day is it?'

'Forgive me, Sire, I'm afraid I've forgotten.'

'The Patriarch Job.'

'Then God be praised Your Majesty's reign will end gloriously, for Job, after piously enduring the most cruel tests of has faith, found blessings and rewards showered upon his head!'

'No, no, Peter Arkadievitch, believe me! I have a presentiment—more than a presentiment, a secret conviction— that I am destined for terrible trials, but I shall not receive my reward on this earth. How often have I not applied to myself the words of Job: 'Hardly have I entertained a fear than it comes to pass and all the evils I foresee descend upon my head.'"[182]

PART II
In the Path of Blood

CHAPTER 5

CAPTIVITY

THE PALACE PRISON

The following morning, on 22 March, elated but also uneasy, Alexandra awaited Nicholas with her children. Alexis in a state of nervous agony constantly looked at his watch and counted the minutes aloud one by one. At last Nicholas' train arrived on time at the Tsarskoe Selo station. There the representatives of the government handed over the prisoner to the commandant of the palace. With the tsar came Prince Vasily Dolgorukov, son of the wife of Count Benckendorff from her first marriage.

The Commandant of the Guard had given orders that the gates of the palace should be locked and that he should be informed by telephone if anybody wished to enter. When the tsar's motorcar arrived, the sentry asked who it was, and the chauffeur told him. The sentry then called the Commandant of the Guard and announced his arrival. Then the commandant went down the steps and asked in a loud voice "Who goes there?" The sentry cried out, "Nicholas Romanov." "Let him pass," said the officer.

After this "offensive comedy,"[1] as Benckendorff called it, the car arrived at the steps and the emperor and Dolgorukov emerged. Entering the antechamber, they met a crowd of people, mostly soldiers, who were noisy and smoking. They all had gathered there to see the tsar up close. According to his custom, Nicholas passing among the crowd saluted them in military fashion without, however, receiving a return salute from those present. He shook hands with Count Benckendorff and entered the empress' apartment without saying a word. He met Alexandra in the children's room, and they embraced with emotion. Alexandra with tears in her eyes assured him that the most precious thing to her was her husband and the father of her children, and not the tsar with whom she had shared the throne. Then, at last, Nicholas let himself weep in the embrace of his wife.

At first Kornilov's plan was to keep the family completely confined to the palace. Count Benckendorff, however, knowing very well of the emperor's great need for physical activity persuaded the general to allow the use of a part of the garden for this purpose. However, for every exit into the garden the officer on duty had to be informed so that more guards would be stationed in the specified area. But right from that first afternoon when Nicholas went out, the terrible face of the revolution began to appear before the eyes of the family.

From the upper floor window, the empress with Lili Dehn and Anna Vyrubova observed Nicholas' first walk in the garden. As he walked, one of the soldiers stood in front of him blocking his way. Nicholas changed direction. Another soldier blocked his passage in the new direction. In a few moments Nicholas was surrounded by six armed soldiers. Vyrubova describes it, "With their fists and with the butts of their guns they pushed the Emperor this way and that as though he were some wretched vagrant they were baiting in a country road. 'You can't go there, Gospodin Polkovnik (Mr. Colonel).' 'We don't permit you to walk in that direction, Gospodin Polkovnik.' 'Stand back when you are commanded, Gospodin Polkovnik.' The Emperor, apparently unmoved, looked from one of these coarse brutes to another and with great dignity turned and walked back towards the palace."[2] Alexandra was not able to say a word seeing this scene. She only grasped and held Lili Dehn's hand tightly.

Among the people who chose to remain with the family and to share their trials with them, apart from Anna Vyrubova and Lili Dehn, were Count Benckendorff with his wife and his adopted son Prince Dolgorukov, the two ladies in waiting, Baroness Sophia Buxhoeveden and Countess Anastasia Hendrikova, the tutors Pierre Gilliard and Miss Schneider, the family physicians Dr Eugene Botkin and Dr Vladimir Derevenko, and Alexis' personal attendant, the sailor Nagorny. After ten years of close ties with the child, the other attendant of the young heir, the sailor Andei Derevenko turned out to be a wretch and an opportunist. Vyrubova describes this shocking scene before his departure from the palace, "I passed the open door of Alexei's room, and this is what I saw. Lying sprawled in a chair was the sailor Derevenko, for many years the personal attendant of the Tsarevitch, and on whom the family had bestowed every kindness, every material benefit. Bitten by the mania of revolution, this man was now displaying his gratitude for all their favors. Insolently he bawled at the boy whom he had formerly loved and cherished, to bring him this or that, to perform any menial service his mean lackey's brain could think of. Dazed and apparently only half conscious of what he was being forced to do, the child moved about trying to obey."[3] Once he took his revenge, Derevenko left the palace.

Clementy Nagorny. Andrei Derevenko.

Later, when the children had sufficiently recovered, the parents decided to continue their lessons, which they, while still prisoners, would have had to take. Nicholas conducted lessons in history and geography, Alexandra religion, Baroness Buxhoeveden English and piano lessons, Miss Schneider arithmetic, and Countess Hendrikova art. Gilliard, in addition to teaching French also served as "headmaster" of the school. On the morning after giving his first lesson, Nicholas greeted Gilliard, saying to him, "Good morning, dear colleague." Gilliard wrote, "Always the same serenity, the same anxiety to be agreeable to those who share his captivity. He is an example and an encouragement to us."[4]

The calm and peaceful conduct of the emperor all during his imprisonment was a shining example to those around him. Everyone knew that in these first days he had gone through a terrible psychological crisis due to all the things that had happened to his country and to his family. For a moment, it seemed that the anchor that had always stabilized all had disappeared. But soon, recovering his spiritual strength, Nicholas again became the unshaken support of all those around him. "The Czar," wrote Gilliard, "accepted all these restraints with extraordinary serenity and moral grandeur. No word of reproach ever passed his lips. ... We felt he was ready to forgive anything to those who were inflicting such humiliations upon him so long as they were capable of saving Russia."⁵

He followed the military and political developments in the local and foreign press, and when he read about setbacks of the troops of his fatherland he wept. He had requested from the priest who held the services at the palace to pray "for the good success of the struggles of the Russian and allied armies." When the priest commemorated the Provisional Government in the place where the name of the Tsar had been, Gilliard noticed that Nicholas "crossed himself piously."⁶ Again Gilliard wrote, "Sunday, April 1st.— ... We went to church this morning, where we found Their Majesties, the Grand-Duchesses Olga and Tatiana, and the various members of the suite who are sharing our captivity. When the priest prayed for the success of the Russian and Allied armies the Czar and Czarina knelt down, the whole congregation following their example."⁷

Alexandra, exhausted by the care of the sick in the house, was in a condition of extreme fatigue. During the day, she spent most of her hours on the sofa reading and knitting. In the evenings Nicholas wheeled her wheelchair to Vyrubova's room. Accustomed to having the rooms full of fresh flowers, she now suffered from their prohibition: they were considered "too luxurious." When from time to time the staff brought her a few lilacs, she wept with gratitude.

The children were very sorry to see their mother in such psychological difficulty. Anastasia wrote in a note to her mother in those days, "23 April [6 May], 1917: My sweet Mama darling, I wish for you all the best things that one could wish for. Christ is with you. I firmly, firmly kiss you and love you. Good night. Your faithful Schwibz."⁸

It took some time for Alexandra to come to the realization that the revolution was an irreversible event. But in the end, her great faith in God helped her to recover her spiritual strengths, "God will help, He will not leave us," she said. Her faith came to her rescue. "Gradually," writes Baroness Buxhoeveden, "out of that terrible mental suffering she [the empress] gained a serenity in which she could bear anything, and could be, in fact, a support to all those round her."⁹

On this point Nicholas' usual good humor helped much. Lili Dehn recalls, "The Emperor was generally able to see the humour of any situation, and he would sometimes laugh at the idea of being, what he called, 'an Ex.'" Alexandra quickly adopted the expression. "Don't call me an Empress any more—I'm only an Ex," she would say. One day when some especially unpalatable ham was served at lunch Nicholas made everyone laugh shrugging his shoulders and saying, "Well, this may have once been ham, but now it's nothing but an 'ex-ham.'"¹⁰

CAPTIVITY

PASSION WEEK

What Alexandra, as well as the rest of the members of the family, desired above all was church services. The fact that permission was granted for services to be held every Saturday evening and Divine Liturgy Sunday mornings was a great blessing for the family. Their joy was even greater when daily services were permitted in Holy Week. Father Athanasius Belyaev was sent to the palace for this purpose with a deacon and four cantors. They would remain there for all of Holy Week.

Father Athanasius was an aged and very virtuous priest. While celebrating his first Divine Liturgy at the palace chapel on Palm Sunday, his tears ran ceaselessly as he participated in the drama of the family. When he emerged from the Royal Doors with the Holy Chalice, at the point where until that time the priest would commemorate the emperor, he could not utter the new, modified, petition for the authorities, and, deeply affected, he reentered the Altar without a word.

The Divine Liturgy of Great Thursday was marked by a strange event. In the park directly across from the palace the burial was to be held of those who fell at Tsarskoe Selo on the day of the revolution. In fact, these "heroes" were nothing more than six or seven drunkards who, after looting the wine shops of the city, died from drinking too much liquor. The selection of the space for the burial exactly across from the palace was not accidental, but was intended as an affront to the royal couple. At first, in fact, they intended to bury the dead precisely outside the windows of the palace, but at last due to the lack of space they buried them across the road in the park.

The funeral lasted from morning until afternoon and thousands of workers and soldiers were present, holding up high placards with socialist and communist slogans and singing revolutionary songs. Before the burial, they began to declaim incendiary speeches before the red coffins of the dead, which gradually reached alarming proportions so that the commandant and the officers of the palace guard were set on watch. Soon the cries and the hostile attitudes of the crowd began to get out of control, and they began to fear a direct assault on the palace.

Baroness Buxhoeveden, who was an eyewitness of the events, relates, "As the roars of the mourners grew louder and louder, the elements intervened, and very probably saved the Imperial Family's lives. A wind arose which developed in the course of half an hour into a hurricane. The sky grew black, and a tremendous snowstorm descended. The army of red banners fluttered desperately in the wind, many were torn from their staves, and the old trees swayed and creaked. The orators were blinded by the snow, and obliged to cling to their caps and comforters in the ever-increasing blast, so the flow of eloquence stopped, and one detachment after another tramped away, till the vast park was empty, leaving only a few torn red flags flapping in the wind on the site of the 'civic graves.'"[11]

CHAPTER 5

On Great and Holy Friday, the service of the Epitaphios (or Plashanitsa)[12] was served as usual. However, under the conditions of captivity and of an uncertain future, the service was particularly moving. The sight of the procession of the Epitaphios through the great passageways and empty halls of the palace was compelling. The procession was preceded by the staff dressed in their black penitential clothes, the priest followed with the deacon, and finally the royal family. The soldiers observed this nearly unearthly sight in silence.

In the evening after the end of the service of the Epitaphios, all the members of the family came up to Father Athanasius Belyaev for the Sacrament of Confession. The children confessed in their rooms. Father Athanasius recorded his experience in his diary:

> In the corner of each Grand Duchess's room was a real iconostasis, filled with a multitude of icons of various sizes, bearing the images of especially venerated saints. Before the iconostasis was a folding analogion covered with a towel, on which were prayer books, service books, and the holy Gospel and a cross. In furniture and decor, the rooms presented an image of a pure and innocent childhood that did not know secular filth.
>
> For the prayers before confession, all four of the children gathered in the room in which lay the ill Olga Nikolaevna.[13] Alexei Nikolaevich, dressed in a blue robe with an embroidered decorative braid edging, sat in an armchair. Maria Nikolaevna lay semirecumbent in a large wheelchair, which Anastasia Nikolaevna easily moved about. After the reading of the prayers and a short sermon before confession, Olga Nikolaevna remained in the room. The Heir went off by himself, and Anastasia Nikolaevna wheeled Maria Nikolaevna away. Then I went to the other rooms to confess the others: Alexei, Maria, and Anastasia N[ikolaevna]. I will not relate how the confessions went. My impression was the following: Grant, O Lord, that all children be on as high a moral level as were the children of the former Tsar. Such was their lack of hatred, their humility, their submission to the will of their parents, unquestioning dedication to the will of God, purity of thought and complete ignorance of secular filth—both passionate and sinful—that I was astounded, and could not decide whether I, as a spiritual father, should remind them of sins perhaps unknown to them, and how I should incline them to repent of sins of which they were not aware.[14]

Afterwards, Father Athanasius was led to the chapel beside the bedroom of the royal couple, where he met Nicholas, Alexandra, and Tatiana. Continuing his description in his diary, he writes of this:

> After the reading of the prayers, the Sovereign and his spouse departed, and Tatiana Nikolaevna confessed. She was followed by

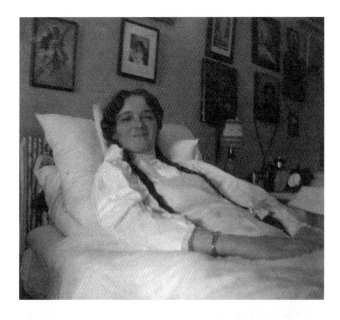

Olga recovering from the measles.

Nicholas with Maria in her wheelchair.

the Empress, who was clearly agitated, and who apparently had fervently prayed and had decided to confess before the holy cross and Gospel all of the ills of her heart, according to the Orthodox rite, fully cognizant of the greatness of the Mystery.

Then the Sovereign came to confession. Oh, how inexpressibly fortunate I felt to have been made worthy through the mercies of God to become the intermediary between the Heavenly King and the earthly one. For next to me stood the one who was loftier than anyone else living on earth. He was even now the Anointed One given to us by God, one who for twenty-three years, by the law of royal succession, was our reigning Russian Orthodox Tsar. And now, the humble servant of God Nicholas, as a meek lamb, wishing good for all of his enemies, not harboring any offense, praying fervently for Russia's prosperity, deeply believing in her glorious future, on bended knees, gazes upon the cross and the Gospel, and in the presence of my unworthiness, relates to his Heavenly Father the hidden secrets of his long-suffering life, and, reduced to dust before the greatness of the Heavenly King, tearfully asks forgiveness for his transgressions, voluntary and involuntary.[15]

On the following day, in his own diary, Gilliard wrote the following: "[Holy] Saturday, April 14th.—In the morning, at half-past nine, Mass and Holy Communion. In the evening, at half-past eleven, everyone went to church for the midnight service. Colonel Korovitchenko, the Commandant of the palace and friend of Kerensky, and the three officers of the guard were also present. The service lasted until two o'clock, when we went to the library to exchange the traditional greetings. The Czar, according to Russian custom, embraced all the men present, including the Commandant and officers of the guard, who had remained with him. The two men could not hide their emotion at this spontaneous act."[16]

Count Benckendorff relates that one of the two officers "was so moved and so much embarrassed that he was unable to eat anything. His hands trembled and he was as pale as death. After supper he told me that, having seen the Emperor at G.H.Q. several months beforehand, he had not been able to master his emotion on seeing him again under circumstances so different and so dramatic."[17]

A few days later, during the month of May, a venerable elder of Sarov Monastery was in great grief over the trials that the royal family was now experiencing. While he was in this condition, and as he was praying with tears, he fell asleep and saw the following wonderful vision: He was in Tsarskoe Selo and looking toward the Alexander Palace, namely toward the dwelling of the royal family, he saw that above it rose a pillar of light that reached to the heavens. The elder then proceeded into the palace. Inside, he saw the tsar sitting at his desk and busy writing. Near him at another smaller table sat Alexis reading some book. With them was the rest of the family, the empress with the girls who were sitting and knitting. Among the members of the family, radiating divine light, stood Saint Seraphim of Sarov who gave them spiritual counsels and was consoling them. When Saint Seraphim saw the elder, he came near and said to him:

"Don't be too grieved, Father, don't be despondent; God will not abandon His chosen and beloved children. He has the power to snatch them away from evildoers, but He desires for them, not earthly happiness, but heavenly. It is easier for the Lord to send legions of angels to destroy all their enemies than it is for us to speak a word, but He only takes away their enemies' reason, so that they destroy themselves. The Lord has sent me for a while to console, strengthen, and protect the Royal sufferers, for 'the spirit is willing, but the flesh is weak,'[18] and they have need of our heavenly assistance in difficult moments of sorrow. Look at the resplendent light that emanates from the faces of the Royal sufferers—this is a sign that they are under God's special care, as righteous ones. Just as, from the beginning of the world, the righteous have been vilified, wronged and slandered by iniquitous people—followers of the first liar and deceiver, the devil; so also have these righteous Royal sufferers been vilified, humiliated, slandered, and wronged by evil people, instigated by the same universal evildoer who rose up against the righteous ones and against our Creator and God Himself, Christ, the Giver of life. Look at the face of the Empress and you will see that the light emanating from her face is brighter than the others'—this is a sign that she has borne more slanders and false accusations than anyone, from followers of the universal slanderer."[19]

SPIRITUAL RESPITE

Father Athanasius Belyaev, who was called regularly to serve the liturgical needs of the family during Holy Week, was finally appointed by the Provisional Government as Rector of the palace for all the time of their imprisonment at Tsarskoe Selo. This came about because Father Alexander Vasiliev was gravely ill, and while, at first, his replacement was temporary, at last he could not return. But this outcome was very important because Father Athanasius preserved valuable details regarding the spirituality, the piety, and the love of the royal family for the liturgical life.

The fact of the intense presence of Saint Seraphim of Sarov with the family, as it appeared in the vision of that virtuous elder from the Sarov Monastery, is also confirmed by Father Athanasius. This occurred at a service at the palace a few days after Saint Seraphim's commemoration in July [20 July Old Style, 2 August New Style], when Father Athanasius mentioned the saint during his sermon. He noted in his diary, "Everyone listened attentively, and I sensed that the spirit of St Seraphim was with those who were praying."[20]

This attestation has special weight because Father Athanasius was known for the sanctity of his own life. This mention gives evidence of a deep spiritual experience, something that is yet revealed more clearly in some other places in his diary. He mentions a similar incident, when he experienced the spiritual intensity of the royal family's prayer, and how this affected his own spiritual state in a wonderful manner. He writes of this:

"One must really be this near to the former Royal Family, must see for oneself, in order to comprehend just how fervently—often on their knees—in what an Orthodox manner, the former Royal Family prays to God. With what obedience, meekness, and humility do they stand during divine services, giving themselves over entirely to the will of God. And in me, a sinful and unworthy servant at the altar of the Lord, my heart becomes still, tears pour forth, and despite the oppressive weight of confinement, the grace of the Lord fills my soul, and words of prayer flow out easily, touching and penetrating the listening faithful."[21]

The same day that Father Athanasius felt the presence of Saint Seraphim in the midst of the family, he also recorded the following beautiful detail in his diary: "The Heir served in the altar, and toward the end of the liturgy went into the nave, where the entire Imperial Family was standing. With them, he listened to my talk on how the memory of St Seraphim had been celebrated in our Feodorovsky Cathedral."[22] Alexis also served as Altar Boy for Father Athanasius on other occasions. Father Athanasius preserved the details of the first time when the child found the courage to participate actively in the Divine Liturgy: "The former Heir Alexei Nikolaevich quietly arrived at the cherubic hymn. He came unnoticed because he used a separate entrance, and went straight into the altar to serve as an acolyte. He would take the censer from the chanter, return it to its place, and would hand it as needed to the protodeacon. This was the first time that his parents' beloved child had shown an inclination to personally participate in divine services."[23]

Father Athanasius' presence in the palace during this period was undoubtedly the work of Divine providence giving the family spiritual support. He supplied the grace of a consoling word and with his sermons instilled in the souls of the imprisoned family the sweetness and the strengthening of Divine grace. Father Athanasius himself refers to this fact, without however noticing—due to his great humility—the great importance of his own personal counsel. He writes, for example:

"Thanks be to God, the entire Imperial Family has recovered, and attends all of the services and attentively listens to the sermons; this is apparent from the fact that as soon as I begin the sermon, they all move forward a little, and stand there until the end."[24]

In another instance he relates: "I was speaking about enduring spiritual suffering, which faces man, abandoned by everyone, in an inexpressible, oppressive state, horrifies him, and the sole comfort he finds is in prayer. At this point there escaped from someone such an irrepressible, loud and powerful, heartrending sigh, that it amazed all of the listeners. And that response of spiritual torment emanated from the place where only the Imperial Family was standing."[25]

Nicholas always thanked Father Athanasius for his spiritual help. When the priest brought out the cross to be kissed, Nicholas would say to him quietly, "Thank you, batiushka, for your kind and comforting words."[26]

These words of consolation came to be a wellspring of great help for the family, because their great trials were still to come...

KERENSKY AND NICHOLAS
A FORESEEN ENCOUNTER

While the family was enduring this first stage of their imprisonment, the maddened crowd of revolutionaries in the capital was not satisfied with the handling of the Romanovs. They thirsted after their blood. The newspapers, more brazenly than ever, published whatever most shameful and provocative material their diseased imagination could conceive. Nicholas was depicted in drawings as applauding enthusiastically at the sight of the hanging of revolutionaries, and Alexandra was depicted as bathing in a tub full of the blood of the victims. All members of all the Soviets with one accord desired nothing less than the death of the royal family and all the rest of the Romanovs. Under these circumstances, the Provisional Government, unable to restrain the outcry of the representatives of the Soviets in meetings, laid the entire responsibility for the protection of the imperial family on the shoulders of Alexander Kerensky, Minister of Justice, and a leading figure in the new government.

Twelve years earlier, Pascha 1905, from the memoirs of Kerensky: "It was Easter and I was returning late at night, or rather in the morning, about four o'clock, from the traditional midnight celebration. I cannot attempt to describe the enchanting spell of St. Petersburg in spring, in the early hours before dawn. ... Happily aglow, I was walking home to the Vassilievsky Island and was about to cross the bridge by the Winter Palace. Suddenly, by the Admiralty, just opposite the Palace, I stopped involuntarily. On an overhanging corner balcony stood the young Emperor, quite alone, deep in thought. A keen presentiment: we should meet some time, somehow our paths would cross."[27]

3 April, 1917. Early in the afternoon Kerensky arrived at the palace prison of Tsarskoe Selo. Going in he assembled the soldiers and the serving staff and made a fiery revolutionary speech saying that they now served the people, who paid them. Therefore, they had the duty to report to the authorities every suspicious thing that they might observe in the palace. Afterwards Count Benckendorff received him in the tsar's waiting room. "Kerensky," the Minister introduced himself. "I have come here to see how you live, to inspect your Palace, and to talk to Nicholas Aleksandrovich"[28] Benckendorff, with a composure irritating to Kerensky, mentioned that he would submit the matter to His Majesty. But wishing to delay the minister

until the family finished their meal, the count suggested to Kerensky a tour of the palace. Benckendorff recalls, "His manner was abrupt and nervous. He did not walk, but ran through the rooms, talking very loudly."[29] With Kerensky a heterogenous unruly mob followed with hostile manner and curious appearance. Some of them were dressed as well-to-do workers wearing black shirts and lambskin hats, some were soldiers, and some were sailors. The latter of these had hanging on them hand-grenades, knives, and revolvers. They went into all the rooms and rummaged through them thoroughly making a lot of noise.

When Kerensky had searched through everything causing a great upheaval, time had passed, and Nicholas and his family had risen from their meal. Benckendorff led the Minister to a parlor and let him wait before a closed double door. Shortly, opening the doors with a grandiose push, the count announced majestically, "His Majesty welcomes you!" Kerensky, as Benckendorff writes, "was in a state of feverish agitation… and seemed like a madman" and "spoke incoherently."[30]

In fact, Kerensky admitted the agitation that had come over him that day. He relates in detail, "To tell the truth, I had been looking forward to the interview with the former Czar with some anxiety, and feared I might lose my temper when I came face to face for the first time with the man I had always hated. …"

"I was trying to pull myself together as we passed through an interminable succession of apartments, preceded by a flunkey. At last we came to the children's rooms. Leaving me before the closed door leading into the inner apartments, the count went in to announce me. …"

"[Once I went in,] my first glimpse of the scene, as I was approaching the Czar, changed my mood altogether. The whole family was standing huddled in confusion around a small table near a window in the adjoining room. A small man in uniform detached himself from the group and moved forward to meet me, hesitating and smiling weakly. It was the Emperor. On the threshold of the room in which I awaited him he stopped, as if uncertain what to do next. He did not know what my attitude would be. Was he to receive me as a host or should he wait until I spoke to him? Should he hold out his hand, or should he wait for my salutation? I sensed his embarrassment at once as well as the confusion of the whole family left alone with a terrible revolutionary. I quickly went up to Nicholas II, held out my hand with a smile, and said abruptly, 'Kerensky,' as I usually introduce myself. He shook my hand firmly, smiled, seemingly encouraged, and led me at once to his family. …

"I inquired about the health of the members of the family, informed them that their foreign relatives were solicitous about their welfare … I begged them not to be anxious or distressed but to rely on me. They thanked me and I began to take my leave. Nicholas II inquired about the military situation and wished me success in my new and difficult office."[31]

Kerensky asked to see Nicholas privately, but did not insist on seeing his daughters when he learned that they were still bedridden due to their illness.

Alexandra was alarmed when Kerensky asked to see Nicholas alone and went next door to the girls' room. Olga and Tatiana, already in somewhat better health hastened to their mother to find out the reason for Kerensky's visit, or, rather, intrusion:

"Mamma, Mamma, what is the matter?"

"Kerensky has insisted upon my leaving him alone with the Emperor," answered the Empress. ... "They'll most probably arrest me,"[32] replied Alexandra.

The two girls literally clung to their mother in fright. Lili Dehn, who had hidden in the girls' room out of fear of arrest, went to the room where the emperor was with Kerensky to learn what had happened. When the emperor emerged, he was already alone:

"Your Majesty," she cried, "tell me, I implore you, if there is anything dreadful in store for Her Majesty?"

"No, no, Lili, and if Kerensky had uttered one word against Her Majesty, you would have heard me strike the table—thus—and" so saying "he struck the writing-table hard with his fist."[33]

This was the first meeting of the two men, which confirmed the premonition that Kerensky had twelve years earlier: their paths had indeed at last crossed. The fervent revolutionary, whose militant attitudes and combative ideology were all turned against the monarchical form of government, had before him, in his hands, to be precise, the embodiment of that very idea that he so hated: the tsar himself. History seemed to have justified him. "Bloody" Nicholas was at his mercy.

At last, as he was leaving Kerensky had Anna Vyrubova and Lili Dehn arrested. Vyrubova's arrest brought some relief to the staff because her presence in the palace was pregnant with serious dangers. The rumors of her involvement both with Rasputin in political matters of state and of their conspiracies with the empress made her extremely hated by the masses. The soldiers threatened openly that they would murder her in the palace, and that after her would come Alexandra's turn. To avoid the danger, Count Benckendorff repeatedly tried to persuade the empress to allow her friend to be transported to some hospital away from the palace. However, Alexandra did not want to even hear of such a thing. At last Anna remained under guard for five months in the Peter-Paul Fortress, while Lili was set free after a few months.

Very little time was given to the two women to bid farewell to the empress. Anna wrote, "The last I remember was the white hand of the Empress pointing upward and her voice: 'There we are always together.'"[34] So also were her final words with Lili, "Lili, by suffering we are purified for Heaven. This good-bye matters little—we shall meet in another world."[35] As they were being taken away, the two women pressed their faces to the windows of the car in a final attempt to see their dear ones who were left behind. They were just able to distinguish the shape of their form behind the

CHAPTER 5

Empress Alexandra with her two beloved friends,
Lili Dehn and Anna Vyrubova.

Alexander Kerensky.

window where they themselves had stood in order to watch their departure. This would be the last time they would see them.

Only six days had passed when a new visit to the palace by Kerensky evoked great unease. It was Holy Tuesday and the family was in church for the morning service. Kerensky called one of the ladies in waiting and told her that as soon as the service ended, he must see Nicholas. Explaining the reason for his visit, he revealed that threatening attitudes toward the imperial couple were growing in the capital, necessitating Nicholas' transfer to some fortress far from Alexandra. They believed that Alexandra was at the head of some counter-revolutionary movement and that she exercised influence over Nicholas in this regard.

Kerensky, in his own words, wished to mollify the situation, but to achieve that in the framework of the investigations that he would conduct to ascertain the pro-German politics of Alexandra, he must isolate Alexandra in some other wing of the palace, away from Nicholas and the children. He would permit their meeting only during meals and at church services, always however with the presence of an officer who would be on duty. The opposition of the entire staff was intense. They considered it inhumane to separate a mother from her children at a time when their illness had not yet completely passed. Kerensky finally yielded and agreed to separate Nicholas from the family for however long the inquests lasted.

The investigation lasted eighteen days. The committee appointed by the Provisional Government responsible for examining all the archives that were kept at the palace, which registered all the activities of the emperor during his reign, could not find any incriminating evidence. Not a single trace of the things his enemies accused him of could be found in Nicholas' records. He was found completely innocent and absolutely faithful in his duty to his country and his people.

As for the long-awaited inquisition of the empress, it lasted only one hour, without it being deemed necessary to call any further sessions. Emerging from the hall where they questioned Alexandra, Kerensky could only say to Nicholas that his wife spoke the truth. This, of course, was not news to Nicholas, but Kerensky, after the whirlwind of slanders against Alexandra, was completely astonished by the clarity and sincerity that characterized the empress' every word. Alexandra, for her part, appreciated Kerensky's courtesy and his decent conduct towards her. After this inquest, Kerensky never again raised the matter of "treason" on the part of the Empress. On the contrary, he assured his colleagues in the Provisional Government that the empress was absolutely faithful to Russia.

Kerensky's contacts with the deposed imperial couple during this time caused all to understand the good intentions that both parties had for Russia's interests. Nicholas appreciated Kerensky and was sorry that he had not known him during his reign. He believed that they would have been able to work together for the good of their country. Kerensky found himself in a state of surprise knowing Nicholas personally. He wrote how he was affected by his "unassuming manner and complete absence of pose. Perhaps it was this natural, quite artless simplicity that gave the Emperor that peculiar fascination, that charm which was further increased by his wonderful eyes, deep and sorrowful. ... It cannot be said that my talks with the Czar were due to a special desire on his part; he was obliged to see me when I came to the palace and visited him. Neither can it be said that his life at that time was an idyll and offered the rosiest of outlooks for the future. Yet the former Emperor never once lost his equilibrium, never failed to act as a courteous man of the world."[36]

CAPTIVITY

UNWANTED UNTO DEATH

Excursion into the garden was an activity precious to the prisoners in the palace. With the coming of spring they were given permission to spend more time outdoors, which brought them much joy because they greatly loved fresh air and physical activity. Thus, they went out daily at 3 o'clock and took walks there and busied themselves with gardening for an hour and a half. This "luxury" however came at a price. Guards were stationed around the garden a short distance apart, and a further detachment came to observe them more strictly. These soldiers taunted the prisoners as they passed by them and constantly bothered them.

On one of these outings, Nicholas took his bicycle and began to ride along the length of the path. When at one point he passed before one of the guards, he bent down and stuck his bayonet through the spokes of the bicycle wheel so that Nicholas tumbled. Thanks to his agility, however, he managed to avoid injury. The guards, of course, broke out into sarcastic laughter over this "exquisite" spectacle. After this episode, Nicholas did not ride his bicycle again.

When the weather was good, Alexandra also came out to the garden, guided by one of the servants on her wheelchair. In those instances, she

The prisoners working in the garden of the Alexander Palace. Gilliard in the center, Nicholas on the right, and the girls far in the back.

Nicholas after cutting wood.

Working in the garden of the Alexander Palace during the permitted outings.
Above: On the left, Tatiana with a guard. Nicholas, on the right.
Below: Tatiana with Maria working under the surveillance of the guards.

Above: Olga, Alexis, Anastasia and Tatiana taking a break from their garden work.
Below: On the left, Tatiana working with Countess Hendrikova.
On the right: Alexis and Tatiana with guards.

Nicholas taking a break from the garden work.

Alexandra doing needlework in her wheelchair.

used to sit on a mat under the shade of a tree. Her sad expression and her wheelchair irritated the soldiers and they taunted her for being unable to walk. The servant who pushed her chair received many abusive attacks. One time when the sailor Nagorny, Alexis' guardian, happened to be pushing her, the soldiers' madness surpassed all previous bounds and they sent letters to this faithful servant threatening him with death. But those who had occasion to come in direct contact with the family only needed to have the barest traces of humanity to discern the quality of these people.

In one of her outings, Alexandra sat under a tree, as was her custom. Next to her sat Baroness Buxhoeveden and they were enjoying the beautiful weather. At one point, however, the baroness rose for a bit, when suddenly a soldier sat heavily next to Alexandra with a hostile growl. "The Empress," writes Buxhoeveden, "edged a little bit away [so that her visitor might sit more comfortably], making a sign to me to be silent, for she was afraid that the whole family would be taken home, and the children robbed of an hour's fresh air."

"The man seemed to her not to have a bad face, and she was soon engaged in conversation with him. At first he cross questioned her, accusing her of 'despising' the people, of showing by not travelling about that she did not want to know Russia. Alexandra Feodorovna quietly explained to him that, as in her young days she had had five children and nursed them all herself, she had not had time to go about the country, and that, afterwards [when they had grown], her health had prevented her. He seemed to be struck by this reasoning and, little by little, he grew more friendly. He asked the Empress about her life, about her children, her attitude towards Germany, etc. She answered in simple words that she had been a German in her youth, but that that was long past. Her husband and her children were Russians, and she was a Russian too, now, with all her heart. When I came back with the officer, who seemed a decent man, and to whom I had risked appealing, fearing that the soldier might annoy the Empress, I found them peacefully discussing questions of religion. The soldier got up on our approach, and took the Empress' hand, saying 'Do you know, Alexandra Feodorovna, I had quite a different idea of you? I was mistaken about you.' It was the more striking because this man was the deputy of the Soviet. When he came on guard the next time he was quite polite."[37]

Day and night the guards ran up and down afraid that at any minute there would be some attempt to free the family. Had any such thing taken place, it would have obviously meant the end of their own lives. As for the prisoners inside the palace, they lived every day with the anxiety that the following day would find them free or thrown into the depth of some soviet dungeon. The Provisional Government hoped that they would soon send them somewhere abroad, but for the present they did not dare to take any such initiative. For the time being the Provisional Government was under continual and close observation by the Soviet. It could not take a single

Baroness Sophie Buxhoeveden.

step behind their backs. They had to await some change in the political stage. Gilliard had somehow perceived the authorities' impotency when he wrote the following:

"Our captivity at Tsarskoie-Selo did not seem likely to last long, and there was talk about our imminent transfer to England. Yet the days passed and our departure was always being postponed. ... Yet we were only a few hours by railway from the Finnish frontier, and the necessity of passing through Petrograd was the only serious obstacle.

"It would thus appear that if the authorities had acted resolutely and secretly it would not have been difficult to get the Imperial family to one of the Finnish ports and thus to some foreign country. But they were afraid of responsibilities, and no one dare compromise himself."[38]

But there was something else that neither Gilliard nor the family knew. Despite the Provisional Government's intention to transport the family abroad, and apart from the opposition of the Soviets, there was yet another insurmountable obstacle. On 20 March, 1917, Kerensky spoke at the session of representatives of the Soviet of Moscow and declared with emphasis: "As general public prosecutor I have the power to decide the fate of Nicholas II. But, comrades, the Russian Revolution is unstained by bloodshed and I will not permit it to be disgraced."[39] 'I will not be the Marat[40] of the Russian

Revolution… and I will take the Czar to Murmansk myself. The Russian Revolution does not take vengeance."[41] However, the conditions for the bold enterprise of the transporting the family to the Finnish border, and from there to England, began to be somewhat more favorable only in June. The Provisional Government, somewhat more established in power, was now able to proceed on this secret mission. But why did no such thing materialize?

Even from the first days after the revolution, the Provisional Government of Russia began to take steps to secure their asylum from the King of England, George V, and his liberal Prime Minister David Lloyd George. King George was Nicholas' first cousin, and their outward resemblance was uncanny. Moreover, their ties were always rather tight, and precisely for this reason the government of Russia was resolved to do this. Lloyd George and the Ministerial Council of England declared to King George that it was inclined to grant asylum to the family, but only because the request came from the new liberal government of Russia. The unique condition was the assumption of the expenses of maintaining the family by the Provisional Government of Russia. Under this condition the Russian Foreign Minister replied that the Provisional Government was willing to advance a very generous amount to cover the needs of the family.

Thus, when at the end of June the necessary arrangements were made to transport the family, the Provisional Government applied once again to England, informing them of this. But in the meanwhile, the diplomatic attitude had changed significantly on England's political stage. And so, in the end, the answer of the English government was negative. The responsibility for the rejection of the request remains to this day a matter of much debate. The certain thing is that not only the Labour Party but also the Liberal Party opposed the acceptance of the request. They were concerned that the extreme Left of Russia would use this event in order to turn public opinion against England.

There is yet one more account. Prince Edward, son of the King of England, remembers an incident that happened one morning while he was having breakfast with his parents, King George and Queen Mary. Prince Edward remembers: "Suddenly an equerry comes in. I meant this was breakfast, for heaven's sake! We looked, I hope, suitably horrified at this breach. Not done, you know, ever. The king was furious, but the man went straight up to him with this note, which the king read and gave my mother, and she read it and gave it back and said, 'No.' The king gave it to the equerry and said, 'No.' Later that day I asked my mother what that was all about and she said the government was willing to send up a ship to rescue that czar and his family but she did not think it would be good for us to have them in England."[42]

Some consider the Queen of England's refusal to be the result of a personal animosity against Empress Alexandra. But if Queen Mary had any serious reasons not to receive the imperial family of Russia in her country, these would, in fact, be purely political.

CAPTIVITY

The Provisional Government's subsequent attempt to secure asylum for the family from the French government foundered on the same negative attitude. Nicholas and Alexandra were not informed of these attempts to bring about their escape. They themselves did not wish to leave Russia. They could not face the prospect of living in European hotels as former royalty, hounded by reporters for snapshots and interviews. "I'd rather go to the uttermost ends of Siberia," said the emperor.[43] As for Alexandra, she prayed daily not to leave Russia. She said that anything of that sort would be a true nightmare. They considered it their duty to remain in Russia and to share her destiny with her.

AN HISTORICAL PARENTHESIS

When Tsar Nicholas abdicated, it seemed that the aim of the conspirators was achieved. But having caused chaos, they soon became its victims. At first, the February Revolution spread a wave of enthusiasm throughout the country. They believed that a new epoch of freedom was beginning. However, not everyone was happy. Most of the population of the huge country did not even understand what exactly had happened. They were wondering why and on what ground the tsar abdicated the throne. Neither the course of war nor economic circumstances demanded such a change.

Russia suffered far less casualties in the war than its enemies or allies. The mobilization rate in Russia amounted to just 39% of all men aged from 15 to 49, while in Germany it was 81%, in Austria-Hungary 74%, in France 79% and in England 50%. In Russia, for every 1000 mobilized soldiers there were 115 dead compared to 154 in Germany, 122 in Austria, 168 in France, and 125 in England.[44]

The Provisional Government was supposed to support the country's order, successfully end the war, and summon the National Constituent Assembly to determine the new form of government in Russia. But at the same time, throughout the country completely new governing bodies spontaneously began to emerge: the Soviets of the deputies of soldiers, sailors, workers, and farmers. The country was ruled by dual power. The Soviets were representative governing bodies elected by the people. The Petersburg Soviet of Workers' and Soldiers' Deputies, established on 1 March, 1917, tried to extend its jurisdiction as a national governing body. In total there were nearly six hundred Soviets established in Russia, headed for the most part by Mensheviks—a faction of the Marxist Social Democratic Party—and the SRs, the non-Marxist Social Revolutionary Party, most numerous of all the leftist parties in Russia. The Soviet regime originally had nothing to do with the Bolshevik Party. Only in the second half of 1917 would the number of Bolsheviks in the Soviets reach 90%.

CHAPTER 5

Within days, the country was swept by economic problems. Everyone understood the so-called "freedom" in their own way. Many took it as an opportunity not to work at all. Instead of artificial food shortages, a real food crisis began. Within one month, "bread cards" were introduced in Petersburg. One person could get 1 pound (400 grams) of bread per day, a half of today's loaf. By September, this amount was reduced to half a pound.

Every next day, the country was drawing closer to chaos and catastrophe, while the Petersburg Soviet issued its first military order, which undermined the Russian army within few months. The order, which was published on the same day as the establishment of the Petersburg Soviet, March 1, transferred all power within military units from the hands of the officers to special committees elected by the soldiers. All orders had to be obeyed only if they did not contradict the committees. All weapons were to be handed over to these committees as well and by no means were to be issued to the officers. The soldiers reported to the committees in case of any misunderstanding with their commanders.

As a result, committees were established everywhere, completely undermining military discipline. It is hard to imagine anything more bizarre that could completely ruin the Russian army at the front, right in the middle of war. Within a few months, the exemplary Russian army changed beyond recognition. There were protests, insubordination, debauchery, excessive drinking, and desertion. Officers' orders were disregarded. Soldiers would refuse to attack, they would refuse to carry their wounded comrades from the battlefield, they would abandon their trench when the enemy began to attack. And all this happened right before the decisive offensive that had been prepared and was expected to bring Russia the much-awaited victory.

Time passed and conditions in Russia were anything but stable. Political support for the Soviets by the masses of workers increased continually and prepared the ground to receive an until now forgotten personality. Vladimir Ilyich Ulyanov, known as Lenin, now appeared actively on the stage not only of Russian, but also of world history.

LENIN
THE FATEFUL RETURN

Vladimir Ulyanov was born in Simbirsk on 22 April, 1870, two years after Nicholas' birth. His family drew their descent from various nationalities. Apart from Russian, they had German and Jewish elements. However, Vladimir was baptized in the Orthodox Church. One of the most important events that sealed the later course of Ulyanov was the execution of his elder brother for participating in an assassination attempt against Tsar Alexander III, Nicholas' father.

In 1892, once he finished his studies in the Department of Law of the University of Saint Petersburg, Vladimir began to work as a lawyer. The focus of his interest was the study of Marxist philosophy. Already from this time, Vladimir envisioned the economic and political development of Russia and of the entire world. Thus in 1894 he moved to Saint Petersburg where he devoted all his energies to propaganda work, for which he was at last arrested in December 1895. In 1896 he was held in prison, and in 1897 he was exiled to Siberia.

In 1900 Vladimir Ulyanov went to Switzerland where he began to work for the creation of a revolutionary social-democratic movement. His goal was to prepare an armed uprising of the masses to overthrow the tsarist regime. In 1903, at a meeting of the Russian Social-Democratic Party of Workers, which took place in Brussels and London, the party split into two factions, the Bolsheviks ["Majority"] and the Mensheviks ["Minority"]. Vladimir Ulyanov, already known under the party name Lenin, was chosen as leader of the Bolshevik faction, from which the Bolshevik Party was later constituted.

When the revolution broke out in Saint Petersburg in March 1917, only two months had passed since Lenin had declared that his generation would not live to see this great event. Despite the events, his conviction remained firm. Neither the abdication of the tsar nor the formation of the Provisional Government persuaded Lenin that the hour had come that he had dreamt of. He considered this change of power as the replacement of one capitalist system by another. Thus, on 25 March he sent his instruction to the Bolshevik Party in Saint Petersburg, "Our tactics: absolute distrust, no support of the new government, Kerensky especially suspect, no rapprochement with the other parties."[45]

Despite his skeptical attitude towards all that was taking place in Russia, Lenin burned with desire to return as soon as possible. He remained awake for entire nights making all sorts of plans for his repatriation. But this was all extremely dangerous. Nevertheless, he did not need to labor for long on this point. The "friend" who would be able to solve his problem was found: Germany. The revolution in Russia, in which Germany had invested so much capital, was not able to bring about the result she so desired, the removal of Russia from the war. Perhaps Lenin could accomplish this, which moreover he promised. But even if their collaborator failed to seize absolute power in his hands and in concluding a peace between them, the Germans knew that his presence was enough to evoke intense turmoil in Russia.

On 9 April, in a sealed German train Lenin, his wife, and seventeen other Bolshevik exiles set out on their return journey. Later the English Prime Minister Winston Churchill wrote: "the German war leaders… had from the beginning used the most terrible means of offence at their disposal…. Nevertheless, it was with a sense of awe that they turned upon Russia the most grisly of all weapons. They transported Lenin in a sealed truck like a plague bacillus from Switzerland into Russia."[46]

CHAPTER 5

After twenty years' absence, on 16 April, 1917 Lenin was received in Saint Petersburg by an immense crowd of people and a sea of red banners. There at the railway station the "prophet" of socialist revolution achieved apotheosis. His preaching began at the same moment: "This war is a shameful capitalist slaughter!" Thus, the fatal microbe that had arrived began to infect Russia.

The following day at the All-Russian Congress of Soviets, Lenin published his famous "April Theses," demanding the overthrow of the Provisional Government, the abolition of the police, of the army, and of the bureaucracy, and the end to the war. The enthusiastic reception of the previous days, however, were not repeated at the congress. His proposals were considered delusional and madness. Even the more distinguished Bolshevik leaders believed that for the transition from the authoritarian [tsarist] regime to socialism a prolonged middle period of bourgeois government was necessary. Lenin left the hall amid jeers! His defeat, however, meant nothing to him.

All that spring and summer Lenin ceaselessly battered the Provisional Government. Putting aside for the moment his extreme Marxist rhetoric, he made his slogan, that which the masses of the people desired more than anything else: "Bread, Land, Peace" and "All power to the Soviets." When the people realized that the Provisional Government did not intend to end the war, the balance began to shift. The Bolsheviks won over significant popular opinion. Then the ministers began to resign, one after the other. With the resignation of the Prime Minister Lvov at the beginning of July, Kerensky took his place. The situation at the front, however, had brought forth worse dangers. Soldiers' commissions, poisoned by Bolshevik propaganda, took control of the situation and pushed the armies into general retreat.

16 July, 1917. A familiar picture was repeated again in the streets of Saint Petersburg. The only difference was the slogans: "Down with the War! Down with the Provisional Government!" Lenin was not ready to manage this sudden outbreak in his favor. The Provisional Government, mainly by issuing a document that presented Lenin as a German spy within the security agencies, succeeded in quashing the uprising. Arrests of Bolshevik leaders began, but Lenin, disguised as fireman, succeeded in escaping to Finland. The first Bolshevik uprising had failed.

UNKNOWN DESTINATION

The Bolsheviks "are after me and then will be after you,"[47] Kerensky had said to Nicholas before the uprising of July. It was now already clear that for the family to remain near the capital was anything but safe. Kerensky decided to transport the family elsewhere, to some distant point of Russia. Nicholas asked whether it would be possible to move to Livadia, their beloved resort.

When Kerensky informed Nicholas on 11 August that they would depart within a few days, and that they should take warm clothes with them, Nicholas realized that their destination was not Livadia. Without letting Nicholas know their destination, Kerensky began to justify his rejection of Livadia. Nicholas however interrupted him and said to him quietly. "I have no fear. We trust you."[48]

Preparations began immediately at fever pitch. At this new stage in their trials, the family was voluntarily accompanied into exile by the tutors, Pierre Gilliard and Miss Schneider, Countess Hendrikova, Prince Dolgorukov, Doctor Botkin, and Alexandra's *valet-de-chambre*, Alexei Volkov. Baroness Buxhoeveden would meet them later, since she had to undergo an operation. However, their parting with Count Benckendorff and his wife was definitive. The Countess's chronic bronchitis and their old age did not permit them to follow the family so beloved to them. Benckendorff's place would be taken by General Tatishchev, who arrived at the palace for this purpose immediately.

On 12 August, 30 July by the Old Calendar, Alexis completed his thirteenth year. The empress, on this opportunity, requested that the Znamenie Icon of the Mother of God be brought to the palace. Colonel Kobylinsky, who was the commandant of the palace at that time says of this, "On July 30 (August 12), the Imperial Family asked me to bring the Znamensky Holy Image of the Virgin from the Znamensky Church to the Palace as they wanted to hold divine service on the birthday of Alexis Nikolaevich."[49]

The Icon arrived accompanied by a procession of clergy who entered the palace and served a moleben at the palace chapel for the good success of the family's journey. Benckendorff remembers, "The scene was moving. The ceremony was as poignant as could be: all were in tears. The soldiers themselves seemed touched, and approached the holy ikon to kiss it. They [the family] followed the procession as far as the balcony, and saw it disappear through the Park. It was as if the past were taking leave, never to come back. The memory of this ceremony will always remain in my mind, and I cannot think of it without profound emotion."[50]

Kobylinsky, thirty-nine years old, was a veteran of the war, who had been wounded twice in action. He was not a revolutionary, but simply an officer who continued to carry out his duties under the new government. In his depths, however, the colonel remained faithfully devoted to the royal family, and insofar as possible, he attempted to make his royal prisoners' life easier. By orders from Kerensky, he was to remain in command of the detachment of guards who would accompany the family. Nicholas wrote of him to his mother, that he was his last friend.

Their departure was scheduled by train on the 14th of August. The previous evening Kerensky left early from a meeting with the Council of Ministers to oversee the last preparations before the trip, of which no one knew except himself and three other trusted persons. His first concern on arrival at the palace at 11 pm was to speak to the guard that was assigned to follow the family to their new destination.

CHAPTER 5

Addressing himself to the guard Kerensky said, "You kept guard over the Imperial Family in Tsarskoe-Selo, and you are to do the same in Tobolsk, where the Imperial Family are to be removed according to the resolution of the Council of Ministers. Remember, don't strike a man when he is down. … Don't forget that your charge is a former Emperor, and he and his Family must want for nothing."[51]

Kerensky took care of one more thing before the family's departure. That last night, as the preparations continued at a fast pace, Grand Duke Michael, Nicholas' brother arrived there. They permitted him to meet with his brother alone to bid him farewell. Kerensky was obliged to be present at the meeting, but he stood discreetly out of the way. He described the meeting: "The brothers… were most deeply moved. For a long time they were silent… then they plunged into that fragmentary, irrelevant small-talk which is so characteristic of short meetings. How is Alix? How is Mother? Where are you living now? and so on. They stood opposite each other, shuffling their feet in curious embarrassment, sometimes getting hold of one another's arm or coat button."[52]

Alexis spotted Michael. Kobylinsky relates, "Suddenly Alexis Nikolaevich ran towards me and asked: 'Is that Uncle Mimi who has just come?'" The Colonel answered that it was, and indicated to him that he would not be able to enter the room where his father was. Then, Kobylinsky continues, "Alexis Nikolaevich asked my permission to hide himself behind the door. 'I want to see him when he goes out,' said the Tsarevitch. So he hid behind the door and looked through the crack of it at Michael Alexandrovich."[53] After ten minutes Michael came out, kissed Alexis hastily and left weeping. That was the last time he would see them alive.[54]

At one point Benckendorff asked Kerensky how long the family would remain in exile. Kerensky replied with all certainty that after a Constituent Assembly that coming November, Nicholas with his family would be free to go wherever they wish. Kerensky spoke with sincerity when he said that. What he did not know, however, was that in November he himself would be a fugitive, hunted by the Bolsheviks.

A few months later, with the family now in exile, Nicholas wrote a moving letter to his sister Ksenia, where he described in short this very period of their imprisonment at the palace:

> My own dear Ksenia,
>
> … As you know, when I arrived from Mogilev, I found all the children quite sick, especially Maria and Anastasia. Naturally, I spent the whole day with them dressed in a white [hospital] smock. The doctors came to see them in the morning and the evening, accompanied at first by a guard officer. Some of them entered the bedroom and were present during the doctor's exams. Later, the officers stopped accompanying the doctors.

Grand Duke Michael Alexandrovich.

I took walks with Valia D. [Dolgorukov] and with one of the officers or with the chief of the guard himself. Since, after the end of February, they no longer cleared the park, there was no place to walk because of the masses of snow—so excellent work turned up for me: clearing paths. A chain of guards stood around the house and another around the pond and the railing of the small garden across from the windows of Mama's rooms. We could walk only inside and along the length of this second chain [of soldiers]. When the ice melted and it became warm, the former commandant, Colonel Korovichenko, said that he would push the chain out a little farther.

CHAPTER 5

Nicholas clearing the paths from the snow.

Three weeks went by without a change. One fine day, four riflemen with their guns followed me; I made use of this and went farther into the park. Ever since, long daily walks in the park have been allowed, as has the chopping down and sawing up of dry trees. All of us would exit through the doors of the round hall, to which the chief of the guard kept the key. We never used the balcony, since the door to it was locked.

Our exit together with all of our people into the garden, to work either in the vegetable garden or in the woods, must have recalled the animals' abandonment of Noah's Ark: next to the sentry box at the bottom of the stairs from the round balcony a crowd of riflemen gathered to observe this procession in a mocking manner. The return home also took place in a group, since the door was instantly locked. At first, I would greet them out of habit, but I soon stopped because they answered unpleasantly or not at all.

During the summer, we were allowed to take the air until 8 o'clock in the evening. I rode bicycles with my daughters and watered the vegetables, since it was very dry. Evenings, we sat by the windows and watched how the riflemen rested on the grass, smoked, read, horsed around, and sang. ...

Naturally, during this long period of time there were many trifling and amusing, but sometimes unpleasant, episodes. But everything can't be described, and someday, should God grant it, we'll tell you in person.⁵⁵

As for Alexandra, a short while before their departure to the unknown destination, she wrote to Lili Dehn:

> It is necessary to look more calmly on everything. What is to be done? Once He sent us such trials, evidently He thinks we are sufficiently prepared for it. It is a sort of examination—it is necessary to prove that we did not go through it in vain. One can find in everything something good and useful—whatever sufferings we go through—let it be. He will give us force and patience and will not leave us. He is merciful. It is only necessary to bow to His wish without murmur and await—there on the other side He is preparing to all who love Him indescribable joy.
>
> You are young and so are our children—how many I have besides my own—you will see better times yet here. I believe strongly the bad will pass and there will be clear and cloudless sky. But the thunderstorm has not passed yet and therefore it is stifling—but I know it will be better afterwards. One must have only a little patience—and is it really so difficult? For every day that passes quietly I thank God.⁵⁶

A FAMILY IN EXILE

On 19 August, after a trip of five days, the family arrived at their new destination: Tobolsk in Siberia. En route, after a journey by train, they set out by boat from the village of Pokrovskoe, Rasputin's hometown. From the deck the family could discern the tall house of the *muzhik*, which easily stood out from the poor izbas of the other villagers.

The family would stay at the house of the governor of Tobolsk, which had been assigned for that purpose. At precisely this house Nicholas had been guest twenty-eight years earlier on his return from his journey to the Far East. Now he would not be a guest, but a prisoner in that house. The house was two-storey with a balcony and a small garden. The family was accommodated on the upper floor. The four sisters shared a corner room and Alexis had his own room next to which was that of the sailor Nagorny. Gilliard was housed on the ground floor, while the remaining staff was assigned a house on the other side of the street. Volkov writes:

"The Governor's house was spacious and very comfortable. The Imperial Family and servants, everyone, was well housed. The suite lived in the Kornilov house, directly across the street from the Governor's house. Tatitchev, Botkin, Dologoruki, Miss Schneider, Countess Hendrikova, and

CHAPTER 5

later Gibbs, the English teacher who arrived in Tobolsk after we did, all lived there [at the Kornilov house]. Gilliard lived in the Governor's house [with the family]."[57] The staff had complete freedom and could go to the city whenever they wished. Some of them rented apartments in the city and Doctor Botkin got permission to set up a clinic in the center of Tobolsk.

Kobylinsky also wished to extend similar liberties to the family. When, though, on the first morning after their arrival, the family visited the staff at the house across the street, the soldiers reacted against the degree of freedom given to the prisoners. Kobylinsky was obliged to permit an enclosure to be built around the house with a tall wooden fence, enclosing in the fenced space some piece of the small street next to the house, so that the prisoners would be able to walk there a little.

One corner in the drawing room, on the first floor of the house, had been converted by the family into a chapel where icons and lamps were placed. The priest of the Church of the Annunciation in Tobolsk came to perform the services with the deacon and four sisters of the Ivanovsky Convent. Very often, however, the singing had to be supplied by the empress with her daughters. Alexandra's letters to her friend Anna Vyrubova during this time give a very living picture of the common prayer life of the family:

"The days fly. It is Saturday again, and we shall have evening service at nine. A corner of the drawing room has been arranged with our ikons and lamps. It is homelike—but not church. I got so used to going almost daily for three years to the church of Znamenia before going on to the hospitals at Tsarskoe."[58] "We had to sing this morning without any preparation, but it went—well, not too badly. God helped. After service we tried to sing some new prayers with the new deacon, and I hope it will go better tonight."[59]

Pankratov, one of the Bolshevik commissars who had a leading place in the house in Tobolsk, preserved a few details from the family's life in exile. He wrote the following:

"When I was free,[60] I often heard it said that Nicholas II's family was very religious. ... The spiritual-moral need of the royal prisoners was initially satisfied by holding services in the hall of the Governor's House, that is, in the same house where the former tsar's family lived [in Tobolsk]. And on the next Saturday [after I went on duty], I happened to attend vigil for the first time."

"All the work of setting up and preparing the hall for worship was taken upon by Alexandra Feodorovna. She placed the icon of the Savior in the hall, covered the wooden icon stand [and] decorated them both with her embroidery, etc. At 8 o'clock in the evening the priest from the Annunciation Church and four nuns from the Ivanovsky Monastery came. ... Candles were lit around the icon stand. The service began. The whole family piously crossed themselves; the suite and the servants followed the movements of their former masters. I remember that this whole situation made a profound first impression upon me. The priest in vestments, the nuns in black, flickering candles, the soft singing of the nuns, the visible

From a service in the chapel set up in the house in Tobolsk.
On the right, the sisters of the Ivanovsky Monastery
chanting at the lectern.

religiosity of the worshippers, the icon of the Saviour. A string of thoughts gave way one to another. 'What are they praying for, what is this former royal family asking for? What do they feel?' I asked myself."

"[When] The nuns sang, 'Glory to God in the highest, and on earth, peace goodwill toward men.'[61] Nicholas II's whole family kneels down and fervently cross themselves. Behind them, all the rest [also] fall on their knees. At the time it seemed to me that the former tsar's whole family immersed themselves sincerely in religious feeling and mood."[62]

As Alexandra often wrote in her letters, their great desire was to be in church and especially at the Divine Liturgy. At the beginning of their settlement in Tobolsk they were not permitted to go to the church for Liturgy, which troubled the family very much, as they wished to receive Communion.

CHAPTER 5

In Tobolsk. From left: Tatiana, Olga, unidentified child, Alexis, Nicholas, Anastasia.

At last on 8 September [Old Style],⁶³ the Feast of the Nativity of the Theotokos, the family was allowed to go to church for the Liturgy for the first time.

Gilliard writes, "[Permission to attend the Liturgy] pleased them greatly, but the consolation was only to be repeated very rarely. On these occasions we rose very early and, when everyone had collected in the yard, went out through a little gate leading on to the public garden, which we crossed between two lines of soldiers. … While going and returning I have often seen people cross themselves or fall on their knees as Their Majesties passed."⁶⁴

Nicholas again writes to his sister Ksenia regarding this matter: "We just returned from liturgy, which begins for us at 8 o'clock, when it is completely dark. "In order to get into our church we must pass by the town garden and cross the street – about 500 paces in all from the house. The riflemen stand in a loose chain along the right and left; when we begin to go home, they gradually leave their places and walk behind us while others remain off in the distance and to the side – all this reminds us of the end of a roundup, so that we laugh every time we walk through our gate. I am very glad that they reduced your guard—both you and they understand it's 'extremely tiresome.' Poor, confused people."⁶⁵

Church attendance was a balm for the family. Maria, in a letter to a certain friend of hers on 10/23 December 1917 wrote, "This morning at 8 we went to Obednya [Liturgy]. We are always so happy when they let us go to church, of course one cannot compare this church with our Sobor [the Feodorovsky Cathedral], but still better than [having service] in the room."⁶⁶

However, permission to attend church was not given often and in her letters, Alexandra describes her pain and longing for this: "We hope tomorrow to go to Holy Communion, but neither today nor yesterday were we allowed to go to church. We have had services at home, last night prayers for the dead, tonight confession and evening prayer."⁶⁷ "On the 6th we had service at home, not being allowed to go to church on account of some kind of a disturbance. I have not been out in the fresh air for four weeks. I can't go out in such bitter weather because of my heart. Nevertheless church draws me almost irresistibly."⁶⁸ "How I long to take Communion."⁶⁹ "I hope nobody will ever see these letters, as the smallest thing makes them react upon us with severity. That is to say we get no church services outside or in."[70]

"On the whole, the inhabitants of Tobolsk," writes Gilliard, "were still very attached to the Imperial family, and our guards had repeatedly to intervene to prevent them standing under the windows or removing their hats and crossing themselves as they passed the house."[71] The more difficult incidents were when the empress or the girls went out on the balcony. In those instances, many gathered to see them, which caused tension in the guard.

Furthermore, many merchants freely sent gifts to the family, the nuns brought them sugar and sweets, and the peasants, butter and eggs. The soldiers at first opposed it, but the family's simplicity of conduct and manner of life gradually began to make an impression on them. Freed from the contagion of the revolutionary atmosphere of the capital, they began to relate to the members of the family, especially the children. The girls asked them about their homeland and families and soon learned the names of their wives and children. When someone from the regiment who was especially friendly to the family was on duty, Nicholas with Alexis and the girls discreetly slipped into their chamber to play various board games with them. Thus, the first months of Siberian exile rolled by fairly quietly.

Little Alexis had a special joy in the period of their stay in Tobolsk. The authorities permitted his beloved friend Kolya to come to the house to play together. Nicholas Derevenko, known by the nickname Kolya, was the son of Alexis' personal physician, Dr Vladimir Derevenko, who followed the family into exile to treat his little patient. Kolya had been Alexis' inseparable friend for years, and his presence here in Siberia was a great consolation to him. In Alexis' letter to his teacher Peter Vasilievich, the liveliness that characterized the relationship of the two boys is apparent: "While I am writing You, Zhylik[72] is reading a newspaper, and Kolya is sketching a portrait of him. Kolya is being rowdy and therefore distracting me from writing to You. Dinner is soon. Nagorny is sending You warm regards. ... Lord keep you! Your loving Aleksei."[73]

This simplicity and intimacy that characterized the members of the Imperial Family made an impression not only on the soldiers, but also on the people considered to be connected to the family. Gilliard writes characteristically, "At tea in the evening with Their Majesties, General Tatichtchef, with a frankness justified by the circumstances, expressed his surprise at finding how intimate and affectionate was the family life of the Czar and Czarina and their children. The Czar, smiling at the Czarina, said, 'You hear what Tatichtchef says?' Then, with his usual good-humour tinged with a touch of irony, he added: 'You have been my aide-de-camp, Tatichtchef, and had ever so many opportunities of observing us. If you knew so little about us, how can you expect us to blame the newspapers for what they say about us?'"[74]

CHAPTER 5

Alexis having a lesson with his tutor Peter Vasilievich Petrov.

FORGOTTEN BY THE WORLD

The family had fallen into a regular routine and the schedule in the far north rolled smoothly. Nearly forgotten by the world, the members of the royal family lived peacefully amid the daily routine of their new reality. Colonel Kobylinsky gave a very detailed description of this reality:

"Our life in Tobolsk went on peacefully. The restrictions were the same as in Tsarskoe-Selo, but everybody felt much happier. The officer of the day remained in his own room, and nobody interfered with the private life of the Imperial Family. They all rose early, except the Empress. In the morning after breakfast the Emperor took a walk and went in for some sort of physical exercise. The children also had a walk. Everybody did what he pleased. In the morning the Emperor used to read and write up his diary, the children had their lessons. The Empress read, embroidered, or painted."

"Lunch was served at eleven o'clock. After lunch the Family usually had a walk. The Emperor frequently used to saw logs with Dolgoruky, Tatishchev, and Gilliard, and sometimes the Grand Duchesses took part in this. Tea was served at four o'clock, and everybody stood at the window and watched the life of the town."

"Dinner was at six, and after dinner, Tatishchev, Dolgoruky, Botkin, and Derevenko joined us and sometimes we played cards. The only card players in the Family were the Emperor and the Grand Duchess Olga. The Emperor occasionally used to read aloud. Sometimes they staged French or English plays. Tea was served at eight o'clock, and conversation became general until eleven, but never later. After eleven o'clock everybody retired for the night; the Tsarevitch went to bed at nine or thereabouts."[75]

Kobylinsky, after a request from Nicholas, took care to bring to the house a great quantity of oak trunks, hatchets and saws to cut the wood that they would need for the kitchen and the hearth. This physical activity, especially in the frozen Siberian winter, was very helpful exercise for those that could participate. The soldiers were astonished when they saw with what dexterity the young princesses could cut wood with hatchets and saws. Often not even peasant women displayed such skill in this masculine work.

The four duchesses—Olga twenty-two years old, Tatiana twenty, Maria eighteen, and Anastasia sixteen—were now young women filled with life and energy. However, their only entertainment was to sit at the window and observe life in the outside world go by normally, oblivious to what the new inhuman regime had in store for them. In order to lighten their mood, their tutors Pierre Gilliard and the Englishman Sidney Gibbes began to stage plays and to "adapt" small excerpts from classic theatrical works in which all took part with especial joy. In the evenings after supper, sitting all around the fire, they listened to Nicholas read from various books. During the reading, the women knitted and all together they attempted to keep warm drinking tea and coffee.

The severe Siberian winter visited the exiles of Tobolsk in December. No door and no window was able to keep out of

Anastasia at a lesson with Sydney Gibbes.

the house the -20°C (-4°F) temperature. Despite the fire that constantly burned in the parlor, the temperature in the house never rose above -6°C (22°F)! Sitting around the fireplace Alexandra shivered throughout and suffered chilblains. Her fingers had become so stiff that they could hardly knit.

Christmas 1917 would be their last. Isolated from the world, they lived the joy of the feast of love, distributing to the members of their staff gifts that they had made themselves. These gifts were projects requiring weeks to make, with the main ingredient being the true love of the members of the family: knit vests, painted handmade ribbons for bookmarks, and all manner of handiwork. On Christmas Eve, Alexandra wrote in her diary: "December 24, 1917—Sunday: Christmas Eve. Got the presents ready. 12 p.m. Liturgy at home... I decorated the tree, laid out the gifts... Later I went to the guard-watch of the 14th Rifle Regiment... I brought them a small Christmas tree, food, and a Gospel reading for each one of them with enclosure, which I drew. I sat there with them."[76] On Christmas morning they had the blessing to attend the morning Liturgy. But an unfortunate incident caused them to lose further opportunities for the heavenly joy of attending church.

The service had nearly ended when the deacon, despite the prohibition against it, dared to proclaim the prayer [Polychronion, or *Mnogoletie*] for the prolongation of the life of the royal family. The congregation in turn repeated the refrain "Many years!" The soldiers became furious, threatening the priest who had commanded the deacon to intone these words. They were shouting, "Drag him out of the church by the hair." Kobylinsky described the event:

"...the soldiers started a riot and made up their minds to kill, or at least to arrest the officiating clergy. It was most difficult to persuade them not to take any aggressive steps and await the decision of an investigating committee. Bishop Hermogen immediately transferred Father Vasiliev to the Abalaksky Monastery, as the situation was so strained, and I went to see the Bishop personally and ask him to appoint another clergyman. ... So, the men decided not to allow the Imperial Family to go to church, and only allowed them to pray in the presence of a soldier. The sole concession I was able to obtain was permission for the Imperial Family to visit church on the *Dvounadesiatye Prazdniky* (important Holy Days in the Orthodox Church [i.e. the Twelve Great Feasts])."[77]

Nevertheless, the family had also a very special blessing on that Christmas. Alexandra writes in her diary: "After the liturgy—there was a prayer before the miraculous icon of Abalatskaya Mother of God."[78] The icon was brought to the house on Christmas Eve from the Ablatsko-Znamenskii Monastery, 17 miles from Tobolsk, and it offered great spiritual consolation to the imprisoned family.

Alexandra wrote to Lili Dehn during this period, "I am already looking forward to those beautiful services—such a longing to pray in church. I dream of our church (at Tsarskoe Selo) and of my little cell-like corner near the altar."⁷⁹

A heavenly helper came to the family in their great spiritual need, Hermogenes, the Archbishop of Tobolsk. Hermogenes had previously been Bishop of Saratov and at first was one of the supporters of Rasputin, but later convinced that the accusations about his debauched life were true, he became his vehement opponent. As a result, he had a rupture with Nicholas, who had relieved him of his episcopal duties in 1915, and Hermogenes was obliged to retreat to the Monastery of Saint Nicholas in Ugresha, in the suburbs of Moscow. In 1917 the Provisional Government assigned Hermogenes as Archbishop of Tobolsk and Siberia.

During the royal family's exile in Tobolsk Archbishop Hermogenes did all he could to ease their living conditions. The most important of these improvements were the efforts undertaken by the archbishop to establish a regular chapel in the house where the Divine Liturgy might be held. Nicholas reconsidered his past attitude against the hierarch "and sent Bishop Hermogenes a bow to the earth, asking him to forgive him that he had been forced to allow his removal from his see. He could not have done otherwise at the time, but he was glad to have the opportunity of asking the bishop's forgiveness now. The bishop was very touched, and sent a bow to the earth to the Tsar together with a prosphora and asked for his forgiveness."⁸⁰

This chapel set up in the house by the archbishop's decree was truly a great blessing for the family. However, in order to assure that even at these private services no similar incident would occur, the soldiers stationed a guard in the house. This fact meant the beginning of a closer and more severe observation of the life of the prisoners.

Despite these new difficulties, life in Tobolsk continued to roll on in its usual rhythm. In December Alexandra wrote to Anna Vyrubova, who had already been released from prison, "Lessons begin at nine (in bed). Up at noon for religious lessons with Tatiana, Marie, Anastasie, and Alexei. I have a German lesson three times a week with Tatiana and once with Marie, besides reading with Tatiana. Also I sew, embroider, and paint, with spectacles on because my eyes have become too weak to do without them. I read 'good books' a great deal, love the Bible, and from time to time read novels. I am so sad because they are allowed no walks except before the house and behind a high fence. But at least they have fresh air, and we are grateful for anything. He [Nicholas] is simply marvelous. Such meekness while all the time suffering intensely for the country. A real marvel. The others are all good and brave and uncomplaining, and Alexei is an angel. He and I dine à deux and generally lunch so, but sometimes downstairs with the others.⁸¹

I am knitting stockings for the small one (Alexei). He asked for a pair as all his are in holes. Mine are warm and thick like the ones I gave the wounded, do you remember? I make everything now. Father's [i.e. Nicholas]

Above and on the left: On the roof of the greenhouse in Tobolsk.
Below: The chapel in the house.

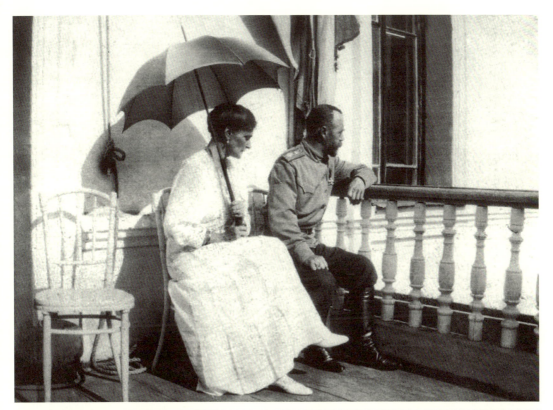

From the period of the captivity in Tobolsk. On the page on the left:
(1) Nicholas cutting wood with Alexis.
(2) Olga cutting wood with an axe.
(3) Nicholas cutting wood with Gilliard.
(4) Olga playing with Alexis. (5) The last known photo of Anastasia.
On this page. Below: The Governor's house on Freedom Street, where the family were held captives. Above: Nicholas with Alexandra at the balcony of the Governor's house.

Hieromartyr Hermogenes, Archbishop of Tobolsk.

trousers are torn and darned, the girls' under-linen in rags. Dreadful, is it not?"[82]

"One by one all earthly things slip away, houses and possessions ruined, friends vanished. One lives from day to day. But God is in all, and nature never changes. I can see all around me churches (long to go to them), and hills, the lovely world. Wolkoff wheels me in my chair to church across the street from the public garden. Some of the people bow and bless us, but others don't dare. … I feel old, oh, so old, but I am still the mother of this country, and I suffer its pains as my own child's pains, and I love it in spite of all its sins and horrors. No one can tear a child from its mother's heart, and neither can you tear away one's country, although Russia's black ingratitude to the Emperor breaks my heart. Not that it is the whole country, though. God have mercy and save Russia."[83]

BOLSHEVIK REVOLUTION

Here in exile Nicholas did not receive newspapers as regularly as he might have wished, or in a timely manner, so as to follow political developments, which caused him acute discomfort. He now drew his information for the most part from rumors circulating in Tobolsk. These were the sources from which he followed the downfall of Kerensky and the Provisional Government with sadness.

In a paradoxical turn of history, it was Kerensky himself who was most responsible for the collapse of the Provisional Government. A mere two weeks after Nicholas and his family were exiled, General Kornilov attempted to persuade Kerensky to collaborate in annihilating the Bolsheviks. Kerensky refused and Kornilov resorted to a coup against the Provisional Government, considering a military dictatorship to be the only way to halt the growing power of the Bolsheviks. Kerensky believed that the only way to overturn Kornilov's coup under the present circumstances was alliance with the Bolsheviks. The Bolsheviks responded with enthusiasm and began to organize the workers in battalions of Red Guards. In the end, Kornilov's threat turned out to be without effect. Instead of fighting, the troops supporting the coup defected to their opponents. And so, after the coup was put down, Kerensky instructed the Red Guard to return the arms that they were issued. They refused.

CAPTIVITY

In September the Bolsheviks gained the majority in the Soviets of most of the large cities, including Saint Petersburg. From Finland Lenin proclaimed, "History will not forgive us if we do not take power now... to delay is a crime!"[84] On 23 October he returned secretly to the capital. The final blow came on 6 November, now known in history as the October Revolution because according to the Old Calendar the coup took place on 24 October, 1917. With no bloody conflict, the Provisional Government was overthrown, and the ministers were arrested. Kerensky alone succeeded in escaping, ending up finally in America. He left, taking with him the dream of the creation of a liberal democratic Russia. The new regime instituted an unprecedented tyranny, a reign of terror and blood, which would remain in power for seventy years: a new Babylonian captivity.

Nicholas was shocked to learn about these dramatic developments. He never believed that Lenin and his collaborators could pose any serious danger to Russia. He considered them paltry German agents capable of only stirring up trouble. When he saw them come to power, he had already regretted and bitterly mourned his wasted sacrifice in abdicating the throne for the good of Russia.

At first, after the Bolsheviks seized power, life in Tobolsk continued unchanged. But the shadow of the Bolshevik Revolution began to fall little by little over the far North. The contagion began to afflict some of the soldiers of the family's guard. Commandant Kobylinsky constantly lost ground in power and authority among the soldiers, who grew ever more hostile to him and to the family. A new incident became the cause of new difficulties. This time the soldiers were bothered by the epaulettes worn by Nicholas and the officers of the guard. A committee of soldiers decided to forbid their use. Nicholas refused. His epaulettes displayed the rank of colonel, which he had received from his father, and he had not taken promotion to a higher rank, not even when he became Commander-in-Chief of the Russian troops. Kobylinsky did all he could to change the soldiers' decision. He explained that Nicholas should not have to undergo this humiliating punishment because, even though he was no longer tsar, he had not ceased to be cousin of the monarchs of England and Germany. But to no avail. The soldiers began to threaten. Not wishing to place his family in needless dangers, Nicholas finally gave in.

The pressure that the soldiers exerted on Kobylinsky finally broke the nerves of the noble colonel. He was obliged to speak to Nicholas about this matter. The conversation and the scene that took place is very moving because it reveals the deeper feelings of both the Colonel and the Emperor. Kobylinsky describes the event:

"I knew that I had absolutely lost all control of the men, and I fully realized my impotence! So I went to the Governor's house and asked Tegleva [a maidservant] to tell the Emperor that I begged him to receive me. The Emperor at once received me in Tegleva's room, and I said to him: 'Your Majesty, all authority is fast slipping out of my hands. The men have removed our shoulder-straps! I cannot be useful to you any more, so I wish to resign, if you do not object. My nerves are strained. I am exhausted.' The Emperor put his arm on my shoulder, his eyes filled with tears. He replied: 'I implore you to remain, Evgeni Stepanovich, remain for my sake, for the sake of my wife and for the sake of my children. You must stand by us. You see how all of us are suffering.' Then he embraced me and we kissed each other, and I resolved to remain."[85]

Kobylinsky's decision to remain turned out to be important, because very soon the Bolshevik regime commanded the removal of all troops of the guard who had been members of the Imperial Army. These soldiers, who had been more friendly to the family, came secretly to bid farewell to the emperor and to the other members of the family. Their removal was heavy blow. A dark future impended.

The new soldiers who were sent were fanatical members of the Revolution. Their vulgar and shameful behavior became apparent. They found pleasure in drawing vulgar sketches on the wooden fence and on other parts of the house so that the girls would see them, and they did not lose any opportunity to taunt and openly challenge the members of the family. Kobylinsky recalls, "Swings had been made for the children, as the Grand Duchesses liked to swing, but the soldiers of the Second Regiment who were on sentry duty, carved most indecent words on the seats of the swings. After the Emperor had seen this the seats were removed."[86]

Furthermore, they set new prohibitions. Economic means of support of the family and staff were drastically reduced, and goods such as butter and coffee were forbidden because they constituted needless luxuries. However, the residents of Tobolsk, learning about this development began to send packets with eggs and sweets, which Alexandra called, "gifts from Heaven."[87]

The sufferings imposed on the prisoners of Tobolsk only served to further cultivate their faith and love for God. Alexandra wrote in one of her letters, "The spirits of the whole family are good. God is very near us, we feel His support, and are often amazed that we can endure events and separations which once might have killed us. Although we suffer horribly still there is peace in our souls."[88]

ROYAL HEART IN GRACE

This sudden turn in the life of the royal family gave to each member a strong push towards the life of the Spirit. Isolated and cut off from the world and responsibilities, they found valuable time to give to their souls abundantly the spiritual food that they had always sought.

This reality is especially powerfully revealed in the person of Alexandra. Her letters in this period of exile in Tobolsk constitute a mental mirror in which one can see a reflection of this inward growth of spirituality and the empress' transformation. The spiritual wisdom that she gained treading the path of martyrdom is astonishing:

"Soon spring is coming to rejoice our hearts. The way of the cross first—then joy and gladness. It will soon be a year since we parted, but what is time? Life here is nothing—eternity is everything, and what we are doing is preparing our souls for the Kingdom of Heaven. Thus nothing, after all, is terrible, and if they do take everything from us they cannot take our souls. … We live here on earth but we are already half gone to the next world. We see with different eyes."[89] "All things for us are in the past, and what the future holds I cannot guess, but God knows, and I have given everything into His keeping."[90] "The more we suffer here the fairer it will be on that other shore where so many dear ones await us."[91] "How can one ask more? We simply give thanks for every day safely ended."[92]

Alexandra's words were the fruit of long-time spiritual struggles. In the course of these struggles, one of the greatest adversaries that must be fought was her unusually powerful personality. Every person is called to subject the passions of his character, but in the case of Alexandra, this was even more difficult. This is something that one can understand once one studies the reality of the empress a little. Who was she?

Five pregnancies in quick succession, all of them bringing to life robust babies in excessively difficult births. If one adds to these heart disease, with the resulting difficulty in breathing, overwork, cyanosis, and swelling of the feet, sciatica to such a degree that very often she could not walk at all, unbearable neuralgia of the trigeminal nerve of the face, earaches, and acute migraine, then it is clear that the effect of these maladies on her psychic world was an unbelievable Golgotha. And all these things in combination with the constant soul-draining agony over the life and health of her child. If one bears in mind the intense struggle that Alexandra was obliged to impose on her shattered psychology, then one may realize the greatness of the majesty of her soul when she wrote these words.

Furthermore, one wonders at her continual spiritual watchfulness and her self-awareness, which constituted the most severe judge of her soul: "In my heart is love and forgiveness for everything, though at times I am not as patient as I ought to be. I get angry when people are dishonest, or when they unnecessarily hurt and offend those I love. Father [i.e. Nicholas], on the other hand, bears everything."[93] "My greatest sin is my irritability. … I want to be a better woman, and I try. For long periods I am really patient, and then breaks out again my bad temper. … I long to warm and to comfort others—but alas, I do not feel drawn to those around me here. I am cold towards them, and this, too, is wrong of me."[94]

This constant severe self-examination made Alexandra a true soldier of Christ who trod the path of holiness to the end. Her only consolation in this last stage of her life was the study of the Divine Word: "I am reading Solomon and the writings of St. Seraph[im of Sarov], every time finding something new."⁹⁵ "There are some beautiful passages in the Proverbs of Solomon. The Psalms also give me peace."⁹⁶ "I get a great deal of consolation reading the Bible. I often read it to the children."⁹⁷

Alexandra's desire to transmit to her children the spiritual riches of the life in Christ remained as intense until the end. She wrote, "I am teaching the children the Divine Service. May God help me to teach it to them so that it will remain with them through their whole lives, and develop their souls."⁹⁸

UNEXPECTED DEVELOPMENTS

From Nicholas' diary: "2/15 March, 1918. Remembering these days last year in Pskov and on the train! How much longer will our poor motherland be tormented and pulled apart by external and internal enemies? Sometimes it seems that there is no more strength to take this, I don't even know what to hope or wish for? Nevertheless, there is no one like God! May His holy will be served!"⁹⁹

"To-day is Carnival Sunday [Sunday of Meat-Fare]," writes Gilliard, "Everyone is merry. The sledges pass to and fro under our windows; sound of bells, mouth-organs, and singing. ... The children wistfully watch the fun. They have begun to grow bored and find their captivity irksome. They walk round the courtyard, fenced in by its high paling through which they can see nothing. ... Never was the situation more favourable for escape, for there is as yet no representative of the Bolshevik Government at Tobolsk. With the complicity of Colonel Kobylinsky, already on our side, it would be easy to trick the insolent but careless vigilance of our guards. All that is required is the organised and resolute efforts of a few bold spirits outside."¹⁰⁰

Is it truly possible that no one wished, or at least did not think about undertaking, an attempt to rescue the family? Indeed, there were several plans, both within and outside of Russia, to liberate the royal captives. Most of these were undertaken without the knowledge of the family. Nevertheless, apart from the various obstacles that hindered—justifiably or not—the plans for any rescue attempt, there was yet another one preventing the realization of these plans: Nicholas himself. ¹⁰¹ Nicholas believed that no Russian should abandon his fatherland in such a critical hour for Russia.¹⁰² As Gilliard characteristically relates, "[The emperor] will not hear of the family being separated or leaving Russian territory."¹⁰³ He did not intend to leave, but he was determined to face within his country that which God would permit. Alexandra resolutely shared Nicholas' determination and said, "I wouldn't leave Russia on any consideration, for it seems to me that to go abroad would be to break our last link with the past, which would then be dead for ever."¹⁰⁴

Nicholas and Alexandra's desire to remain was not only their own personal decision, but it was the determination of the whole family regarding that possibility. This truth is reflected clearly in a reference in the recollections of Pankratov, where he mentions a conversation that he had with one of the girls:

"One morning, [when] I went to the Governor's House to hand over letters and journals, one of the princesses asks me:

'Is it really true that the Constituent Assembly will send us all abroad?'

'From where did you get such information?'

'They write it in the newspapers.'

'What does it matter what they write in the newspapers? The Constituent Assembly has not been convened yet, and nobody knows how they will resolve this issue,' I answer. The princess feels embarrassed, and after a few minutes, she suddenly declares:

'It would be better if they sent us even further somewhere in Siberia, but not abroad.' I looked at the princess and involuntarily asked myself what that meant.

'You don't want to leave Russia?'

'It's best if we stay in Russia. Let us be sent deeper into Siberia.'"[105]

Five days after the above-mentioned excerpt from Gilliard, Nicholas in turn wrote in his diary, on 9/22 March: "Today is the anniversary of my arrival in Tsarskoe Selo and of my imprisonment with my family in the Alexander Palace. Willing or not, one bears in mind this difficult time which has passed! And what other thing awaits us in the future? All things are in the hands of God. All our hope is placed in Him. At 8 o'clock in the morning we went to Liturgy. We spent the day as always. We took supper at 7 o'clock in the evening, afterwards we had Vespers and then confession in the living room: the children [confessed], the staff, and we."[106]

In the meanwhile, the time of Great Lent began, and the family enjoyed the special joy that characterizes these days of the liturgical year. Nicholas wrote in his diary in this time, "In the first week [of Lent] I started reading the Bible from the beginning."[107] Alexandra wrote to Vyrubova, "The weather is so fine that I have been sitting out on the balcony writing music for the Lenten prayers, as we have no printed notes. ... On Wednesday, Friday and Saturday mornings [of the first week] we were allowed to go to the eight o'clock morning service in church—imagine the joy and comfort! The other days we five women will sing during the home service."[108]

Despite the difficult conditions of exile, the family took care to keep the fast as much as possible. Anastasia wrote to some person known to her, "In the first week of Lent, we fasted and they let us go to church. At all the [other] services through the week we sang by ourselves, as it is difficult to get the cloisters to come over with such frequency for services at home."[109] Furthermore, amid such deprivations, Alexandra worried that they did not have the possibility of keeping the abstinence that her soul sought,

Commissar Vasily Yakovlev.

"We are allowed one and a half pounds of sugar every month, but more is always given us by kind-hearted people here. I never touch sugar during Lent, but that does not seem to be a [voluntary] deprivation now."[110]

From a letter written by Anastasia, where she makes mention of a new situation in the house, it appears how developed the spiritual understanding of the children was. Their attention did not rest only on the evil at all, but they looked on everything with good disposition: "For the moment, thank God, we are living well. A detachment of Red Army men came from Omsk, up until now they behaved themselves, and on the whole everything is calm."[111] One very old enemy, however, much older than the Bolsheviks, appeared suddenly once more: Alexis' hemophilia. An injury caused him internal bleeding in the groin. The days that followed recalled all the terrible days and nights in Spala in 1912. Alexis' pains again became unbearable and the child desperate with his terrible condition shouted, "I would like to die, Mama; I'm not afraid of death, but I'm so afraid of what they may do to us here."[112] One might ask, perhaps the pure soul of the child forebode the coming tragedy.

Echoing the same presentiment Alexandra wrote in a letter to Anna Vyrubova, which was her last to her, "The atmosphere around us is fairly electrified. We feel that a storm is approaching, but we know that God is merciful, and will care for us. ... Though we know that the storm is coming nearer and nearer, our souls are at peace. Whatever happens will be through God's will."[113]

In fact, very soon it appeared that these worries were not unjustified. On 9/22 April, Nicholas wrote in his diary, "We learned about the arrival of the extraordinary authorized [commissar] Yakovlev from Moscow; he settled in Kornilov house. The children imagined that he will come today to do a search, and burned all letters, and Maria and Anastasia even [burned] their diaries. The weather was revolting, cold with wet snow. Alexei felt better and even slept for two to three hours during the day."[114]

Commissar Vasily V. Yakovlev arrived at the house in Tobolsk on 22 April, at the head of 150 cavalry. On the following day he asked to see the family. Nicholas writes in his diary on that day, "10[23] of April. Tuesday.

At 10:30 o'cl. in the morning Kobylinsky showed up with Yakovlev and his suite. I received him in the hall with the daughters. We expected him at 11 o'cl., therefore Alix was not yet ready. He came in, clean-shaven face, smiling and embarrassed, asked if I am happy with the guards and the building. Then, almost running he stopped by to see Alexei, without stopping, looked around the rest of the rooms, and, having apologized for bothering us, went downstairs. In the same hurried manner, he also stopped by the others' [rooms] on the rest of the floors. In a half hour he appeared again, in order to present himself to Alix, again hurried to Alexei and went downstairs. This was the extend of inspecting the house for now."[115]

The language and behavior of Yakovlev were cultured, and he addressed Nicholas as "Your Majesty." However, Gilliard wrote that "Everyone is restless and distraught. The commissary's arrival is felt to be an evil portent, vague but real."[116]

Two days later, on 25 April, Yakovlev summoned Kobylinsky and presented him the documents relating to his mission. They were signed by the notorious Yakov Sverdlov, President of the Central Executive Committee of the All-Russian Congress of Soviets, and a close collaborator of Lenin. The orders to Kobylinsky and the guard were unequivocal: absolute obedience to Yakovlev or death executed on the spot. The following day Yakovlev communicated to Kobylinsky his mission in detail. He informed him that his principal orders were to transfer the entire family elsewhere, far from Tobolsk. But when he understood that Alexis' injury did not permit him to be moved, he received new orders from Moscow, according to which he must leave the family in Tobolsk and to take with him only the sovereign.

Now was the time to inform Nicholas. Kobylinsky later wrote, "At two o'clock Yakovlev and I entered the hall. The Emperor and Empress stood in the middle of the hall, and Yakovlev stopped a little distance away from them and bowed. Then he said: 'I must tell you' (he was talking to the Emperor only) 'that I am the Special Representative of the Moscow Central Executive Committee, and my mission is to take all your Family away from Tobolsk, but, as your son is ill, I have received a second order which says that you alone must leave.' The Emperor replied: 'I refuse to go.' Upon hearing this Yakovlev said: 'I beg you not to refuse. I am compelled to execute the order. In case of your refusal I must take you by force or I must resign my position. In the latter case the Committee would probably send a far less scrupulous man to replace me. Be calm, I am responsible with my life for your safety. If you do not want to go alone, you can take with you any people you wish. Be ready, we are leaving to-morrow at four o'clock.' Yakovlev again bowed to the Emperor and the Empress and left their presence."[117]

Alarm sounded in Alexandra's heart. What could this sudden development mean? She began to think that the reason they wanted to separate Nicholas from his family and especially from herself was to pressure him into taking some decision alone, making threats against the safety of his family, subjecting him to blackmail. As for Nicholas, he believed that the Bolshevik regime would compel him to sign the Treaty of Brest-Litovsk.

A little earlier, on 3 March, in Brest-Litovsk in Belorussia, where the Germans had their General Headquarters of the Eastern Front, a delegation of Lenin's government had signed a peace treaty with Germany. The terms were unbelievably humiliating for Russia, which lost Poland, Finland, the Baltic states of Estonia, Latvia and Lithuania, the Ukraine, the Crimea, and the greater part of the Caucuses. 56 million people lived in this vast territory of four hundred thousand square kilometers, more than one-third of the population of the former Russian Empire. Thus, Lenin kept his promise to his German saviors!

During the rule of Romanov dynasty, from 1613 until 1917, Russia participated in about forty wars. And although the empire did not always win, not once did it leave a single piece of land to its enemy, not even after defeat. The country's territory only kept growing. In these three hundred years, Russia never paid a dime of war reparations. And now, so that a cabal of Bolsheviks could secure their position in power, Soviet Russia was giving to its enemy a territory that comprised 27% of its agricultural lands, 26% of the railroad network, and 33% of the textile industry, where 73% of steel were manufactured, along with 89% of coal mined, and 90% of sugar produced. This territory was the home of 40% of all workers.

When news of the treaty reached Tobolsk, Nicholas was horrified. "It is such a disgrace for Russia and amounts to suicide,"[118] he said, and he added, "to think that they called Her Majesty a traitor."[119] Nicholas was also terribly disturbed over what the German emperor, who was the most steadfast defender of the monarchical form of government, had come to, by condescending to sign an accord with the Bolsheviks. "I should never have thought," he said, "the Emperor William and the German Government could stoop to shake hands with these miserable traitors. But I'm sure they [the Germans] will get no good from it; it won't save them from ruin!"[120] Nicholas' words came true very soon, that very year, when Germany was defeated by her adversaries. But his own life, and the life of his family remained in the hands of these traitors who had no interest at all in his signing the treaty. They only wished his complete extermination.

Alexandra found herself in an unbelievably difficult position. The dilemma was terrible. Could she let Nicholas leave completely alone without knowing where he was and why? But if she went with him, what would become of Alexis, who was in such a difficult condition with his health? The unexpected tidings spread like lightning within the house. Tatiana, weeping, called on Gilliard to go up to her mother, who, visibly shaken, informed him of the situation. Gilliard assured her that if she decided to leave with the tsar, he himself, as well as all the remaining members of the family and staff would take the best care of Alexis. Alexandra then replied,

"'Yes, that will be best; I'll go with the Czar; I shall trust Alexis to you...' A moment later the Czar came in. The Czarina walked towards him, saying: 'It's settled; I'll go with you, and Marie will come too.' The Czar replied: 'Very well, if you wish it.'"[121]

The decision that Maria was to accompany her parents was made by the girls. In an urgent consultation, they decided that one of them must necessarily accompany their parents. They concluded that Olga was not sufficiently healthy. Tatiana would have to remain in order to take care of the housekeeping and of Alexis. Anastasia was the youngest. So, under these conditions the most suitable to provide help to their parents was Maria. Furthermore, three servants of the staff would accompany the three members of the family: Chemodurov, the tsar's valet, Anna Demidova, the tsarina's maid, and Sednev, the footman to the girls. Finally, Prince Dolgorukov with Doctor Botkin would also go with them.

Alexandra undertook to inform Alexis of the developments. The entire family remained in the boy's room until late in the evening. At 10:30 PM the members of the staff who were most closely tied to the family came for evening tea. They found Alexandra on the divan and around her the girls with faces swollen from crying. But Nicholas and Alexandra were now calm and peaceful. That evening Gilliard wrote in his diary, "We all did our best to hide our grief and to maintain outward calm. We felt that for one to give way would cause all to break down. The Czar and Czarina were calm and collected. It is apparent that they are prepared for any sacrifices, even of their lives, if God in his inscrutable wisdom should require it for the country's welfare. They have never shown greater kindness or solicitude. This splendid serenity of theirs, this wonderful faith, proved infectious."

"At half-past eleven the servants were assembled in the large hall. Their Majesties and Marie Nicolaievna took leave of them. The Czar embraced every man, the Czarina every woman. Almost all were in tears."[122] According to Sydney Gibbes "they knew it was the end."[123] And even though no one expressed it openly Anna Demidova said with evident fear to Gibbes, "I am so frightened of the Bolsheviks, Mr Gibbes. I don't know what they will do to us."[124]

That last night, no one in the house slept. The children wrote farewell notes and gave them to their father. From Olga: "My dear Papa! May the Lord protect You, bless You and have pity on you, my dear, beloved Papa. Do not worry about Aleksei. I cannot express to You how painful it is, but the Lord knows the reasons why we are going through all of this. I kiss you and I love you as much as I can, my angel, my Papa. Your Olga."[125] From Anastasia: "My dear Papa! May the Lord and all Saints protect You, my dear and beloved Papa. In our thoughts and prayers, we are always with You. I cannot even imagine how we can be without You. I believe and hope that the Lord will help us all. Good night my precious and wonderful Papa. I kiss you a thousand times, strongly, strongly as strong as my love is for you. May the Lord be with You and bless You, darling. Your loyal and devoted, Shvybz/Anastasia."[126] From Alexis: "My dear and sweet beloved Papa, I hope that You will arrive soon. I will try to eat a lot and heal quickly. How good it is you travel with our good soldiers. May God may keep you. I hug you strongly and make the sign of the cross upon you. I pray for You. Your Alexei."[127]

Before dawn the galloping of horses was heard and the creaking of carriages that would convey the prisoners. Yakovlev preserved in his memoirs the scene of the family's separation: "All the residents of the house were up and about. In all corners of the house one could hear sobbing. The Romanov daughters and their entire 'court' staff came out on the porch to see off their 'patrons.' Nicholas Romanov was bewilderingly pacing around in his wobbly gait from one person to another, and with sort of convulsive movements crossed [made the sign of the Cross over] his daughters as goodbye."[128]

All things were now ready, and the carriage drivers drove the horses with their lashes. The carriages began to move. The daughter of Doctor Botkin, who was living with her brother in the staff house across the street from the family, stood in the door to see her father from afar as they left: "My father noticed me and, turning around, he blessed me several times [with the sign of the Cross]."[129] That was the last time she saw her father.

The stay in Tobolsk had come to an end. No help came, no one took notice. Three girls remained behind, alone with their little brother. As the carriage was departing Alexis, lying in his bed, had his face turned toward the window and wept bitterly, uncontrollably…

Dr Eugene Botkin with his children Tatiana and Gleb.

CAPTIVITY

A MYSTERIOUS JOURNEY

The journey of the imperial couple and of their companions followed a curious path. Yakovlev's mission was to transfer the family to Moscow. There the great collaborator of Lenin, Leon Trotsky, was eager to stage a spectacular public trial, which would certainly have no outcome other than the conviction of Nicholas and the apotheosis of revolutionary justice. However, certain other very important factors of the new reality also desired a part in the "management" of the royal family: the members of the Soviet of Ekaterinburg in the Urals, who had the reputation—and justly—of being the harshest faction of the Bolsheviks.

For years now, the coal miners and workers of the Urals, toiling in the depths of the earth or at blast furnaces, acquired a tradition of resentment and rebellion that won them the title of the Red Urals. They formed the hard-core center of Bolshevism in all of Russia. Hence the desire of the Soviet of Ekaterinburg was not the setting-up of a political show trial with Nicholas and his family as victims. They wanted to expend all their ferocity on their victims, being persuaded that this family was responsible for their own misery. They wanted their blood.

Moscow, or better yet, Lenin, was in a dilemma. On the one hand, they did not wish to be seen as officially responsible for the final fate of the family without having gone through the necessary judicial trials, because that could create serious problems with the Bolshevik regime's external relations. On the other hand, the Soviet of Ekaterinburg constituted the strongest bastion of the new regime, which, besides the fact that it should not be disregarded, it was also not easy—if not impossible—to make them comply with orders from the capital. What then must happen? The events that followed remain inexplicable to this day.

On 1 April, 1918, the president of the Central Executive Committee of the Soviets gave command to transfer the family to Moscow as soon as possible. The relevant official document with the decision, which was not communicated, specifically stated: "To immediately transport all the arrested to Moscow."[130] However, on 9 April, Sverdlov in his communication with the Soviet of the Urals reported:

"9 April 1918. Dear comrades! Today via the direct line I am informing you in advance of a messenger coming to you, c.[omrade] Yakovlev. We charged him with transferring Nicholas to the Urals. Our opinion is that you should settle him in Yekaterinburg for now. Decide for yourselves whether to place him in prison or to outfit some mansion. Do not take him anywhere outside Yekaterinburg without our direct order. Yakovlev's assignment is to deliver Nicholas to Yekat.[erinburg] alive and to hand him over either to Chair.[man] Beloborodov or to Goloshchekin. Yakovlev has been given the most precise and detailed instructions. Do everything that is necessary. Talk over the details with Yakovlev. With com.[radely] reg.[ards], Ya. Sverdlov."[131]

CHAPTER 5

Regardless of whatever played out in the political arena, the journey of the group of prisoners from Tobolsk had begun. From Tobolsk Yakovlev and the prisoners were to arrive at Tyumen, where they would take the train for their unknown final destination. The conditions of the journey were terribly difficult. Nicholas sat with Yakovlev in front in the open part of the carriage. Alexandra with Maria were in an enclosed carriage without seats. The only relief offered was a few cushions and a little hay on the floor, which constituted a dreadful trial for her because the carriages proceeded with great speed on the terribly uneven Siberian roads. The jarring caused by the passage over frozen, rocky roads literally shattered Alexandra. So ugly was the condition of the roads that several times the wheels of the carts broke and every time they were obliged to repair them.

They travelled all day, exposed to the tormenting cold of the north. At one station some people saw Maria descend to adjust somewhat the cushions of her mother. Her hands were so cold that she had to rub them for a long time before they began again to move a little, so that she could then help her mother. In many cases the ice on the surface of some puddles were not solid enough, and the travellers had to go across on foot, walking on boards. At one point of the journey, Nicholas had to take Alexandra in his hands to take her across a puddle whose frozen water covered the passers by up to the knees. When at last they stopped for the night to rest a few hours in the house of some peasant, the women were completely frozen.

In the meanwhile, the Bolsheviks of the Ural Soviet were under terrible pressure. They did not trust Yakovlev. Despite the assurances of Sverdlov, they wanted to follow the mission up close, so that if anything went wrong, they might immediately intervene drastically and seize the prisoners. Thus, they decided to send two detachments of soldiers to assure the handing over of the prisoners to Ekaterinburg. Yakovlev began to worry when he saw the detachments from Ekaterinburg. He knew that the Urals were not especially interested in the secure transfer of the prisoners to their final destination, but that they wished to exterminate them.

Two days later, on 27 April, when they arrived at Tyumen, Yakovlev immediately sent a telegram to Goloshchekin at the Regional Soviet of the Urals, strongly objecting to plan to send detachments of soldiers. He also mentioned that he had information that these detachments planned to attack the train and kill the prisoners: "Your detachments have only the single wish of destroying that baggage [i.e., the prisoners]. ... I have one prisoner from Gusiatsky's detachment who admitted everything. ... I am convinced, of course, that I will break these lads of their nasty intentions. But there is among the detachments you have in Yekaterinburg a strong inclination to destroy the baggage. Do you guarantee the preservation of this baggage? Remember that the Council of Commissars vowed to keep me safe."[132]

Then Yakovlev sent a telegram to Moscow to Sverdlov asking him, "The route remains the same, or did you change it? Inform Tiumen immediately.

CAPTIVITY

I am going by the old route. An immediate answer is necessary."[133] What, then, was this "old" route? Why did Yakovlev wish confirmation whether he would proceed according to this route and not some other? And what was the alternative choice? At any rate, Sverdlov's reply was unambiguous, "The route is the old one; tell me whether you are carrying the baggage [the family] or not."[134]

Yakovlev's reply: "I have just brought part of the baggage [Nicholas, Alexandra, and Maria] here. I want to change the route because of the following extremely important circumstances. Certain people arrived in Tobolsk from Yekaterinburg before I did in order to destroy the baggage. The special purpose detachment repulsed their attack—barely avoiding bloodshed. …

"The entire route from Tobolsk to Tiumen was guarded by my detachments. Having failed to achieve their goal in Tobolsk, on the road, and in Tiumen, the Yekaterinburg detachments decided to prepare to ambush me outside Yekaterinburg. They decided that if I didn't hand over the baggage to them without a fight, they would massacre us. …

"I have warned you; now decide: either I take the baggage to Simsky Gorny district immediately, where there are good places in the mountains that are exactly and purposely suited for this, or I head to Yekaterinburg. It is up to you. And I cannot vouch for the consequences. If the baggage falls into the hands [of the Yekaterinburg detachment], it will be destroyed. Since they've gone so far in preparing to wipe out me and my detachment, then of course the end result will be the same. So answer: do I go to Yekaterinburg or through Omsk to Simsky Gorny district? I'm waiting for an answer. I'm at the station with the baggage."[135]

Sverdlov: "Let me know whether you are too nervous; perhaps fears are exaggerated and the old route can be retained." Finally, however, he gives Yakovlev new instructions: "Go to Omsk, telegraph when you get there. Appear before the chairman of the soviet, Vladimir Kosarev. Transport everything secretly; I'll give further instructions in Omsk. Get going."[136]

Thereafter, Sverdlov informed Omsk regarding Yakovlev's mission:

"To Vladimir Kosarev, chairman of the soviet, Omsk.

"Yakovlev, [about] whose powers I informed you, will arrive [in] Omsk with the baggage; trust [him] completely. Follow only our orders [and] no one else's. I place full responsibility on you; conspiracy is necessary. Yakovlev is acting in accordance with our direct orders. Send an order immediately up the Omsk-Tiumen line: assistance must be rendered in every possible way to Yakovlev.

"Sverdlov."[137]

In accordance with Sverdlov's instructions, the train would now proceed to Omsk. Omsk, however, was east of Tyumen, in the opposite direction from the destination of the mission, which according to the last official decision of Moscow was Ekaterinburg.

CHAPTER 5

Despite all that, when the train departed it proceeded to the west taking the standard route toward Ekaterinburg. The Soviet of Ekaterinburg had been informed of the route of the journey and was waiting. At some point, however, Yakovlev changed the route. He set off eastward with the goal of heading to Omsk. This change, as expected, surprised Ekaterinburg, which began to send urgent telegrams to all the Soviets denouncing Yakovlev as a "traitor to the revolution." For Ekaterinburg the matter was clear: Yakovlev had ignored the written approval of Moscow and the instructions to hand the prisoners over to their local Soviet. What Ekaterinburg did not know was the secret instructions of Sverdlov to Yakovlev.

Ekaterinburg communicated immediately with Omsk, giving instructions not to permit Yakovlev to pass, because he was a traitor to the revolution. Then the chairman of the Ekaterinburg Soviet, Alexander Beloborodov, communicated with Moscow: "On 28 April, a special train number 8 VA set out along the Omsk line under the command of commissar Yakovlev, who was escorting the former tsar, Nicholas Romanov. Commissar Yakovlev was under orders from the All-Russian Sovnarkom to deliver the former tsar from Tobolsk [to] Yekaterinburg, to turn him [over] to the control of the Ural Regional Soviet. ... According to letters from Sverdlov, chairman of the TsIK [Central Executive Committee], dated 9 April, the former tsar was not to be taken [to] any other place without direct orders from the center—and we received no such orders. Having taken Romanov [from] Tobolsk, commissar Yakovlev rushed [to] Tiumen, directed the train [to] Yekaterinburg, but [at] the next closest switching point, turned the train [in] the opposite direction, east toward Omsk. Having discussed commissar Yakovlev's behavior, the Ural Regional Soviet of Workers, Peasants, and Soldiers, by unanimous verdict, sees [in] him outright betrayal of the revolution, a desire to transport the former tsar [beyond] the bounds of the revolutionary Urals for reasons unknown and contrary to the exact written instructions of the TsIK chairman. This is an act that puts commissar Yakovlev outside the ranks of revolutionaries."[138]

Sverdlov's reply was explicit: "Everything being done by Yakovlev ... is in direct fulfillment of an order I have given. I will inform [you] of the details by special courier. Issue no orders concerning Yakovlev. He is acting in accordance with an order rec.[eived] from me today at 4 o'clock in the morning. ... Yakovlev is to be trusted completely. Once again, no interference. Sverdlov."[139]

Now the expectation was that Omsk, in accordance with instructions from Moscow, would allow Yakovlev to pass without interference because his mission proceeded in accordance with the orders that he was given. However, when Yakovlev's train arrived at Omsk, he was surrounded by troops! Surprised, Yakovlev sought to communicate immediately with Sverdlov in order to find the explanation of this development. His surprise at Sverdlov's reply was even greater:

"Immediately go back [to] Tiumen; I reached an understanding [with the] Uralites; they adopted measures [and] guaranteed that they will be personally responsible for the actions of the regional men; hand all the baggage over [in] Tiumen to the chairman of the Ural regional committee; this is essential."[140]

Having received these unexpected new instructions, Yakovlev considered it his duty to clarify his position and to give for the last time a description of the situation. Accordingly, he reported the following to Sverdlov:

"Without question I submit to all orders from the center. I will deliver the baggage wherever you say. But I consider it my duty to warn the Council of Peop.[le's] Commissars once more that the danger is entirely well founded, which both Tiumen and Omsk can confirm. One more thought: if you send the baggage to Simsky district, then you can always transport it to Moscow or wherever you want. If the baggage is taken by the first route, then I doubt that you will be able to drag it out of there. ... Thus, we warn you one last time and free ourselves from any moral responsibility for the future consequences. I am going by the first route. We are departing at once."[141]

Even though no official document survive, it is not difficult to conclude from the above that Yakovlev's secret instructions were to guide the prisoners to Moscow. It appears that the letter that Sverdlov sent to the Ekaterinburg Soviet on 9 April was only intended to allay the impatient Uralians, so that they would not cause problems in the actual mission, which was the transfer of the prisoners to Moscow. That Moscow was the actual final destination of the mission is also apparent in Yakovlev's final message to Sverdlov when he said, "If you send the baggage to Simsky district, then you can always transport it to Moscow."[142]

One question is whether the original route that the mission would have followed—which in their communications Yakovlev and Sverdlov named "original" or "first"—was through Ekaterinburg. However, this does not seem very likely, because it is not possible that Moscow hoped the Urals would allow the mission to pass through the station without seizing the prisoners. Moreover, they had the written assurance of Sverdlov that they would hand over the family.

The explanations of these events can be summarized in two scenarios: According to the first, the Central Executive Committee in fact intended to bring the prisoners to Moscow, but at last the mission failed and they were compelled to submit to the claims of the Uralites.

The second likely scenario is much more dramatic: According to this version, the initial written assurance to Ekaterinburg that the family would be handed over to them was not deceptive, but actual! This was the Moscow's official, but extremely secret, decision. It should not, for any reason, become known. This would have made Moscow responsible for what followed in Ekaterinburg, namely the extermination of the entire family. Moscow for the present did not wish this. So, with this plan, it appeared that Moscow "wished" to bring the family there, but the Ekaterinburg Soviet "forced" it to hand over the victims. In this manner neither could Yakovlev be considered a traitor, for he operated in accordance to orders from Moscow, nor could Moscow be accused of the fate of the family, because Ekaterinburg "seized" the captives, nor could Ekaterinburg have demands because it had in its hands what they sought!

Yakovlev had no other option. He had to hand the prisoners over to the bloodthirsty Uralites. It seems, however, that this development did not especially please Yakovlev. The respect that he showed to the family from the beginning and all his comportment during his mission leaves a question mark in history: Perhaps in the end Yakovlev intended to lead the prisoners from Omsk to the borders out of Russia towards freedom? The question remains unanswered.

Returning from the train, Yakovlev informed Nicholas and Alexandra that he had received orders to hand them over to Ekaterinburg. Nicholas, who had been learned about the atmosphere of the Urals in the local press, said, "I would go anywhere at all, only not to the Urals."[143] But the pen of decision had already been dipped, not in ink, but in blood...

CHAPTER 6

THE CHAPTER OF BLOOD

THE HOUSE OF SPECIAL PURPOSE

The arrival of the train at Ekaterinburg was the first ominous signal of what the prisoners would experience in that city. The curtain had now officially opened on the last act of the drama of the royal family. Yakovlev preserves the details in his memoirs:

"On the morning of the 30th [of April] we arrived in Ekaterinburg without any incident. Despite our early arrival, the Ekaterinburg station was overflowing with people. As it turned out, the residents of Ekaterinburg found out about our pending arrival—we had no idea about this. The crowd concentrated at the freight platform as especially large. Our train was standing on the fifth track from the platform. When they saw us, they started demanding for me to bring Nicholas out and show him to them. There was a roar in the air, and here and there threatening cries could be heard: 'Strangle them all!,' 'Finally they are in our hands!'

"The guards who stood on the platform weakly restrained the pushing crowd, which started chaotically moving towards our train car. I lined up my guard team around the entire train [and] prepared machine guns. To my great horror I saw that somehow the station commissar ended up at the head of the crowd. He yelled out to me, still from afar: 'Comrade Yakovlev, bring the Romanovs out of the train. Let me, at least, spit in his face!'

"The situation was becoming extremely dangerous. The crowd was pushing against us and kept getting closer to the train. Its mood was becoming more threatening. To wait for someone from the Soviet was useless—no one among the local leaders came to our aid, although they were already warned not only of our arrival, but also of what was going on

CHAPTER 6

at the train station! It was necessary to take some decisive measures. I went to see the station head, comrade Kasyan, with a demand to immediately put a freight train between the platform and our train, and then send our train towards Ekaterinburg [station] II as soon as possible.

"The shouts were getting more insistent. Persuasions did not work. The crowd kept demanding to see the Romanovs more and more insistently. In order to at least temporarily restrain them, until Kasyan returns, I shouted loudly to my lined-up guards: 'Prepare the machine guns.' The pushing crowd fled, but threatening shouts towards me could be heard. The same fat commissar with a big stomach yelled in a frenzied voice: 'We are not afraid of your machine guns. We have prepared cannons against you. See them sitting on the platform.' I looked in the direction he was pointing. Indeed, three-inch muzzles were moving there, and someone was swarming nearby.

"While we were exchanging these niceties, trying to somehow stall for time, Kasyan returned; he was able to persuade the station manager to fulfill our demands, despite the chaos taking place at the station. Right after Kasyan's arrival we saw that a freight train was moving towards us. In a few minutes we were behind a wall of train cars, isolated from the crowd. Shouts and curses could be heard towards the train driver, and while the rushing people were trying to get to our side through the buffers of the freight train, we, having an attached locomotive, took off and disappeared in the endless tracks of the Ekaterinburg train station, and in 15 minutes were already in complete safety of Ekaterinburg [station] II."[1] Twenty minutes later two automobiles came to the station to transfer the captives to their new prison.

The city of Ekaterinburg is located on a series of low hills on the eastern side of the Urals. On the highest hill of the series, near the center of the town, a prosperous engineer had built an imposing two-storey house; his name was Nicholas Ipatiev. The house was built on the side of the hill; one side of the house was on the same level as the adjacent street, while the other side looking towards the hill made a half-basement. The windows of the rooms on this half-basement just barely overlooked the level of the street.

A few days earlier, an order had suddenly been given to Nicholas Ipatiev to abandon his house in 24 hours. Subsequently, a very high wooden fence was built around the house, so that the only thing one could see from the interior of the upper floor of the house was the end of the domes of the churches and the crosses on their peaks. Just across from the house was the Church of the Ascension, from which the neighborhood, as well as the street on which Ipatiev's house was built, took their name. In fact, the Ipatiev house was built on the ruins of the old Church of the Ascension. Five of the rooms of the upper storey were converted into prisons and the ground floor of the house into outposts and offices. The building was officially named "the House of Special Purpose."

THE CHAPTER OF BLOOD

Holy Tuesday, 30 April, 1918. There, outside of the Ipatiev House, a little before noon, two automobiles of the local Soviet came to a stop. They transferred some captives who were intended for something very "special." The captives with the special purpose were, for the present, Nicholas with Alexandra, their daughter Maria, Doctor Botkin, and their three servants. Prince Dolgorukov was not given permission to accompany the prisoners. Immediately after their arrival in Ekaterinburg he disappeared. The rest did not know what happened to their beloved prince. They were told that he was in prison, but as much as they tried, through Doctor Botkin, they were not able to find out if he was well. "By the ambiguous hints of those around us we understood that poor Valya is not free and that he will be investigated, after which he will be set free,"[2] Nicholas wrote in his diary.

The rest of the prisoners were made to open all their baggage for inspection as soon as they arrived at the house. Nicholas attempted to object, but they cut him off immediately, informing him that he was no longer at Tsarskoe Selo. His next provocative act would cause him to be placed in isolation.

After the inspection, the prisoners were led to their rooms. Nicholas and Alexandra would remain in the corner room, which had four windows toward Ascension Avenue, and two towards the street of the same name, Ascension Street. But because of the height of the fence, their only view was the cross of the church's bell tower. Next to their parents' room, with a view towards Ascension Street, would be the girls' room, and the next one, the dining room, would be assigned to Anna Demidova. Doctor Botkin with the servants Chemodurov and Sednev shared the living room, next to Nicholas and Alexandra's room, along the length of the Avenue. Maria, for the time being, stayed in the same room with her parents until the rest of the children would arrive.

The commandant of the Ipatiev House was thirty-year-old Avdeev, who lived in a world of boasting and wine. He used very harsh language and gave great performances of Bolshevik zeal. Avdeev displayed his harsh vocabulary at every opportunity. One of the guards at the Ipatiev House remarked:

"Avdeev was a drunkard. He loved drinking and drank all the time. … Avdeev talked about the tsar with malice. He cursed him in any way he could, called him 'bloody' and 'bloodthirsty.' The main thing he cursed him for was the war: that the tsar wanted this war and for three years he spilled the blood of the workers, and that masses of these workers were shot in this war, and also for the strikes."[3]

The first day of captivity at the Ipatiev House dawned, Holy Wednesday. Because it was the First of May [i.e., "May Day," or International Workers' Day], it was a public holiday. Various groups of curious inhabitants of Ekaterinburg stopped at the Ipatiev House and tried to see the captives. The guards' instructions were clear. No one was to approach the house. So they shouted to the people:

CHAPTER 6

'Keep moving, citizens, keep moving! It's not allowed to stop here!'
'Why is it not allowed to stop here? What is here?'
'Nothing, but it's not permitted to stop here!'
'Tell us the truth, comrades, is it the tsar that you are guarding here?'
'You have been told to keep moving!'[4]

This was not only the royal family's first day in Ekaterinburg. By daybreak Hermogenes, Archbishop of Tobolsk, who had been arrested on Palm Sunday, had arrived and been put in ward in the central jails of the city. That day Olga wrote to her mother, who was on the road towards her unknown destination: "Today there was an enormous religious procession, with banners, icons, many members of the clergy and the faithful. It was very beautiful, under the sky sparkling with sun and the bells ringing. In the evening, I do not know why, the local bishop was arrested."[5]

The authorities had forbidden the archbishop to carry out the usual litany for the Feast. Nevertheless, the bishop was impetuous. Singing "Save, O Lord, Thy people" [a hymn that includes the words "grant victory to kings"], the procession arrived at some point at the hill above the city where was the Kremlin of Tobolsk. From that height the governor's house was clearly visible, where only the children of the royal family now remained. The bishop, with an intense feeling of sacred awe, turned toward the house and blessed it from afar. A little later he was arrested for his disobedience and three days later he was sent to Ekaterinburg, where he was jailed. On 29 June, as the Bolsheviks were transporting him by riverboat from Tyumen back to Tobolsk, they brought him to the deck, stripped him, tearing off his cassock, abused him, and, as the hierarch was praying for them and blessing them, they tied a heavy stone to his hands and threw him into the River Tura where he met a martyr's death.

Utterly exhausted, Alexandra spent the greater part of this first day in bed. She passed the afternoon arranging her icons, photographs, and books that she had brought with her from Tobolsk. That first day they were not allowed to go outside for a walk. Thus, the prisoners found themselves in their new reality, which could only be described as mysterious and unforeseen. And when this day reached its end, the family in Ekaterinburg wrote their first letter to the children back in Tobolsk, addressed to Anastasia:

[Maria writes:] "Христос Воскресе! [Christ is risen!][6] I send you my greetings for the feast of light, my sweet Anastasia. We arrived here by car after the train. We had lunch at 4:30 in the cafeteria. ... We took tea together at 9:30 in the evening. After that we rested a little; we put up camp beds ourselves and went to bed at 11 o'clock. Papa read to us, the Gospel of the week. Mama teased Mashka,[7] imitating, with success, Pankra[tov]'s enthusiasm, but despite all of that, everything again is a little depressing.

[Alexandra]: I bless you and kiss you affectionately, my little soul. ...

[Nicholas]: I am bored without you, my dear Shvybz. I miss the funny faces you make at meals. How were the religious celebrations during the Holy Week? Did you set up a good icon altar? See you soon. I kiss you thrice. Your Papa."[8]

From Nicholas' diary: "19 April/2 May. Holy Thursday. ... continued reading the Bible. Breakfast was brought late—at 2 o'clock. Then all of us, except Alix, took advantage of permission to go out into the little garden for an hour. The weather got cooler, there were even a few raindrops. It was nice to breathe the fresh air. Hearing the bells tolling made one sad to think that it is Passion [week] and we do not have the chance to be at these wonderful services, and besides we cannot even fast. ... In the evening, all of us residents of the four rooms gathered in the hall, where Botkin and I took turns reading the Twelve Gospels, after which we went to bed."[9] This service at home the prisoners held before a table that Alexandra covered with an embroidered cloth, on which she set the family's icons.

The schedule at Ekaterinburg may have gradually settled into a routine, but back in Tobolsk the agony had now come to a climax. Up until this day, Holy Thursday, the children did not know anything about where their parents were. The last time they received a message from them was a few hours before arriving in Tyumen, on 27 April. When they received the telegram, they believed that their destination was Moscow, where they expected to arrive on 30 April. The days passed without newer tidings. Gilliard wrote in his diary, "Thursday, May 2nd.—Still no news since they left Tioumen. Where are they? They could have reached Moscow by Tuesday!"[10]

The following day, Good Friday, those remaining behind in Tobolsk received the first message from the authorities in Ekaterinburg. Gilliard writes, "Friday, May 3rd.—Colonel Kobylinsky has received a telegram saying that the travellers have been detained at Ekaterinburg. What has happened?"[11] Kobylinsky openly expressed their unease: "On April 20 (May 3) the committee of our detachment received a telegram from Matveiev, who informed it of their arrival at Ekaterinburg. I cannot remember the exact words of the telegram, but we were all greatly surprised at the contents, as we had fully believed that the Emperor and Empress had been taken to Moscow and not to Ekaterinburg."[12]

The following day Olga immediately hastened to write to her parents, "Saturday, 6 o'clock, April 21st/ May 4th. We learned through a telegram from Matv. [Bolshevik commissar Matveev] that everything is fine. Oh my God, how are you? It is horrible not to be together and to know nothing about you, because what we are told generally is not always the truth.... May God protect you."[13] Olga did not finish this letter, but set it aside to complete the following day, on the Feast of Pascha.

In Ekaterinburg, the authorities allowed Fr Anatoly Meledin and his deacon to be sent to the Ipatiev House for the service of Pascha. "21st of

April. Great Saturday. ... At the request of Botkin, they let in for us a priest and a deacon at 8 o'clock. They served Matins quickly and well; it was a great consolation to pray even in such conditions and to hear 'Christ is Risen.'"[14] Sunday of Pascha, instead of the bright celebrations and greetings in the palace, this year passed with reading, an hour's walk in the garden in the afternoon, and evening tea. At the hour of the Paschal meal, on the "festive" table one small *kulich* was set out. But Avdeev cut the larger part of the *kulich* and ostentatiously devoured it before the eyes of the prisoners.[15]

Back in Tobolsk, the children would pass their first Pascha separated from their parents. It would also be their last. In expectation of the midnight Paschal Service, the girls and the staff decorated the makeshift iconostasis in the corner of the parlor with flowers and fir branches. In the evening a priest came and held the service for the small group of prisoners. However, the absence of their parents did not leave them room to especially enjoy the Feast. Gilliard writes, "Saturday, May 4th.—A sad Easter eve. We are in low spirits. Sunday, May 5th.—Easter Day. Still no news."[16]

Continuing her previous day's letter, Olga wrote, among other things, "22 April /5 May (letter continued) Христос Воскресе [Christ is Risen]! Dear beloved ones. We would love so much to know how you celebrated your Easter. Dear Mama, when will we finally be together? May God look after you. The midnight service and the liturgy afterwards were well done. It was beautiful and intimate. We put on all the side lights, except for the chandelier and there was enough light. The Little One slept during the service and did not participate in the Easter supper and did not even notice that we moved him to his bedroom. ... The candles were beautiful with the golden stripes, and it was for you that we lit them in turns during the Easter service ... Mama, my little soul, how are things with you? I feel sad—when I think about you—why do we have everything and you, what do you have? Dear and beloved Mama, how I would love to see you and kiss you!!"[17]

Finally, after a week with no communication, Gilliard notes, "Tuesday, May 7th.—At last the children have had a letter from Ekaterinburg saying that all are well but not explaining why they are held up [in Ekaterinburg]. What agony can be read between the lines!"[18] Alexandra wrote this letter to Olga already from the 1st of May, namely the first day after their arrival in Ekaterinburg: "April 18 [May 1st], 1918. Your old mother is always with you in her thoughts, my dear Olga. The three of us are constantly talking about you and wonder what all of you are doing. The beginning of the trip was unpleasant and depressing; it was better after we got into the train. It's not clear how things will be there."[19] That last sentence, as Gilliard understood, hid great agony.

Along with Alexandra's letter, Anastasia also received a note from Maria, who had written on 19 April/2 May: "Христос Воскресе [Christ is Risen], my little and dear soul. I kiss you three times. I hope you receive all my little eggs and icons. We think about you all the time and dream about the happy day when we will see each other again. Did you receive all our letters? It is already a week and we have not seen each other and we have written [to you] every day. It is silly, what there is to write about, but we cannot write everything. There were some amusing incidents. Every night I wish you a good night's sleep. And you? In the entire house there is no water and we wait a long time for the samovar to be brought in, which is slow to heat. Mama takes her meals in the camp bed and I take mine with Papa, Nyuta [Demidova], Evg.[eny] Serg.[eyevich Botkin], Sednev and Chemod[urov] in the dining room and Nyuta sleeps there. She sends her greetings to all of you."[20]

In the days after they received letters from Ekaterinburg, the children in Tobolsk set to writing. From Anastasia to Maria, 24 April/7 May: "Aleksei is so sweet as a boy and tries so [hard]… (remember how it was on the little bench when you were here?). We take turns having breakfast with Aleks[ei] and making him eat, although there are days when he eats without encouragement. We are always with you in our thoughts, dear ones. It is terribly sad and empty; I really don't know what is going on. The baptismal cross is with us, of course, and we got your news, so the Lord will help and is helping. We arranged the iconostasis awfully nicely for Easter, all in spruce, the way it should be here, and the flowers. We took pictures. I hope they come out. I continue to draw, not too badly they say, so it's very pleasant. We swung on the swings, and when I fell it was such a wonderful fall!… Yes, indeedy! I told the sisters about this so many times yesterday, that they got tired of hearing about it, but I could tell again and again, although there is no one left to tell. … I apologize of course that this is such a jumbled letter, you understand that my thoughts are racing and I cannot write everything so I jump on whatever comes to mind. Soon we will go for a walk, summer has not arrived yet and nothing is blooming, it is being a real slouch. I want to see you all so much, (you know) it's sad! … My sweet dear ones, how we pity you all. We trust that the Lord will help—His very own—!!!… I am unable and cannot say what I want, but you will understand I hope. Your regards were transmitted [to us] word for word, and we send you big thanks and the same. It is so pleasant here, they bless one in almost all the churches, it ends up being very cozy. When we sing amongst ourselves, it comes out badly because we need a fourth voice, but you are not here and therefore we make terribly witty comments about this. Much weaker but we have funny anecdotes too. … Goodbye for now. I wish you all the best, happiness, and all good things. We constantly pray for you and think [of you], may the Lord help. May Christ be with you, precious ones. I embrace you all very tightly and kiss you."[21]

From Tatiana to her mother, 25 April/8 May: "Mama, my dear, my beloved little soul. Thank you immensely for the little icons and egg. I miss you terribly, my beloved ones. The rooms are so sad and empty. We spend the evenings with Nastenka [Anastasia Hendrikova] downstairs, and then we all have tea. We go to bed early. I help Zhylik [Gilliard] when he is in

Letter by Nicholas from Tsarksoe Selo, 1913.

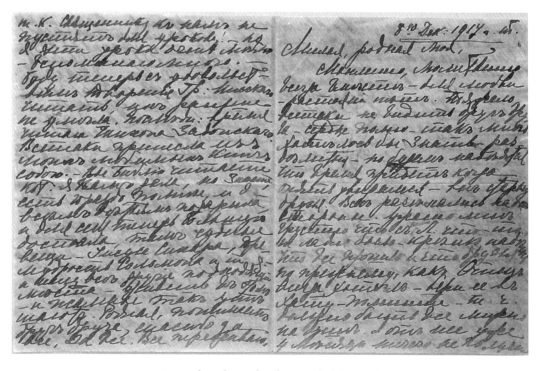

Letter by Alexandra from Tobolsk, 1917.

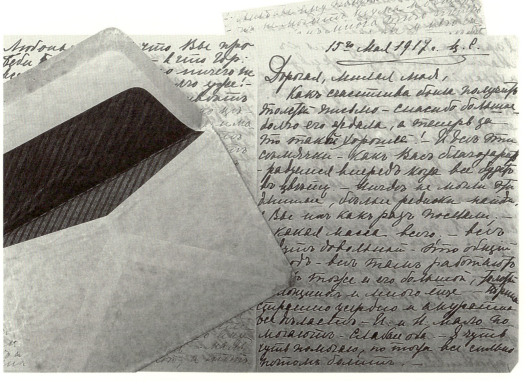

Letter by Olga from Tsarskoe Selo, 1917.

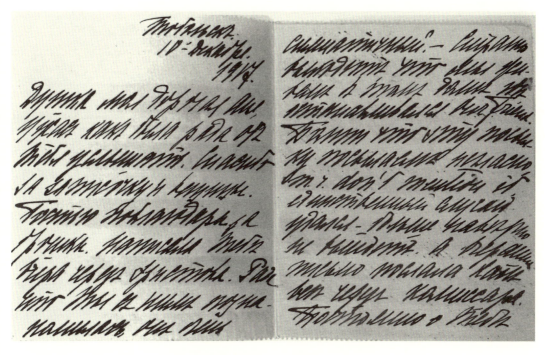

Letter by Tatiana from Tobolsk, 1917.

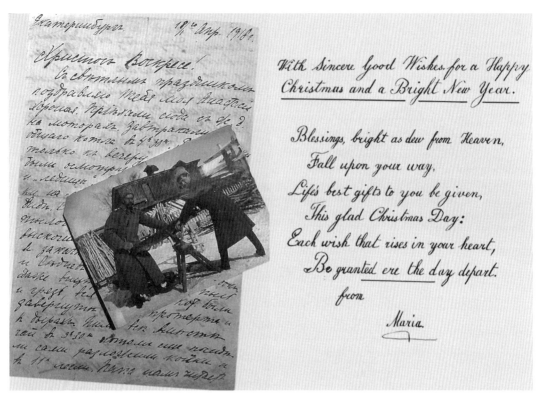

Letters by Maria. On the left: From Ekaterinburg, 1918. On the right: Christmas wishes.

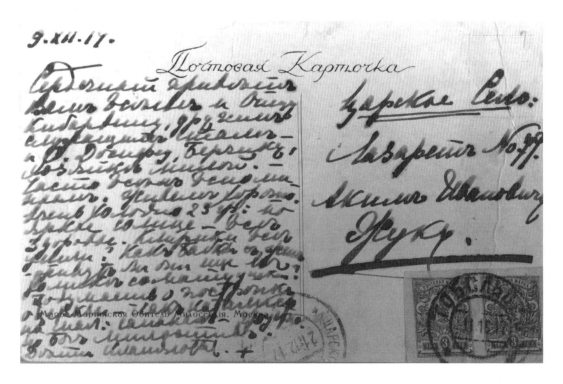

Postcard by Anastasia, Tobolsk, 1917.

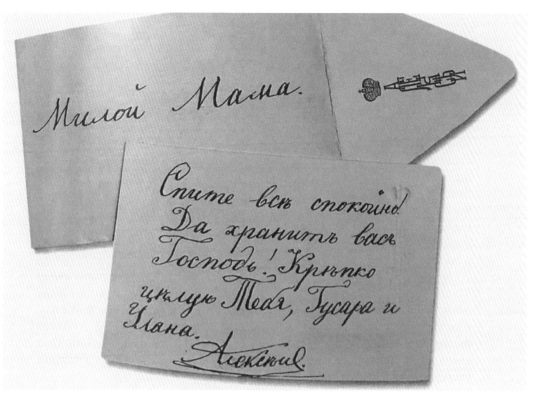

Note from Alexis to his mother.

Postcard by Alexis, Tobolsk, 1918.

need. ... Mama, my dear little soul, we are very lonesome without you and we torment ourselves with the thoughts that we do not know how you are doing. I pray a lot for you so that God will come to help you all, our dear angels. Do you have books to read or should we send some to you? ... I hope that the sugar was useful. How do you get fresh supplies? Can we bring something that you need or are you able to buy it yourselves? We think about you all the time and talk about you. In fact, we cannot even imagine how you live nor what you do. For you it is easy because you know how we live. I hope Mama, little soul, that you have no difficulty in deciphering my charming handwriting which you love so much!! What will we do with the bags of [ill.]? Now goodbye, may Christ protect you from all evil. I kiss you my beloved dear ones as much as I love you. I miss you. Your daughter who loves you very much, Tatiana."[22]

From Alexis to his mother on 28 April/11 May: "My dear and sweet Mama, I am doing better, but I can't yet walk. Thank you very much for the letter and for the card. The weather isn't great. It snows and it's icy. We had a service today. They did not let Kolya and Tolya come. ... I send greetings to everyone. I strongly hug Papa and Mashka. I hope that Gracious God keeps and watches over you! [Soon] we will all be in each other's arms and everything and all will be fine. Your Alexei."[23]

These letters would be long delayed before they even reached Ekaterinburg. The children's parents and Maria would still to be longing to learn in detail news from the children. However, their agony was greatly assuaged because the same day that the children in Tobolsk wrote their letters, on 8 May, by some unexpected intervention, they were able to receive a telegram from Olga.

In the person of the assistant commandant of the house, the family recognized a former soldier of the Imperial Guard, Constantine Ukraintsev, who, as Alexandra noted in her diary, "as a little boy Olga played with him at Gagri 15 years ago."[24] Beyond his friendly attitudes towards the prisoners, Ukraintsev secretly gave them the telegram from Olga, on 8 May: "Thanks letters. All well. Little One already been garden. We are writing. Olga."[25]

The joy over this telegram was very great. The next day Maria wrote to the children: "26 April/9 May, 1918. Ekaterinburg. Thank you, our little souls, for the telegram which we received yesterday before dinner; we are very happy, because this is the first news we received from you since we [have been] here. We are happy to learn that you received our letters." In the same letter Alexandra also wrote a few words, "We were very happy to receive Olga's telegram. Finally we know something about you and now we wait for a letter. My dear little souls, tomorrow it will be two weeks since we said goodbye. We are sad without you and miss you. Did you ask for a bag for the 'medicines'? ... We do not know with whom, or how you are going to arrive, and that worries us a lot. But the Lord is merciful and will protect you. I hope that Tatiana and Zhylik have finished everything.

Yachka probably does not understand anything. My dear ones, it is difficult to write and therefore my heart overflows. I hold you all tightly in my arms and bless you. My wishes with affection to all. Mama."[26]

Alexandra in this letter of hers asks the girls if they took care of a bag, in which they would transport the "medicines." That was the code for the jewels, the only remaining belongings of value that the family held, which they brought with them from Tsarskoe Selo. Fleeing from Tobolsk to the unknown, Alexandra avoided taking these jewels with her, not knowing what sort of inspection they would be subject to when they arrived at their destination. Thus, she told the girls that if in her letters she mentioned the transportation of "medicines," this meant that they must sew the jewels inside their clothes, so that they would not be subject to inspections.

In fact, arriving at Ekaterinburg and seeing the thorough inspections to which they were subjected, Alexandra took care to inform the girls about this. Thus, when the girls received this letter of their mother, they set to work. For entire days they took apart their clothes and placing diamonds, emeralds and other precious stones inside, they again sewed them in, wrapping them inside another layer of fabric. When they finished their work, those blouses that contained the jewels weighed two or more kilograms [four or more pounds] apiece.

The same day that Alexandra and Maria expressed their joy over the telegram that they received in their letter to the children, Ukraintsev was relieved of duty. The authorities learned of his "bad" behavior and now the family lost one person so valuable to them in their new reality. Alexander Moshkin took the position of Assistant Commandant. Moshkin found great joy in humiliating his captives. Avdeev did not spend the night at the Ipatiev House, but Moshkin remained there. Thus, in the evenings after the departure of Avdeev, Moshkin gave himself over to drinking and singing along with other guards. The sounds of their revelry then filled the house.

These provocative episodes did not only take place at night, but sometimes also during the day. According to a witness, "one day a student of the gymnasium was photographing the Ipatiev House. The Bolsheviks seized him and threw him into one of the rooms of the house. ... While he was sitting there, that student saw the Red Guards gathering in the room where there was a piano, and playing balalaikas they sang indecent songs with loud voices."[27]

Anatoly Yakimov, one of the guards at Ipatiev House, said of such incidents, "While drunk, they made a lot of noise in the commandant's room, yelled, slept in a pile, wherever they fell, and made the place a dirty mess. They sang songs that could not have been pleasant to the tsar. They sang 'You fell victim in a fatal battle,' 'Let's deny the old world,' 'Walk together, comrades.' At times when Avdeev was absent, a member of the imperial family petitioned Moshkin with some request, and he always said that they need to wait until Avdeev returns. When Avdeev came back and Moshkin passed on the request, Avdeev had the response: 'To the devil with them!' Returning from the imperial family's rooms, Avdeev would often tell us that he refused one of their requests. This refusal apparently gave him pleasure. He talked about it happily. For example, they asked him to permit them to open windows, and he was telling us how he refused it. I don't know how he referred to the tsar directly, but behind his back he called him 'Nikolashka.'"[28]

Maria wrote to her sisters, "We miss the quiet and peaceful life in Tobolsk. Here we have unpleasant surprises almost daily. Just now the members of regional committee were here and asked each of us how much money we had with us. We had to sign off on it. As you know, Papa and Mama did not even have one kopek with them so they signed, nothing, and I [had] 16 r[ubles] 75 k[opeks], which Anastasia gave me for the road. They took all the money from the rest to [give it to the] committee for safekeeping, left each one a little, [and] gave them receipts. They warn [us] that we are not guaranteed not to have new searches. Who would have thought that after 14 months of captivity they [would] treat us this way?"[29] Another one of these surprises occurred when on 15 May all the windows of the floor where the prisoners were held—which were sealed with glue so that they would not open—were now painted white so that they could not even see outside. Maria wrote the following day, "I write to you in semi-darkness as we do not have any light because the windows have been whitewashed. The white color is very unpleasant. It is, above all, bad for Mama because she suffers constantly from headaches."[30]

Another change that the authorities wished to impose was shortening the time for walks in the garden, something that Nicholas found very difficult. Used to vigorous physical activity, he was not able to adjust to the new situation. He repeatedly requested to be given permission to work in the garden cutting wood, but it was not possible for them to allow him to use tools. Finally, Avdeev showed some flexibility and did not reduce the time outside in the garden.

As time passed, the severe monotony, the absolute confinement, and the unpleasant surprises began to take their toll. These difficult hours required great spiritual reserves to keep mental equilibrium, and the family in Ekaterinburg revealed their hidden treasure: their great faith in God. In her letter to Alexis, Maria wrote, "It is difficult to write anything pleasant, because there is very little of it here to report, but on the other hand, God does not abandon us, the sun shines and the birds sing. This morning we heard the church bells. That was the only pleasant and agreeable event. ... My dear, how I would love to see you. I hope you feel better quickly and start running around again. I hold you very tightly in my arms, my dear little brother. How is Zhylik's cough? May Christ protect you. Your Masha."[31]

On 6/19 May, Nicholas completed his fiftieth year. From his diary: "I have lived for fifty years, and even to me it seems strange. ... At 11:30 the same priest and deacon held a moleben, which was very nice. ... We have not received any news about the children, and we are beginning to wonder whether they left Tobolsk."[32]

During those three weeks Nicholas and Alexandra received very few telegrams and letters from the children in Tobolsk. To the question of when would they be brought there, the reply was always that preparations were being made. On 21 May, however, Avdeev told them that the children were expected within a few days and three other rooms were opened for the staff.

THE SECOND DEPARTURE FROM TOBOLSK

On 11 May, Colonel Kobylinsky was relieved of his duties as commandant of the house in Tobolsk. In his place the stiff-necked Commissar Rodionov was sent with a detachment of Red Guards from Ekaterinburg, who were "vulgar and crude men," as Alexei Volkov writes.[33] Rodionov's perverseness became apparent at every instance. When the priest came with the nuns to hold services at the house, Rodionov found special pleasure in stripping the nuns for "inspection." Colonel Kobylinsky recalls, "Once after divine service had taken place in the house, they searched the priest and the nuns in a very indecent manner and touched everything in the sanctuary. Rodionov placed one Lett on duty near the sanctuary to watch the priest. This created such unhappiness that the Grand Duchess Olga wept and said that if she had known beforehand that this sort of thing would happen she would never have made a request for divine service."[34]

On the very first day of his installation in Tobolsk, he called Volkov and communicated to him one of his paranoid demands regarding the girls. Volkov wrote of this:

"One day, Rodionov came to find me and declared: 'Tell these young girls not to close the door to their room at night.' I replied that this was completely impossible. 'I told you to do it' he insisted.

'It is absolutely impossible, since your soldiers would pass by there all the time in front of the open doors where the young girls would be sleeping.'

'My soldiers will not pass by the open doors. But, if you do not do exactly as I have ordered you to do, I have the authority to shoot you where you stand.' As he spoke these words he took out his revolver.

'I will place a watchman at the door of the bedroom,' [he continued].

'But, that is abominable!' I shouted at him.

'That is my business' he replied."[35]

Rodionov's order never allowed margin. For this reason, fearing the worst, the men of the staff took care to take turns in the evening to make sure that nothing happened to the children.

Finally, on 19 May, Alexis had recovered sufficiently and was now able to travel. Furthermore, the ice on the river had melted and so the trip from

CHAPTER 6

Tobolsk to Tyumen could take place normally by steamship. So before dawn of 20 May, a line of carts stood along the length of the street to load the luggage. A little after 11 in the morning, a car arrived at the central entrance of the house and stopped amid the lined-up regiment of soldiers who stood holding their rifles. Then the prisoners appeared. Nagorny, holding Alexis in his hands, proceeded ahead and he put him tenderly and gently into the car. The young duchesses followed and the staff that would accompany them. One of them was also Baroness Sophia Buxhoeveden, who until now had not been permitted to enter the house where the family stayed. From the day when she came to Tobolsk she stayed at the Kornilov house across the street where the remaining staff resided.

When they were settled in the car, Alexis noticed that they had loaded crates with plates, paintings, and furniture that belonged to the owner of the house. Volkov relates, "Seeing this, the Tsarevich said to Rodionov: 'Why are you taking these things? They don't belong to us, they belong to other people.' 'The Master is gone, it is all ours' replied Rodionov."[36]

The steamship Rus awaited the company at the pier on the River Tobol, the same that brought the family to Tobolsk the previous August. Along with the children, twenty-seven members of the staff followed, among whom—apart from Buxhoeveden—were Pierre Gilliard and Sydney Gibbes, Countess Anastasia Hendrikova, Miss Schneider, General Tatishchev, Alexei Volkov, Dr Derevenko, Kharitonov the cook, Trupp the footman, and Leonid Sednev, a kitchen boy of fourteen.

As she boarded the Rus, Baroness Buxhoeveden saw the children for the first time after their departure from Tsarskoe Selo, nine months earlier. She wrote about this meeting, "I was horrified to see how ill the Tsarevich still looked. He was terribly thin and could not walk, as his knee had got quite stiff from lying with it bent for so long. He was very pale and his large dark eyes seemed still larger in the small narrow face. Olga Nicolaevna had also greatly changed. The suspense and anxiety of her parents' absence, and the responsibility she bore when left as head of the house with her sick brother to look after, had changed the lovely, bright girl of twenty-two into a faded and sad middle-aged woman. She was the only one of the young girls who acutely realised the danger that their parents were in."[37]

At the time of boarding the steamship, as Baroness Buxhoeveden remembers yet again, Olga "was in despair when she saw the archbishop's carriage and horse, which he had lent to take the Tsarevich to the boat, also being taken on board. 'But he will need it. It is not ours, please tell them,' she said. I assured her that my protestations would not help."[38]

Waiting for the baggage to be loaded, the girls began to settle into the cabins, while Alexis sat in his mother's wheelchair on deck and enjoyed the spring sunshine. The soldiers on the boat sang and played the accordion. But as the hours passed, their entertainment grew noisier. Drink had begun to ignite their cheer and now they amused themselves with gunshots in the air, tossing hand grenades into the river, and target practice with automatic firearms aimed the trees on the riverbank, and at passing birds. When at last the sun began to go down and touch the far horizon, the Rus set its bow toward the dark waters of the Siberian north for its destination, Tyumen.

Night settled. This would be one of the most terrifying nights the young princesses would experience. Alone, without their parents, with absolutely no protection, in the middle of the dark waters of the frozen Siberian river. The soldiers went completely out of control. Their mood was ugly. Their voices and their uncontrolled gunfire shook the ship. But the innocent and pure souls of the girls were much more terrified of the shameful behavior of the soldiers, who sought to show by any means that that evening they would have the fun they sought. Rodionov, despite the intense protests of Nagorny, whom the soldiers locked in with Alexis in their cabin, again did not allow the girls to lock their doors in the evening. But God preserved them and with the first light of day the girls' terrible agony of soul came to an end.

Sydney Gibbes.

At dawn on 22 May, the ship came to land at Tyumen. At the railway station of Tyumen, a special train awaited the company. Here the company was separated. The girls, Alexis with Nagorny, General Tatishchev, Miss Schneider, Countess Hendrikova, and Dr Derevenko were placed in one second-class car. Gilliard, Gibbes, Baroness Buxhoeveden, Kharitonov with his helper Leonid, Volkov, Trupp, and the rest were placed in fourth-class seats. The same day Nicholas wrote, "May 9 [22]. Wednesday. ... We still don't know where the children are, or when they will arrive? The uncertainty is strenuous!"[39]

THE NEW INMATES OF EKATERINBURG

In the afternoon the train set forth and left Tyumen behind, heading towards the Urals. Final destination, Ekaterinburg. Around midnight it entered the thick and dark forest that surrounds the eastern peaks of the Urals, and finally, at 2 o'clock in the morning, the train arrived at Ekaterinburg Station 2. Nearly a month earlier, the first group of captives had also arrived here, where they had fled to escape the threatening demonstrations of the raging mob that had gathered at the central station. Again, Station 2 did not turn out to be as safe this time. By 9 o'clock in the morning, it was filled with a hostile crowd that had been informed of the arrival of the children. Their faces were frightful. Men and women looked like they had escaped from the prisons, where only the most vicious and bloodthirsty criminals were held.

From Nicholas' diary that same day: "May 10 [23]. Thursday. In the morning during the course of an hour we were continuously told that the children were a few hours from the town, then that they had arrived at the station and, finally, that they had arrived at home, although their train had been here since 2 o'clock [am]!"[40]

The soldiers began to unload the baggage. Someone from the crowd seized one of the crates and opened it. Inside were pairs of boots that belonged to the emperor. "'He has six pairs, and I have none!' shouted a man, pointing to his bare feet. At this, one of the crowd cried 'Death to the tyrant! Death to the bourgeois!' 'All these boxes contain the gold dresses of these wanton women!' another cried. ... 'Off with their heads!'"[41] The shouts then became terrifying: "Hang them; drown them in the lake!"[42] At last, with great difficulty they brought the crowd under control and the soldiers were able to transport the baggage.

At 10 o'clock, Rodionov entered the car where the girls were together with the members of the staff who had traveled with them in the same car. Next to him was Alexander Beloborodov, Chairman of the Regional Soviet of the Urals. Rodionov commanded them to come out carrying their baggage and to proceed to the wheelbarrows that awaited them across the road.

Gilliard describes what followed: "Several carriages were drawn up alongside our train, and I saw four men go towards the children's carriage. A few minutes passed and then Nagorny, the sailor attached to Alexis Nicolaievitch, passed my window, carrying the sick boy in his arms; behind him came the Grand-Duchesses, loaded with valises and small personal belongings. I tried to get out, but was roughly pushed back into the carriage by the sentry. I came back to the window. Tatiana Nicolaievna came last, carrying her little dog and struggling to drag a heavy brown valise. It was raining, and I saw her feet sink into the mud at every step."[43]

Another eyewitness likewise described the scene: "[The girls] were wearing beautiful dark dresses with big fabric buttons. They walked unsteadily, or rather unevenly. I decided that this was because each one was carrying a very heavy suitcase and also because the surface of the road had become squelchy from the incessant spring rain. Having to walk, for the first time in their lives, with such heavy luggage was beyond their physical strength. ... They passed by very close and very slowly. I stared at their lively, young, expressive faces somewhat indiscreetly—and during those two or three minutes I learned something that I will not forget till my dying day. It felt that my eyes met those of the three unfortunate young women just for a moment and that when they did, I reached into the depths of their martyred souls, as it were, and I was overwhelmed by pity for them—me, a confirmed revolutionary. Without expecting it, I sensed that we Russian intellectuals, we who claim to be the precursors and the voice of conscience, were responsible for the undignified ridicule to which the Grand Duchesses were subjected. ...

"We do not have the right to forget, nor to forgive ourselves for our passivity and failure to do something for them. ... [E]verything was painted on those young, nervous faces: the joy of seeing their parents again, the pride of oppressed young women forced to hide their mental anguish from hostile strangers, and, finally, perhaps, a premonition of imminent death."[44]

Once he had placed Alexis in the car, Nagorny hurried back to help the girls. "He was roughly pushed back by one of the commissaries," writes Gilliard. "A few minutes later the carriages drove off with the children in the direction of the town. How little I suspected that I was never to see them again."[45]

Also from Nicholas' diary on 10/23 May: "Nighttime! It was a great joy to see them again and embrace them after four weeks of separation and uncertainty. There was no end to our mutual questions and answers. Very few letters reached them from us, and us from them. They had endured a lot of moral suffering, poor things, both in Tobolsk and during the three-day journey."[46]

FAITHFUL UNTO DEATH

As time passed, Gilliard expected that at any moment they would come back and take them also, so that they would drive them to the place where they held the Royal Couple and the children. He was eager to be again with these people so beloved to him, who had already become his true family. But the hours passed, and no one came. Much later, the train came into the station and there Rodionov with other soldiers took away Volkov, General Tatishchev, Countess Hendrikova, and Miss Schneider, whom they drove to the prison, while cook Kharitonov with his fourteen-year-old helper Leonid Sednev were taken to the Ipatiev House.

At 5 o'clock in the afternoon Rodionov returned to the train

Ivan Kharitonov.

From left. Seated: Catherine Schneider and Anastasia Hendrikova. Standing: General Tatishchev, Pierre Gilliard, Prince Dolgorukov.

---

to announce to the remainder that they were free to go! With the sole exception of Doctor Derevenko, to whom they gave permission to remain free in Ekaterinburg, so that he could visit Alexis and provide the necessary medical care, all the rest were obliged to leave the city. However, they were forced to remain for over a month inside the rail car, until the railway lines were restored and they were able to travel. Finally, Gilliard, Gibbes, and Buxhoeveden departed for Tobolsk where they settled temporarily. Later they returned to Ekaterinburg. But before then, all would be finished.

Two days later, on 28 May, two guards came to take General Tatishchev from prison. Volkov gave him his fur coat to protect himself on the way, whatever his destination might be. That coat became the identifying element later, when Tatishchev was found dead, not far from prison. With him was Dolgorukov. The son of one of the executioners of the Cheka was a witness: "The young Chekist Grigory Nikulin… took Dolgorukov out with his suitcases into a field. … [T]here was snow, and after the execution Nikulin himself had to carry Dolgorukov's suitcases across a snowy field. The snow was deep and [as his feet sunk in] he cursed all the way."[47]

Much later, when the terrible events at the Ipatiev House had already taken place, they took Volkov, Schneider, and Hendrikova together with eight other prisoners out of the prison. They told them that they would take them to the central jails. They walked on foot in the middle of a forest near Perm when night began to fall. Volkov understood the purpose of their nighttime march. In the middle of forests there were no jails, of course. And then he tried his luck leaving the line of prisoners and running into the forest. Gunshots followed in his direction. But he was fortunate and after a difficult journey, he managed to escape. But not the rest—neither the two noble women. The Bolsheviks murdered them in cold blood in the depth of night. Miss Schneider, the dedicated teacher who thirty years earlier had taught Russian to Princess Elisabeth, the Empress' sister, and later to Alexandra herself, was fortunate: she was killed by a bullet. As for Countess Hendrikova, they did not waste a single bullet. The "brave" Red Guards shattered her skull with their rifle butts.

A few weeks earlier, when Baroness Buxhoeveden met Nastenka Hendrikova in Tobolsk, she said of her, "[Nastenka] said openly to me that she had a premonition that all our days were numbered. She, personally, had gone through much sorrow that year. She was passionately devoted to the Empress, and the long months of captivity had tried her to the utmost and had developed intensely the religious side of her nature. Indeed she now lived an entirely spiritual life, and had so fixed her thoughts on approaching death that it had no terror for her. She was very pretty and looked younger than her twenty-eight years, but she welcomed the thought of death, so weary had she become of life and so much detached from earthly interests. I felt her drifting away to higher planes."[48]

THE NEW REALITY

The first four days, the girls slept on the floor on their coats until they brought mattresses for their folding beds. Alexis was settled in Maria's bed in his parents' room. The following morning, on 24 May, they brought Nagorny and Trupp to the Ipatiev House. Trupp took the place of the elderly Chemodurov who had taken ill and could not endure the constraints of imprisonment. They took him to the city hospital.

CHAPTER 6

Aloise Yegorovich Trupp.

Alexis had not recovered sufficiently from his latest wound, when on the very first day at the Ipatiev House he once again bumped his foot as he was climbing into his bed. This new wound worsened, and Dr Derevenko visited him to relieve his pain. In the evenings Alexandra kept watch again by her child. It finally took twelve days before this new episode passed.

On his visit of 26 May, Dr Derevenko "was accompanied by a dark[-haired] gentleman, whom we recognized as being a doctor,"[49] Nicholas wrote in his diary. However, this visitor was not a doctor, but a member of the local Soviet and the Cheka. His name was Yakov Yurovsky. That day, without at all suspecting it, Nicholas and his family had met for the first time the man who in six weeks would undertake their execution.

The following day, only three days after his arrival at the Ipatiev House, Nagorny was taken to the Ekaterinburg jail along with the servant Ivan Sednev, the uncle of little Leonid. No explanations whatever were given for the arrest of these two men. As for Nagorny, one of the guards in his deposition testified: "The typical Slavic appearance of this peasant in sailor's uniform was overprinted with an infinite tenderness. Nagorni single-mindedly wanted to cheer up and distract his young charge and to lessen the bitterness of the prison. The sailor smiled frankly and his small grey eyes were lit with a tender love. I will never forget this likable fellow."[50] His separation from his beloved Alexis cost Nagorny much. However, this pain of the devoted and good-hearted servant did not last long. On 28 June, he was murdered along with Sednev a few kilometers outside the city.

Clementy Nagorny, the faithful servant.

Soon the family and the few members of their company entered—as much as possible—into the rhythm of their new reality in their new prison. After rising in the morning, around 8 or 9 o'clock they gathered in the parlor of the house for common prayer and the reading of Holy Scripture. Often, they also sang hymns. The guard Anatoly Yakimov recalls:

"One thing I witnessed first-hand in the life of the imperial family: they

Anna Demidova.

used to sing sometimes. I had the chance to hear their spiritual singing. They sang the Cherubic hymn. They also sang some secular song. I did not hear the words, but the melody was sad.... I heard only female voices, never any male ones."[51]

Subsequently they were obligated to present themselves for inspection by the commandant or his assistant, after which they took their breakfast all together. Their breakfast consisted of black bread, usually left over from the previous day, and tea. There was no coffee. When on 16 May the prisoners received a package with coffee and cocoa from Alexandra's sister Elisabeth, who was also in Ekaterinburg as an exile, Alexandra noted in her diary: "Great treat, cup of coffee."[52]

After breakfast, the young princesses helped Demidova with household chores. They made the beds, did the general cleaning and washed their sheets and clothes by hand. The rest of the morning, up to the time of their first recess for a walk in the garden, the prisoners read, wrote letters—even though nearly none of them arrived at their destination—and played board games.

Undoubtedly the excursions in the garden constituted the most pleasant event of the day for the captives. But Alexandra, did not often go out because of her health. Taking their turn, one of the girls remained inside with her reading aloud from some spiritual book. Of the Holy Scripture, she preferred the books of the Prophets, and especially that of the Prophet Hosea. The few times she went out of the house, the empress sat on the steps of the entrance, because she could not walk as far as the garden.

The guard Alexander Strekotin recorded: "The prisoners were taken outside for a walk twice a day, at 10 in the morning and at 4 in the afternoon. Thirty minutes each time. At this time, in the garden and in the yard, the guard was increased from among the volunteers in the team; there were always plenty of volunteers. The prisoners did not all always go outside for a walk. In particular, the four people who were imprisoned along with the imperial family went out most rarely. Also, the tsaritsa rarely went out, and always not for long. The ex-emperor always wore the same military khaki uniform.... The tsarevich—Alexei, wore the same [uniform] as the tsar in the same colonel rank, [he was] brunet, with black unhappy eyes, thin, ill-looking. His severe untreatable illness completely paralyzed both of his legs, apparently even before the revolution,[53] which was why he was always carried outside by the tsar himself. He carefully picked him up, pulled him close to his wide chest, and the other would grab his father's thick short neck with his arms, while his thin, whip-like, weak legs hung limply. ... He [the tsar] sat him in a wheelchair and wheeled him around the garden, stopping at paths to give him pebbles, he [the heir] then tossed them into bushes, or he [the emperor] picked flowers for him, or branches from the bushes."⁵⁴

After the second walk in the afternoon, the company took their tea. At that time, the exact same background of the past twenty and more years was repeated. Nicholas read aloud from some book, while Alexandra and the girls knitted and Alexis played with his toy soldiers. Finally, the entire company took their supper together, which, as the lunch, was prepared by the kitchen of the local Soviet. The girl who volunteered to deliver the food to the house remembers:

"One day while I was taking the meals, I saw the former heir Alexis Nikolaevich sitting in his wheelchair. He seemed weak, having an ill expression on his face. I saw the empress only two times. She was tall, dark-haired and thin. But I often saw Maria, Anastasia, and their brother Alexis, the former heir. They pushed him in his wheelchair. Once I whispered to him, 'Do your feet hurt?' and nodding his head affirmatively he replied to me, 'Yes.' One guard saw it and told me that it is not permitted to speak with them. I did not see the two older daughters, although they told me that they too were in the house. … We were not permitted to speak, and so the prisoners were always silent. But they always seemed kindly and smiled when they saw me."⁵⁵

With the departure of Avdeev at 9 o'clock in the evening, Moshkin's time came, who, along with his companions, gave themselves over to drink and rowdiness until dawn. And so yet another day ended in the Ipatiev House, the "House of Special Purpose," in expectation of the day when that special purpose should be accomplished.

"There were prayer services in the house," Yakimov recalled, "but the entire time I stayed at the [Ipatiev] house, there were only three services. Twice they were given by the priest Storozhev and once by the priest Meledin. But there were services before us. I know this because I was the one who went to get the priests when there was to be a prayer service. During Avdeev, there were two services at the house, while I was there. During Yurovsky—one. During the service, from a distance I heard female and male voices: they must have sung themselves."⁵⁶

One of those services took place on Sunday, 2 June, with Priest John Storozhev. The service was Typica [Obednitsa].⁵⁷ Father John later testified regarding this visit of his:

> On Sunday, 20 May/2 June, 1918, I performed the regular Divine Liturgy at the Ekaterininsky Cathedral, and just having returned home at 10 o'clock in the morning, I settled in to have tea, when someone knocked at the front door of my apartment. I personally opened the door and saw in front of me a soldier of nondescript appearance, with a red face and small shifty eyes. He was wearing an old jacket of khaki colour, on his head, a worn military cap. There

were no epaulets, nor cockade, of course. No weapons were seen on him. To my question of what he needs, the soldier responded: "You are requested to perform a service for Romanov." Not understanding whom he is referring to, I asked "Which Romanov?" "You know, the former tsar," he explained. From subsequent discussion it turned out that Nicholas Alexandrovich Romanov was asking to perform the next Typica. "He wrote over here asking for some kind of Typica service," the visitor announced.

Having agreed to perform the service, I told him that it would be necessary to bring a deacon with us. The soldier insistently objected for a long time against inviting a deacon, stating that "the commandant" ordered him to bring only one priest, but I insisted, and together with this soldier we went to the Cathedral, where I got everything necessary for the service, and I called for Deacon Buimirov, with whom, accompanied by the same soldier, we went to the Ipatiev House.

From the time the Romanov family was placed here, the [Ipatiev] house was surrounded by a double plank fence. ... [Once we passed the first fence] we entered behind the second fence right at the gate of the Ipatiev House. Here stood numerous young men armed with rifles, dressed in general civilian clothes; on their belts hung hand grenades. These armed men apparently were the guards. They took us through the gates into the courtyard and from here through a side door into the ground floor of the Ipatiev house. Having ascended the staircase, we entered the upper [floor] towards the main door, and then through the hallway—into the study that "the commandant" occupied. Everywhere, on the stairs as well as on the platform, and in the front room were guards—the same type of young men armed with same rifles and hand grenades in civilian clothes. ...

The commandant stared at me silently, without greeting, I saw him for the first time and did not even know his surname, and now memorized it. To my question of which service we need to perform, he replied, "They are asking for Typica." Neither I nor the deacon engaged in any conversation with the commandant, but I only asked if I would be allowed to give prosphora to the Romanovs after the service, which I showed him. The commandant quickly looked over the prosphora and after a long thought returned it to the deacon, saying: "It can be given to them, but I must warn you there will be no other conversations." I could not help but respond that I do not plan to have any conversation at all. My response apparently bothered the commandant a bit and he said a few times "That's right, no other ones besides those about religious subjects."

...Having put on our vestments, and taking with us all that was necessary for the service, we walked out of the commandant's room into the hallway. The commandant himself opened the door that led

CHAPTER 6

into the hall, letting me go in first. With me walked father deacon, and the commandant entered last.

The hall into which we entered through an arch was connected with a smaller room—a sitting room, where close to the front corner I noticed a table set up for the service. But I was distracted from looking at the hall and the sitting room, because as soon as we stepped into the hall we saw that three figures walked from the window: they were Nicholas Alexandrovich, Tatiana Nikolaevna, and another older daughter, but which one exactly I did not have a chance to see.

In the next room, separated from the hall by an arch, was Alexandra Feodorovna, two younger daughters and Alexei Nikolaevich. The latter was lying down on a camp [folding] bed and I was amazed by his appearance: he was pale to a point of transparency, thin, and he surprised me by his great height. In general, his appearance was extremely sickly and only his eyes were lively and bright and looked at me with obvious curiosity—a new person. He was dressed in a white undershirt and covered with a blanket down from his waist. His bed stood by the right wall from the entrance, just past the arch.

Near the bed stood an armchair, in which Alexandra Feodorovna sat, wearing a loose dress, of dark lilac colour. There were no jewels on her at all, and I did not notice any on the daughters either. Alexandra Feodorovna's great height was noticeable, as was her manner of holding herself, the manner that cannot be called anything but "majestic." She sat in an armchair, but got up cheerfully and steadily when we entered and exited, as well as when during the service I proclaimed "Peace to all," read the Gospel or when we sang the more important prayers. ...

Nicholas Alexandrovich was dressed in a khaki tunic, the same color trousers, and tall boots. On his chest was an officer's St George Cross. There were no epaulets. All four daughters wore dark skirts and simple white blouses. Their hair was cut rather short in the back;[58] they looked cheerful, and I must say, almost merry. Nicholas Alexandrovich impressed me by his firm gait, his calmness, and especially his manner of looking directly and openly into one's eyes. I noticed no sign of emotional oppression in him. It seemed to me that I saw some barely noticeable grey hairs in his beard. ... As for Alexandra Feodorovna, her appearance was somehow tired, even sickly.

I forgot to mention one thing that constantly caught my attention—the special reverence for my priestly office with which every member of the Romanov family bowed in response to my silent greeting to them at the exit of the hall after the service ended. ...

Having taken our places [with the deacon] in front of the table with the icons, we began the service, and the deacon said the petitions of the Litany of Peace while I sang. Two female voices sang along with me (I think it was Tatiana Nikolaevna and one of the other [girls]). Occasionally Nicholas Alexandrovich sang along in a low bass (he sang the "Our Father" this way, for instance, and other hymns).

The service passed pleasantly and well; they prayed fervently. At the end of the service, I did the usual dismissal with the Holy Cross and for a moment I paused in bewilderment: should I approach the congregation with the Cross so they could kiss it, or was this not allowed, and with this wrong step I might perhaps create difficulties for the Romanov family in being able to satisfy their spiritual needs in holding future services?

I cast a glance at the commandant, to see what he was doing and how he might feel about my intention to approach them with the Cross. It seemed to me that Nicholas Alexandrovich also cast a quick glance towards the commandant. The latter stood in his place, in the farthest corner, and calmly stared at us. Then I took a step forward and simultaneously Nicholas Alexandrovich approached the Cross first with firm and even steps, without moving his steady gaze away from me, and kissed the Cross, behind him approached Alexandra Feodorovna and all four daughters, while I myself approached Alexei Nikolaevich lying in his bed. He was looking at me with such lively eyes that I thought, "Doubtless he will now say something," but Alexei Nikolaevich silently kissed the Cross.[59]

During this period, the Lord took care to send a heavenly consolation to His faithful servants. From 18 June and on, with the intervention of Dr Derevenko, the novice nuns Antonina and Maria from the Novo-Tikhvin Convent arrived daily at the Ipatiev House bearing fresh eggs, milk, butter, and cream for the prisoners from their farm, and also freshly baked bread, vegetables and meat.

The history of the Novo-Tikhvin Convent began fairly recently, at the end of the eighteenth century. However, the fervent zeal of the nuns and the assistance of the faithful of Ekaterinburg soon contributed to the property development of the convent, making it the greatest monastic community of the Urals. More notable, however, was the spiritual growth of the convent. People from all classes found—and still find—in the bosom of the convent the heavenly consolation that the Orthodox spiritual tradition offers and they receive blessing from the wonderworking icon of the Mother of God of Tikhvin. Before the outbreak of the Revolution, there around a thousand nuns lived there, who were especially distinguished for their works of charity.[60]

It was very natural then that the genuine Christian love of the sisters of the convent did not leave the Batiushka-Tsar of Russia and his family entirely to the mercy of the revolutionaries. So, with the initiative of the Abbess Magdalena,[61] and under the guidance of Nun Augustina, every morning the two sisters Antonina and Maria arrived from the southern

CHAPTER 6

The Novo-Tikhvin Monastery in the 1920s.

suburbs of the city where their convent was, to the Ipatiev House with their blessed supplies.

In 1919, Nun Augustina mentioned the following in her testimony: "I am the director of the iconographic section of our convent. Once, last summer, there came to our convent a gentleman unknown to me, who wished to order from us the icon of the Venerable Martyr Margarita. On his very first visit he told us about the Tsar's family. He began to say that we should save them, and for this purpose we should rally the officers and do whatever is possible to avert the danger that might threaten them. I introduced this man to Dr Derevenko as the only person who would be able to say anything definite. He himself intended to go to the officers at the Academy of the Army Command. This gentleman visited Dr Derevenko and when he returned from him he told us that the royal family, according to Derevenko, had need of food.

"We began to send the royal family milk. The Commandant of the house, Avdeev, with whom Derevenko had spoken beforehand of the matter, willingly permitted the delivery of milk to the Royal family. He only asked of us that the nuns not be wearing the monastic habit, but worldly clothes: he must have feared his own Red Army soldiers. So we began to bring milk. Two of our nuns, Maria and Antonina brought it.

"The first time we sent milk was 5 June by the Old Calendar [18 June].[62] They received the milk, if I make no mistake, either Avdeev himself or his aide. And since Avdeev, according to the nuns, treated them well, we made these offerings of ours richer. Along with a quart of milk we also began to send a bottle of cream, and then other produce: eggs, butter, bread, various baked goods (pies, cheese bread),[63] radishes, cucumbers, green soup [Ботвинья], meat, kielbasas. All these things Avdeev or his aide received willingly."[64]

From the deposition of novice Maria: "Last year abbess Augustina summoned me and commanded me, 'Dress in worldly clothes. You will take milk with Antonina to the Ipatiev House.' And she told us that this milk will go to the tsar's family. I put on worldly clothes, and so did Antonina, and we took the milk. ... They let us in through the fence; we go up to the porch, the guard rings, out comes either Avdeev or his aide, they take the provisions from us, and we leave. Once Avdeev said to us, 'Now Alexis Nikolaevich is better. Can you also bring rum?'"[65]

The rum certainly was not intended for Alexis. Avdeev and his aide who received the food kept nearly all of it for themselves and the other soldiers. Only a few of these provisions reached the family. But beyond keeping the food, the men of Avdeev's guard resorted to other systematic thievery. According to Yakimov, "They would often go to the cupboards and take things from there into big bags, which they drove away in automobiles or horses. They brought these things to their houses."[66] Chekist Isai Rodzinsky likewise related that "the children of the workers began to appear wearing Alexis' clothes."[67]

Mother Augustina.

COUNTERPOINTS

Valentine Speranski, former professor at the University of Saint Petersburg, who emigrated to Paris after the Revolution, visited Ekaterinburg in 1924 to give a series of lectures. While he was there, he held interviews with people of various political parties and stations, including the Bolsheviks, who had at one time any connection with the terrible events that had taken place there only six years earlier. One of the most important persons who gave information to Speranski was Anatoly Yakimov, who served as guard at the Ipatiev House.

Yakimov preserved very important details from the period of his service at Ipatiev. He included some of these in his deposition when he was interrogated by the special investigator Sokolov in 1919. But one very important part of these he also gave to Speranski in 1924. According to Yakimov, soon a known phenomenon was observed in the Ipatiev House. The unaffected kindness and the natural simplicity of the comportment of the members of the Royal Family did not pass unobserved by the soldiers. As time passed, some of the guards at Ipatiev began to perceive the situation differently, a fact that finally affected their attitude towards the prisoners. He relates:

"Some answered [the tsar] gently, the others with a boorish taunt. I have seen such scenes: head to head with Nicholas Alexandrovich, one of our comrades spoke to him humbly, but as soon as he saw one of the others approaching, he changed his tone. At the beginning, some of our young people were happy to be cheeky in front of the prisoners and to cause them inconvenience, but little by little, if we cannot say that they became faultless, at least they were correct in behavior and we finally avoided acting casually in the presence of the imperial family."[68]

Yakimov also related the following revealing details: "Nothing was left of my ideas about the tsar that I had before I became a guard. I started to think differently of them after I saw them with my own eyes. I started to feel pity for them as human beings. In my head an idea was born: let them escape; what can I do to allow them to escape. I never told anyone, but I had an idea to talk to the doctor, Derevenko, who used to visit them. But then I was wary of him. I thought I don't know what kind of person he is. His face had no expression when he was leaving them, and he never said a word about them. So I was too wary. Before I got hired as a guard, having not seen or known them, I was also somewhat guilty towards them. Avdeev and the comrades would be singing revolutionary songs at times, and I would sing along with them a bit. But once I saw what's what, I quit all that, and almost all of us, if not all, used to criticize Avdeev for that."[69]

The propagandistic image of the bloodthirsty Romanovs that circulated among the masses of people had already begun to fall apart. The revolutionary rhetoric about the arrogant disdain of the emperors for Russia and their oppressive malevolence crumbled at the sight of this loving family, so easily approachable and—if conditions permitted – ready to relate with every person who approached them. Yakimov said of Nicholas:

"His eyes were nice, kind, as was his entire face. In general, he gave the impression of being a nice person, simple, sincere and talkative. He looked like he wanted to talk to us."[70] "He would sit in the sun, his eyes lowered, and we could feel an innate strength in him. I often thought that he had to despise from the bottom of his soul all of these peasants, these rascal scoundrels who became his guardians. However, Nicholas Alexandrovich was master of himself, and so to each person he could quietly say the appropriate word in an affable way. His voice was sweet and clear, his manners excessively pleasant. His eyes were blue and very pleasing. When one of our stupid men, under the influence of drink, made him out as a villain, or spoke to him rudely, he replied politely and patiently. His clothes were patched, and his boots completely worn out. The *valet-de-chambre* of the emperor said that before the revolution he liked to wear the same clothes and the same shoes for a long time."[71]

"I managed to speak with him twice. The first time, I was on guard in the garden, one day in the spring. I came on duty just as the emperor and his family were let out for their walk. I stood at a distance as they walked around speaking in English quietly, admiring the green and fresh branches of the trees. The emperor, understanding from my demeanour that I was neither insolent nor braggart, came near me, looked at me quietly, and spoke to me as if we had known each other for a long time and said, 'This is a beautiful time for working the fields.' 'That's right' I said to him politely; 'for the peasants it is the time for the most profitable work.' Then by and by we spoke of harvests and the price of wheat. I started to take a real interest in our conversation, but suddenly Commandant Avdeev harshly yelled out that the time for walking was over.'"[72]

Alexandra seemed distant, closed within herself. Her stance became even more intensely felt due to the precisely opposite attitude of Nicholas and the girls. At first Alexandra would often come out into the garden for a walk. But when some of the guards began to ask her offensive questions she stopped going out. Yakimov says of Alexandra: "Her gaze was stern, her figure and manners were those of a proud and haughty woman. At one time a group of us talked about what we thought of all of them, that Nicholas Alexandrovich was a simple man, while she [Alexandra] was not simple: and that she looked like a tsaritsa. She appeared older than him. On her temples grey hairs were noticeable, her face was not that of a young woman, but of an old one."[73] Strekotin expressed the same opinion declaring that Alexandra "was serious, haughty and silent."[74] In saying these things, the guards obviously were not able to comprehend the terrible condition of Alexandra's health, which did not allow her any room to behave differently. She was but a sick and nearly crippled woman, something that also became apparent from the following witness. The publisher of the newspaper *The Ural Worker*, a certain V. Vorobev, who served for a short time as guard at the Ipatiev House, relates that Alexandra was "constantly suffering from migraine and indigestion… [and] she reclined on the couch, her head bound with a compress."[75]

Yakimov said the following about the children: "It seemed that Tatiana was similar to the tsaritsa. She also looked stern and proud like her mother."[76] "However, she smiled pleasantly when she met decent and appropriately acting guards."[77] "The rest of the daughters: Olga, Maria, and Anastasia did not have any haughtiness. One could tell by looking at them that they were simple and kind."⁷⁸ "The older Olga Nicholaevna was, like her brother, pale and sickly, but that did not stop her from being restless. Her eyes, most of the time, looked sad and tired. During the walks she stood apart from her sisters and looked sadly off in the distance. She played the piano more often than her sisters and when she wanted to play a piece for herself, she chose something catchy and plaintive. ...

"Maria Nicholaevna was more friendly to me. ... A true Russian beauty, although in her veins flowed a blood rather more German, Danish, and English than Russian. When Maria Nicholaevna smiled, her eyes shined so brightly that it was a pleasure to see. Her face was more often pink than her sisters. Her laughter was so cheerful and so infectious, that it would have been fun to play and joke with her. One could see an invincible force drove her temperament. I remember one day, in the garden, she strongly grabbed on to a huge tree branch and she began to swing on until Yurovsky yelled at her angrily: 'Citizen! Stop damaging the trees!'

"[Anastasia] was a charming little devil. She was so mischievous that with her, I think, you could not get bored. Lively and restless, she continually made comic mimes with her favorite dog, as one does at the circus."⁷⁹ "The heir was always ill; I cannot say anything about him. The tsar would carry him out to the wheelchair, and in it he was covered by a blanket."⁸⁰

When they were off duty, these men in the barracks, at the taverns, and at their homes, would speak openly with sympathy about the emperor and his family. A certain female friend of Yakimov declared with manifest displeasure, "Yes, but it was not only in the last days that I began to notice that not only him, [Yakimov] but also the other guards of my acquaintance were gradually becoming counterrevolutionary. They began to have troubled consciences, like old women poisoned by religion, and became less rigid. Instead of remembering the great crimes committed by Nicholas the Bloody and Alix with her Rasputin, they began to argue like real bourgeois. They lost their direction completely, those idiots!"⁸¹

Later when the tragic events occurred, these guards felt horror that they were not able to help the family. They said in desperation, "Yes, we had pity for them, but what could one do? When you are the guard, you have to perform your duties."⁸² Furthermore the security measures at the Ipatiev House were draconian. Any attempt to save the family would have been doomed from the start and would have resulted in an inevitable bloodbath.

Despite all of this, not all the soldiers nursed the same feelings for the family. Furthermore, these few soldiers who held friendly attitudes towards the family did not have any power to express this to them because all communication with the prisoners was strictly forbidden. There were very few instances when the prisoners exchanged a few words with the guards. Most of the guards were truly deeply poisoned with the revolutionary zeal of the time and used every opportunity to display it. Yakimov relates:

THE CHAPTER OF BLOOD

"It is a shame to admit it, but all of us to the last man, we were more or less guilty as to those unfortunates. It was difficult for these young boorish peasants, elevated to this role of guards to stop themselves, if only in their heads, from the temptation to satisfy their animal instincts. They made fun of the defenseless girls. Our comrades from the factory later became more humane, but Zlokazov's young studs stayed as vicious as before, they would keep on continually offending those young girls and watched their every move. I often pitied those girls. If, for example, they were playing dancing music on the piano they smiled, but tears from their eyes dropped onto the keys."[83]

The girls found it very difficult to understand and to adapt to this new atmosphere. Their narrower surroundings from the time they were born until then had always consisted of officers and soldiers of the imperial guard. It was very natural for them to approach these men and to begin conversations with them. Moreover, even in the period of their captivity up until then, especially in Tobolsk, their relationship with their guards was fairly good. So their surprise was great when they tried to approach the soldiers at the Ipatiev House.

Strekotin characteristically relates, "The prisoners constantly tried to start conversations with the red guards. One time, during the time of walk in the garden, the tsar approached me quietly and said: 'Tell me, is Ekaterinburg a big city?' 'Like Moscow'— I responded, and having tossed the rifle up on the belt, walked away. The most eager to talk were the daughters (except Olga). They would often start a conversation like this: 'We are bored, it was merrier in Tobolsk. Can you guess what this little dog's name is? They always brought dogs outside with them, which lived with them. When [one time] they approached the Red Guard Sadchikov Nicholas Stepanovich with this type of talk, he responded roughly: 'There is no need to distract me, you can just stomp along.' They looked at each other fearfully, and continued walking along the path silently. ...

"The indoor upstairs post where the prisoners lived was especially difficult. There, almost every minute, the prisoners walked by the guard post, and the daughters especially would smile at the guard every time and start a conversation, they would stop at the post and it was all very repulsive and annoying. I stood at that post only once, and declined after that."[84]

In another instance, as Nicholas sat at the table with his daughters, Avdeev, drunk as usual, elbowed him in his face. Yakimov commented on the incident, "It's better that Alexandra Feodorovna did not see this shame. Her husband and daughters felt that they needed to hide the truth [of what happened] from her."[85]

The illness of the servant Chemodurov led to his replacement by Trupp, which saved Chemodurov's life, thus preserving details about the life of the prisoners at the Ipatiev House. In his descriptions, he characterized the soldiers who guarded the family as "completely dissolute: they were rude, without any barriers, with lit cigars in their teeth and their

CHAPTER 6

Terenty Ivanovich Chemodurov.

shameful comportment; they breathed disgust and revulsion. ... When members of the family passed next to the guards, they would rattle their weapons to frighten them."[86]

Some of them devoted their time of service to drawing and writing whatever was most shameful on the walls of the hallways and bathrooms. A favorite theme of their vulgar drawings was to make shameful depictions of the empress with Rasputin. Even though the guards wrote and drew these where it was impossible for the prisoners not to see them, they found it especially pleasing to ask the girls if they had noticed their "artwork." The worst annoyances of this sort were mainly by the guards who stood in the halls outside the bathroom. As Chemodurov explained, "When one of the girls went to the bathroom, the guard began to amuse himself by asking where she was going and why. When the girl went inside, the guard turned toward the door of the bathroom and 'waited' until [the girl] came out."[87]

Yakimov confirmed the truth of these events. Remembering these sorrowful events, as Speranski writes, "with an undisguised confusion, [he] confessed that he and his companions had allowed themselves the lowest and the most unhealthy curiosity, when they stood guard at the door of the bedroom of the grand duchesses, or near to the family boudoir. One day Grand Duchess Tatiana Nicholaevna, pale as death, gave them a look so rude that they were ashamed, they turned on their heels and did not continue their attempts at insolent debauchery."[88]

Valentin Speranski relates that according to the witness of the interviews, "the most shocking erotic language was carried into the Ipatiev House by means of improper graffiti on the walls of the hallways, on the garden walls and on the poles of the garden swing.[89] Maria Nicholaevna once silenced two of the crudest persecutors when she said boldly, glaring at them: "How can you stomach repeating these shameful words? Do you think that it is with such words that a well-bred woman can be moved and think kindly of you and put you in her favor? Be polite and decent people; then we can talk with you."[90]

ANOTHER HISTORICAL PARENTHESIS

While the flow of daily life went on in the Ipatiev House according to its own rhythm, all of the rest of Russia passed through one of the most critical turning points in its history. Displeasure over the shameful Treaty of Brest-Litovsk, Lenin's shut-down of the Constituent Assembly (because he had lost the majority), and indignation over the political terror perpetrated by the Bolsheviks, all combined with the famine in Russia, which had resulted from the government's seizure of wheat, to provoke an unprecedented series of strikes and demonstrations. In June of 1918, the reins of power had begun to slip dangerously from the hands of Lenin and the Bolsheviks. At the same time, above the conflict in the political arena, another dismal reality threatened their authority: civil war had already begun in Russia.

The White Army was formed at the beginning of 1918, which included former tsarist generals, soldiers of the imperial Army, monarchists, democrats, and various other factions that were bound together by a common hatred for the Bolsheviks. Another force was soon added to this alliance, which shook the balance of power: the Czechoslovak Legion, which consisted of 37,000 former prisoners of war who were trapped in the Ukraine after the Treaty of Brest-Litovsk. Although they were now free, their departure was almost impossible due to the general paralysis of transport and of all of other services in Russia.

Terribly resenting the Bolshevik government for this circumstance, the Czechs finally revolted when Trotsky commanded them to disarm and compelled them to join the Red Army. Allying, then, with the White Army, the Czechs began to push into Siberia, occupying one city after another. On 6 June, they occupied Ufa, on 7 June, Omsk, and on the next day Samara. In the first week of July, they already had nearly the entire zone along the length of the Trans-Siberian Railroad from Penza to Vladivostok under their control. Now only two cities remained, Perm and Ekaterinburg, whose capture was now a matter of days.

Lenin's agonizing anxiety was certainly to hold on to power. But the agony of the Soviet of Ekaterinburg centered on the possibility of the liberation of the royal family by the advancing White Army. That must never be permitted.

THE GAME OF ESCAPE

From Nicholas' diary: "May 31 [June 13]. Ascension Day. For a long time during the morning, but in vain, we expected the arrival of a priest to hold the service; all of them were occupied at [their] churches.[91] For some reason, we were not allowed to go into the garden during the day. Avdeev came and talked a long time with Evg.[eny] Serg.[eyevich Botkin]. According to him, he and the Regional Soviet are apprehensive about demonstrations by the anarchists and, therefore, perhaps we might have an untimely departure, probably—to Moscow! He asked [us] to prepare for departure. We immediately started packing, but quietly, so as not to attract the attention of the guards.

"About 11:00 in the evening he returned and said that we would have to stay a few [more] days. Therefore, on June 1, we remained bivouacking without unpacking anything. The weather was fine; the walk took place as always, two times. Finally, after dinner Avdeev, slightly drunk, announced to Botkin that the anarchists had been captured and that the danger had passed and our departure was canceled! After all the preparations this was very annoying."[92]

In this case the Bolsheviks told the truth. The general opposition to the dictatorial measures of the government and the reign of terror began to reach large dimensions. The Bolsheviks were proved liars and traitors to the ideology of Revolution. However, even though it was against the Bolsheviks, this anarchist movement in Ekaterinburg was not at all favorable to Nicholas and his family. The mood of the crowd that demonstrated all over the city was threatening and intended, in fact, to attack the house and kill Nicholas.

The general ferment that had now appeared persuaded the Bolsheviks of the Urals that they needed to hasten their proceedings regarding the fate of the prisoners. But it was necessary to find justification for any drastic measures they might undertake. Thus, about a week after this episode, they began to build their "case."

Around 20 June, when they opened the provisions that the nuns had brought them, they found a note, written in French, inside the stopper of the bottle of the cream:

> Friends are no longer sleeping and hope that the hour so long awaited has come. The revolt of the Czechoslovaks threatens the Bolsheviks ever more seriously. Samara, Cheliabinsk, and all of eastern and western Siberia are in the hands of the provisional national government. The army of Slavic friends is eighty kilometers [50 miles] from Yekaterinburg. The soldiers of the Red Army cannot effectively resist. Be attentive to any movement from the outside; wait and hope. But at the same time, I beg you, be careful, because the Bolsheviks, before being vanquished, represent real and serious danger for you. Be ready at every hour, day and night. Make a drawing of your three bedrooms [showing] the position of the furniture, the beds. Write the hour that you all go to bed. One of you must not sleep between 2:00 and 3:00 on all the following nights. Answer with a few words, but, please, give all the useful information for your friends from outside. You must give your answer in writing to the same soldier who transmits this note to you, but do not say a single word.
> From someone who is ready to die for you,
> Officer of the Russian Army.[93]

Two other similar letters came to the family, one around 24 June and the last around the 27th. On the first two letters, the purported replies of the family survive, also written in French, addressed to the letters of those "friends," inviting their rescue. The purpose of the letters was to see what their response would be. The Cheka did not hesitate to admit that they themselves wrote these letters from the "Russian officer." The reply letters gave the Cheka the necessary grounds to justify whatever decision they would make regarding the fate of the family. They had already set up their case.

The family was alarmed by this matter and for several hours they remained in a constant state of disquiet. Obviously, whatever attempt for their rescue meant enormous mortal danger for all. One or two days before the receipt of the last letter from their "friends," Nicholas wrote in his diary, "14 [27] June. Thursday. ... We spent an anxious night and we remained awake [and] dressed. All this happened due to the fact that the other day we received two letters, one after the other, in wh.[ich] we were informed that we should prepare to be abducted by some loyal people! But the days passed, and nothing happened, and the wait and uncertainty were very tormenting."[94]

After this entry in his diary, completely unexpectedly, Nicholas wrote nothing else for seven whole days in a row. After making daily entries into his personal diary with absolute regularity for thirty-seven years, this sudden gap was a mysterious phenomenon.

The event of the sudden gap in Nicholas' diary has puzzled many historians. The reason for this is that this habit of his did not have as its purpose a simple preservation of memories. In fact, he wrote in his diary very perfunctorily, mentioning events in a telegraphic manner with nearly no personal content. Nicholas' main purpose in the systematic keeping of his diary was to train himself to maintain absolute self-discipline. Even Kerensky realized that, to a certain degree, and he wrote: "It is usual to picture the murdered Czar as a man of very limited capacity and intellectual development, the favorite reference in this connection being his peculiarly shallow diary, which has now been published. Particularly famous is the entry made on some very important historical day: 'Had a walk in the park, shot two crows.' But the diary was a tedious habit ingrained since childhood, practically a duty for all the members of the royal family. It was written in merely as a matter of form; the most trivial and ordinary things were entered."[95]

How, then, is this serious change in the emperor's behavior to be explained? Nicholas understood that the end was approaching. Even from the first days of June he had begun to pass over some days in his diary. The awareness of his impending end did not inspire him to continue to write any longer the small details of his daily life. Military discipline no longer had a place in his life, which was now ending, but his mind had fixed on the fact of his departure. As is apparent from evidence of this period, Nicholas had given himself over to a deep, nearly absolute introspection that was nothing other than prayer.

CHAPTER 6

From the time of the very first years of his reign, Nicholas had often mentioned that he had the absolute conviction that God had foreordained him to sacrifice himself for the sins of his people. He always and absolutely gave himself over to the will of God, as is also apparent from his very own words, "God knows what is good for us, we must bow down our heads and repeat the sacred words 'Thy will be done.'"[96]

But what Nicholas apparently did not ever believe was that his family would share the same fate as himself. His children were completely uninvolved in responsibility for anything that his enemies accused him of. He could not at all believe that the malice and injustice of men would reach the point that they would hurt his children. He did not believe that even when the hour had arrived.

Gunshots could already be heard from the fighting a few kilometers outside of Ekaterinburg. The obviously inevitable assault on the city by the White Army and the Czechs at any moment could only force the Bolsheviks to take some definitive action on the fate of their prisoners. The fact of their nearly immediate transport only a few days before pointed to the same thing. Both Nicholas and Alexandra were well-versed in history and knew that similar situations in revolutions of the past settled for nothing less than to deprive monarchs of their very lives.

Confirmation of the premonition that something would happen very soon finally arrived with the third letter that the prisoners received from their "friends" on 27 or 28 June. In this letter, the author suggests a plan of escape that was completely insane, if not outright ridiculous. Among other things, it asked them to make a homemade rope to climb out of the window when they received a signal, but first to barricade the door of their room with furniture from within! Nicholas obviously suspected a trick of the Bolsheviks and understood that the time was near. So, he stopped writing any more in his diary.

The evening of the 3rd of July, Avdeev was summoned with Moshkin to an extraordinary meeting of the regional Soviet. There the members of the Presidium informed them that they were relieved of their duties. The reason given was the systematic thefts practiced by the guard at the Ipatiev House. At the second session that same evening, Yakov Yurovsky was summoned, who was informed of his appointment as new Commandant of the Ipatiev House. His instructions from the presidium were focused on only two points. The first was to strengthen the guard, which had direct contact with the prisoners. The second was to prepare for the "special purpose": murder.

THE CHAPTER OF BLOOD

A FINAL COUNTDOWN

4 July 1918. One more usual morning at the Ipatiev House. Having gathered for common morning prayer, the prisoners awaited the routine morning inspection that followed. However, Avdeev and Moshkin were absent. The prisoners took their breakfast and continued with their usual activities until noon. They were ready to sit down for their meal when Beloborodov entered into the dining room with some men announcing that Avdeev had been relieved of his duties and from that time on Yakov Yurovsky would take his place as new commandant with Gregory Nikulin as his assistant. These two men were present. Nicholas and Alexandra recognized Yurovsky immediately. He was not, after all, a doctor, as they had believed at his first visit.

Yurovsky seemed intelligent and decisive. He did not make idle conversation and was not informal with anyone. He had a faultless gift of speech and this, combined with the propriety of his comportment, gave him the ability to easily crush anyone. His character, however, was hypocritical and disingenuous. Apart from his polite manners, he evoked a sense of intense fear and nursed an enduring hatred for the royal family in his heart.

"Once Yurovsky took over the house," Yakimov relates, "immediately he set up a machine gun post in the attic, put a new guard post in the back yard [and] ended the drunken antics. I never saw him drunk or drinking. But he did change something else, which worsened conditions for the imperial family. He decreased the deliveries from the monastery, or completely stopped them, I can't remember [exactly]."[97]

Novice Antonina says of the event, "On 22 June [4 July] we were bringing various provisions. They received them. I think Avdeev's assistant took them, but [it] was obvious that there was some confusion: take them or not? We left, but soon two Red soldiers with rifles caught up with us, sent from the Ipatiev House, and they took us back. There the new commandant came out—yes, this is he whose picture I see [a picture of Yurovsky was presented to her]—and he questioned us sternly, 'Who authorized you to bring these?' I said, 'We bring them with Commandant Avdeev's permission and at the direction of Dr Derevenko,' Then he said to us, 'Other prisoners in jails, do you go to them?' I reply 'When they ask, we bring them.' Nothing else happened and we left.

"The next day, the 23rd [5th of July] and the 24th of June [6th of July] again we bring provisions. We brought a quart of milk and cream in a bottle. On the 24th [6th] when we brought milk and cream, Yurovsky nagged us again: 'What are these things you bring?' We say, 'Milk.' 'And what is that inside the bottle? More milk?' 'That is cream!' Well, after that, under Yurovsky we only brought milk."[98]

Three days after assuming command, Yurovsky took care to fulfill the first part of his mission. All of Avdeev's old guard was transferred to the

CHAPTER 6

basement of the Ipatiev House and to the house across the street where the remaining part of the guard stayed. On the floor where the captives were kept, he installed new men. And the days passed. The first part of the mission was accomplished. It was now time to set the mechanism in motion to advance the second part of the mission.

9 July 1918. Dr Botkin began to write a letter to his brother. It would be his last, and it would never reach its intended recipient:

> "I am making the last attempt to write a real letter, at least from here, although this caveat is completely redundant; I do not think that it is in the cards for me to ever write from anywhere else again— my voluntary imprisonment here is limited to my existence on this earth. In actuality, I have died—dead to my children, my friends, my work... I have died, but have not been buried yet, or rather was buried alive, whichever you prefer: the consequences are almost identical, i.e., both one and the other have their negative and positive sides. If I were literally dead, that is to say, anatomically dead, then according to my faith I would know what my children are doing, would be closer to them and undoubtedly more useful than now. I rest with the dead only civilly, my children may still have hope that we will see each other sometime in this life, while I, other than thinking that I can still be useful to them somehow, do not personally indulge myself with this hope, do not humor myself with illusions, but look directly into the face of unadorned reality... as Abraham did not hesitate to sacrifice his only son to God on His demand. I strongly believe that the same way God saved Isaac, He will save my children too and be a father to them."[99]

12 July 1918. As the White Army and the Czech Legion approached Ekaterinburg closer by the hour, Ekaterinburg was as if on the crater of a volcano. At 5 o'clock in the afternoon, Goloshchekin called an extraordinary meeting of the Regional Soviet of the Urals. At that time in room 3 of the Amerikanskaya Hotel, now headquarters of the Soviet, the most important members of the Ural Soviet and of the local Cheka met. Goloshchekin had just returned from Moscow, where he hastened to inform the Central Executive Committee of a terribly burning issue: Ekaterinburg was in danger of falling into the hands of the Czechs and the Whites very soon. To avoid attempts to rescue the Tsar, the Soviet of the Urals resolved to expedite his immediate execution. Does Moscow approve this decision?

Less than twenty-four hours earlier, a former miner saw Yurovsky together with the bloodthirsty Commissar Peter Yermakov and one other soldier in the Koptiaki forest. The three men were going around near the abandoned Four Brothers mine. They were searching for a suitable place for their purpose: the disposal of the bodies.

Dr Eugene Botkin.

What was the official position of Moscow? There was never an official mention of this on paper. As was the case in similar circumstances, where a serious decision might negatively affect public opinion on the world stage, as well as the foreign policy of the Bolshevik regime, the same thing happened now. Moscow quietly, but fatally, nodded affirmatively: if in fact it had come to the point at which the security of Ekaterinburg could no longer be assured, then the resolution of the Ural Soviet to execute the tsar was "justified."

The meeting at the Amerikanskaya hotel came to an end. The matter was settled. The only question that remained was how and when. The first question was left to Yurovsky. The second depended on the military situation of Ekaterinburg and the reply could only be given by Reinholds Berzins, the military commander of the northern front of the Urals. So, a telegram

CHAPTER 6

Yakov Yurovsky.

was sent to the front. But the reply was delayed, and as the days passed the members of the Presidium of the Soviet of the Urals burned with agony.

14 July 1918. Sunday. Father John Storozhev narrates: "On 30 June/13 July I found out that the next day, 1/14 July, on Sunday, Fr Meledin had to perform a liturgy at the Ipatiev house, that he already had a warning about this from the commandant, and the commandant at the time was infamously cruel, a certain Yurovsky—former military medic. I assumed that I would replace Fr Meledin at the cathedral and perform the Liturgy for him on 1/14 July."[100]

The guard Anatoly Yakimov, however, makes mention of an extraordinary change in the schedule: "Something confusing happened with the priest. The prayer service under Yurovsky happened just once. This was on Saturday, 13 July, Yurovsky called me to him and instructed me to find a priest. First, he asked me which priests are serving. I named Fr Meledin and Fr Storozhev. Then he asked me to get one of them. Back then Meledin lived the closest (Vodochnaya 168), so on that same Saturday evening I asked him. In the morning... Yurovsky [found out] and sent me to tell Meledin not to come, [to tell him] that Typica was cancelled. And if he asks who cancelled it, 'tell him that it was them, not I. Instead of Meledin, go ask Storozhev,' [he said]. ... So I went to Storozhev and asked him. What this meant, I do not know."[101]

Father John Storozhev continues:

> Around 8 o'clock in the morning on 14 July, a soldier came to see me, and requested I serve Typica at the Ipatiev house. At 10 o'clock, I was already at the Ipatiev house with Deacon Buimirov. Inside, behind the fence, at the bottom of the stairs and inside the house, there were lots of armed young men, standing on guard. When we entered the commandant's room, we saw disorder, dust, and mess. Yurovsky was sitting at the table, drinking tea and eating bread with butter. Another man was sleeping on the bed, fully dressed.
>
> Having entered the room, I said to Yurovsky: "The clergy were summoned, so here we are. What do we need to do?" Yurovsky stared directly at me without a greeting, and said "Wait here, then you will serve Typica" I asked "Liturgy [Obednya] or Typica [Obednitsa]?" "He wrote Typica," said Yurovsky.

THE CHAPTER OF BLOOD

When we had vested and a bucket with coals was brought in [for the censer], Yurovsky invited us into the hall for service. I was the first to enter the hall, then the deacon and Yurovsky. Simultaneously, Nicholas Alexandrovich with two daughters came in through a door that led into inner rooms. Yurovsky asked Nicholas Alexandrovich: "Are all of you gathered?" Nicholas Alexandrovich answered firmly, "Yes—all."

Ahead, behind the arch, already standing were Alexandra Feodorovna with two daughters and Alexei Nikolaevich, who was sitting in a wheelchair, wearing a sailor jacket. He looked pale. Alexandra Feodorovna, wearing a dress, looked livelier than in the past. Olga Nikolaevna, Tatiana Nikolaevna, Maria Nikolaevna, and Anastasia Nikolaevna were wearing black skirts and white blouses. Their hair reached their shoulders in the back.

To me Nicholas Alexandrovich, as well as his daughters, looked exhausted this time.

During the service the family members arranged themselves [this way]: Alexandra Feodorovna's chair stood next to the wheelchair of Alexei Nikolaevich, which was farther away from the arch, hers was a bit behind his. Behind Alexei Nikolaevich stood Tatiana Nikolaevna. Olga Nikolaevna, Maria Nikolaevna, Anastasia Nikolaevna stood near Nicholas Alexandrovich, who took his usual place on the right side of the wall arch. Behind the arch, in the hall stood Dr Botkin, the maid, and three servants. At the far corner window stood Yurovsky.

We performed the service at the table set up in the center of the room behind the arch. This table was covered with a silk cloth of antique Russian design. On the table, in proper order and the usual church symmetry stood numerous icons. …

The deacon and I started the Service of Typica. The order of Typica is usually performed for the army when for some reason or another it is impossible to serve a Liturgy. In essence this prayer service is similar to the service of the Divine Liturgy, but it is significantly shorter, since at Typica the Holy Eucharist is not offered.

According to the order of service for the Typica, it is customary to read "With the Saints give rest" at a certain point. For some reason, instead of reading, the deacon sang this prayer. But as soon as we started singing, I heard that the members of the Romanov family, who were standing behind us, fell to their knees, and here I suddenly felt a deep spiritual comfort afforded by shared prayer.

On an even deeper level one felt this when at the end of the service I read the prayer to the Mother of God, which expresses in highly poetic, touching words the supplication of one greatly afflicted to support him in his sorrows, and to give him strength to bear with dignity the cross sent by God.

After the service all kissed the Holy Cross. When I was leaving and walked very close by the former grand duchesses, I heard barely

CHAPTER 6

audible the words "Thank you."

Silently the deacon and I reached the art school building, and here he said to me, "You know Father Archpriest, something happened to them in there." In these words there was confirmation of my own impression, I stopped and asked him why he thinks so. "Not sure. It is as if they are different somehow. And no one sang." And I must say that for the first time no one in the Romanov family sang with us at the prayer service on 14 July.[102]

15 July 1918. At 7 o'clock in the morning, as always, the sisters from the Novo-Tikhvin Convent arrived. Nun Augustina relates, "On the second of July by the Old Calendar [15 July] Yurovsky ordered our novices to bring half a hundred eggs in a basket and a quart of milk the next day."[103] The eggs, indeed, he wanted packed carefully. For whom did the commandant provide them?

A little later at 10:30 in the morning, four women arrived from the Union of Professional Cleaners to clean the basement of the house. One of them, Evdokia Simeonova, remembers that that day the girls' disposition was very good:

> We went up to the first floor and immediately we saw the emperor, empress and all their children who were in the dining room, sitting around the table as though they were having a meeting. We bowed politely, and they responded with a friendly smile. The grand duchesses got up immediately and all four rushed into their bedroom to help move their beds for us. As I remember it, they were neither in the least scared, nor in the least sorrowful. Their bright eyes gleamed with happiness, their short hair was in disorder, their cheeks were rosy like apples. They were not dressed like princess in a fairy tale, but wore simple black dresses that weren't very short, with lightweight white silk blouses with rather high necklines.
>
> The commandant, Yurovsky, was a weasel. During our time there he stood listening at the open door, and would look in to glare at us when we attempted to speak with the grand duchesses. As a result we spoke in low voices after that. At the very moment when Yurovsky turned his back to us the smallest grand duchess, Anastasia, turned to the doorway and made such a grimace at him that we all almost died of laughter, then she put out her tongue and thumbed her nose at his back. I myself burst into laughter, but stopped myself right away.
>
> All the girls treated us simply, were friendly and welcoming. Each of their smiles and looks were a gift for us. They told us in low voices, poor dears, that they were not only moving the beds, but after were going to help us wash the floor. 'We regret not having any physical work and our father suffers the most from it. We would have done the hardest work with the greatest pleasure; washing of the dishes

is not enough for us. ... At Tobolsk we liked to saw wood and put it in piles, and here we are not allowed it.'

...I said very quietly to the oldest Grand Duchess: May God cause you to no longer suffer under the yoke of these monsters! At that time we could hear Yurovsky in the dining room asking, his voice hard, about the health of the heir and giving medical advice. My words gave them great joy. Their eyes glittered and they said to me very quietly, gently, 'Thank you my dear for your kind words. We are also hopeful.'

[Later] the beds needed to be put back in place. The duchesses quickly came running happy to help us. I don't remember which one of them said to one of her sisters jokingly, 'You! Urchin, move the cots faster!' Their eyes brimmed with joy.

Poor Alexei stayed in bed all day long. His father moved him from room to room. When I saw the poor sick child, it made me sigh: His face was the color of wax, it was transparent, and his eyes were like those of the prey being stalked by wolves. He smiled at me pleasantly when I bowed profoundly to him. His sisters were spirited and breathed love of life, but he—he seemed to be no longer of this world.

I could see clearly that they were not gods, but were actually ordinary people like us, simple mortals but layered with an immense sorrow. And I love them deeply, which I will do until my last breath.[104]

16 July 1918. Afternoon. After four agonizing days for the Bolsheviks in Ekaterinburg, the awaited reply came from the front. The forecast of Commandant Berzins was timely: the fall of Ekaterinburg could come within the next three days. Inside Room 3 of the Amerikanskaya Hotel silence spread. In a few moments the decision was taken for the great "when"—that very evening.

A little after the meeting, at 7 o'clock in the evening, Goloshchekin sent a telegram to Saint Petersburg, because the lines to Moscow were not working regularly that day, in which he wrote:

> To Moscow, Kremlin, to Sverdlov, copy to Lenin.
> The following has been transmitted over the direct line from Yekaterinburg: ["]Let Moscow know that for military reasons the trial agreed upon with Filipp [Goloshchekin] cannot be put off; we cannot wait. If your opinions differ, then immediately notify without delay.
> Goloshchekin, Safarov.["][105]

Moscow's reply: Silence...

Leonid Sednev.

The last day of the life of the royal family began as all the previous ones of their imprisonment. At 7 o'clock in the morning the sisters came from Novo-Tikhvin and brought the fifty eggs and the milk that Yurovsky required. Then the morning walk followed. Alexandra as usual did not emerge but remained inside with Olga. Yakimov remembers, "The last time I saw the tsar and his daughters was 16 July. They were taking a walk in the garden at four o'clock in the afternoon. I cannot remember if I saw the heir at this time. I did not see the tsaritsa, she did not go out then."[106] In the afternoon Tatiana remained inside with Alexandra. One hour earlier, at 3 in the afternoon, an automobile arrived at the Ipatiev House and drove Yurovsky to the Amerikanskaya Hotel. An extraordinary final meeting took place there.

At 7:00 PM, Yurovsky returned and at 8:00 PM he entered the dining room as the prisoners were taking their supper. He informed them that little Leonid Sednev should get his things ready immediately for departure. His uncle Ivan Sednev wanted to take him home. No one knew that Ivan Sednev had already been dead for six weeks. Despite the assurances of Yurovsky that the child was in no danger, the family was greatly worried. Alexandra wrote in her diary that evening, "Suddenly Lyonka Sednyov was fetched to go and see his Uncle and flew off—wonder whether it's true and we shall see the boy back again!"[107] This time, however, Yurovsky spoke the truth. The child did not suffer any harm in the end.

From the deposition of Yakimov: "On 15 July, Monday, at our barracks at the Popov house a boy who lived with the imperial family appeared, he used to take the heir around in his wheelchair. It caught my attention then, the other guards also noticed it. Nevertheless, no one knew what it meant, why the boy was brought here. But it was undoubtedly done on Yurovksy's orders."[108]

As night fell, the gunshots from the battles of the Bolsheviks with the Whites were heard more menacingly. The Czechs with the White Army were now only thirty kilometers away from Ekaterinburg. However, inside the Ipatiev House, the prisoners passed a usual quiet evening. Before lying down to sleep Alexandra wrote in her diary for the last time, "10:30, to bed."[109] Around 11 PM all the rooms of the prisoners at the Ipatiev House yielded to the dark of night. The prisoners had put out the lights... for the last time.

THE CHAPTER OF BLOOD

THE AGONIZING WAIT

During those final nights in Ekaterinburg "the very air around the sunken house became heavy with a sense of impending tragedy," reported the British Vice Consul Arthur Thomas, who was in the city. "According to all the neighbours this feeling reached its climax on the night of July 16, 1918, the night of the murder. Although all traffic on the streets was not stopped till midnight, the obvious nervousness of the sentries and the fact that machine-guns were being placed all around the villa as well as on the roof and on the balcony drove most people indoors, where they cowered till daybreak."[110] After midnight, the only thing heard was the gunshots of the Czechs and the Whites who approached menacingly.

Earlier the same evening, Yurovsky made the necessary preparations for the murder. However, there was one important detail, if it could be called a detail. Neither Yurovsky nor any one of his comrades had any experience with mass murders. That would turn out fatally terrifying for their victims. Yurovsky chose a room on the ground floor as the most suitable for his purpose, directly underneath the girls' room. For the planned murder, however, that room was small, a fact that made the dimensions of the tragedy yet more terrible.

A little after 8:00 that evening, Yurovsky summoned the man in charge of the guard, Paul Medvedev. From Medvedev's deposition: "I took up duty the night of 16 July, and around 8 o'clock the same evening, Commandant Yurovsky ordered me to confiscate all the Nagant revolvers in the detachment and to bring them to him. I took … a total of twelve revolvers, and brought them to the commandant's office. Then Yurovsky said to me: 'Today we'll have to shoot everybody. Warn the detachment so they won't worry if they hear shots.'"[111] For the impending murder it would be necessary to inform them only a few minutes before the event. Some of the revolvers that were collected for this purpose used gunpowder to fire, causing an ejection of smoke and caustic fumes—a third element which would contribute to the intensity of the tragedy.

The Regional Soviet of the Urals chose yet one more man to participate in the murder along with Yurovsky and his men, the bloodthirsty Peter Yermakov. When Beloborodov summoned Yermakov earlier that evening to the Amerikanskaya Hotel he told him characteristically: "You are a lucky man. You have been chosen to execute them and to bury them in such a manner that no one will find their bodies. This is your personal responsibility, which we entrust to you as an old revolutionary."[112] Yurovsky chose the remaining men for the mission, forming a squad of eleven men, one for each victim. On each of them he laid the murder of a specific victim, so that "everything was to be orderly,"[113] according to his words. But they encountered an unexpected difficulty, as he himself reported: "When I allotted their roles, the Letts said that I spare them from the responsibility of shooting the girls, because they would not be able to do that. Then I decided it would be for the best to completely free these comrades from the shooting, as people who are not capable of performing their revolutionary duty at the most decisive moment."[114]

After the selection, Yurovsky withdrew to his office with some members of the Regional Soviet and the Cheka of Ekaterinburg. Goloshchekin was present. All being seated in nearly absolute silence, they chain smoked nervously, constantly glancing at their watches. Only one snag remained. Exactly at midnight the "chimneysweep," Serge Lyukhanov, the authorized driver of the Ipatiev House, was supposed to arrive, driving a truck. The truck that was to convey the bodies of the victims to the woods.

Lyukhanov, however, was nowhere to be seen. The tension at the Ipatiev House stretched the nerves of the comrades even more, as Yurovsky wrote: "The fact that we waited longer than expected couldn't help but create anxiety, in addition to the anxiety of waiting in general, but the main thing was that the [summer] nights were so short."[115] "Having completed all the necessary preparations, we waited for the 'chimneysweep' to appear. However, neither at 12:00, nor at 1:00 AM did the 'chimneysweep' appear, and the time was passing. ... I thought that he would not come that night [after all]."[116]

The penetrating ringing of the telephone shattered the agonizing quiet. It was Lyukhanov. Certain delays came up, he said, but he would depart immediately. A few minutes before 1:30 AM, the men were surprised when the telephone rang again. And again, it was Lyukhanov. He was leaving for the house. That was it. Yurovsky got up quickly and proceeded to the parlor that Dr Botkin used as a bedroom.[117]

ETERNAL PRESENT CONTINUOUS

Yurovsky stands outside the double door of the salon. The time is 1:30 AM. He knocks on the door. Doctor Botkin, surprised, awakens and comes out. He asks what is the matter.

"The situation in the city is bad. There are disturbances and unrest. The family's stay here on the first floor is insecure. They must all come downstairs. I must transfer them to a safer location. Wake the rest and tell them to get ready. They do not need to take anything with them for now."[118]

Botkin goes inside to awaken the rest and Yurovsky returns to his office. A few minutes later, Lyukhanov's truck is heard approaching. It is the only vehicle that moves outside at this hour. Passing into the open entrance of the fence, the truck enters the yard of the house. Yurovsky gives final instructions to his men for their assignment. The hour approaches 2:00 AM and Medvedev makes a round to inform the guards of the events that would follow.

THE CHAPTER OF BLOOD

A little after 2:00 AM, the prisoners are ready and leaving their rooms. None of them seems uneasy. None of them speaks. Nicholas emerges first, carrying Alexis on his chest. Both are wearing military tunics and peaked caps on their heads. Alexandra follows, holding Olga by the arm; then the girls, Tatiana, Maria, and Anastasia holding her little dog. They are all wearing long dresses and blouses without jackets or hats. With them they are holding cushions, purses, and other small items. Anna Demidova follows the girls, also holding a cushion or two. Finally, Dr Botkin, Alexei Trupp, and Ivan Kharitonov emerge.

Yurovsky leads the prisoners toward the stairs on the other end of the floor. From there they descend to the ground floor, emerge into the yard and walk three or four meters, and Yurovsky opens the double doors making a sign to the prisoners to pass on again into the house. Then they descend a few steps and pass into a hallway leading back again to the other end of the house where "that" room was located, under the girls' bedroom. Adjoining, the men of the assassination squad are inside a second room.

At the south end of the corridor, Yurovsky opens another double door. This is now the last door that will open to the family in this life, it is the door to "that" room. He makes a motion for them to pass on in. There, in the depth of the room is one more double door, locked. The room, strangely enough, is completely empty and Alexandra asks if it is permitted to sit while they wait. Yurovsky asks one of the men to bring two chairs. Nikulin, emerging from the room to bring the chairs, whispers wryly to Strekotin who is there outside, "The heir needs a chair. Apparently, he wants to die in a chair. Well, let's bring them, please."[119]

As soon as the chairs are brought, the girls place the cushions they are carrying on them. In one chair, next to the arched window, Alexandra sits. In the second, at the center of the room, Nicholas affectionately places Alexis and stands directly in front of him, as if he wishes to hide him. Behind Alexis stands Dr Botkin. The girls stand behind their mother. Next to them in front of the locked door stands Demidova holding her cushions. Trupp and Kharitonov lean on the north wall of the room. The only light in the room comes from an electric lamp that hangs from the center of the ceiling. The light in the room is so dim that the women who passed into the far side of the room seem like shadows. Only the cushions that Demidova is holding are clearly discernable.

When all the prisoners are inside, Yurovsky realizes that the room is too small for his "special purpose." But there is now no margin for changes. However, it is necessary to space out the victims, so that the murderers would be able to do their deed. With a calm and low voice, he begins to indicate to each one the proper place to take: "You, please, stand here, and you, here; like that, in a row."[120] It seems that at that hour Yurovsky remembers the time when he worked as a photographer and uses this knowledge for his purpose.[121] Once the scene is set, he leaves the room, closing the double door behind him.

CHAPTER 6

Going into the adjoining room where the men waited, Yurovsky sends Yermakov to command Lyukhanov to step hard on the gas in order to cover the noise that a few moments hence would horrify history. Yermakov returns, and all the men follow Yurovsky out into the hallway, right in front of the closed doors of "that" room. The truck's engine shatters the absolute silence. With a quick motion, Yurovsky opens the doors of the room and enters the room suddenly. Behind him follow the rest of the men, who crowd in front of the surprised prisoners. Some of these men, such as Yermakov, are new faces, unknown to the prisoners. They look at them with bewilderment as they take their places, one next to the other, forming two lines.

Yurovsky commands all the prisoners to stand upright. Alexandra arises, but Alexis remains seated. Yurovsky takes out a sheet of paper from his pocket. This is the most important moment in his life, his very own hour in history. Unfolding the paper that he is holding, he begins to read loudly:

"In light of the fact that your relatives in Europe continue their assault against Soviet Russia and your close collaborators, both within and outside the country, attempt to liberate you, the Presidium of the Regional Soviet of the Urals has resolved to condemn you to death by firing squad."[122]

Before Yurovsky is even finished, Nicholas turns toward the back and looks with terror at his family. He turns again forward. With a face as white as a sheet, he interrupts Yurovsky, "Lord, my God! What?! What?!" Behind him are now heard voices, "O my God! No!" Dr Botkin, with a choking voice asks, "So you are not transporting us anywhere?"[123] Nicholas, who seems nearly unable to comprehend what he just heard, continues to ask, "What?" Yurovsky reads the document quickly for the second time and, having given command to the men to get ready, shouts loudly, "Fire!"

Alexandra and Olga raise their hands to make the sign of the Cross. The same second, contrary to their orders, all the men fire ceaselessly at Nicholas. They all wish the great honor of the murder of the Tsar. Just as his chest erupts and his blood spurts out, his body remains for a moment upright as it is shaken and then collapses downward, dead.

The weapons of the murderers immediately turn clumsily in all directions. The bullets hit Alexandra mortally. Just as the first gunshots kill his parents Alexis remains seated in his chair petrified. Across from him stands Nikulin, who was assigned to execute him. With shaking hands, he shoots him repeatedly until he empties his revolver. The child sags somewhat and remains motionless in his chair. The bullets continue to fall as rain in all directions and mortally wound Kharitonov and Trupp, who falls on his knees and sags down dead.

The girls gather back into the right corner of the room screaming with fright for help. But there is none. Maria breaks away from the rest and hurls herself with force on the locked doors in the back part of the room. She pounds them with all her strength, pulling and pulling on the knobs as she cries for help. Seeing her, Yermakov begins to fire in her direction. Maria falls to the floor, dead.

THE CHAPTER OF BLOOD

Only a few minutes have passed when the room fills with smoke and caustic fumes. There is absolutely no visibility. Chaos now reigns, and all shoot blindly in the dark room. Only women's screams of terror are heard, loud cries, moans of the dying. Yurovsky, with a loud voice commands, "Cease fire!"

The murderers go out and open the double doors. Their eyes burn from the smoke, the dust from the plaster walls, and the toxic fumes of the gunpowder, they cough, some feel nauseous. But their work is not yet done. Inside the room, voices and cries are still heard. The tragedy now reaches its tensest moment.

When the men return to the room, the smoke has dispersed somewhat. But the sight is terrible. Absolute terror. The terrified victims are crawling and wallowing on the floor in puddles of blood. Yurovsky sees Dr Botkin soaked in blood trying to get up from the floor, supporting himself on his right elbow. He approaches him and shoots him point blank in the left side of his skull.

Olga and Tatiana and Anastasia are also still alive. They are undergoing the most frightful suffering that the human mind can grasp. The men again begin to shoot at them. But while they hit the girls in the chest, the bullets ricochet in all directions. The murderers stand stunned before this inexplicable phenomenon. Yermakov, who approaches them like a demonized beast, tries to solve the problem. The girls, having their backs pressed to the wall sit on the floor squatting and weeping attempting to cover their heads with their hands.

Yermakov begins to stab them in the chest with his bayonet. Drunken and carried away as he is from blood lust, he hits the girls without being able to kill them, but only wounding them randomly. Being unable to stab them with his bayonet, he begins to club them in the face with the butt of his rifle. The terrified voices and cries of the girls continue dramatically. While Anastasia is lying on the floor, Yermakov stands over her and stamping her two hands with his feet he tries to kill her. Seeing the inability of Yermakov to finish his satanic work, Yurovsky approaches with cold calm and successively pumps a gunshot into the heads of each of the three girls. The bullets pass through their skulls and the girls fall down lifelessly.

Suddenly the voice of Demidova is heard. The pillows she was holding had saved her life from the bullets and she had simply fainted. As soon as she regains her senses, she cries out: "Thanks be to God! God has saved me!"[124] She attempts to rise when one of the murderers' bayonet descends on her. In a last hopeless attempt, Anna tries to defend herself grabbing the bayonet with her bare hands. Finally, they shatter her head with their riffles' butts.

From Demidova's cries, Alexis, who is still alive and sagged into his chair, revives! He begins to moan painfully. Yurovsky approaches him and shoots him point-blank three times. The child slides slowly from his chair and his lifeless body falls next to the feet of his father. And so, the scene of the slaughter is now finished.

On the left page:
Above: The Ipatiev House
fenced by high wooden palings.
Below: On the far left, the door through which
the family with their retainers came out of the
house. On the right, the double door
through which they re-entered.

Picture on the left:
The staircase which lead to the murder room.
Below: The Ipatiev House, where the window
of the murder room is visible, its greater part
being below the level of the ground.

On the next pages: The room of the murder.

CHAPTER 6

As the dust and smoke begins to disperse completely, the murderers could now admire their great feat: bodies mangled, and punctured by countless bullets, shredded with knife wounds, and disemboweled. Faces with expressions of extreme agony, eyes wide open with the terror of the final chapter of this tragedy. On the floor, masses of warm, clotted blood, brains, and bodily fluids: The majesty of revolutionary justice that has triumphed tonight.

This task, which, had the executioners been professionals, would normally not have taken more than a mere thirty seconds, lasted more than fifteen minutes at the Ipatiev House, transforming the suffering of the innocent victims into a hideous tragedy.

Finally, Yurovsky tested the pulse of all the victims, and once he had ascertained that they were all dead, he commanded the men to begin moving the corpses to the truck. But no one had considered the matter of their transportation ahead of time. They began by wrapping the corpses in blankets and tried to move them in this manner. Once they moved some of the victims, the blankets had become completely soaked in blood and slipped out of their hands. Then they made improvised stretchers to continue their macabre work.

As they were moving the victims, some of the soldiers began to steal various articles that were on the corpses: diamond brooches, pearl necklaces, gold watches and whatever was in the pockets or purses of the victims. When Yurovsky threatened to execute on the spot those that did not immediately return the loot, one by one they began to give up the spoils.

The truck was already prepared with its horrible cargo. When they counted the corpses once more, they covered them with a khaki sheet. Normally at this point, Yurovsky's mission would be finished. Goloshchekin, knowing that Yurovsky was sick, had told him that it was not necessary to go to the forest to deposit the corpses. This mission would be undertaken by Yermakov. However, Yermakov was completely beside himself. As Yurovsky wrote, "I was worried that he [Yermakov] would not be able to accomplish this work in the necessary manner, so I decided to go myself."[125] Yurovsky sat in front with Yermakov and the driver Sergei Lyukhanov. Three other men of the guard came, riding in the back with the bodies. Lyukhanov put the truck in gear and went out from the Ipatiev House taking the road for the Koptyaki forest. The time was exactly 3:00 AM.

Among the few personal effects of the family that remained behind scattered at the Ipatiev House, the prison of their martyrdom, there was a notebook of Olga's. On one of its pages, written in the hand of the young girl, was the following prayer:

Grant us Thy patience, Lord,
In these our woeful days,

The mob's wrath to endure,
The torturer's ire;

Thy unction to forgive
Our neighbors' persecution,
And mild, like Thee, to bear
A bloodstained Cross.

And when the mob prevails,
And foes come to despoil us,
To suffer humbly shame,
O Saviour, aid us!

Master of the world, universal God,
Bless us in prayer
And grant rest to our humble soul
In this unbearable, dreadful hour.

And when the hour comes
To pass the last dread gate,
Breathe strength in us to pray,
"Father, forgive them."[126]

MARTYRDOM AFTER DEATH

The truck took two hours to cover the distance of 15 kilometers to the Koptyaki forest. To the unbelievably unpleasant surprise of Yurovsky, Yermakov had brought only one shovel with him. There was nothing else with which to bury eleven bodies. Entering the wood, the truck encountered twenty-five men, workers, and local Bolsheviks. It was Yermakov's cavalry troop that came with their carts to undertake the task. All of them drunk, they believed that they would pass an entertaining evening with the girls of the family. Yermakov, in order to whet their appetite for the work had promised them that he would bring the victims alive, so that his men might revel first by violating them before proceeding with their murder. But when they understood that they were dead they began to make trouble.

At last Yurovsky imposed order and commanded Yermakov's men to load some of the bodies in the carts that they had brought with them. Continuing their way into the forest, after nearly two kilometers the truck got stuck in the mud from the recent rain. Yurovsky gave command to unload the bodies so that they might free the truck. When they had thrown the victims on the muddy ground, they attempted to push the truck, but

CHAPTER 6

without success. Now, worse yet, the engine had dangerously overheated. In that area there was a railway line and Lyukhanov was compelled to go to the nearest guard station to ask for water from the guard. He returned with water and boards, which they laid under the wheels of the truck, so that they were able to free it by pushing hard. When they had tossed the bodies into the truck again, they once more continued their macabre journey.

But what ensued was even worse. A little further down, the truck was wedged between two trees and it was now impossible to proceed. Yurovsky told the men to unload the bodies again and to put them in their carts and he sent two men ahead with horses to find the Four Brothers, the mine where they would bury the bodies. At last they came back without success, and when the bodies were transferred to the carts they set forth once again to look for the mine.

When at last they found the Four Brothers, the sun had already risen. But a new surprise awaited Yurovsky, when they met some peasants from the village Koptyaki, who had camped in the woods since the evening to cut hay along the length of the road toward the village. The absolute secrecy that the mission required had already been lost. Yurovsky fiercely threatened the villagers and evicted them from the area, hoping that he would be able to continue his task undisturbed. Then he sent Yermakov's men to the village to tell the villagers that the Czechs had come very near, and for this reason they must not go into the woods at all.

Remaining behind with his own men, Yurovsky shared the fifty eggs and milk that he had requested the nuns to bring him the previous day. Thus, the murderers of the family shared the last meal from the convent sitting by their bodies, under the Siberian morning sun. Yurovsky did not drive off Yermakov's men merely for security from passers-by. He had begun to suspect that the fabulous jewels of the family would be hidden on them.

When the men had eaten quickly, they unloaded the bodies and began to strip off their clothes completely. From the girls' tattered camisoles, diamonds, emeralds and other precious stones began to pop through. These were the mysterious shields that did not permit the hysterical stabbings of Yermakov to pass easily into the bodies of the girls. The men, astonished at the sight of this unbelievable treasure, tore up the clothes of the victims with madness, pulling and jerking their bodies savagely with their muddy hands, in order to uncover more jewels. Alexandra also wore a belt with hidden pearls.

The men's temptation to seize some of these precious finds was great. But Yurovsky's pervasive eyes observed all these things closely. He carefully gathered and catalogued all the jewels as the men continued their work. It was impossible, however, that they would not have dropped some of those things onto the wet ground. Later the villagers and those who investigated the crime found a few of them scattered on the ground.

The girls were no longer beautiful: "There was no beauty to see in the dead,"[127] one of the men of the mission later said. These deformed bodies with their dislocated extremities, the clotted blood in the hair, the punctured heads did not remind anyone of those charming and lively children who just that last evening smiled with innocence at their murderers as they were being led to their slaughter. Finally, they threw the bodies one after another into the abandoned mineshaft, which was full of water.

As soon as they had thrown all the bodies into the hole, Yurovsky shuddered to realize that his adventures with the Romanovs had just begun. The water inside the mineshaft was not enough to hide the bodies of the victims because the water had frozen at the bottom of the mineshaft. In desperation, Yurovsky first poured sulfuric acid on the bodies, which burned the flesh that was on the surface, and then he threw a few hand grenades into the mineshaft, hoping that they would make the walls collapse and so cover the bodies. But the walls turned out to be quite strong. The only thing the explosions succeeded in doing was to dismember some of the bodies' extremities. The investigators of the crime would later find some of these bone fragments.

They threw earth and branches on the mouth of the mineshaft, to temporarily hide its terrible contents. No alternative solution to the problem had been thought of. Now Yurovsky had to act quickly. The traces of the wheels of the cart, the horses and of the men, as well as the curiosity of the villagers who saw their strange visitors in the woods would soon reveal what none should ever learn. They now needed tools and ropes to remove the bodies from the mineshaft and to bury them at some other point in the wood. Leaving three men who would guard the region, at 9:30 AM, Yurovsky departed on foot for Ekaterinburg.

Faithful to their duty, the novice nuns of the New Tikhvin Convent, Antonina and Maria, arrived that morning at the Ipatiev House with the milk for the family. Sister Maria narrates:

"We brought our provisions on 4 [17] July, we passed through the fence; there stands a truck. The guard and someone else were somewhat confused. They rang; no one comes out of the house. That had never happened before. Before, as soon as we came, they would ring, [and] Yurovsky would come out and take them. Now they ring, and ring, [but] nobody comes. We ask: 'Where is Yurovsky?' They say somewhat confusedly, 'Having breakfast.' We waited a bit and went to the side door. There on the other side of the door stands the guard. He looks at us and says, a bit confused, 'They don't need milk any more. They are sick. But wait.' And now he ran off. I could hear as he asks someone in the yard, 'What should I tell them?' Then he comes out and agitated he shrugs and says, 'You know what? Don't bring any more. Leave!' Nothing was taken from us, and we left."[128]

Sister Antonina continues: "We leave, and we see some printed notices pasted up in various places. We began to read and we see: The emperor had been shot and his family was taken away. We ran to Dr Derevenko, we told him, 'They did not take the milk. There seems to be no one at the house, and in the notices it says that the tsar is shot and his family taken away.' The doctor knew nothing, he was stunned and his face changed."[129]

At the offices of the Regional Soviet of the Urals, in Room 3 of the Amerikanskaya Hotel, the members of the Presidium had already gathered to compose their first official communication to the capital regarding the successful fulfillment of their historical obligation to the Revolution. The telegram that was sent to Moscow reported the following:

"Received on 17 July 1918 at 2 o'clock.

"To chairman of the Sovnarkom [Council of People's Representatives], comrade Lenin, and chairman [of the Supreme Executive Committee] Sverdlov.

"From Yekaterinburg.

"In view of the enemy's proximity to Yekaterinburg and the exposure by the Extraordinary Commission [Cheka] of a serious White Guard plot with the goal of abducting the former tsar and his family. The documents are in our hands. Nicholas Romanov was shot on the night of the sixteenth of July by decree of the Presidium of the [Ural] Regional Soviet. His family has been evacuated to a safe place."[130]

Later, in the evening at 9 o'clock, a second, unofficial, telegram from Beloborodov to the secretary's office in Moscow declared, "Inform Sverdlov that the entire family suffered the same fate as its head. Officially [however] the family will die during evacuation [of the city]. Beloborodov."[131] So began an official process of disinformation and lies that lasted for decades.

When Yurovsky reached the town, it was already noon. The news of the failure of the second part of his mission had already reached the Regional Soviet, and Yurovsky was summoned to give account of the events. At the extraordinary meeting of the Soviet, Yermakov received a severe rebuke for his insubordination. Now it was immediately necessary for Yurovsky to assure a favorable settlement of the matter. The decision was to completely disfigure the bodies with sulfuric acid and to burn them before taking them to another place. They hoped that in this manner even if the White Army found the bodies, they would not be able to recognize them. But nobody knew that the burning of a body outdoors was not a simple matter.

From one member of the local Soviet Yurovsky learned of a copper mine about five kilometers from the Four Brothers, which would be suitable for the disposal of the bodies. Along with another comrade, Yurovsky hastened on horseback to examine the suggested location. On the way to the wood, their horses had an accident and threw their riders. Both hurt, they needed an hour before they were able to ride their horses again and continue their way. When they returned to Ekaterinburg it was 7 o'clock in the evening. As soon as Yurovsky ordered new trucks, carts, barrels of sulfuric acid and firewood to the Four Brothers mine, he took a horse with a cart—he could not find an automobile—and thirty minutes after midnight he set forth for the Koptyaki forest. Around 4 o'clock in the morning, he was back in

THE CHAPTER OF BLOOD

the wood. Yurovsky had already spent another twenty-four hours without sleep since the beginning of the tragedy at the Ipatiev House.

The drama of the family and of their faithful servants again turned a new chapter. The men began to drag the bodies from the bottom of the flooded mineshaft. Goloshchekin was also present, along with other cadres of the Cheka, to assure that the work would be done right this time. One of the men was obliged to descend into the freezing water of the mineshaft to tie ropes around the bodies, so that they would be able to draw them out. The meager light of torches was not enough to illumine the thick darkness of the Siberian forest, and that comrade was not able in his blindness to grasp any body's extremity to tie up. One more comrade went in and was able to make a beginning. The first body that they managed to secure was the tsar's. One by one, in sequence all the victims were drawn from the deep and laid on a waterproof cover on the ground.

The water of the mineshaft had washed the the blood from the victims' faces, and some of them were once again recognizable. Naked, laid out on the ground, the bodies of the martyred family once more saw the morning sun rise on the transient reality of earthly things. Being yet more disfigured by the abuse of these last two days, these bodies, already holy and martyric relics, once again indicted the inhuman malice and injustice of men, having now entered the bounds of divine justice.

But the day had progressed, and Yurovsky feared that perhaps there was not enough time to transport the bodies to a new mine. He attempted to dig there to dispose of the bodies, but the ground was rocky and hard. As the men dug, a noise was heard from nearby. When after the shouts of Yurovsky startled a villager, Yermakov hastened shouting that that man was a friend and acquaintance of his. Yurovsky's patience had reached its limits. Once more he had to return to the city to put the matter to the Cheka. He commanded the bodies to be camouflaged with branches and leaving his men yet again to stand guard over the area, he set forth for Ekaterinburg.

The decision was to continue the plan of removal to a new mine. They would load the bodies on carts and would drive them to the point where the truck was stuck the first night, where Lyukhanov, after getting the truck free from the two trees, awaited new instructions. From there, the bodies would continue to the new mine with Lyukhanov. Returning to the forest, the truck that Yurovsky drove broke down and stopped in the road. Judging that it was absolutely necessary to have a second vehicle for the mission, he was obliged to return to the city on foot, still limping from his sprain. There he was able to secure an automobile to return to the forest and to order the delivery of a truck to transport the men.

At that same hour in Moscow, a meeting of the Central Executive Committee was taking place, presided over by Lenin, to consider some new proposal. At some point Sverdlov entered the hall and sat behind Lenin whispering something in his ear. "Comrade Sverdlov wants to make a statement," Lenin said to the council. Sverdlov read the message of 17 July from the Ural Soviet, which notified of the execution of the former tsar. The councillors raised their hands approving the decision and action of the Ural Soviet. With absolutely no comment Lenin continued, saying, "Let us now go on to read the draft clause by clause."[132]

It is evening once more, 10:00 PM; Yurovsky returns to his victims, beside whom he has lived the last three days without any sleep. The men dragged the bodies through the muddy ground of the clearing and loaded them once more onto carts. The dismal procession set forth once more through the narrow lanes of the forest. Shortly before dawn the bodies were once more in Lyukhanov's truck and on their way to their final destination. How final, however would that be at last? Arriving in a clearing that was called Pig's Meadow, Lyukhanov's truck once again got stuck in the muddy ground. The same thing also happened to the truck that followed, transporting the men. These implacable, merciless, and cold-blooded murderers seemed to be fighting with God Himself.

For Yurovsky the case was closed. He decided that the bodies must be buried by any means possible that very moment, at that very place. There was no more time to waste. The Czechs and the Whites were already very near and at any moment it was likely that they would appear before them. The mission must be accomplished for good before the sun rises. To avoid the likely recognition of the victims by their number, in case the Whites discover them, Yurovsky decided to separate two of the smaller bodies of Alexis and Maria, and to burn them at a distance of 16 yards [15 meters] from the common grave. So, if the Whites find the grave with the nine bodies, they would not be certain of their identity.

In a short time, the grave, if it could be called such, was ready. It was square with dimensions two and a half by two and a half meters. They threw the bodies of their victims in and poured abundant quantities of sulfuric acid over them, which would consume their flesh and disfigure their faces. In the end they threw lime over them and closed the pit with dirt. To erase every trace of the location of the grave they covered it with boards and ran the truck over it many times. Again, they threw dirt and brushwood over it to erase completely any hint of the location of the grave.

At the location of second burial, the bodies of Alexis and Maria sizzled within the fire, smoldering without burning. The ingenious murderers did not know that it can take many hours to burn bodies in the open air. Understanding that their attempt had failed, the heroes of the Revolution proceeded to more drastic measures. With shovels and pickaxes they chopped up the bodies of the two children and threw the pieces into a small pit that they had dug. They scattered the ashes from the fire in all directions to erase all their traces from that location.

Around 6 o'clock in the morning of 19 July, the martyrdom of the family of the Romanov Royal Martyrs and of their faithful servants had come to an end. Yermakov, extremely proud of their historic feat, in order to dramatize the historicity of the moment, took a little ash with his shovel and threw it flamboyantly into the air. He said later, "The wind caught them like dust and carried them out across the woods and fields."[133] Without realizing it, this action of his was truly symbolic, but also prophetic, because according to the church hymn, "Their sound of their deeds hath gone forth into all the earth."

The story of the Romanovs did not come to a close at that moment, as their bloodthirsty and inhuman murderers would have liked to believe. Their lives were extinguished from the earth, but the glory with which God has crowned them would soon enfold not only the historical reality, but also timeless eternity. At that moment the Romanov Royal Martyrs passed from earthly tragedy to heavenly glory.

A few months earlier, when the family was still in Tobolsk, Olga wrote the following letter on behalf of Nicholas, which essentially constitutes his last will and testament:

> Father asks to have it passed on to all who have remained loyal to him and to those on whom they might have influence, that they not avenge him; he has forgiven and prays for everyone; and not to avenge themselves, but to remember that the evil which is now in the world will become yet more powerful, and that it is not evil that conquers evil, but only love.[134]

THE HOUR OF REVELATION

The Red capital of the Urals, Ekaterinburg, fell on the night of 25 July. Officers of the White Army arrived nearly immediately at the Ipatiev House to examine it. Scenes of desolation were everywhere. Burnt and scattered remnants of the personal effects of the family were strewn on the floors of the upper storey. Icons, photographs, books, notes.

Then, one room in the basement. It was clear that something gruesome had taken place here. Despite the care with which the Red guards attempted to carefully clean the place, it was impossible to achieve this. Traces of blood splatters were discernable everywhere. The walls and the floor were riddled with bullet holes and bayonet scars. A special inquest was immediately begun to investigate the matter.

Pierre Gilliard arrived at the Ipatiev House with Sydney Gibbes only a few days after the fall of Ekaterinburg. The White forces had already forbidden entrance to the house because of the investigations that were already being conducted at the site. However, entrance was permitted to the two tutors.

Gilliard describes this experience of his, "I went through the first-floor rooms, which had served as the prison; they were in an indescribable state of disorder. It was evident that every effort had been made to get rid of any traces of the recent occupants. Heaps of ashes had been raked out of the stoves. Among them were a quantity of small articles, half burnt, such as tooth-brushes, hairpins, buttons, etc. ... If it was true that the prisoners had been sent away, they must have been removed just as they were, without any of the most essential articles of toilet. ...

"I went down to the bottom floor, the greater part of which was below the level of the ground. It was with intense emotion that I entered the room in which perhaps—I was still in doubt—they had met their death. Its appearance was sinister beyond expression. The only light filtered through a barred window at the height of a man's head. The walls and floor showed numerous traces of bullets and bayonet scars. The first glance showed that an odious crime had been perpetrated there and that several people had been done to death. But who? How?

"I became convinced that the Czar had perished and, granting that, I could not believe that the Czarina had survived him. ... But the children? They too massacred? I could not believe it. My whole being revolted at the idea."[135]

That same day little Kolya Derevenko, Alexis' closest friend, also went into the Ipatiev House with his father, Alexis' physician, Dr Derevenko. Years later, already an old man, he described the scene:

"I was a little boy, just twelve years old. I didn't know anything about evil in people. We lived in the Popov house, very close the Ipatiev house. In the middle of summer 1918, I was afraid and I was worried for Alexis. I wanted to see him. And, I am sure, he wanted to see me. Until that sad 17th of July, 1918... In that last week of July 1918, I, my father, Gilliard, Gibbes, and others entered the Ipatiev house. Terrible scene. The house was in complete chaos. Diaries, letters, albums, and other items were all around the house.

'But where is Yeskela?'[136] I asked my father. But he didn't answer me. ... But Leonid Sednev ... I saw him. He cried. He cried so loud, so loud!

'Papa, where is my Yeskela?' I cried.

'They killed him,' he cried.

'H-how?'

'They killed the tsar, the tsarina and the grand duchesses also. All of them are dead,' my father said.

'I don't understand, where... where are their bones?'

'We do not know, maybe we'll never find them.'

"My world was destroyed. They destroyed Russia, no more illusions. I found Yeskela's last letter to me. Especially one sentence in that letter, 'I hug you warmly,' made me cry. I thought: 'And I hug you warmly, too, my dear friend, and my tsar.'

"I was in shock. In later years, I thought just about him, 'Why did they kill you? There was no little space in the USSR for my Yeskela? We'll be forever friends, my dear tsarevich. I want to see you just one more time, and I can die in peace. ..."[137]

THE CHAPTER OF BLOOD

From the investigations of N. Sokolov at the "Four Brothers" mine, 1919.

Alexis' last note to his little friend Kolya:
"Dear Kolya, all the sisters send greetings to you, your Mama, and Grandma. I feel well myself. My head was aching all day, but now the pain is gone completely. I hug you warmly. Greetings to the Botkins from all of us. Always yours, Aleksey
"The END"[138]
The conclusion of the note with the word "END" (конецъ), which was written after his signature was something that Alexis noted for the first time in a letter of his. This was also one more of the curious things that little Alexis displayed at the end of his life.

The investigations to resolve the matter continued, but without leading to any definite conclusion. The first special investigator who attempted to follow the traces of the crime was Nicholas Sokolov, to whom the case was assigned somewhat later, in April of 1919. The depositions of eyewitnesses, mainly the peasants from the village of Koptyaki, guided Sokolov to the Four Brothers mine.

Inside the mine and in the area around it, Sokolov located some important clues: bone fragments, a woman's finger, the upper denture and glasses of Dr Botkin, traces of human fat, corsets, belt buckles, shoes, keys, marbles and diamonds, spent bullets, and other small items. Among them was also found the corpse of Anastasia's pet dog. However, Sokolov's further investigation was interrupted a few months later when in July 1919 the Bolsheviks recaptured Ekaterinburg. Sokolov finally escaped to Paris, taking with him the box with his findings, among which were also minuscule fragments of remains. For the next five years he continued his work on the case until his untimely death in 1924.

CHAPTER 6

In the time that followed, the unknown fate of the family gave occasion for the creation of unacceptable inaccuracies and deceptions of public opinion. On all the world stage, there was huge interest in the fate of the Romanovs and those who believed that some of the members of the family escaped from the Bolsheviks were innumerable. The situation took on even greater dimensions when a girl appeared in Berlin in 1922 claiming that she was Anastasia. This affair, which was of the most serious of its type,[139] marked the appearance of various persons claiming to be one of the children of the royal family.

The terrible mystery of the Koptyaki forest began to be uncovered sixty years later. On 30–31 May of 1979, the amateur investigator Alexander Avdonin, after many years of investigation and collection of evidence, with the help of the cinematographer Geli Ryabov, succeeded in locating the mass grave of the nine victims. However, they had to wait another ten years, until the time of Mikhail Gorbachev's Perestroika, to officially announce their discovery. Then a new prolonged period of scientific analysis began through genetic (DNA) testing of the discovered remains. The results finally confirmed the identity of the remains of Nicholas, Alexandra, the two older girls, and one of the younger ones, but without being able to ascertain whether these were Maria's or Anastasia's. The government performed an official burial of the members of the Royal Family in Saint Petersburg on 17 July, 1998, the eightieth anniversary of their martyrdom.

However, new waves of theories began to flood worldwide attention concerning the possible survival of Alexis and one of the girls, whose remains were not found in the common grave. Finally, on 29 July, 2007, a team of members of the Military and Historical Club of Ekaterinburg succeeded in locating the second grave where the dismembered bodies of Alexis and one of his younger sisters were found. The confirmation of the identity of the remains was established again through genetic testing.[140] Thus all the remains of the members of the martyred family once again saw the light of our finite reality.

Dr Sergei Nikitin, one of the most noted criminologists in all of Russia, was engaged for many years in the study of the skulls that were found in 1991. According to the results of his studies, the remains of the unidentified girl from the first burial site belong to Anastasia. The methods used by Dr Nikitin were those of Forensic facial reconstruction and photographic superimposition.

Forensic facial reconstruction is the process of recreating the face of an individual, whose identity is often not known, from their skeletal remains through an amalgamation of artistry, anthropology, osteology, and anatomy. The method is based on the measurement of the thickness of the soft tissues of the face at various points on the skull. The measurements are taken with needles or by using computed axial tomography and magnetic resonance imaging (CAT, MRI). Then, the reconstruction is completed through the use of modelling clay depicting the soft tissue on the skull.

Photographic superimposition is based on overlaying the skull onto a photograph that was taken in life. The examiner investigates the outline, the facial tissue thickness at various anthropometric points, and the positional relationships between skull and face, based on anatomical data after the skull to comparison photograph orientation is achieved.[141]

'THEM THAT HONOUR ME I WILL HONOR'[142]

A multitude of reported miracles of the Royal Martyrs began to appear even soon after their martyrdom. Healings of the sick, reunion of separated families, myrrh-streaming and fragrant icons, all testify to their great boldness before the throne of God. So the official recognition of their sanctity remained the great desire of the fullness of the Church. In fact, the first act of the glorification of the Royal Family was held on 1 November, 1981 by the Russian Church Abroad,[143] and the corresponding glorification by the Patriarchate of Moscow followed on 15 August, 2000.

In 2001, on the grounds of the Four Brothers mine, known as Ganina Yama, the Holy Monastery of the Royal Martyrs was erected. Apart from the catholicon of the monastery, i.e., its central church, seven other chapels were erected on the grounds of the monastery, equal in number to the members of the royal family.

During the period of Communist rule, the Ipatiev House was renamed the Museum of the People's Revenge and was used as a center of anti-monarchist propaganda. However, even as of the beginning of the decade of the 1970's, some groups of faithful began to arrive at this house of martyrdom from all over Russia to lay a few flowers and to seek the intercession of the Royal Martyrs. This grew to the point that it provoked the atheist regime, and so in 1977 the Ipatiev House was razed by the government authorities. But soon it came about that this same regime was shaken to its foundations, and so on the grounds of the Ipatiev House the famed Church on the Blood was built and dedicated in 2003.

The Church on the Blood is a huge and magnificent structure. The main church is dedicated to the Synaxis of All Saints that Shone Forth in Russia. But in the basement of the church is the Church of the Royal Martyrs, whose Holy Altar is on the very spot of the martyrdom of these saints. Apart from the icons of Christ and the Theotokos, the iconostasis of this church is decorated only with icons of the members of the Royal Family.

An All-Night Vigil is held every year on the memorial of the holy Royal Martyrs, and at the end of the Divine Liturgy, around 3 o'clock in the morning, a great procession follows from the church to the wood where the

Monastery of the Holy Royal Martyrs stands on the spot of their first burial. This procession lasts around four hours and immediately after the arrival of the procession at the monastery, a service of supplication (*moleben*) is served to the saints. A little later, at 9:00 AM, the Divine Liturgy is served in the catholicon of the Monastery of the Royal Martyrs and in the evening another All-Night Vigil is served there. In 2017, at this night-time procession more than sixty thousand faithful participated. In 2018, on the centennial of their martyrdom, the number of faithful reached a hundred thousand.

PART III
In the Words of the Saints

SAINT JOHN OF KRONSTADT

In 1901 Saint John of Kronstadt saw an apocalyptic vision of the end of the world. In this vision, God also revealed the coming sorrows of Russia. Here follows an excerpt from the vision in which Saint John mentions the Holy Royal Martyr Nicholas Romanov.

After evening prayers, I laid down to rest a little in my dimly lit cell since I was fatigued. Hanging before the icon of the Mother of God was my lit lampada. Not more than a half hour had passed when I heard a soft rustle. Someone touched my left shoulder, and in a tender voice said to me, "Arise servant of God John and follow the will of God!"

I arose and saw near the window a glorious starets (elder) with frosty grey hair, wearing a black mantia, and holding a staff in his hand. He looked at me tenderly, and I could scarcely keep from falling because of my great fear. My hands and feet trembled, and I wanted to speak, but my tongue would not obey me. The starets made the sign of the cross over me, and calm and joy soon came over me. Then I made the sign of the cross myself.

He then pointed to the western wall of my cell with his staff. …
Suddenly the wall vanished, and I walked with the starets. …
I followed after the starets. "Look!" he said pointing with his hand. I saw a mountain of human corpses stained in blood. I was very frightened, and I asked the starets, "What is the meaning of these dead bodies?" He replied, "These are people who lived the monastic life, were rejected by the Antichrist, and did not receive his seal. They suffered for their faith in Christ and the Apostolic Church and received martyrs' crowns dying for Christ. Pray for these servants of God!"

Without warning, the starets turned to the north and pointed with his hand. I saw an imperial palace around which dogs were running. Wild beasts and scorpions were roaring and charging and baring their teeth. And I saw the tsar sitting on a throne. His face was pale and masculine. He was reciting the Jesus Prayer. Suddenly he fell like a dead man. His crown fell. The wild beasts, dogs, and scorpions trampled on the anointed sovereign. I was frightened and cried bitterly. The starets took me by my right shoulder. I saw a figure shrouded in white—it was Nicholas II. On his head was a wreath of green leaves, and his face was white and somewhat bloodied. He wore a gold cross around his neck and was quietly whispering a prayer. And then he said to me with tears, "Pray for me, Fr John. Tell all Orthodox Christians that I, the Tsar-martyr, died manfully for my faith in Christ and the Orthodox Church. Tell the Holy Fathers that they should serve a Panikhida for me, a sinner, but there will be no grave for me!"

Soon everything became hidden in the fog. I cried bitterly praying for the Tsar-martyr. My hands and feet trembled from fear.

Then the starets began to quickly depart from the earth to the heights of heaven. As he did so, I remembered that I did not know his name, so I cried out loudly, "Father, what is your name?" He tenderly replied, "Seraphim of Sarov!"

That is what I saw, and this is what I have recorded for Orthodox Christians.[1]

SAINT MACARIUS OF MOSCOW

Saint Macarius Nevsky was Metropolitan of Moscow before Saint Tikhon, from 1912 until 20 March, 1917. In his last year as metropolitan, he saw the following vision.

I saw a field. The Savior was walking along a path. I went after Him, affirming, "Lord I am following you!" And He, turning to me, replied, "Follow Me!" Finally, we approached an immense arch adorned with stars. At the threshold of the arch the Savior turned to me and said again, "Follow Me!" And He went into a wondrous garden, and I remained at the threshold and awoke.

Soon I fell asleep again and saw myself standing in the same arch, and with the Savior stood Tsar Nicholas. The Savior said to the tsar, "You see in My hands two cups: one which is bitter for your people and the other sweet for you."

The tsar fell to his knees and for a long time begged the Lord to allow him to drink the bitter cup together with his people. The Lord did not agree for a long time, but the tsar begged importunately. Then the Savior drew out of the bitter cup a large glowing coal and laid it in the palm of the tsar's hand. The tsar began to move the coal from hand to hand and at the same time his body began to grow light, until it had become completely bright, like some radiant spirit. At this I again woke up.

Falling asleep yet again, I saw an immense field covered with flowers. In the middle of the field stood the Tsar, surrounded by a multitude of people, and with his hands he was distributing manna to them. An invisible voice said at this moment: "The tsar has taken the guilt of the Russian people upon himself, and the Russian people is forgiven."[2]

SAINT ANATOLE OF OPTINA

Elder Anatole said to Prince N. D. Zhevakhov, before his being named to the post of Assistant Ober-Procurator of the Holy Synod in 1916: "There is no greater sin than to oppose the will of God's Anointed. Protect him, for the land of Russia and the Orthodox Faith are supported by him. … But…" Fr Anatole became lost in thought, and tears appeared in his eyes. With great emotion he finished his unspoken thought, saying, "The destiny of the tsar is the destiny of Russia. If the tsar rejoices, then Russia will rejoice. If the tsar weeps, then Russia will also weep. … Just as a man with his head cut off is no longer a man, but a stinking corpse, so also Russia without a tsar will be a stinking corpse."[3]

SAINT NEKTARY OF OPTINA

From the recollections of Fr Basil Shoustin, a spiritual child of St Nektary.

In 1914, my older brother became a novice in the Optina Skete and occasionally had the position of cell-attendant to Fr Nektary. He often sent my father letters with a request to send him money, since he was buying a variety of books of spiritual content and was putting together a spiritual library. I was always outraged at this and said that, now that he had left the world, according to his calling, he should make a break with his passions. And my brother had such a passion—buying books. I wrote Fr Nektary a letter, and a fairly sharp one, expressing my indignation and surprise. He did not answer. My brother continued to send his requests and, occasionally, outright demands. Then I wrote the Elder an even sharper letter, accusing him of not suppressing my brother's passions, but catering to them. He again did not answer. And then, when I was on leave from the front, I succeeded in travelling with my wife to Optina. This was already in 1917, at the time of the Provisional Government. We arrived at the Monastery and Fr Nektary met us with a low, low bow and said, "Thank you for your sincerity. You wrote without any embellishments concerning what was on your soul, what was disturbing you. I knew that after these letters you yourself would visit, and I'm always happy to see you. You write such letters ahead of time and you appear after them yourself for the answer. So now I'm telling you that there will soon be a famine of spiritual books. You won't be able to obtain spiritual books. It's good that he's collecting this spiritual library—a spiritual treasury. It will come in very, very handy. A grievous time is coming now. In the world the number six has past and the number seven is approaching. The age of silence is approaching. Be silent, be silent," said the Elder, and tears flowed from his eyes. ... "And the Tsar is beside himself; how much humiliation he is now enduring for his mistakes. The year 1918 will be even worse. The Tsar and his whole family will be killed, tormented. One pious young woman had a dream: Jesus Christ was sitting on a throne, and near Him were the twelve Apostles; and horrible torment and groans could be heard from the earth. And the Apostle Peter asked Christ, 'O Lord, when will these punishments cease?' And Jesus Christ answered him, 'I will give them until 1922, but if the people do not repent, do not come to their senses, then all will perish in this way.' Suddenly our Emperor was standing before the throne of God with the crown of a great martyr. Yes, this Tsar will be a great martyr. He has redeemed his life of late, and if people do not turn to God, then not only Russia, but all of Europe will collapse. ... The time for prayer has come. While you're working, say the Jesus Prayer. At first with your lips, then with your mind and finally, it will go on by itself in your heart."[4]

SAINT TIKHON, PATRIARCH OF MOSCOW

Saint Tikhon, Patriarch of Russia, nurtured a deep love and great reverence for Tsar Nicholas, something that is especially evident in his sermons from the time he was still archbishop of America. When he mentioned Nicholas, he called him "the meek and kind Nicholas II." An excerpt of his sermon of 6 May 1904 on the occasion of Nicholas' birth follows:

Today we, brethren, celebrate the birthday of our Sovereign. The day of birth is important in the life of every man, and a joyful day it happens to be. "A woman when she is in travail hath sorrow, because her hour is come: but as soon as she is delivered of the child, she remembereth no more the anguish, for joy that a man is born into the world."[5] Life is a precious gift of God, the greatest good, which opens for man a number of other blessings – in nature around him; in his own being, spiritually and bodily; and in the society of people that surround him. Nevertheless, after the fall of our forefathers, there is no complete and perfect joy on earth. "Which earthly joy is not related to sorrow?"[6]

In the life of each one of us there happen to be quite a few sorrows and sufferings, and they are the lot of all born on earth. And since, according to the word of the most wise Solomon, the tsar himself is a mortal person as well, similar to all, and equally with everyone else has a common entrance into life and the same going out; and having been born, the first voice he reveals is crying, similar to all.[7] Then, of course, there are sorrows and sufferings in the life of our beloved Sovereign.

May it not seem strange, brethren, that on this joyful day of our Sovereign's birth, we speak of his sorrows and sufferings. An excuse for this may be found in the fact that the birth of the Sovereign falls on the day when the Orthodox Church remembers the Long-suffering Job. Of course, this coincidence perhaps seems random to some. But there is nothing that is random to the eye of the believing man. And even more so in such important events as the birth of rulers, whom God Himself raises up, the right ones for the time.[8] Therefore, it is not a random but rather a mysterious coincidence of the birthday of our Sovereign with the day of remembrance of the Long-suffering Job.

The Holy Righteous Job: who has not heard how this "opulent man, abounding in wealth and cattle, was shorn of riches and glory; he who had many children is childless and homeless; he who was formerly on the throne is now naked and covered with sores."[9] Through the permission of God, terrible afflictions overtake this righteous man, and blow after blow strike him. One after another, the messengers come to him with sad news about the loss of his entire estate; and "while he was yet speaking, there came also another"[10] telling about the death of all his children and servants; and after some time he himself is stricken with a terrible disease (leprosy).

Was it easy for Job to endure all of this? Was his flesh of brass, and was his strength the strength of stones?[11] If one weighed his grief, it would surely be heavier than the sand of the sea.[12] And yet Job courageously endures the misfortunes that have befallen him: "in all this he did not sin with his lips";[13] and he does not grumble against God.

But there still are wounds that await him, more painful than the external misfortunes. Three friends of his, who came to visit him in his misfortune, instead of comforting him, started accusing him of various vices, since they thought that the Lord was punishing him for his sins. ... These kinds of reproaches they threw at him of whom the Lord Himself spoke that "there is none like him in the earth – a perfect and an upright man, one that feareth God, and escheweth evil".[14] ...

Let us [now] bring ourselves, brethren, from the ancient times to the present days – from "the greatest of the sons of the east"[15] to the Supreme Leader of our motherland. ... According to the unknown designs of God, lately misfortunes strike various places of our vast motherland. To our Tsar, as at one time to Job, one after another word has come – now of harvest failure, now of destruction due to earthquake, avalanches, now of floods. And in very recent days a war has joined all of it,[16] with all its horrors, losses, victims – a war that was forced upon our Most Peace-Loving Tsar.

And is it easy for our Tsar to bear all these misfortunes? Does he not suffer for his native land?

But even more painful wounds are inflicted upon his heart. Just as Job was not understood by his friends, and suffered terribly from that, in the same way the Russian people and their Crown-Bearing Leader until this day cannot gain proper estimation from other nations. The best of their intentions are met with mistrust and suspected of insincerity; terrible designs are attributed to them; the most honorable of their undertakings are misinterpreted, twisted, laughed at. Everything that is good is met with silence, and their shortcomings are blown exceedingly out of proportion and announced for the whole world to hear. Our country is presented as being the most uneducated, while some Asian nations, like Japan, are said to be far more culturally advanced than we are. Our government is, supposedly, the most ineffective, which only the Russian people can tolerate.

Let us not enumerate further these mindless words – they are already well-known to all of us who live abroad. "Plead my cause, O Lord, with them that strive with me: fight against them that fight against me."[17] And to our beloved Tsar, together with the well-being of Moses, the courage of David, and the wisdom of Solomon, give the "patience of Job" as well. Help him and the whole of the Russian nation to believe in the truth of Christ, in the righteousness of their cause, and to adhere to the right paths of the Lord as before, no matter what our ill-wishers say.[18]

An excerpt from the sermon of Saint Tikhon immediately after notice of the execution of the Tsar. The sermon was given at the Divine Liturgy on 21 July, 1918, in which Saint Tikhon, already Patriarch of Russia, served the first official Memorial Service (Panikhida) for the murdered tsar.

Our happiness and blessedness consist in our observing the Word of God, in inculcating in our children the Lord's commandments. Our forebears thoroughly understood this truth. It is true that they, as all people, may have strayed from His teachings, but they knew how to acknowledge sincerely that this is sin, and they knew how to repent.

We, however, to our sorrow and shame, have lived to see such a time when the blatant violation of Divine commandments is now not only not acknowledged as sin, but is justified as something lawful. And so, a few days ago, a horrible deed was committed: the former Sovereign, Nicholas Alexandrovich, was killed by firing squad by decree of the Ural Regional Soviet of Workers' and Soldiers' Deputies, and our supreme government – the Executive Committee – has approved it and recognized it as lawful.

But our Christian conscience, guided by the Word of God, cannot agree to this. We must, in obedience to the teaching of the Word of God, condemn this action, otherwise the blood of him who was shot will fall on us, and not just on those who committed this act.

We will not here evaluate and judge the actions of the former Sovereign: the dispassionate judgement on him belongs to history, and he now stands before the impartial judgement of God, but we know that when he abdicated the throne, he did it with a view to the good of Russia and out of love for her. He could have, after abdication, found himself in safety and in a fairly tranquil life abroad, but he did not do this, wishing to suffer together with Russia. He did nothing to improve his situation, he uncomplainingly submitted to fate… and suddenly he is condemned by some gang of people to a firing squad somewhere in the depths of Russia; not for any fault, but only because someone might have wished to snatch him away [rescue him]. This command was put into effect, and this deed – now after the execution – was approved by the supreme authority.

Our conscience can never be reconciled to this, and we must, in the hearing of all, proclaim this as Christians, as sons of the Church. Let them call us counterrevolutionaries for this, let them throw us into prison, let them put us before a firing squad. We are ready to endure all this in the hope that the words of our Saviour may apply to us: "Blessed are they that hear the word of God and keep it."[19]

A Sermon Preached at the New York Cathedral, on the Anniversary of the Holy Crowning, on May 14, 1905, at the time when Saint Tikhon was still the archbishop of America.[20]

Today, beloved compatriots, we remember the Holy Crowning of our Sovereign, and on this day I consider it appropriate to talk to you about the autocratic power which is distinctive of the Russian Tsars.

We who live far from the motherland, in a foreign land, among people who know little or nothing at all about our country and its regulations, quite often have to hear criticism, censure, and ridicule of the institutions that are native and dear to us. These kinds of attacks are most often directed against the autocracy, which is one of the foundations of the Russian State. To many here it seems to be some sort of a "scarecrow," an Eastern despotism, a tyranny, an Asian thing. All of the failures, shortcomings, and disorderliness of the Russian land are attributed to it. Russia, they say, will always remain a colossus with clay feet until it introduces in its land a Western-style constitution, order based on law, and a constituent assembly. And following the words of these kinds of faultfinders, our homegrown politicians have started to yell lately in Russia, "away with autocracy."

We cannot dissuade all those who wish to remain under delusion—those whose eyes do not see and ears do not hear. But on you, who live abroad and love your native land from this faraway place, lies a special duty to explain and acquaint the local honest thinkers with what the autocracy in Russia really is.

Autocratic power means that this power does not depend on any human power; it does not draw anything from the latter, is not limited by it, and has within itself the source of its being and strength. And for what purpose does it exist? The Jews asked the Prophet Samuel for a king for themselves so that he might judge and protect them.[21] And the psalm singer David prays for his son Solomon, "Give the king Thy judgments, O God, and Thy righteousness unto the king's son, that he shall judge Thy people with righteousness; he shall judge the poor of the people, he shall save the sons of the needy and humble the oppressor; he shall rescue a poor one from a mighty one and a needy one who has no helper."[22]

This means the tsar's power must guard the law and righteousness, protecting the subjects from violence and especially those who are destitute and crippled, who do not have any other intercessors and protection. And for this reason it has to be autocratic and independent, not limited by either the powerful or the rich. Otherwise, it could not fulfill its purpose, since it would have to constantly tremble for its fate. For in order not to be deposed, it would have to please the rich, the powerful, and the influential, and to serve the truth in the way it is understood by the latter, to deliver the judgment of men and not of God.

It is this kind of autocratic power that exists in our motherland, which arrived at it by way of long suffering from the internal strife of the princes and from the heavy yoke of non-Orthodox enemies. The tsar in Russia possesses power and freedom of action in such a measure as it is possibly allowed for a man. Nothing and nobody restrains him—neither the claims of the parties, nor the benefits of any class at the expense of another. He stands immeasurably higher than any party, any titles, and any fortunes. He is impartial and unbiased; ingratiation, servility, and mercenary motives are foreign to him. He does not have any need for any of that, since he is standing at the height that is inaccessible, and nobody can add or take anything away from his majesty. "He does not accept favors from the hands of his subjects, but on the contrary gives them gifts himself."[23] He cares not for his personal interests, but for the well-being of the people, so that "everything is well arranged for the benefit of the people entrusted in his care and for the glory of God."[24] The rights and the interests of all his subjects are equally dear to him, and each one of them has in him a protector and benefactor.

The tsar is the "batiushka" for the people; this is how the people lovingly call him. Autocracy is based on the feeling of fatherly love for the people, and this love removes any hint of despotism, enslavement, and mercenary possession, which some are trying to attribute to the Russian autocracy.

And how would it not be shameful to talk about the despotism of the tsar's power when its bearers—let's take the sovereigns who have reigned closest to our time: Great Tsar Liberator Aleksandr II, Wise and Righteous Tsar Aleksandr III, and Meek and Kind Nicolas II—are the cause of amazement and admiration of sensible people even outside of Russia! Is it not strange to speak about the tyranny of the tsarist power when a Russian person imbibes love for his tsar with the "milk of his mother," when he then nurtures within himself this love until it reaches exalted adoration, when he displays complete obedience and loyalty towards his tsar, when our own troublemakers even deceive him and incite him to rebellion using the name of the tsar, when he is always ready to give his life for the tsar? No, despots and tyrants are feared and trembled at, but are not loved.

But they say, and especially frequently lately, that the tsarist power is only autocratic in theory, since in practice the autocracy is in the hands of the bureaucratic officials, who rule everything, who rule poorly, who create a dividing wall between the tsar and the people, so that the voice and the needs of the people do not reach the tsar ("The Lord is too high and the tsar is too far").[25] The people know their needs better than the officials or the tsar, and better understand their own benefit and usefulness; and therefore the people themselves should be in charge of all of that and rule, as is done in other states.

Indeed, the tsarist power has its own agencies, and these agencies are run by humans who are not deprived of shortcomings and imperfections, and who arouse fair criticism against themselves sometimes. But let us ask if there is a place where this does not happen? Let somebody show us this blessed land! We, here, live in a state where people rule themselves and choose their officials. Are they always up to the mark? And has serious abuse of power never taken place here?

They say that under tsarist power this type of abuse is more common since with it there is a great opportunity for bureaucracy, which has seized all the reins of government into its hands. The bureaucracy is especially attacked these days, although bitter historical experience shows that the criticizers of bureaucracy become just as bureaucratic, and sometimes even worse, as soon as they receive power into their hands.

The bureaucracy, however, is not associated with the essence of the autocratic power; and the tsar, apart from it, enters into "direct" contact with the people. He listens to the voice of the people regarding the "questions of the state organizational improvement," and he receives representatives even from the "strikers" (which does not always happen even in the republics). And in tireless caring about the well-being and improvement of the state, "he draws upon the most worthy persons who are invested with the trust of the people, selected from the folk to take part in the preliminary formulation and discussion of legislative proposals."[26]

And as far as people's government that is so pleasing to them is concerned, it is a complete delusion to suppose that the people themselves rule the state. It is supposed that all of the people in public meetings work out the laws and elect the officials, but this is only according to theory; and this just might be possible only in the smallest of states, consisting of one small town.

In reality, this is not the case. The masses of people, burdened with cares to provide the means for daily life and not familiar with the preeminent goals of the state, do not use their personal "autocracy"; rather, they transfer their rights to a few favorite people, those who are elected. The way the elections are held, what kinds of methods are used in order to become elected, there is no need to tell you; you have seen it here yourselves.

So the people do not rule, but those who are elected rule. And since they are not elected by all of the people but only a part of them (the majority), by a party, so then when they rule, they express the will not of all of the people but only of their party (and sometimes even purely their own will, since they even forget about the promises which they had poured out before their elections), and care only for the well-being and interests of their own party. And the opposing party they treat in a despotic manner, oppressing it in every way and pushing it out of power.

And this kind of imperfect state some want to introduce even in our country—often only for the reason that other people, who are more knowledgeable than we are, have it. They forget, however, that every people have their own special qualities and their own history, and what might be good for one turns out to be unsuitable for another. Only those institutions are sound and valid whose roots are established deep in the past of a particular nation, and which have emerged from the qualities of its spirit.

The rule of law (constitution, parliamentarianism) has these kinds of roots in some western nations. But in our country, Russia, autocracy emerged from the depths of the people's spirit and is most common to it. Everyone must consider this. And to experiment with changing the order of the state is not a trivial matter; it could disturb the very foundations of the state instead of improving things and fixing some shortcomings. May he who has ears, hear!

As for us brethren, let us pray to the Lord that He further preserve the Autocratic Tsar for Russia and grant him wisdom and power to judge the people in truth, and that He preserve the Russian state in peace and without sorrow.

SAINT JOHN MAXIMOVITCH

The sermon that follows was given by Saint John Maximovitch at Vespers of 16 July, 1934. At the time Saint John was in Serbia, where just two months earlier, on 28 May of 1934, he had been consecrated bishop for the Diocese of Shanghai. The sermon was given on the occasion of the Memorial Service for the slaughter of the Royal Martyrs.

Tomorrow (July 4/17) the Holy Church praises Saint Andrew, the Bishop of Crete,[27] the author of the Great Canon of Repentance, and at the same time we gather here to pray for the souls of the Tsar-Martyr and those assassinated with him. Likewise, people in Russia used to gather in churches on the day of the other Saint Andrew of Crete (Oct. 17),[28] not the writer of the Great

Canon whose day is celebrated tomorrow, but the Martyr Andrew, martyred for confession of Christ and His Truth. On the day of Martyr Andrew, people in Russia thanked God for the miraculous delivery of Emperor Alexander III from the train wreck at Borki on October 17, 1888. In the terrible derailment which occurred during his journey, all the carriages of the train were wrecked, except the one carrying the Tsar and his Family.

On the day of the Martyr Andrew of Crete, martyred by enemies of Christ and His Church, the Heir to the throne and subsequent tsar, Nicholas Alexandrovich, was saved, and on the day of Saint Andrew of Crete the Canonist, who reposed in peace, the Tsar was assassinated by atheists and traitors. On the day of Martyr Andrew, Russia also celebrated the day of the Prophet Hosea, who foretold Christ's Resurrection. Churches were built in honor of these saints wherever Russian people thanked God for the delivery of their Sovereign. Thirty years later, on the day of Saint Andrew the Canonist, who taught repentance, the Sovereign was assassinated before the eyes of the whole nation, which did nothing to save him. It is especially dreadful and incomprehensible since the Sovereign, Nicholas Alexandrovich, incarnated the best virtues of those Tsars whom the Russian people knew, loved, and esteemed.

Most of all the Tsar-Martyr resembled Tsar Alexis Michailovich[29] Tishayshiy (the Most Meek, 1645–76) excelling in unshakable meekness. Russia knew Alexander II (1855–81) as Liberator, but Tsar Nicholas II liberated even more nations of the fraternal Slavic tribe. Russia knew Alexander III (1881–94) as Peacemaker but Sovereign Nicholas II did not limit himself to care for peace in his own days but made a significant step towards establishing peace in Europe and in all the world so that all nations should solve their controversies peacefully. To that purpose, by his dispassionate and noble initiative, the Hague Conferences[30] were called. Russia admired Alexander I (1801–25) and called him the Blessed One because he liberated Europe from the alien rule of a tyrant, Napoleon. Sovereign Nicholas II, under much more difficult circumstances, rose against another ruler's attempt, Kaiser Wilhelm II, to enslave Slavic nations, and in the defense of that nation showed a determination that was devoid of compromises.[31] Russia knew the Great Reformer Peter I but if we recall all the reforms of Nicholas II, we would be uncertain whom to give preference and the latter's reforms were conducted more carefully, more thoughtfully, and without abruptness. John Kalita (1328-40) and John III (1449-1505), Grand Princes of Moscow, were known for uniting the Russian people, but their cause was finally accomplished only by Sovereign Nicholas when in 1915 he returned to Russia all her sons, though only for a short time.[32]

Sovereign of All Russia, Nicholas II was the first Pan-Russian Tsar. His inner, spiritual, moral image was so beautiful that even the Bolsheviks in their desire to blacken him could blame him only for his piety.

It is known for certain that he always began and ended the day with prayer. He always received Communion on the days of the Church's great holidays and often went to receive the Great Sacrament in a crowd of commoners, as for instance during the opening of the relics of Saint Seraphim of Sarov. He was an example of marital fidelity and the head of an exemplary Orthodox family, bringing up his children to be ready to serve the Russian people and strictly preparing them for the future labors and feats of that calling. He was deeply considerate towards his subjects' needs and always wanted to ascertain clearly and acutely their labor and service. Everyone knows that he once marched alone many miles in soldier's full equipment in order to better understand the conditions of a soldier's service. He walked alone, which refutes the slanderers who say that he was afraid for his life. Peter I said: "know about Peter, that life is not precious for him, but may Russia live" and Sovereign Nicholas II indeed fulfilled his words. Some people say that he was credulous. But the great father of the Church, Saint Gregory the Great, says that the more pure the heart, the more credulous it is.

What did Russia render to her pure-hearted Sovereign, who loved her more than life? She returned love with slander. He was of great morality, but people began to talk about his viciousness. He loved Russia, but people began to talk about his treason. Even the people close to the Sovereign repeated the slander, passing on to each other rumors and gossip. Because of the ill intention of some and the lack of discipline of others, rumors spread and love for the Tsar began to grow cool. They started to talk of the danger to Russia and discuss means of avoiding that non-existent danger, they started to say that to save Russia it would be necessary to dismiss the Sovereign.

Calculated evil did its work: it separated Russia from her Tsar and in the dread moment at Pskov he was alone; no one near to him. Those faithful to him were not admitted to his presence. The dreadful loneliness of the Tsar… But he did not abandon Russia; Russia abandoned him, the one who loved Russia more than life. Thus, in the hope that his self-belittling would still the raging passions of the people, the Sovereign abdicated. But passion never stills. Having achieved what it desires, it only inflames more. There was an exultation among those who desired the fall of the Sovereign. The others were silent. They succeeded in arresting the Sovereign; succeeded, and further events were almost inevitable. If someone is left in a beast's cage, he will be torn to pieces sooner or later. The Sovereign was killed, and Russia remained silent. There was no indignation, no protest when that dread, evil deed happened, and this silence is the great sin of the Russian people, and it happened on the day of Saint Andrew, the writer of the Great Canon of Repentance, which is read in churches during Great Lent.

In the vaults of a basement in Ekaterinburg the Ruler of Russia was killed, deprived by the peoples' insidiousness of the tsar's crown, but not deprived of God's Sacred Anointment. Hitherto, all the cases of regicide in the history of Russia were committed by cliques, not by the people. When Paul I was killed, people knew nothing about it and when it became known, for many years they brought to his grave compassion and prayers. The assassination of Alexander II produced in Russia a storm of indignation that healed the people's morality and assisted the reign of Alexander III. The people remained innocent of the blood of the Tsar-Liberator Alexander II. But in the case of Nicholas II the entire nation is guilty of shedding the blood of its tsar. The assassins did the terrible deed; their masters approved the murder, sharing the same sin; the people did not prevent it. All are guilty and indeed we must say: "His blood is on us and on our children."[33] The garland with which the Russian people crowned their Tsar was made of treason, treachery, the breaking of the oath of allegiance to Tsar Michael Theodorovich, the first Tsar of the Romanov dynasty and his heirs, passivity, hardness of heart, and insensitivity.

Today is a day of sorrow and repentance. Why—we could ask—did the Lord save the Tsar [previously] on the day of Martyr Andrew and not save him on the day of the other Saint Andrew, the teacher of repentance? With deep grief we answer: The Lord could have saved him, but the Russian people did not deserve it.

The Sovereign received a martyr's crown, but this neither justifies us, nor reduces our guilt, as the Resurrection of Christ does not justify, but condemns Judas, Pilate, and Caiaphas and those who demanded from Pilate the murder of Christ. ...

Perhaps the day will come when not just the patron saints but also the Royal Martyrs themselves will be depicted on icons in remembrance of the event we recollect today.[34]

EPILOGUE
Nicholas B. A. Nicholson
Researcher and Author
New York

"Nicholas II was not stupid. Nor was he nearly as weak as is commonly thought. The dilemmas of ruling Russia were vast and contradictory, and it was an illusion to think that simply by agreeing to become a constitutional monarch Nicholas could have preserved his dynasty and empire."
                                                                                                              Dominic Lieven.

The most common representation of Emperor Nicholas II and his reign depicted by historians is invariably colored by the end of his empire and the violent death of the imperial family. This death is sometimes presented as tragic, but usually as inevitable, and in some way justified. Because the reign of the last emperor ultimately resulted in World War and collapsed into revolution, of necessity he is judged to be an utter failure. From his first words as emperor that indicated that he felt himself unprepared to rule, to the unanswered question just after his abdication, "What else could I have done when everyone has betrayed me?" Nicholas is generally presented as weak-willed and inept, and any attempt to portray him otherwise is regarded as historical revisionism or from a false perspective.

For the Orthodox world, the questions are different ones, based not on the quality of his achievements, but on the measure of his personal sacrifice. The elevation of Nicholas II and his family to sainthood was first proposed in Serbia as early as 1927, and the first formal request arrived in March of 1930. The imperial family were canonized as Holy Martyrs by the Russian Orthodox Church Abroad in 1981, and in 2000 they were recognized as passion-bearers by the Moscow Patriarchate. There were objections at every stage at the time both inside and outside the Church, and the issue of the canonization of Nicholas Romanov has often strengthened the divide on any presentation of the Tsar-Martyr and his reign. To some Orthodox, he is now crystallized as perfect and infallible, and the inconvenient truths about his life must be crushed at any cost. To others, he is seen as so flawed an individual and so close to living memory, it is almost impossible to see him as a positive historical, moral, or spiritual model.

EPILOGUE

Between these two opposing positions lie facts and figures that paint a contradictory portrait of the complicated reign of Nicholas II. It is wisely considered a fruitless exercise to extol the achievements of a society that has perished, but neither are lost societies entirely without merit or unworthy of consideration. We must remember that Nicholas II reigned for twenty-three years before his abdication, and in that span, Russia saw enormous leaps forward as a nation, and experienced unprecedented economic, demographic, and cultural growth, which, as Lieven rightly notes, would have presented difficulties for any sovereign.

It would be wrong however, to ignore the fact that alongside this great progress, the Russian peasantry and the working poor faced deplorable conditions that were becoming unusual in other countries. The squalor of their circumstances and the contempt for their human rights were considerable, and while Nicholas evidenced concern for this situation, he and his government did very little to alleviate it. After 1905 and leading up to 1914, the massive economic growth and widening gap between the rich and poor sat alongside the systemic corruption within the government and throughout society. At the same time, it would be unfair to refuse to recognize the myriad of achievement of the reign of Nicholas II and to note their positive and continuing effect on Russia.

In the tumultuous reign of the Emperor Alexander II, Russia saw the liberation of its serfs, the end of Russia's old agrarian economic structure, and the beginning of what might have been a slow and progressive move towards the concession of rights to Russian subjects. Extreme resistance from both the right and the left made this impossible, and hopes for this were dashed with the assassination of Alexander II in 1881. His son, the reactionary and charismatic Alexander III found himself obligated to rule "with an iron fist in a velvet glove" over a period of social and political change. Alexander III successfully navigated the complicated social and political situation for only thirteen years before his untimely death placed the throne in the hands of his young recently married son only twenty-six years of age.

Nicholas II was surrounded by the forceful presence of his mother, the Dowager Empress, and his uncles the Grand Dukes Vladimir, Alexis, Serge, and Paul. Other relatives such as Grand Duke Nicholas Nikolaevich held significant political influence, while others such as Grand Duke Konstantin Konstantinovich held cultural and social prestige. The generation of Alexander III was in its prime at the time of the sovereign's untimely death, and both the Dowager Empress Maria Feodorovna and Nicholas' eldest and most beloved and brilliant uncle, Grand Duke Vladimir, were only forty-seven years old. This generation of Romanovs could have, under normal circumstances, expected another two decades of service to and influence over their nation, and it was with both regret and misgivings that they kissed the hands of their new young sovereign and his Hessian bride.

EPILOGUE

The House of Romanov's internecine struggle began almost immediately, and Nicholas II found himself faced with dissent not only from without, but from within. Some tragedies of the earliest days of his reign (such as the expulsion of the Jews from the capital preceding the coronation of 1896, and the official response to the Khodynka tragedy) were really decisions taken on the advice of the sovereign's uncles and extant ministers, and thus reflected Alexandrine policies rather than those of Nicholas II. While interpersonal struggles remained within the Romanov dynasty, and Russia wrestled with its changing role in Europe, there came, however, enormous leaps of demographic, social, economic and cultural progress.

Nicholas II instigated the first (and only) imperial census, which gives us a very good look at the last days of the empire. In 1894, the population of Russia was 122,000,000. By 1917, the population had grown to 182,000,000, with substantial increases to the educated urban centers.[1]

In 1894, the budget of the Imperial Ministry of Education was 25,200,000 rubles, the number of students in secondary schools was 224,179, and there were 13,944 students in universities. At the start of the war in 1914, the budget had grown to 161,200,000 rubles (an increase of 628%), with 733,367 students in secondary schools (an increase of 227%), and 39,027 students in university (an increase of 180%). Under the reign of Nicholas II, primary education became free of charge, and after 1908, it was mandated and made obligatory for all subjects. Almost 10,000 primary schools were founded every year after 1908. By 1913, there were 130,000 in Russia, and this figure does not include the military academies, Orthodox church schools and seminaries, or the many private Roman Catholic, Muslim, and Jewish educational institutions permitted to operate within the empire.[2] The strides in education were massive in the reign of Nicholas II. In 1920, the Soviets took a survey and established the fact that 86% of Russians between the ages of 12 and 16 were able to read and write. While this is frequently touted as the "first great achievement of the Soviet State" it is clear from these facts that it was the assiduous attention to primary school education at the height of Nicholas II's reign that made this possible.

In the period between 1896 and 1913, the Russian economy boomed at a rate unknown in its history. The most rudimentary facts demonstrate tremendous growth and the slow, but stable rise in the standard of living. In 1894, there were 1,664,000 savings accounts in Russia, with a total capital of 333,000,000 rubles. By 1908, the security of these institutions had prompted growth to the point of 6,560,000 accounts with over 1.2 billion rubles in savings. In 1910, there were 104 newly organized joint stock companies with 119.3 million rubles invested. By 1913, there were 240 stock companies with over 403.1 million rubles invested.[3]

In the reign of Nicholas II, the Russian Orthodox Church saw enormous growth due to the personal involvement of the emperor and empress, as well as state funding. Hundreds of churches were built in Russia and abroad from the personal funds of the imperial family, and Nicholas II took an active interest in the life of the Church, attending Synodal meetings, and involving the imperial family closely in important Church affairs, such as the canonization and glorification of St Seraphim of Sarov in 1905.[4]

The cultural legacy of the reign of Nicholas II is perhaps the most lasting. The "silver age" of arts and letters remains among the most compelling of Russia's great periods, and includes the efforts of countless artists and architects, writers, historians, and poets, too many to mention here, whose works remain recognized today as masterpieces both inside and outside of Russia.

While it is not often noted, I believe that there was one lasting gift of the reign of Nicholas II that was a direct result of the end of the empire. The men "gifted and daring… ambitious and fierce" had been either condemned or exiled, and it was in their dispersal that we recognize the one remaining jewel of Nicholas' reign. The revolution and Russian Civil War forced millions of Russians into exile throughout the world, and it is impossible not to acknowledge the contributions of the Russian diaspora to any society that saw large groups of exiled Russians settle among them. Western Europe and the United States were fortunate to receive into their societies some of the greatest Russian minds and talents of the reign of Nicholas II, without whom the twentieth century might have looked very different.

Educated in the modern Russian schools of Nicholas' reign, and brought up in the Russian faith, this "first wave" of the emigration gave the west Nabokov, Stravinsky, Rachmaninoff, Balanchine, Pavlova, Nijinsky, Chagall, Diaghileff, Malevich, Sikorsky, Florovsky, and Pomazansky. The extraordinary talents of the writers, historians, theologians, artists, architects, mathematicians, and philosophers of the two generations raised in the period between 1894 and 1918 are of enormous importance, not just to Russia, but to the world.

Anywhere the diaspora settled, they brought with them cuttings of the seeds that were first sown during the reign of Nicholas II, and it is, perhaps, this legacy that is the greatest testament to what the reign of Nicholas II "might have been."

It would be destructive and pointless to point to achievements of the reign of Nicholas as a success "if only" the First World War and the February and October revolutions had not occurred. Are there then no lingering positive effects of the reign of Nicholas II? His reign is all too easy to dismiss, but Sir Winston Churchill, perhaps the greatest statesman of the twentieth century had this to say:

> *"It is the shallow fashion of these times to dismiss the Tsarist regime as a purblind, corrupt, incompetent tyranny. But a survey of its thirty months' war with Germany and Austria should correct these loose impressions and expose the dominant facts. We may measure the strength of the Russian Empire by the battering it had endured, by the disasters it had survived, by the inexhaustible forces it had*

EPILOGUE

developed, and by the recovery it had made. In the governments of states, when great events are afoot, the leader of the nation, whoever he be, is held accountable for failure and vindicated by success. No matter who wrought the toil, who planned the struggle, to the supreme responsible authority belongs the blame or credit.

"Why should this stern test be denied to Nicholas II? He had made many mistakes, what ruler has not? ... But the brunt of supreme decisions centered upon him. At the summit where all problems are reduced to Yea or Nay, where events transcend the faculties of man and where all is inscrutable, he had to give the answers. His was the function of the compass needle. War or no war? Advance or retreat? Right or left? Democratise or hold firm? Quit or persevere? These were the battlefields of Nicholas II. Why should he reap no honor from them? The devoted onset of the Russian armies which saved Paris in 1914; the mastered agony of the munition-less retreat; the slowly regathered forces; the victories of Brusilov; the Russian entry upon the campaign of 1917, unconquered, stronger than ever; has he no share in these? In spite of errors vast and terrible, the regime he personified, over which he presided, to which his personal character gave the vital spark, had at this moment won the war for Russia.

"He is about to be struck down. A dark hand, gloved at first in folly, now intervenes. Exit Tsar. Deliver him and all he loved to wounds and death. Belittle his efforts, asperse his conduct, insult his memory; but pause then to tell us who else was found capable. Who or what could guide the Russian state? Men gifted and daring; men ambitious and fierce, spirits audacious and commanding—of these there were no lack. But none could answer the few plain questions on which the life and fame of Russia turned."[5]

RUSSIA'S CZARINA

BY ISABEL F. HAPGOOD

WHENEVER my thoughts fly back, like homing pigeons, from a trip to Russia which includes a mental visit to the Imperial family, I ponder on the illustration of the old adage "extremes meet" furnished by the Tzaritza and one of our American empresses. Here are the outlines of the picture: Two young girls, each married in the home of the ruler over a vast country, on their wedding-day ascending the throne, and reigning over millions of subjects, yet with lives as different otherwise, in most respects, as it is possible for lives to be — Princess Alix of Hesse, now Empress of All the Russias, and Frances Folsom, now Mrs. Grover Cleveland. Could any contrast be greater, could any likeness be more close? Both women models of wifely and motherly devotion — but one hampered and bound at every turn by etiquette; the other free to lead her own life as she will.

Of the two, the Tzaritza was, probably, the more simply reared, on the whole. Assuredly more so than the children of most American millionaires. At the time of her birth her father was not even the ruler over the little Grand Duchy of Hesse; and the glimpses of the plain family life which one derives from the letters of her mother, Princess Alice, of England, show how plain, wholesome, and even ideal were her early surroundings. The Grand Duchess Alice, writing to her mother,

PRINCESS ALIX, OR "SUNNY."

Queen Victoria, often mentions items which demonstrate to us almost straitened circumstances. She returns thanks for a whole set of furniture; she says they must take their outing at horrid Blankenberghe, which has neither tree nor bush, only sand, because they cannot afford the prices at Scheveningen; she tells how the children of the coachmen and servants are brought in to share with her own children, when the Christmas tree is divided, because keeping the family together as one household is so important.

The future Empress was a very pretty baby, her mother writes, and received her name of "Alix" in the hope that, in that form, it would not be so easily spoilt as in her own case (the Germans persisted in pronouncing "Alice" as "Alicé"). Later on she came to be called, in jest, "Aliky," but more often by the nickname "Sunny," because of her sweet, merry disposition and constant laughter. Portraits of her in her childhood and up to the time of her marriage show her with a very mobile face, full of spirit and cleverness, beautifully expressive, and ranging from joy to pensiveness. Her great beauty, fine dark eyes, black lashes, exquisite complexion, masses of dark chestnut hair, and an extremely elegant, graceful figure, added to her special accomplishments as a fine singer and instrumental performer, would have rendered her a most attractive person in any walk of life. When

---

The first page of the article by I. Hapgood in *Harper's Bazzar*, 1906.

APPENDIX

RUSSIA'S CZARINA

BY ISABEL F. HAPGOOD

Isabel Florence Hapgood was born in Boston on November 21, 1851. She graduated from Miss Porter's School in Farmington, Connecticut, in 1868. Hapgood showed considerable language abilities, mastering many Romance and Germanic as well as Slavic languages, including Russian, Polish and Church Slavonic. She became a major translator of French and Russian literature. Between 1887 and 1889, she traveled through Russia. While there, she met several significant Russian literary and clerical figures. After that trip, she began traveling about annually to Russia. On that long first trip, ahe spent several weeks with the famous Russian novelist Leo Tolstoy on his country estate, and continued publishing translations of his works. For 22 years, Hapgood wrote for the *New York Evening Post* and the *Nation*, as a journalist, foreign correspondent and editorial writer. Particularly impressed by the Russian Orthodox liturgy and choral singing, Hapgood wanted to translate them for American audiences. Saint Tikhon, then Archbishop of Alaska and the Aleutian Islands, supported her efforts and became her friend. In 1916-1917 Hapgood was visiting Saint Tikhon, who had become Patriarch of Moscow, when the February Coup broke out. She became one of the first to report on the murder of the Romanov family. She escaped with the assistance of the American Consul and returned to the United States. She died in New York City on June 26, 1928. The following article was published in *Harper's Bazzar*, Vol. XL, No. 2, February 1906, pp. 103-109.

WHENEVER my thoughts fly back, like homing pigeons, from a trip to Russia which includes a mental visit to the Imperial family, I ponder on the illustration of the old adage "extremes meet" furnished by the Tzaritza and one of our American empresses. Here are the outlines of the picture: Two young girls, each married in the home of the ruler over a vast country, on their wedding day ascending the throne, and reigning over millions of subjects, yet with lives as different otherwise, in most respects, as it is possible for lives to be — Princess Alix of Hesse, now Empress of All the Russias, and Frances Folsom, now Mrs. Grover Cleveland.

Could any contrast be greater, could any likeness be more close? Both women models of wifely and motherly devotion — but one hampered and bound at every turn by etiquette; the other free to lead her own life as she will.

Of the two, the Tzaritza was, probably, the more simply reared, on the whole. Assuredly more so than the children of most American millionaires. At the time of her birth her father was not even the ruler over the little Grand Dutchy of Hesse; and the glimpses of the plain family life which one derives from the letters of her mother, Princess Alice, of England, show how plain, wholesome, and even ideal were her early surroundings. The Grand Duchess Alice, writing to her mother, Queen Victoria, often mentions items which demonstrate to us almost straitened circumstances. She returns thanks for a whole set of furniture; she says they must take their outing in horrid Blankenberghe, which has neither tree nor bush, only sand, because they cannot afford the prices at Scheveningen; she tells how the children of the coachmen and servants are brought in to share with her own children, when the Christmas tree is divided, because keeping the family together as one house-hold is so important.

The future Empress was a very pretty baby, her mother writes, and received her name of "Alix" in the hope that, in that form, it would not be so easily spoilt as in her own case (the Germans persisted in pronouncing "Alice" as "Alicé"). Later on she came to be called, in jest, "Aliky," but more often by the nickname "Sunny," because of her sweet, merry disposition and constant laughter. Portraits of her in her childhood and up to the time of her marriage show her with a very mobile face, full of spirit and cleverness, beautifully expressive, and ranging from joy to pensiveness. Her great beauty, fine dark eyes, black lashes, exquisite complexion, masses of dark chestnut hair, and an extremely elegant, graceful figure, added to her special accomplishments as a fine singer and instrumental performer, would have rendered her a most attractive person in any walk of life. When we add great strength of character and charm of manner (though, possibly, in a less degree than possessed by her lovely mother), we may concede that she has most of the attributes which are demanded of the perfect woman. But in her position, naturally, she is the target of criticism, like her unfortunate husband, the Emperor. If the poor man accepts suggestions, he is said to be weak and under the thumb of some one; if he rejects advice, he is pronounced obstinate and autocratic. The chief charges against the Tzaritza are, that she is "cold," and does not devote herself sufficiently to philanthropic objects— though even her critics can hardly define what they would have her do. Her portraits, as Empress, all give the impression of impassiveness and deep melancholy; but they misrepresent her through exaggeration of these characteristics. The truth is that she is terribly shy; and the circumstances under which she was married and first met her new country-people as her subjects, and has lived ever since, have not tended to decrease her diffidence. To sum it up in a manner familiar to Americans, I may compare her position to that of the unhappy "new clergyman." He has up-hill work for a long time with his parishioners, who are bewailing the loss of the former rector, and refuse to have their affections won by any merits whatsoever. The Tzaritza had to contend not only with the popularity of the Dowager Empress — a very fascinating woman — but with the limitations imposed on young wives and mothers, who are physically unable to devote themselves to society. For years the Dowager Empress had had no young family to hamper her efforts to render the court gay and provide a "good time" for the aristocracy, who are the chief critics in such cases, as well as the chief adorers. Then, consider the very trying surroundings of her first days in Russia. She had become engaged to the Tzarévitch in the summer of 1894, with all prospects of being able to undergo a long apprenticeship to her new duties (as Tzarévna), in the ordinary course, before being called upon to become the cynosure of all eyes, both at home and abroad. But in the autumn Alexander III suddenly sickened, and the Princess Alix was sent for to his death-bed in the Crimea. After his death, after that heartrending and protracted journey with the funeral train to St. Petersburg, she was married within a week of the terribly trying and exhausting funeral, all the court doffing their deep mourning weeds for that day.

All this had been preceded by the necessity of joining the Eastern Catholic Church, to which the Russian State Church belongs—a necessity quite proper in the case of the sovereign, but no longer required (as of old) except of the bride of the heir to the throne. I doubt if any one ever had more falsehoods printed about her on such an occasion than did the young bride. The German papers asserted that she had positively refused to marry the Tzarévitch when she discovered that she must change; then, that she had been shut up on bread and water to compel her to "anathematize" the Lutheran Church which she was leaving (as she had nobly refused to do); and that, at the last moment, she had balked at some dogma and point-blank declined to be baptized. One English paper stated that she would be compelled to don a nightdress and, in the presence of all the grand dukes and court officials, "get into a bath"—meaning the baptismal font, presumably. Now, Alexandra Feodorovna—as her Russian name is, forever dropping "Alix"—is the third Empress whom Hesse has furnished to Russia; and her elder sister, the Grand-Duchess Sergius, had joined the Russian Church voluntarily two or three years previous to this time, having remained a Lutheran for seven or eight years after her marriage. Moreover, princess-brides are put through a regular preliminary course of instruction by a competent court chaplain. Hence it is self-evident that she could not have made any surprising discoveries as to the necessity for change, at the last moment, even admitting that the fact was not perfectly well known. Having been very well grounded in her own religion, and a thoughtful person, she, naturally, asked many keen questions, and quite properly insisted on having every point made clear; that is all. As she had been baptized in the name of the Trinity, all she had to undergo was chrismation (confirmation) with the Holy Chrism; and the "nightgown," or long white garment prescribed by the ecclesiastical ritual, would have been dispensed with (it always is, nowadays), even had baptism been necessary; which baptism would have taken place behind a screen, with even the priest outside the screen. But chrismation can be administered to a person clad in ordinary raiment—as is proven by its administration to both Emperor and Empress in their imperial robes, after crowning, on their coronation day. And no one who joins that Church has to "anathematize" the Church he or she is leaving.

One reason for the change of name was, that there is no "Alix" in the calendar of the saints for the Eastern Catholic Church (though, curiously enough, the Empress's mother always referred to the present Queen of England as "Alix" in her home letters), and the celebration of the "name day," or Day of the Guardian Angel, is of great importance in Russia, especially the festival celebration of such a "name day." Feodorovna, "daughter of Feodor" (also used for Frederick), is an instance of the indispensable patronymic which accompanies all Christian names, for accurate definition of relationship. The wives of Paul I, Alexander II, and Alexander III all bore the name of *Marie Feodorovna*; while the wives of Alexander I and Nicholas I bore the other favorite imperial combination, as does the reigning Empress.

If the Tzaritza is sadder, somewhat less "sunny" than of yore, one can pardon her and understand it; it is a trying position for a young woman of two-and-twenty to feel that every eye is watching her slightest gesture and movement, with critical intent—especially for a shy young woman. Some of my court friends who were received by her privately, soon after her marriage, and therefore had a better opportunity to judge than at a general reception, wrote me: "She is extremely shy. One can see that she does her best —but one has to help her in conversation." Surely such an attitude, joined to her youth, sweetness, and helplessness, should have appealed to the chivalry of the men and the warm-heartedness of the women, as far more sympathetic than a perfectly self-possessed, imperial air. No doubt it did; but people at a distance are apt to hear of—or to remember—only the harsh criticisms; and the Empress's half-English extraction has, indubitably, militated against her popularity with many Russians, because England and all that is hers is generally unpopular in Russia. Hence her shy reserve has often been credited to English coldness, enmity, and an overstern code of conduct.

I remember the Tzaritza otherwise—as a girl of sixteen, shy, with delicious little awkwardnesses which added to her grace and charmed irresistibly. She, her father, and her brother (now the reigning Grand Duke of Hesse) came to St. Petersburg to spend the gayest bit of the winter season with the Grand-Duchess Sergius. The Tzarévitch was twenty-one, and the most engrossing topic of conversation and speculation that winter, in court circles and elsewhere, was his future bride. Four princesses of Montenegro were in the capital; two in society, having been invited by the Empress to visit her after they had finished their school there the previous spring; two in the aristocratic Smolny Institute for noble girls, the third of them being the present Queen of Italy. A good many people jumped to the conclusion that one of these would become Tzarévna, especially as they already belonged to the Eastern Church, and Alexander III had recently toasted Prince Nicholas of Montenegro (at a banquet in Berlin) as his "only friend in Europe." Among others who assumed it was the Shah of Persia, who came on a visit a little later, and at a court banquet (as one of the court ladies who was present informed me) pointed, most embarrassingly, at a Princess of Montenegro, then at the Tzarévitch, and naïvely inquired, in his faulty French, "Fiancée, Grand Due?" But there were intrigues, if one may believe what one heard. Not only was the Russian court, in general, opposed to such a match, but Germany had other views, judging from a detailed and decisive discussion of the matter at which I was present, between an emissary from Berlin and a mightily influential court lady, who had direct access to and power with the Imperial family.

When spring came, this particular aspect of the question was neatly disposed of: the Grand-Duke Peter married the eldest Montenegrin Princess, and shortly afterward the widowed Duke of Leuchtenberg married the second. It was currently reported in St. Petersburg that at the betrothal banquet one of the grand dukes undertook to chaff the Tzarévitch, remarking: "It's your turn next, Nicky. They'll be marrying you off pretty soon!" To which he haughtily replied: "*You* will all obey orders. But I shall choose my own bride." And it is believed that he did it, and that the marriage is really one of affection. Certainly, the Emperor could not have chosen better. Meanwhile, of course, every one attributed the Princess Alix's visit to her sister as "with an object." She was a charming creature, with distinction as well as rare beauty. I remember one amusing incident at the court ball where I had my best view of her. A pretty girl slipped and fell, in the waltz, and lay prone on the floor opposite me, and directly in front of the Grand Duke of Hesse. Her partner and other officers sprang to raise her; but observing that the Grand Duke had risen for the same purpose, they drew up and saluted profoundly, leaving the girl for a brief but appreciable and comical moment where she was, until the royalty reached her and exercised his privilege. She, on regaining her feet, was obliged, naturally, to make the little bob-curtsey to her royal rescuer before she went on with her dancing. But that visit came to nothing—assuming that it had an object—and the Princess returned home after her first (and, if I am not mistaken her only) glimpse of the Russians before she was called to reign over them.

Almost immediately after their marriage the young couple took up their permanent residence in the Alexander Palace at Tzárskoe Seló, sixteen miles from St. Petersburg, and there they have continued to live ever since; except during the brief winter season (from January 1 to Lent) and at other rare intervals; and during the hottest months of summer, when they remove to "The Cottage" —the simple seaside palace in the Alexandria Park at Peterhoff, twenty miles from the capital on the Gulf of Finland. The Alexander Palace is a moderately large, low, and plain white building, situated in the lovely

"English" Park, where the Siberian buttercups grow large, double, and fragrant as roses; where the lawns of the private garden are blue with forget-me-nots, and a miniature fort, various athletic apparatus, a gay little peasant cottage (glorified, of course!) and stable, and garden beds for childish experiments in housekeeping, agriculture, and floriculture, furnish amusement to the five children with which the marriage has been blessed; and the long, wooded avenues give opportunity for exercise by horse, carriage, wheel, or motor-car. At the end of one broad, grassy ride, from the windows of the great semicircular hall, where the children's miniature toboggan-slides (for bad weather) are installed, a glimpse may be had of the "Chinese Village" built by Katherine II, whose low stuccoed houses, with curving Chinese roofs, shelter favored courtiers and screen lovely private gardens in the rear. There is also a little village of houses for the scarlet kazáks of his Majesty's bodyguard, always on duty. The magnificent Great Palace hard by, in the Old Park of formal plan, last used as a residence by Alexander II, is employed only for the reception of royal visitors, foreign ambassadors, and the like, and contains a church (which the Alexander Palace lacks), with five cupolas something in the shape of imperial crowns, that seem to float like golden bubbles above the trees. In this park, also, is the lake, where the Imperial children (and the general public) can have any style of boat from the Norwegian "snowshoe" to the Chinese sampan.

A charming, simple home is the Alexander Palace. But there is one room which must, I think, have been — must still be — supremely painful. It is the library, panelled with mirrors, against which are affixed, like brackets, small half models of all the vessels in the navy—the mirror completing the image. I had the use of that library during the summer I spent at Tzárskoé Seló, and paused most frequently (after selecting my book) before the odd circular *Popóvka*, named after its designer, Admiral Popóff. Not in this palace does the Tzaritza have to wear the adaptation of the national costume which Katherine II established as the court dress; that is reserved for "national" days at court, such as New-year's day, the Epiphany, Easter, and so forth. That is the costume which, in miniature, and in pretty adaptation of the *kokóshnik* (or coronet), the Empress has provided for her four intelligent and attractive little daughters on special occasions. Such is the coronation gown (in cloth of silver), which is preserved, together with all accessories, down to the gloves, fan, stockings, and slippers, in the Museum of the Kremlin in Moscow, in one of the most sumptuous collections of personal adornment to be found in the world. It is enough to make any young girl shy to reflect that even her clothing is of such vital importance that it must be preserved for future generations, and that she is expected to live up to infinitely numerous and diverse ideals!

As it is, the Tzaritza has wisely contented herself with doing her full ceremonial duty and being a devoted and ideal wife and mother; and if people say, "nobody knows her," it may be regarded as praise. If she really tiers and screen lovely private gardens in the rear. There is also a little village of houses for the scarlet kazáks of his Majesty's bodyguard, always on duty. The magnificent Great Palace hard by, in the Old Park of formal plan, last used as a residence by Alexander II., is employed only for the reception of royal visitors, foreign ambassadors, and the like, and contains a church (which the Alexander Palace lacks), with five cupolas something in the shape of imperial crowns, that seem to float like golden bubbles above the trees. In this park, also, is the lake, where the Imperial children (and the general public) can have any style of boat from the Norwegian "snowshoe" to the Chinese sampan.

A charming, simple home is the Alexander Palace. But there is one room which must, I think, have been—must still be — supremely painful. It is the library, panelled with mirrors, against which are affixed, like brackets, small half models of all the vessels in the navy—the mirror completing the image. I had the use of that library during the summer I spent at Tzárskoe Seló, and paused most frequently (after selecting my book) before the odd circular *Popóvka*, named after its designer, Admiral Popóff. Not in this palace does the Tzaritza have to wear the adaptation of the national costume which Katherine II. established as the court dress; that is reserved for "national" days at court, such as New-year's day, the Epiphany, Easter, and so forth. That is the costume which, in miniature, and in pretty adaptation of the *kokóshnik* (or coronet), the Empress has provided for her four intelligent and attractive little daughters on special occasions. Such is the coronation gown (in cloth of silver), which is preserved, together with all accessories, down to the gloves, fan, stockings, and slippers, in the Museum of the Kremlin in Moscow, in one of the most sumptuous collections of personal adornment to be found in the world. It is enough to make any young girl shy to reflect that even her clothing is of such vital importance that it must be preserved for future generations, and that she is expected to live up to infinitely numerous and diverse ideals!

ONE OF THE CZARINA'S EARLY PORTRAITS.

As it is, the Tzaritza has wisely contented herself with doing her full ceremonial duty and being, a devoted and ideal wife and mother; and if people say, "nobody knows her," it may be regarded as praise. If she really exerts political influence on her husband (as some of my court and official friends maintained that she did, in preventing Russia from making an advance on Herat and diverting English troops from the Boers, for example), one can only say that other wives exert influence — when they can or possess it. But then there are other people who assert that she steadfastly refuses to put forward her opinions or advice. In short, "happy is the woman who has no story" may be said of her most emphatically, in one sense, and our sympathies are due to her for accomplishing that much, amid the trials and anxieties which have beset her country and harassed her husband—would have harassed Solomon himself.

ACKNOWLEDGMENTS

Our first debt of gratitude goes to the brotherhood of the Holy Monastery of St Herman of Alaska, in Platina, California, for the labor they have undertaken in gathering and sharing with us all the requested materials. Their most brotherly love towards our monastery has always been, and continues to be, exceptional.

Continuing, we would like to thank the founder and creator of the Alexander Palace Time Machine website, Bob Atchison, and the administrator of the site, Rob Moshein. Beyond offering at our disposal all the greatly valuable materials from their website, they have also kindly and willingly shared with us their unique knowledge and the fruit of their long-term research with regard to the life of the Royal Martyrs. Rob Moshein was also kind enough to translate from French, especially for our book, numerous excerpts from various primary sources. In addition to the above, Bob and Rob have introduced us to other notable historians and researchers in the field, who have become our main colleagues in this project.

Among those who excel in the above are Helen Azar and Nicholas B. A. Nicholson. Both Helen and Nicholas have dedicated a significant amount of their time to locating and collecting materials from the primary sources for our book. They, furthermore, shed light on difficult historical issues in relation to the life and death of the Royal Martyrs. We are also indebted to Helen for her translations from the Russian primary sources and to Nicholas for writing the Epilogue to our book.

Dr. Helen Rappaport –the acclaimed author, historian, and Russianist– has also been remarkably helpful and supportive to our humble efforts. She kindly answered all our questions and offered us her experienced historical consultation for the needs of our project. We are deeply grateful to her for her continuous and invaluable help.

A most warm and immense portion of gratitude goes to our very dear colleague, Sophie Law, Russian Arts Specialist and writer. Sophie has worked on the chapter on St Elisabeth Feodorovna, in which we present previously unpublished letters of the saintly Grand Duchess to her brother-in-law, Tsar Nicholas II. Sophie has also translated various Russian texts for our book and has been involved in almost every step of our project.

ACKNOWLEDGMENTS

We are greatly indebted to George Hawkins, one of our very important research colleagues, who has elaborated diligently on the Russian primary sources that deal with the February Coup, 1917, and the crucial topic of the plots to overthrow Tsar Nicholas II from his throne. This subject has never before been presented in any other English language Romanov biography and we consider it a great blessing that George has joined our project team undertaking this most significant part of it.

A very significant member of our project team is Dr Pyotr Multatuli, renowned Russian author, journalist, historian, and Professor at the Moscow State Institute for Culture and Arts. Pyotr has devoted all his career in researching and writing about the distorted truths in relation to the personality and the reign of Tsar Nicholas II. His works on these subjects are unparalleled and it has been a great honour to have his contribution in our project.

We would also like to express our most genuine appreciation to Dr. Michael Coble, former Chief Scientist of the US Armed Forces DNA Laboratory, who has been very kind in sharing with us all the necessary information with regard to his forensic DNA testing on the skeletal remains of the Royal Martyrs.

This book would not have the form and outlook that it now presents if our dear colleague Dr Olga Shirnina did not entirely take over the artwork of the project with such great enthusiasm and complete dedication. The methodical coloring of the pictures, which was executed by Olga under the consultation of historical specialists, breathed life into the written part of the project. In addition to her artwork, Olga has contributed to the historical research for the book. She has been able to locate most of the Russian archival material used in our book and has undertaken the transcription work of many handwritten manuscripts that were almost illegible.

We are profoundly grateful to Paul Gilbert, Founder of the Royal Russia Website and publisher and editor of Royal Russia Publications, who has been most supportive of our project from the very beginning of our efforts. Through his uniquely excellent website he has repeatedly posted articles, special tributes, and announcements in relevance to our book.

We especially thank Charalambos Iakovou for his technical processing of the photographic material of this book and his continual collaboration in all the work of the Monastery.

We owe special thanks to Maria Papaefstathiou, from Stamoulis and ATHOS Publications, for her excellent design of the book and her most gracious disposition and inspiration with which she worked for the present publication.

Our thanks also must go to Reverend Ignatius Green, Editor at SVS Press, for undertaking gratuitously the editing work of the text; to Captain Peter Sarandinaki, President of SEARCH Foundation Inc., for his valuable contribution to our research in the field of forensic studies; to Michael Perekrestov, Executive Director of the Russian History Foundation at Holy

ACKNOWLEDGMENTS

Trinity Orthodox Seminary, for providing us with all material requested for our project; to Nicholas Chapman, Director of Publications at Holy Trinity Publications, for his valuable advice concerning significant publishing issues; to Mother Cornelia Rees and Jesse Dominick, Editors of the Orthodox Christianity Website, for their continuous support through their posts and articles about our project; and to Constantine Gregory for his exceptionally wonderful narration for our book's trailer.

A most special thanks goes to Tasos Savva, who administers all the social media accounts of our book and is literally engaged in each and every action relating to our work, offering practical help and invaluable advice on all topics and fields in the course of our project.

During the research process of this and every other project, on our side we always have a very special friend and brother in Christ, who contributes to our efforts nothing less than all his exceptional skills, filled with his genuine brotherly love, which seal our work with their highly scholarly marks. This is Matthew Namee, who dedicates much of his time, working together with us in every stage and every field of our projects. We thank him from the depths of our hearts.

Eternally Living Past

Pictures Colorization
Olga Shirnina

Nicholas and Alexandra posing in 17th-century costumes of Tsar Alexei I and Tsaritsa Maria Miloslavskaya. Winter Palace ball, 1903.

16

Ольга.

Татьяна.

Марія.

Анастасія

Алексѣй

C. E. DE HAHN & Co.   TZARSKOE SELO.

From Alexis' visits at the GHQ at Mogilev. Picture on next page: From the left, with French language tutor Pierre Gilliard, Alexander Palace Commandant Major General Vladimir Nikolaevich Voeikov, English language tutor Sidney Gibbes and Russian language tutor Pyotr Vasilievich Petrov.

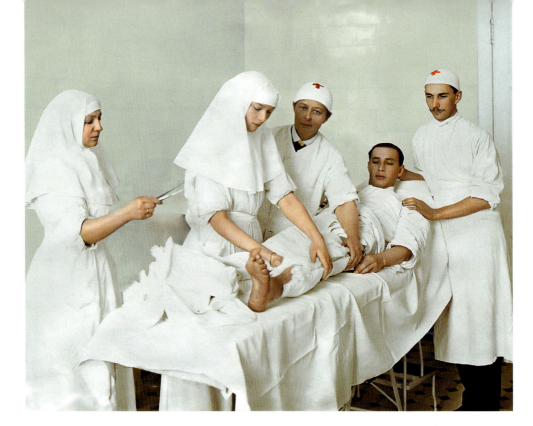

Above: Tatiana attending a wounded officer. Below: Olga and Tatiana with wounded officers. On the photo next page, with Red Cross uniforms. From the left: Anna Vyrubova, Tatiana, Alexandra, and Olga on the back.

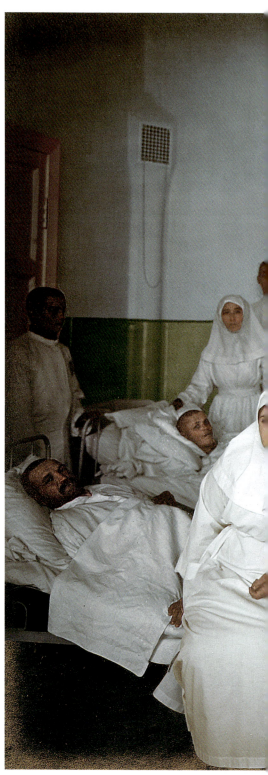
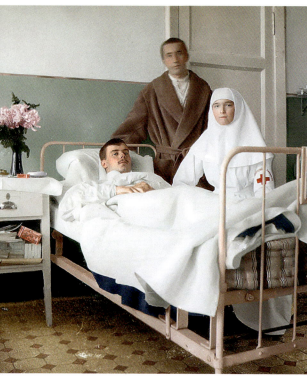

Above: Alexandra with Alexis. Below: Olga with wounded officers.

From the left: Anna Vyrubova, Tatiana, Olga and Alexandra with wounded officers.

Tsar Alexander III.

Empress Maria Feodorovna.

Grand Duchess Ksenya Alexandrovna.

Grand Duchess Olga Alexandrovna.

Grand Duke Michael Alexandrovich.

St Tikhon, Patriarch of Moscow and All Russias.

St John of Kronstadt.

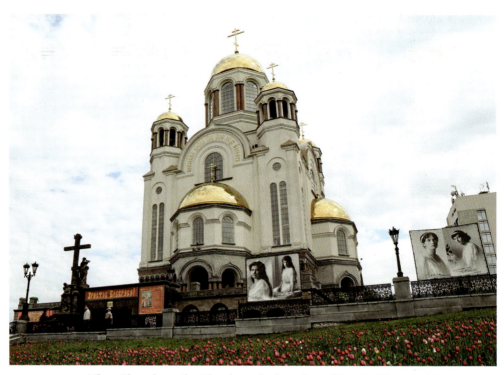

The «Church on the Blood» at the location of Ipatiev House.

Royal Procession after the All-Night Vigil on July 17th, 2017, from the «Church on the Blood» to the Monastery of the Royal Martyrs at Ganina Yama.

The Royal Martyrs chapel at the lower level of the «Church on the Blood».

The holy altar of the Royal Martyrs chapel in the «Church on the Blood» at the exact location of the room where the family with their retinue were murdered.

Troparion of the Royal Martyrs — Tone 1.

Most noble and sublime was your life and death, O Sovereigns; / Wise Nicholas and blest Alexandra, we praise you, / Acclaiming your piety, meekness, faith, and humility, / Whereby you attained to crowns of glory in Christ our God, / With your five renowned and godly children of blessed fame. / O passion-bearers decked in purple, intercede for us.

NOTES

CHAPTER 1 – LOVE WITHOUT BOUNDS

1. The Zemsky Sobor (English: "Assembly of the land," Russian: Земский Собор) was a parliament of the Tsardom of Russia's Estates of the realm active during the 16th and 17th centuries.
2. The dates are given according to the Old Calendar, which was in use at that time in Russia. The members of the royal family also used it in their diaries and letters to the end of their lives.
3. ГА РФ. Ф. 677. Оп. 1. Д. 301. Л. 168 об.-169.
4. "Tsar-Martyr Nicholas II And His Family," St Nicholas Russian Orthodox Church, McKinney, Texas, at https://www.orthodox.net/russiannm/nicholas-ii-tsar-martyr-and-his-family.html
5. Lieven, *Nicholas II: Emperor of all the Russias*, p. 33.
6. Сургучев, "Детские годы Императора Николая II," Бежин Луг, № 1 (1992), С. 40.
7. Mossolov, *At the Court of the Last Tsar*, pp. 17-18.
8. The office of Ober-Procurator was established by Peter the Great in 1722 after he abolished the Patriarchate. The Ober-Procurator, as representative of the Tsar at Synod, constituted its highest office, without whose approval no decision of the Synod would take effect. In this way Peter the Great effectively put the Church under his direct control.
9. Mossolov, *At the Court of the Last Tsar*, p. 16.
10. The title in Russian is Тишайший (Tishayshy).
11. People's Will (Russian: Нароодная воля) was a 19th-century revolutionary political organization in the Russian Empire, which conducted targeted killing of government officials, in attempt to promote reforms in the country. The organization declared itself to be a populist movement. People's Will was composed primarily of young revolutionary socialist intellectuals believing in the efficacy of terrorism.
12. Pares, *A History of Russia*, p. 441.
13. *Ibid*.
14. Namely, the father of Nicholas, who was later Tsar Alexander III.
15. "Tsar-Martyr Nicholas II And His Family," St Nicholas Russian Orthodox Church, McKinney, Texas, at https://www.orthodox.net/russiannm/nicholas-ii-tsar-martyr-and-his-family.html
16. Pares, *A History of Russia,* p. 445.

NOTES

17. Radzinsky, *The Last Tsar*, p. 15.
18. Price, "Diary of Nicholas II, 1917-1918, an annotated translation," p. 5.
19. The correct title of the heir apparent or presumptive in the Russian Empire is "Tsesarevich" (Russian: Цесаревич). It eventually got confused with "Tsarevich," which is a distinct word with a different meaning. Tsarevich was the title for any son of a tsar, including sons of non-Russian rulers accorded that title, e.g. Crimea, Siberia, Georgia. However, in our book we shall make use of the title as it is now commonly known.
20. Mossolov, *At the Court of the Last Tsar*, pp. 17-18.
21. Bing, *The Letters of Tsar Nicholas and Empress Marie*, pp. 33-34.
22. *Ibid.*, p. 32.
23. Radzinsky, *The Last Tsar*, p. 18.
24. *Ibid.*, p. 29.
25. *Ibid.*, pp. 29-30.
26. ГА РФ. Ф. 601. Оп. 1. Д. 2321. Л. 175-176.
27. Radzinsky, *The Last Tsar*, p. 30.
28. Maylunas and Mironenko, *A Lifelong Passion*, p. 6.
29. Pares, *The Fall of the Russian Monarchy*, p. 33. Note that Pares gives the wrong year of this diary entry. Instead of 1890 he writes 1891.
30. Prince Albert, the eldest son of the Prince of Wales, who had courted Alix, was known as Eddy within his family circle.
31. ГА РФ. Ф. 601. Оп. 1. Д. 227. Л. 107-108.
32. Millar, *Grand Duchess Elizabeth*, p. 84
33. Massie, *Nicholas and Alexandra*, pp. 32-33.
34. Maylunas and Mironenko, *A Lifelong Passion*, pp. 24-25.
35. *Ibid.*, pp. 26-27.
36. Мироненко, *Дневники императора Николая II, 1894–1918*, Том 1 (1894-1904), С. 64.
37. Bing, *The Letters of Tsar Nicholas and Empress Marie*, p. 75.
38. Мироненко, *Дневники императора Николая II, 1894–1918*, Том 1 (1894-1904), С. 66.
39. Bing, *The Letters of Tsar Nicholas and Empress Marie*, p. 76.
40. Maylunas and Mironenko, *A Lifelong Passion*, p. 42.
41. *Ibid.*, pp. 45-46.
42. Мироненко, *Дневники императора Николая II, 1894–1918*, Том 1 (1894-1904), С. 92. Entry of July 6, 1894, written by Alix in English.
43. 1 John 1:9.
44. Мироненко, *Дневники императора Николая II, 1894–1918*, Том 1 (1894-1904), С. 93. Entry of July 8, 1894, written by Alix in English.

CHAPTER 2 – AT THE HEIGHT OF GLORY

1. *Ibid.*, С. 120-121. Entry of October 12, 1894.
2. *Ibid.*, С. 120.

NOTES

3. Vorres, *The Last Grand Duchess*, p. 52.
4. Мироненко, *Дневники императора Николая II, 1894–1918*, Том 1 (1894-1904), С. 123.
5. Spiridovitch, *Last Years*, Vol. I, p. 263.
6. Мироненко, *Дневники императора Николая II, 1894–1918*, Том 1 (1894-1904), С. 123.
7. Vorres, *The Last Grand Duchess*, p. 52.
8. Saint Herman of Alaska Brotherhood, *The Royal Passion-bearers of Russia*, p. 7.
9. Vorres, *The Last Grand Duchess*, p. 55.
10. Мироненко, *Дневники императора Николая II, 1894–1918*, Том 1 (1894-1904), С. 124.
11. Fülöp-Miller, *Rasputin: The Holy Devil*, p. 80.
12. Мироненко, *Дневники императора Николая II, 1894–1918*, Том 1 (1894-1904), С. 131.
13. *Ibid.*, С. 134. Entry of November 26, 1894, written by Alix in English.
14. *Ibid.*, Entry of November 27, 1894, written by Alix in English.
15. Buxhoeveden, *The Life and Tragedy*, p. 44.
16. Millar, *Grand Duchess Elizabeth*, p. 84.
17. Fabritsky, *Of Bygone Days*, p. 51.
18. Batiushka (Russian: батюшка) means literally "little father." It has always been used to address an Eastern Orthodox priest, abbot, or monastic elder in Russia. The term, one of affection, was often also applied to the reigning tsar as a term of endearment. Matushka (Russian: матушка) is the feminine equivalent and it means "little mother." The term is used to address either an abbess or a priest's wife. It has also likewise been used as a term of endearment for the reigning tsarina.
19. This is what happened in the Time of Troubles, when the people rejected the false Dmitri.
20. Мироненко, *Дневники императора Николая II, 1894–1918*, Том 1 (1894-1904), С. 272 and 273.
21. Woolley, *Coronation Rites*, pp. 22-23. (For the original text in Greek, see J. Goar, Εὐχολόγιον *sive Rituale Graecorum*, Venetiis 1730, p. 726.)
22. Liebmann, "Martyrology of the Communist Yoke: The Life of Tsar-Martyr Nicholas II," *The Orthodox Word*, #153. Platina, California: Saint Herman of Alaska Brotherhood, 1990, p. 200.
23. Мироненко, *Дневники императора Николая II, 1894–1918*, Том 1 (1894-1904), С. 273.
24. Bing, *The Letters of Tsar Nicholas and Empress Marie*, p. 167.
25. Steinberg and Khrustalev, *The Fall of the Romanovs*, p. 16.
26. Мироненко, *Дневники императора Николая II, 1894–1918*, Том 1 (1894-1904), С. 274.
27. Buxhoeveden, *The Life and Tragedy*, p. 68.
28. *Ibid.*, p. 158.
29. Azar and Nicholson, *Tatiana Romanov*, pp. 137-138.

30. Spiridovitch, *Last Days*, Vol. I, pp. 26-27.
31. Vorres, *The Last Grand Duchess*, p. 102.
32. Мироненко, *Дневники императора Николая II, 1894–1918*, Том 1 (1894-1904), С. 234.
33. Eagar, *Six Years at the Russian Court*, p. 108.
34. *Ibid.*, p. 197.
35. *Ibid.*, p. 66.
36. Мироненко, *Дневники императора Николая II, 1894–1918*, Том 1 (1894-1904), С. 343-344.
37. Eagar, *Six Years at the Russian Court*, p. 137.
38. See Azar and Nicholson, *Tatiana Romanov*, pp. 152-153.
39. Eagar, *Six Years at the Russian Court*, p. 270.
40. Azar and Nicholson, *Tatiana Romanov*, p. 151.
41. Eagar, *Six Years at the Russian Court*, p. 38.
42. *Ibid.*, pp. 39-40.
43. *Ibid.*, pp. 40-41.
44. *Ibid.*, pp. 177-178.
45. Vorres, *The Last Grand Duchess*, pp. 98-99.
46. Hanbury-Williams, *The Emperor Nicholas II as I Knew Him*, p. 57.
47. Buxhoeveden, *Life and Tragedy*, p. 153.
48. Vyrubova, *Memories of the Russian Court*, p. 66.
49. Dehn, *The Real Tsaritsa*, pp. 86-87.
50. Fabritsky, *Of Bygone Days*, p. 115.
51. ГА РФ. Ф. 601. Оп. 1. Д. 721. Л. 1.
52. Бразоль, *Царствование Императора Николая II в цифрах и фактах*, С. 9.
53. Fabritsky, *Of Bygone Days*, pp. 119-120.
54. Vyrubova, *Memories of the Russian Court*, p. 55.
55. Fabritsky, *Of Bygone Days*, p. 123.
56. Aide-de camp P.P. Orlov, who was ultimately promoted to Major-General of the emperor's suite.
57. Spiridovitch, *Last Days*, Vol. I, pp. 55-57.
58. Coudert, "The Human Side of the Tsar," *Century Magazine*, Vol. LXXII. New York: The Century Co., 1906, p. 852. In addition to her paintings, Coudert is remembered for this specific article, in which she wrote about her experience painting Nicholas II and Alexandra, in March 1899. In significant detail, Coudert describes the royal lodgings, her interactions with the royal family and staff, and the process of painting their portraits, giving a rare glimpse into the personal lives of the family.
59. Fort Ino on Cape Inonemi, Finland.
60. Fabritsky, *Of Bygone Days*, p. 123.
61. Buxhoeveden, *Life and Tragedy*, p. 47.
62. Dehn, *The Real Tsaritsa*, p. 51.
63. *Ibid.*, p. 85.
64. Fabritsky, *Of Bygone Days*, p. 128.
65. See Spiridovitch, *Last Days*, Vol. I, p. 36.

66	Eagar, *Six Years at the Russian Court*, pp. 38 and 32.
67	Ashton, Janet, "God in All Things: The Religious Beliefs of Russia's Last Empress and Their Personal and Political Context," *Electronic British Library* (2006), art. 4, p. 11.
68	ГА РФ. Ф. 651. Оп. 1. Д. 55. Л.1-3об.
69	ГА РФ. Ф. 651. Оп. 1. Д. 56. Л. 4-5.
70	ГА РФ. Ф. 685. Оп. 1. Д. 37. Л. 25.
71	Venerable Simeon of Verkhoturie lived in the 17th century and is the patron of the Urals. His memory is celebrated on 18 December Old Style/31 December New Style.
72	Azar and Nicholson, *Tatiana Romanov*, pp. 151-152.
73	*Ibid.*, pp. 191-192.
74	Dehn, *The Real Tsaritsa*, p. 54.
75	*The Ladder of Divine Ascent* is an ascetical treatise on avoiding vice and practicing virtue so that at the end, salvation can be obtained. Written by Saint John the Sinaite (ca. 579-649) initially for monastics, it has become one of the most highly influential and important works used by the Orthodox Church as far as guiding the faithful to a God-centered life, second only to Holy Scripture.
76	Dehn, *The Real Tsaritsa*, p. 71.
77	See Vyrubova, *Memories of the Russian Court*, p. 15.
78	Spiridovitch, *Last Days*, Vol. I, p. 29.
79	Fabritsky, *Of Bygone Days*, p. 122.
80	Polsky, *The New Martyrs of Russia*, p. 117.
81	Acton, Cherniaev and Rosenberg, *A Critical Companion to the Russian Revolution, 1914-1921*, p. 416.
82	Saint Herman of Alaska Brotherhood, *The Royal Passion-bearers of Russia*, p. 10.
83	N.A. Motovilov (1809–1879), a hereditary noble and owner of estates in several provinces.
84	See *A conversation of Saint Seraphim of Sarov with N.A. Motovilov: A Wonderful Revelation to the World* Jordanville, New York: Holy Trinity Monastery, 1962.
85	Timofievich, Dr. A.P., "A Pilgrimage to Diveyevo," in Kontzevitch, *Saint Seraphim Wonderworker of Sarov*, p. 334.
86	The accounts that follow are from the personal recollections of two nuns who were novices in the Diveyevo Convent before it was closed by the Communists. The first, Nun Seraphima Bulgakova, reposed on March 4, 1991 at the age of 85, and the second, Nun Margarita Lakhtionovna, reposed on February 9, 1997 at the age of 98. See Kontzevitch, *Saint Seraphim Wonderworker of Sarov*, pp. 236-243; Damascene (Orlovsky), "Blessed Prascovia Ivanovna of Sarov," *New Confessors of Russia*, Vol. 1, pp. 260-263. Both Kontzevitch and Orlovsky draw much of their information from Летопись Серафимо-Дивеевского монастыря, by Metropolitan Seraphim Chichagov.
87	Kontzevitch, *Saint Seraphim Wonderworker of Sarov*, p. 241.
88	Born into a military family, Leonid Mikhailovich Chichagov enlisted as an

artillery officer after finishing his schooling. Influenced by his experiences in the Russo-Turkish War and meetings with John of Kronstadt, he resigned from the military and became a clergyman. Following the death of his wife, he became a monk at the Trinity Lavra of St Sergius and received the monastic name Seraphim. In 1928 he was appointed Metropolitan of Petrograd. He retired in 1933 due to age and ill health. Four years later, during Stalin's 'five-year plans of atheism' (1932-1937), he was arrested and sentenced to death by firing squad. He was executed on 11 December 1937 at the Butovo firing range and was one of the first to be canonized by the Church in the 1990s as a New Martyr. As a priest, Fr Chichagov made several pilgrimages to Diveyevo Monastery and the Sarov monastery in Sarov. During these visits he wrote a history of the Sarov monastery and a biography of the monk Seraphim of Sarov based on interviews with nuns who had known the saint. The book, entitled Летопись Серафимо-Дивеевского монастыря (Chronicles of Seraphim-Diveyevo Monastery), was published in 1903, saved from destruction by communists.

89 Kontzevitch, *Saint Seraphim Wonderworker of Sarov*, p. 241; see also: Damascene (Orlovsky), "Blessed Prascovia Ivanovna of Sarov," *New Confessors of Russia*, Vol. 1, pp. 261-262.

90 Damascene (Orlovsky), "Blessed Prascovia Ivanovna of Sarov," *New Confessors of Russia*, Vol. 1, p. 261.

91 Kontzevitch, *Saint Seraphim Wonderworker of Sarov*, p. 241; see also: Damascene (Orlovsky), "Blessed Prascovia Ivanovna of Sarov," *New Confessors of Russia*, Vol. 1, pp. 261-262.

92 Kontzevitch, *Saint Seraphim Wonderworker of Sarov*, p. 243; see also: Damascene (Orlovsky), "Blessed Prascovia Ivanovna of Sarov," *New Confessors of Russia*, Vol. 1, p. 262.

93 Damascene (Orlovsky), "Blessed Prascovia Ivanovna of Sarov," *New Confessors of Russia*, Vol. 1, p. 262.

94 Kontzevitch, *Saint Seraphim Wonderworker of Sarov*, p. 242.

95 *Ibid.*

96 Timofievich, Dr. A.P., "A Pilgrimage to Diveyevo," in Kontzevitch, *Saint Seraphim Wonderworker of Sarov*, pp. 333-335.

97 Dossier from the Third Department of His Imperial Majesty's Office: Titular-Councillor N.N. Motovilov's Report on the Prophecies of St Seraphim of Sarov, 1854. ГА РФ. Ф. 601. Оп. 1. Д. 2. Л. 1-2.

98 The closest term in English for "metochion" is "compound." A monastic metochion is a dependent monastery of a particular monastic community that is being given the blessing (permission) and support to develop into an autonomous monastery or a monastic society. The Russian term is подворье.

99 Kontzevitch, *Saint Seraphim Wonderworker of Sarov*, pp. 234-235.

NOTES

CHAPTER 3 – THE BEGINNING OF SORROWS

1. Witte, *Memoirs*, p. 250.
2. Mansergh, *The Coming of the First World War*, p. 103.
3. Мироненко, *Дневники императора Николая II, 1894–1918*, Том 1 (1894-1904), С. 787.
4. *Ibid.*
5. *Ibid.*
6. *Ibid.*, С. 788.
7. *Ibid.*
8. "Czar to appeal for the remains of Russian saint to turn the fortunes of his Manchurian legions", *The San Francisco Call*, May 7, 1905, p. 1.
9. Bing, *The Letters of Tsar Nicholas and Empress Marie*, p. 177. The italics are from the original.
10. Vorres, *The Last Grand Duchess*, p. 111.
11. Spiridovitch, *Histoire du Terrorisme Russe*, p. 207.
12. Vorres, *The Last Grand Duchess*, pp. 111-112.
13. Трусовой, *Начало первой русской революции*, С. 35.
14. Spiridovitch, *Histoire du Terrorisme Russe*, p. 215.
15. *Ibid*, p. 207.
16. Mazour, *Rise and Fall of the Romanovs*, p. 356.
17. Раппопорт С. А., *Мое знакомство с Г. Гапоном*, т. 5, pp. 327-365.
18. For the connection between Gapon and the Okhrana and the Socialist Revolutionary Party, as well as on his death, see also Ruud and Stepanov, *Fontanka 16*, pp. 141-142.
19. Мироненко, *Дневники императора Николая II, 1894–1918*, Том 2, Часть 1 (1905-1913), С. 15.
20. Buxhoeveden, *The Life and Tragedy*, pp. 108-109.
21. Седова, Яна, "В Плену Мифов и Стереотипов," *Наша Страна*, 17 July, 2010, pp. 1-2.
22. Pipes, *The Russian Revolution 1899-1919*, pp. 36-37.
23. Риазофор-Монах Анемподист, "Священномученик митрополит Владимир (Богоявленский) и борьба с революции," *Православная Жизнь*, 53, N 1 (636), January, 2003, pp. 2-10.
24. Izvolsky, *Recollections of a Foreign Minister*, pp. 208-210.
25. ГА РФ. Ф. 640. Оп. 1. Д. 2328. Л. 11-14 об.
26. Ольденбург, *Царствование Императора Николая II*, pp. 312-313.
27. Witte, *Memoirs*, p. 247; Pares, *The Fall of the Russian Monarchy*, pp. 85-86.
28. Spiridovitch, *Last Days*, Vol. I, p. 41.
29. Steinberg and Khrustalev, *The Fall of the Romanovs*, p. 10.
30. *Ibid.*, p. 11.
31. *Полное Собрание Законов Российской Империи*, Собрание третье, Т.25, Отд-ние 1, №26803, С. 754-755.
32. See Vyrubova, *Memories of the Russian Court*, p. 27.
33. Douglas, *Former People: The Last Days of the Russian Aristocracy*, p. 58.

34 Spiridovitch, *Last Days,* Vol. I, pp. 41-43.
35 Peter Stolypin, interview with Bernard Pares, published in *The Russian Review* (1913), retrieved from https://spartacus-educational.com/RUSduma.htm
36 Fischer, *The Life of Lenin,* p. 54.
37 One fact that stirs intense suspicions of the involvement of members of the Okhrana or even other government workers in the murder of Stolypin is the unprecedented summary judgement and execution of the murderer. The trial of twenty-year-old Dimitry Bogrov, who murdered Prime Minister Stolypin, took only six hours and his execution followed only three days later. In contrast, the murderer of Grand Duke Serge Alexandrovich, Ivan Kalyaev, was executed three months after his conviction, while the murderer of Plehve, the Minister of Justice, escaped execution completely and was condemned to hard labor. This sharp contrast in the handling of Bogrov easily gave the impression that keeping the murderer alive and prolonging the investigative process might have exposed some higher member, who had ties with the event of the assassination. Beyond these suspicions, however, there were also other facts which support the possibility of a wider conspiracy, which also included members of the Okhrana or the government. See Ruud and Stepanov, Fontanka 16, pp. 196-197, but also the entire chapter "The Assassination of Stolypin," pp. 173-200.
38 Мироненко, *Дневники императора Николая II, 1894–1918,* Том 1 (1894-1904), С. 817.
39 Spiridovitch, *Last Years,* p. 264.
40 "Czar Rewards Father John," *New York Times,* 27 August, 1904, p. 6.
41 "St. Seraphim's Gift", *The Washington Post,* July 14, 1907, p. 13.
42 Eagar, *Six Years at the Russian Court,* p. 282.
43 Мироненко, *Дневники императора Николая II, 1894–1918,* Том 1 (1894-1904), С. 824.
44 Vyrubova, *Memories of the Russian Court,* pp. 40-41.
45 Vorres, *The Last Grand Duchess,* pp. 115-116.
46 Spiridovitch, *Last Days,* Vol. I, p. 179.
47 *Ibid.,* p. 242.
48 *Ibid.,* p. 178.
49 *Ibid.,* pp. 30-31.
50 *Ibid.,* p. 343.
51 Buxhoeveden, *The Life and Tragedy,* p. 151.
52 Fabritsky, *Of Bygone Days,* p. 129.
53 Bing, *The Letters of Tsar Nicholas and Empress Marie,* pp. 276-277.
54 Buxhoeveden, *The Life and Tragedy,* p. 132.
55 *Ibid., p.* 132.
56 Vyrubova, *Memories of the Russian Court,* p. 93.
57 Gilliard, *Thirteen Years,* pp. 29-30.
58 Bing, *The Letters of Tsar Nicholas and Empress Marie,* p. 277.
59 Ashton, Janet, "God in All Things: The Religious Beliefs of Russia's Last Empress and Their Personal and Political Context," *Electronic British Library* (2006), art. 4, pp. 7 and 11.

60 Vorres, *The Last Grand Duchess*, p. 137.
61 Vyrubova, *Memories of the Russian Court*, p. 94.
62 Bing, *The Letters of Tsar Nicholas and Empress Marie*, p. 277.
63 Fabritsky, *Of Bygone Days*, p. 124.
64 Spiridovitch, *Last Days*, Vol. I, pp. 323-324.
65 Fabritsky, *Of Bygone Days*, pp. 126-127.
66 Шавельский, *Воспоминания*, Том II, С. 159-160.
67 Grand Duchess Militsa Nikolaevna was the sister of Grand Duchess Anastasia (Stana), wife of the cousin of the tsar, of the very tall Grand Duke Nicholas Nikolaevich, known as Nikolasha. The two sisters descended from Montenegro.
68 Мироненко, *Дневники императора Николая II, 1894–1918*, Том 2, Часть 1 (1905-1913), С. 68.
69 Cf. Luke 9:62.
70 ГА РФ. Ф. 601. Оп. 1. Д. 1254. Л. 24-34 об.
71 ГА РФ. Ф. 601. Оп. 1. Д. 1254. Л. 48-55 об.
72 ГА РФ. Ф. 601. Оп. 1. Д. 1254. Л. 56-57 об.
73 ГА РФ. Ф. 601. Оп. 1. Д. 1254. Л. 58-59 об.
74 This date is given in Almedingen's book, *An Unbroken Unity*, p. 63. Countess Olsoufieff gives the 2nd of April (1910) as the date of the tonsure, but it seems not to be correct, because Elisabeth's last letter to Nicholas before her tonsure was written on April 7.
75 Olsoufieff, *H.I.H The Grand Duchess Elisabeth*, pp. 6-7.
76 ГА РФ. Ф. 601. Оп. 1. Д. 1254. Л. 152-153 об.
77 ГА РФ. Ф. 601. Оп. 1. Д. 1254. Л. 105-106 об.
78 Vyrubova, *Memories of the Russian Court*, pp. 98-99.

CHAPTER 4 – MARCH TO THE END

1 From this point on, dates will be given according to the New Calendar because world historical events are known under these dates. Where, however, entries are listed from the diaries and correspondence of the Royal Martyrs, both dates will be given. A few individual exceptions will be indicated in the relevant notes.
2 Mitrovic, *Serbia's Great War: 1914-1918*, p. 46.
3 Gilliard, *Thirteen Years*, p. 142.
4 See Vyrubova, *Memories of the Russian Court*, p. 104. Rasputin encountered the same negative attitude from the royal couple towards his advice in other circumstances as well, as for example when he advised the empress to dismiss Dr Botkin on account of the hostility that the doctor nursed against him.
5 Lieven, *Towards the Flame*, p. 337.
6 Pares, *The Fall of the Russian Monarchy*, p. 195.
7 According to the Old Calendar it was the eve of 19 July.
8 Azar and Nicholson, *Tatiana Romanov*, p. 32.
9 Ryasa or riassa (Russian: ряса, from the the Greek ράσον) is the outer cassock,

a voluminous garment worn over the inner cassock by bishops, priests, deacons, and monastics as their regular outer wear. A Kalimavkion (Greek: καλυμμαύχιον), or, by metathesis of the word's internal syllables, kamilavka (Russian: камилавка), is worn by Orthodox Christian monks, nuns, and priests. The kalimavkion is a stiff cylindrical head covering, similar to a stovepipe hat but without a brim. The kalimavkion is worn during services; at other times, the softer skufia is worn in its place. The specific shape and coloring will differ between the various ethnic traditions.

10   Kontzevitch, *Saint Seraphim Wonderworker of Sarov,* p. 235.
11   See the section of this present work, "The Orthodox Tsar, Patron of the Church."
12   Мироненко, *Дневники императора Николая II, 1894–1918,* Том 2, Часть 2 (1914-1918), С. 47.
13   Gilliard, *Thirteen Years,* p. 105.
14   See *Начало войны 1914 г.,* Т.4, С. 3-62.
15   Gilliard, *Thirteen Years,* pp. 106-107.
16   The Patriotic War of 1812, when Russia defeated Napoleon.
17   Gilliard, *Thirteen Years,* pp. 110-111.
18   *Ibid.,* pp. 112-114.
19   Azar and Nicholson, *Tatiana Romanov,* p. 38, Footnote 55.
20   Gilliard, *Thirteen Years,* pp. 114-117.
21   Мироненко, *Дневники императора Николая II, 1894–1918,* Том 2, Часть 2 (1914-1918), С. 51-52.
22   Buxhoeveden, *The Life and Tragedy,* p. 197.
23   *Ibid., p.* 180.
24   "Znamenie" (Russian: знамение) is translated in English as "sign." The church was therefore dedicated to the Mother of God of the Sign (named after the words of Isaiah 7:14, "the Lord himself shall give you a sign; behold, a virgin shall conceive in the womb, and shall bring forth a son, and thou shalt call his name Emmanuel").
25   See Vyrubova, *Memories of the Russian Court,* p. 111.
26   *Ibid., p.* 110.
27   Azar and Nicholson, *Tatiana Romanov,* pp. 170-171.
28   The dates in the following citation are recorded based on the original, namely in accordance with the Old Calendar.
29   A moleben (Russian: Молебен) is a supplication prayer service (service of intercession, or service of supplication) in honor of either our Lord Jesus Christ, the Mother of God, or a particular saint or martyr. It is a Slavic service and it is usually served by an ordained priest, but laymen can also do a moleben, although in a modified form (Greeks have an analogous service, called the paraklesis; both are ultimately patterned on the Matins service).
30   *Ibid.,* pp. 80-82. Saint Joasaph of Belgorod lived in the 18th century. His canonization took place under Emperor Nicholas II, on 4 September 1911.
31   Buxhoeveden, *The Life and Tragedy,* pp. 196; 202.
32   *Ibid., p.* 194.

33 *Ibid.*, p. 126.
34 The dates in the following quotation are given as in the original, namely in accordance with the Old Calendar.
35 Azar and Nicholson, *Tatiana Romanov*, pp. 94, 101-102.
36 *Ibid.*, p. 92.
37 *Ibid.*, p. 120.
38 Azar, *Maria and Anastasia*, p. 17.
39 Her initials plus, possibly, initials of her nicknames.
40 *Ibid.*, p. 9.
41 *Ibid.*, pp. 16-17.
42 Azar and Nicholson, *Tatiana Romanov*, p. 78.
43 *Ibid.*, p. 155.
44 Gilliard, *Thirteen Years*, p. 130.
45 Luke 7:32.
46 Pares, *The Fall of the Russian Monarchy*, p. 232.
47 Gilliard, *Thirteen Years*, p. 137, Footnote 1.
48 Buxhoeveden, *The Life and Tragedy*, p. 208.
49 Мироненко, *Дневники императора Николая II, 1894–1918*, Том 2, Часть 2 (1914-1918), С. 146.
50 *Ibid.*, С. 149.
51 Gilliard, *Thirteen Years*, p. 139.
52 The day of his official assumption of duties as Commander-in-Chief.
53 Fuhrmann, *The Complete Wartime Correspondence*, p. 181.
54 See Алферьев, *Император Николай II как человек сильной воли*, С. 109; Записка генерала М. В. Алексеева Николаю II, ГА РФ. Ф. 601. Оп. 1. Д. 657. Л. 3; Бескровный, *Армия и флот России в начале XX века*, С. 90, 101-102, 110; Уткин, *Первая Мировая война*, С. 249; *Очерки истории Ленинграда*, Т.3, С. 934-937; Марков, *Русская армия 1914–1917*, С. 98, 194; Ипатьев, *Работа химической промышленности на оборону во время мировой войны*, С. 4; Лященко, *История народного хозяйства СССР*, Т.2, С. 606; Яковлев, *1 августа 1914*, С. 225-226.
55 Azar and Nicholson, *Tatiana Romanov*, p. 169.
56 Churchill, *The World Crisis 1916-1918*, Vol. 3, Part 1, pp. 102-103.
57 Fuhrmann, *The Complete Wartime Correspondence*, pp. 553-554.
58 Hanbury-Williams, *The Emperor Nicholas II as I Knew Him*, pp. 72-73.
59 *Ibid.*, pp. 62-63.
60 *Ibid.*, p. 83.
61 *Ibid.*, p. 67.
62 Lieven, *Towards the Flame*, p. 347.
63 See Мультатули, *Внешняя политика Императора Николая II: 1894-1917 гг. Этапы, достижения, итоги*, С. 650-651; *Международные отношения в эпоху империализма* (МОЭИ), Серия III. Т. 10, С. 2, 12.
64 "President recalls WW1 retreat, thanks Greece, other allies," retrieved from https://www.b92.net/eng/news/politics.php?yyyy=2016&mm=04&dd=18&nav_id=97720

65 Шумило & Сальник, "Нет больше той любви, как если кто положит душу свою за други своя," retrieved from http://catacomb.org.ua/modules.php?name=Pages&go=page&pid=966; See also, Patriarch Kirill, "The Fates of Russians and Serbs Have Been Intertwined by Divine Providence," at http://pravoslavie.ru/106399.html

66 Azar and Nicholson, *Tatiana Romanov,* p. 123.

67 Azar, *Maria and Anastasia,* p. 39.

68 *Ibid.,* p. 59

69 *Ibid.,* p. 100.

70 *Ibid.,* p. 53.

71 Vorres, *The Last Grand Duchess,* pp. 145-146.

72 Шереметев, *Изъ Воспоминаній о Государѣ Императорѣ Николаѣ II,* С. 11-14.

73 *Ibid.,* С. 14.

74 Buxhoeveden, *The Life and Tragedy,* p. 218.

75 Vyrubova, *Memories of the Russian Court,* pp. 131-132.

76 ГА РФ. Ф. 601. Оп. 1. Д. 1756. Л. 2.

77 Vyrubova, *Memories of the Russian Court,* p. 132.

78 Gilliard, *Thirteen Years,* p. 170, Footnote 1.

79 Fuhrmann, *The Complete Wartime Correspondence,* p. 577.

80 1 Peter 3:4.

81 In English it is rendered as "the Monastery of the Tithes."

82 Fuhrmann, *The Complete Wartime Correspondence,* p. 670.

83 Vyrubova, *Memories of the Russian Court,* p. 148.

84 Ludendorff, *My War Memories, 1914-1918,* Vol 2, p. 413.

85 Gilliard, *Thirteen Years,* p. 188, Footnote 1.

86 *Ibid.,* pp. 188-189.

87 Dehn, *The Real Tsaritsa,* p. 113.

88 It is a fact, as becomes apparent in their correspondence, that the relationship of Elisabeth with Nicholas and Alexandra suffered from their opposing views regarding Rasputin. However, this difference between them never became a cause for a definite rupture of the love between them. When she returned to Moscow, Elisabeth related the following to the Vicar Bishop of Moscow Athanasius, "That wretched man [Rasputin] wished to separate me from my family. Glory be to God; he did not succeed." See Almedingen, *An Unbroken Unity,* pp. 101–102.

89 Saint Elisabeth received a martyr's death at the hands of the Bolsheviks in the town of Alapaevsk in the Urals at the dawning of 18 July, 1918. Along with Saint Elisabeth, Nun Barbara Yakovlevna, three sons of Grand Duke Konstantin Konstantinovich (John, Konstantin, and Igor) Grand Duke Serge Mikhailovich, with his secretary and Prince Vladimir Paley, also met a martyr's death.

90 Joan of Arc (c. 1412 - 30 May 1431), in French Jeanne d'Arc, is considered a heroine of France for her role during the Lancastrian phase of the Hundred Years' War, and was canonized as a Roman Catholic saint, but not by the Orthodox Church.

NOTES

91 ГА РФ. Ф. 601. Оп. 1. Д. 1254. Л. 136-139 об.
92 Dehn, *The Real Tsaritsa*, p. 120.
93 Kerensky, *The Crucifixion*, p. 261.
94 Payne, *The Life and Death of Lenin*, p. 252.
95 Buxhoeveden, *The Life and Tragedy*, p. 246.
96 *Ibid.*
97 See Мельгунов, *На Путях к Дворцовому Перевороту*, С. 94-102.
98 Брачев, *Русское масонство XVIII-XX веков*, С. 299.
99 *Царственные мученики в воспоминаниях верноподданных*, С. 226.
100 Яковлев, *1 августа 1914*, С. 248.
101 Mikhail Tereshchenko was the chairman of the Military Industry Committee of the Kiev district and deputy chairman of the All-Russian Military Industry Committee. Aleksandr Mikhailovich Krymov was a Russian Imperial Lieutenant General, a military commander of Russo-Japanese War and World War I.
102 Смирнов, *Государственная Дума Российской империи, 1906-1917*, С. 529.
103 Anton Ivanovich Denikin was a Russian Lieutenant General in the Imperial Russian Army (1916) and afterwards a leading general of the White movement in the Russian Civil War.
104 See Деникин, *Очерки Русской смуты*, С. 106.
105 Лемке, *250 дней в Царской Ставке*, прим. 4 к гл. 3., С. 470.
106 Fuhrmann, *The Complete Wartime Correspondence*, p. 589.
107 *Ibid.*, p. 591.
108 See Деникин, *Очерки Русской смуты*, С. 107-108.
109 Andrei Ivanovich Shingaryov was a Russian doctor, publicist and politician. He was a Duma deputy and one of the leaders of the Constitutional Democratic party.
110 Родзянко, *Государственная Дума и Февральская 1917 года революция. // Архив Русской революции (АРР)*, Т. 6., С. 75.
111 Данилов, *Великий Князь Николай Николаевич*, С. 158.
112 Fuhrmann, *The Complete Wartime Correspondence*, p. 643.
113 Данилов, *Великий Князь Николай Николаевич*, С. 316.
114 Мельгунов, *На Путях к Дворцовому Перевороту*, С. 106.
115 *Ibid.*, С. 109, 258.
116 See *Ibid.*
117 Nikolai Nikolaevich Yanushkevich was a Russian General who served as Chief of Staff of the General Headquarters (Stavka) of the Imperial Russian Army from August 1914 to September 1915. He was dismissed from his post in September 1915 as Tsar Nicholas II took personal charge of the Russian armies with M. V. Alekseev as his Chief of Staff. At the insistence of Grand Duke Nikolai Nikolaevich, Yanushkevich continued to serve as his chief-of-staff after the latter's dismissal as Supreme Commander and appointment to the post of Viceroy of the Caucasus.
118 Мельгунов, *На Путях к Дворцовому Перевороту*, С. 161.
119 See *Ibid.*

120 Vladimir Iosifovich Gurko was a Russian government official and a member of the Russian Assembly, a right-wing party. Since 1906, as an Assistant minister of Interior, he worked with ministers Pyotr Durnovo and Pyotr Stolypin.
121 Кобылий, *Анатомия измены*, С. 122.
122 Dehn, *The Real Tsaritsa*, p. 139.
123 *Отречение Николая II, Воспоминания очевидцев*, С. 85.
124 Воейков, *Со царем и без царя*, С. 120.
125 ГА РФ. Ф. 1807. Оп. 1. Д. 278. Л. 1.
126 ГА РФ. Ф. 1807. Оп. 1. Д. 248. Л. 2.
127 Керенский, "Россия на историческом повороте", *Вопросы истории*, 1990, №6, С. 148 (Сноска 10); С 118.
128 ГА РФ. Ф. 102. ДП ОО. 1917 (247). Д. 307. ЛА. Л. 109.
129 See Николаев, "Кто профинансировал Февральскую революцию", *Национальные интересы*, №2, 2007.
130 See Керенский, "Россия на историческом повороте", *Вопросы истории*, 1990, №6, С. 133.
131 Холяев, "Три февраля 1917 года", *Вопросы истории*, 2003, №7, С 26-38.
132 Платонов, *Николай Второй. Жизнь и царствование*, С. 413
133 Fuhrmann, *The Complete Wartime Correspondence*, p. 696.
134 Steinberg and Khrustalev, *The Fall of the Romanovs*, "Document 6", pp. 76-77.
135 Nikolai Aleksandrovich Artabalevsky was Colonel of the Life Guards 2nd Tsarskoe Selo Infantry Regiment.
136 Верцинский, *Памятные дни*, С. 40-41.
137 ГА РФ. Ф. 601. Оп.1. Д. 2109. Л. 126.
138 Хрусталёв, *Великий Князь Михаил Александрович*, С. 348.
139 Dehn, *The Real Tsaritsa*, pp. 148-149.
140 Воейков, *Со царем и без царя*, С. 126.
141 Мироненко, *Дневники императора Николая II, 1894–1918*, Том 2, Часть 2 (1914-1918), С. 295.
142 Alexander Alexandrovich Bublikov was a railway engineer, from the Perm province, member of the 4th State Duma. He played an important role in the capture of the Sovereign's train and was among the commissars of the Provisional Government, who arrested the Sovereign on May 8, 1917 in Mogilev.
143 Nikolai Vissarionovich Nekrasov was a Russian liberal politician and the last Governor-General of Finland. Nekrasov became a member of the Provisional Committee of the State Duma on February 27, 1917.
144 Брачев, *Русское масонство XVIII-XX веков*, С. 305.
145 Архив Русской революции (АРР), Т. 3-4, С. 252.
146 Gilliard, *Thirteen Years*, p. 211.
147 Dehn, *The Real Tsaritsa*, p. 155.
148 *Ibid.*, p. 158.
149 *Ibid.*
150 Катков, *Февральская революция*, С. 418.
151 *Отречение Николая II, Воспоминания очевидцев*, С. 104.
152 Steinberg and Khrustalev, *The Fall of the Romanovs*, p. 60.

NOTES

153 ГА РФ. Ф. 601. Оп. 1. Д. 2102. Л. 1.
154 Damascene (Orlovsky), "Blessed Prascovia Ivanovna of Sarov", *New Confessors of Russia*, Vol. 1, pp. 261.
155 Dehn, *The Real Tsaritsa*, pp. 194-195.
156 Steinberg and Khrustalev, *The Fall of the Romanovs*, p. 61.
157 Gilliard, *Thirteen Years*, p. 195.
158 Steinberg and Khrustalev, *The Fall of the Romanovs*, pp. 61, 97.
159 Pares, *The Fall of the Russian Monarchy*, p. 467.
160 Steinberg and Khrustalev, *The Fall of the Romanovs*, Document 26: "Nicholas II's manifesto of abdication from the throne, 2 March 1917", pp. 100-102; See also: Pares, *The Fall of the Russian Monarchy*, pp. 467-468.
161 Pares, *The Fall of the Russian Monarchy*, p. 468.
162 Мироненко, *Дневники императора Николая II, 1894–1918*, Том 2, Часть 2 (1914-1918), С. 296.
163 Shakespeare, *The Tragedy of King Richard II*, Act III, Sc. ii, 54-57, p. 62.
164 Dehn, *The Real Tsaritsa*, p. 163.
165 Michailitschenko, *The Romanovs Under House Arrest*, pp. 15-16.
166 Vyrubova, *Memories of the Russian Court*, p. 209.
167 Воейков, *Со царем и без царя*, С. 190.
168 Dehn, *The Real Tsaritsa*, p. 165.
169 Buxhoeveden, *The Life and Tragedy*, pp. 261-262.
170 Dehn, *The Real Tsaritsa*, p. 191.
171 Note dated 13/26 March 1917. ГА РФ. Ф. 683. Оп. 1. Д. 7. Л. 6 об.
172 Dehn, *The Real Tsaritsa*, p. 174.
173 Buxhoeveden, *The Life and Tragedy*, p. 264.
174 Родзянко, *Государственная Дума и Февральская 1917 года революция*. // Архив Русской революции (АРР), Т. 6., С. 75.
175 Деникин, *Очерки Русской смуты*, С. 130-131.
176 Benckendorff, *Last Days*, p. 38.
177 Dehn, *The Real Tsaritsa*, p. 177. She echoes the words of the Lord from the Cross, "Father forgive them, for they know not what they do" (Luke 23:34), and the first martyr, St Stephen, "Lord, lay not this sin to their charge" (Acts 7:60).
178 Gilliard, *Thirteen Years*, p. 214.
179 *Ibid.*, pp. 214-215.
180 ГА РФ. Ф. 5827. Оп. 1. Д. 10. Л. 1.
181 Dehn, *The Real Tsaritsa*, pp. 193-194.
182 Paleologue, *An Ambassador's Memoirs*, Vol I, p. 98. The biblical quote is *Job* 3:25: "For the thing which I greatly feared is come upon me, and that which I was afraid of is come unto me" (KJV or AV, following the Hebrew); or, "For the fear which I feared hath come upon me: and that which I was afraid of, hath befallen me" (Douay-Rheims following the Latin Vulgate and the Greek Septuagint).

NOTES

CHAPTER 5 – THE PALACE PRISON

1. Benckendorff, *Last Days*, p. 43.
2. Vyrubova, *Memories of the Russian Court*, p. 213.
3. *Ibid.*, p. 222.
4. Gilliard, *Thirteen Years*, p. 228.
5. *Ibid.*, p. 216.
6. *Ibid.*, p. 225.
7. *Ibid.*, p. 221.
8. ГА РФ. Ф. 640. Оп. 2. Д. 38. "Schwibz" was a teasing nickname for Anastasia of German origin, from the word "Beschwipst," which means "tipsy." It is sometimes written as "Schwibsik." The Russian has it as follows: Швыбз and Швыбзик.
9. Buxhoeveden, *The Life and Tragedy*, p. 263.
10. Dehn, *The Real Tsaritsa*, p. 199.
11. Buxhoeveden, *The Life and Tragedy*, p. 296.
12. The Epitaphios (Greek: Επιτάφιος, Slavonic: Плащаница) is an icon, today most often on a large cloth, embroidered and often richly adorned, which is used during the services of Great Friday and Holy Saturday. The icon depicts Christ after he has been removed from the cross, lying supine, as his body is being prepared for burial.
13. Olga suffered a relapse after her first recovery from the measles.
14. Michailitschenko, *The Romanovs Under House Arrest*, p. 24.
15. *Ibid.*, pp. 25-26.
16. Gilliard, *Thirteen Years*, pp. 224-225.
17. Benckendorff, *Last Days at Tsarskoye Selo*. Ontario: Gilbert's Books, 2012, p. 44.
18. Matthew 26:41.
19. "Miracles of the Royal Martyrs," *The Orthodox Word*, #202. Platina, California: Saint Herman of Alaska Brotherhood, 1998, p. 217.
20. Michailitschenko, *The Romanovs Under House Arrest*, p. 51.
21. *Ibid.*, pp. 21-22.
22. *Ibid.*, p. 51.
23. *Ibid.*, p. 47.
24. *Ibid.*, p. 38.
25. *Ibid.*, pp. 37-38.
26. *Ibid.*, p. 43.
27. Kerensky, *The Crucifixion*, pp. 162-163.
28. Benckendorff, *Last Days*, pp. 55-56.
29. *Ibid.*
30. *Ibid.*, p. 59.
31. Kerensky, *The Catastrophe*, pp. 263-265.
32. Dehn, *The Real Tsaritsa*, p. 210.
33. *Ibid.*, pp. 210-211.
34. Vyrubova, *Memories of the Russian Court*, p. 225.

35 Dehn, *The Real Tsaritsa*, p. 215.
36 Kerensky, *The Crucifixion*, p. 171.
37 Buxhoeveden, *The Life and Tragedy*, pp. 300-301.
38 Gilliard, *Thirteen Years*, pp. 217-218.
39 Kerensky, *The Catastrophe*, p. 259.
40 A French radical politician, one of the most important figures of the French Revolution.
41 Kerensky, *The Crucifixion*, p. 161.
42 Vidal, *Palimpsest*, pp. 207-208.
43 Dehn, *The Real Tsaritsa*, p. 198.
44 Бандиленко, *Первая мировая*, Star Media, Сер. 8.
45 Fischer, *The Life of Lenin*, p. 108.
46 Churchill, *The World Crisis, The Aftermath*, Vol. 4, p. 73.
47 Benckendorff, *Last Days*, p. 98.
48 Kerensky and Bulygin, *The Murder of the Romanovs*, p. 121.
49 Kobylinsky, "The Depositions of Colonel Kobylinski" in R. Wilton, *The Last Days*, p. 182.
50 Benckendorff, *Last Days*, p. 103.
51 Kobylinsky, "The Depositions of Colonel Kobylinski" in R. Wilton, *The Last Days*, p. 183 and 189.
52 Kerensky and Bulygin, *The Murder of the Romanovs*, p. 129.
53 Kobylinsky, "The Depositions of Colonel Kobylinski" in R. Wilton, *The Last Days*, p. 184.
54 Very soon, in May 1918, Michael would be the first Romanov to be murdered by the Bolsheviks.
55 "Переписка Царственныхъ Мучениковъ съ Вел. Кн. Ксеніей Александровной", *Православная Жизнь*, Jordanville, New York: Holy Trinity Russian Orthodox Monastery, Вып. 1, January 1961, pp. 7-9.
56 Dehn, *The Real Tsaritsa*, pp. 239-240.
57 Volkov, *Memories*, at http://www.alexanderpalace.org/volkov/16.html
58 Vyrubova, *Memories of the Russian Court*, p. 305.
59 *Ibid.*, pp. 335-336.
60 Vasily Semenovich Pankratov, prior to the Revolution, spent many years of his life in prison and in exile for revolutionary action.
61 Luke 2:14.
62 Панкратов, *С царем в Тобольске*, С. 18-19.
63 The Old Calendar date is used here on account of the feast. The corresponding date according to the New Calendar is 21 September 1917.
64 Gilliard, *Thirteen Years*, pp. 241-242.
65 "Переписка Царственныхъ Мучениковъ съ Вел. Кн. Ксеніей Александровной", *Православная Жизнь*, Jordanville, New York: Holy Trinity Russian Orthodox Monastery, Вып. 1, January 1961, p. 7.
66 Azar, *Maria and Anastasia*, p. 158.
67 Vyrubova, *Memories of the Russian Court*, pp. 298-299.
68 *Ibid.*, p. 303.

69 *Ibid.*, p. 314.
70 *Ibid.*, p. 312.
71 Gilliard, *Thirteen Years*, p. 242.
72 Gilliard's nickname.
73 Azar and Eva & Dan McDonald, *Russia's Last Romanovs,* p. 96.
74 Gilliard, *Thirteen Years*, p. 254.
75 Kobylinsky, "The Depositions of Colonel Kobylinski" in R. Wilton, *The Last Days*, pp. 188-189.
76 Angelis, *Empress Alexandra Feodorovna, Her Diaries: 1917&1918,* Entry of December 24, 1917.
77 Kobylinsky, "The Depositions of Colonel Kobylinski" in R. Wilton, *The Last Days*, p. 195.
78 Angelis, *Empress Alexandra Feodorovna, Her Diaries: 1917&1918,* Entry of December 25, 1917.
79 Dehn, *The Real Tsaritsa*, p. 245.
80 Tsar-Martyr Nicholas II And His Family," St Nicholas Russian Orthodox Church, McKinney, Texas, at https://www.orthodox.net/russiannm/nicholas-ii-tsar-martyr-and-his-family.html
81 Vyrubova, *Memories of the Russian Court,* pp. 311-312.
82 *Ibid.*, p. 316.
83 *Ibid.*, p. 313.
84 Florinsky, *Russia: A History and an Interpretation*, Vol. II, p. 1445.
85 Kobylinsky, "The Depositions of Colonel Kobylinski" in R. Wilton, *The Last Days*, pp. 197-198.
86 *Ibid.*, p. 198.
87 Buxhoeveden, *The Life and Tragedy,* p. 323.
88 Vyrubova, *Memories of the Russian Court,* p. 305.
89 *Ibid.*, pp. 333-334.
90 *Ibid.*, p. 315.
91 *Ibid.*, p. 298.
92 *Ibid.*, p. 312.
93 *Ibid.*, p. 313.
94 *Ibid.*, p. 334.
95 *Ibid.*, p. 315.
96 *Ibid.*, p. 303.
97 *Ibid.*, p. 299.
98 *Ibid.*, pp. 329-330.
99 Мироненко, *Дневники императора Николая II, 1894–1918,* Том 2, Часть 2 (1914-1918), С. 413.
100 Gilliard, *Thirteen Years*, p. 256.
101 It must be mentioned that various attempts to free the family that took place within Russia during this time foundered on one more serious obstacle: Lieutentant B. S. Soloviev. Alexis Volkov says regarding this, "Soloviev married the daughter of Rasputin and by reason of this marriage succeeded in penetrating into the midst of the monarchists. His sole purpose was to

extract money from the monarchists by staging a supposed 'rescue' of their Majesties in Tobolsk. In reality he did not have any plan for rescue." Tatiana Melnik-Botkina, daughter of the martyred Doctor Eugene Botkin, accused Soloviev of wasting precious time and of betrayal of the Royal family. Soloviev as "head" of this non-existent group compelled all the monarchists to resort to him, both officers and others, and he deceived them, keeping them idle for entire months. All those who did not conform to his orders he betrayed to the Bolsheviks and they paid with their lives for their disobedience. See Volkov, *Memories*, at http://www.alexanderpalace.org/volkov/16.html

102 For a complete account of the matter regarding various plans for rescuing the royal family, both by monarchist factions within Russia as well as the royal relatives of the Romanovs in European scene and background, see the entire study by Helen Rappaport, *The Race to Save the Romanovs: The Truth Behind the Secret Plans to Rescue Russia's Imperial Family,* London: Hutchinson, 2018.
103 Gilliard, *Thirteen Years*, p. 256.
104 *Ibid.*
105 Панкратов, *С царем в Тобольске,* С. 54-55.
106 Мироненко, *Дневники императора Николая II, 1894–1918,* Том 2, Часть 2 (1914-1918), С. 414.
107 *Ibid.*
108 Vyrubova, *Memories of the Russian Court,* pp. 335-336.
109 Azar, *Maria and Anastasia*, p. 165.
110 Vyrubova, *Memories of the Russian Court,* pp. 341-342.
111 Azar, *Maria and Anastasia*, p. 165.
112 Trewin, *The House of Special Purpose,* p. 95.
113 Vyrubova, *Memories of the Russian Court,* p. 341.
114 Мироненко, *Дневники императора Николая II, 1894–1918,* Том 2, Часть 2 (1914-1918), С. 418.
115 *Ibid.,* С. 419.
116 Gilliard, *Thirteen Years,* p. 259.
117 Kobylinsky, "The Depositions of Colonel Kobylinski" in R. Wilton, *The Last Days,* p. 205.
118 Gilliard, *Thirteen Years,* p. 257.
119 Kerensky and Bulygin, *The Murder of the Romanovs,* p. 202.
120 Gilliard, *Thirteen Years,* p. 257.
121 *Ibid.,* p. 261.
122 *Ibid.,* p. 262.
123 Rappaport, *Four Sisters,* p. 360.
124 Trewin, *The House of Special Purpose,* p. 98.
125 Azar and Eva & Dan McDonald, *Russia's Last Romanovs,* p. 110.
126 *Ibid.*
127 Eugenie de Greece, *Le tsarevich: Enfant Martyr,* pp. 251-252.
128 Воспоминания В.В. Яковлева (Стоянович-Мячин, «Антон»), «Перевозка Николая Романова из Тобольска в Екатеринбург» [5 сентября 1929], ГА РФ. Ф. 601. Оп. 2. Д. 31. Л. 26-73, 75-81 об.

	129	Мельникъ, *Воспоминанiя о царской семье и ея жизни до и послѣ революцiи*, Бѣлградъ: Стефановичъ и ко., 1921, С. 58.
	130	ГА РФ. Ф. 1235. Оп. 34 Д. 36 Л. 7-13.
	131	ГА РФ. Ф. 601. Оп. 2. Д. 33. Л. 1.
	132	ГА РФ. Ф. 601. Оп. 2. Д. 33. Л. 44-48.
	133	ГА РФ. Ф. 130. Оп. 2. Д. 1109. Л. 54-55 об.
	134	*Ibid.*
	135	ГА РФ. Ф. 601. Оп. 2. Д. 32. Л. 17 об., 88 об., 99-100.
	136	ГА РФ. Ф. 601. Оп. 2. Д. 32. Л. 2.
	137	ГА РФ. Ф. 601. Оп. 2. Д. 32. Л. 7.
	138	ГА РФ. Ф. 601. Оп. 2. Д. 27. Л. 5.
	139	ГА РФ. Ф. 130. Оп. 2. Д. 1109. Л. 22.
	140	ГА РФ. Ф. 601. Оп. 2. Д. 32. Л. 71.
	141	ГА РФ. Ф. 130. Оп. 2. Д. 1109. Л. 16-16 об.
	142	*Ibid.*
	143	*Ibid.*

CHAPTER 6 – THE CHAPTER OF BLOOD

1. Воспоминания В.В. Яковлева (Стоянович-Мячин, «Антон»), «Перевозка Николая Романова из Тобольска в Екатеринбург» [5 сентября 1929], ГА РФ. Ф. 601. Оп. 2. Д. 31. Л. 26-73, 75-81 об.
2. Мироненко, *Дневники императора Николая II, 1894–1918*, Том 2, Часть 2 (1914-1918), С. 422.
3. Жук, *Исповедь цареубийц*, С. 472; 468.
4. Воспоминания красногвардейца караульной команды дома Ипатьева А.А. Стрекотина о расстреле царской семьи [1934], ЦДООСО Ф. 221 Оп. 2. Д. 849. Л. 3.
5. Azar and Eva & Dan McDonald, *Russia's Last Romanovs*, pp. 127-128.
6. Despite the fact that this letter was written on Great Wednesday, Maria begins with the Paschal greeting, knowing that by the time the letter reaches the children it would already be Pascha.
7. She means herself.
8. Azar and Eva & Dan McDonald, *Russia's Last Romanovs*, pp. 106-107.
9. Мироненко, *Дневники императора Николая II, 1894–1918*, Том 2, Часть 2 (1914-1918), С. 421.
10. Gilliard, *Thirteen Years*, p. 264.
11. *Ibid.*
12. Kobylinsky, "The Depositions of Colonel Kobylinski" in R. Wilton, *The Last Days*, p. 210.
13. Azar and Nicholson, *Tatiana Romanov*, p. 224.
14. Мироненко, *Дневники императора Николая II, 1894–1918*, Том 2, Часть 2 (1914-1918), С. 422.
15. Соколов, *Предварительное следствие, 1919-1922 гг.*, Российский Архив.

Вып. VIII, С. 112.
16 Gilliard, *Thirteen Years*, p. 264.
17 Azar and Nicholson, *Tatiana Romanov*, pp. 224-225.
18 Gilliard, *Thirteen Years*, p. 264.
19 Azar and Nicholson, *Tatiana Romanov*, p. 224.
20 Azar, *Maria and Anastasia*, p. 169.
21 *Ibid.*, pp. 170-173.
22 Azar and Nicholson, *Tatiana Romanov*, pp. 225-226.
23 Eugenie de Greece, *Le tsarevich: Enfant Martyr*, p. 277.
24 Massie, *The Last Diary of Tsaritsa Alexandra*, p. 120.
25 ГА РФ. Ф. 673. Оп. 1. Д. 74. Л. 1. The proper form would be: "Thanks [for the] letters. All [is] well [here]. [The] Little One [has] already been [in the] garden. We are writing [to you]. Olga."
26 Azar and Nicholson, *Tatiana Romanov*, pp. 226-227.
27 Росс, *Гибель царской семьи*, С. 368.
28 Жук, *Исповедь цареубийц*, С. 476.
29 Azar, *Maria and Anastasia*, p. 176.
30 *Ibid.*, p. 180.
31 Azar, *Maria and Anastasia*, p. 179.
32 Мироненко, *Дневники императора Николая II, 1894–1918*, Том 2, Часть 2 (1914-1918), С 425-426.
33 Volkov, *Memories*, at http://www.alexanderpalace.org/volkov/19.html
34 Kobylinsky, "The Depositions of Colonel Kobylinski" in R. Wilton, *The Last Days*, p. 213.
35 Volkov, *Memories*, at http://www.alexanderpalace.org/volkov/19.html
36 *Ibid.*
37 Buxhoeveden, *Left Behind*, pp. 68-69.
38 *Ibid.*
39 Мироненко, *Дневники императора Николая II, 1894–1918*, Том 2, Часть 2 (1914-1918), С. 426.
40 *Ibid.*
41 Buxhoeveden, *Left Behind*, p. 75.
42 *Ibid.*
43 Gilliard, *Thirteen Years*, p. 269.
44 Speranski, *La 'Maison à destination spéciale,'* pp. 158-160.
45 Gilliard, *Thirteen Years*, pp. 269-270.
46 Мироненко, *Дневники императора Николая II, 1894–1918*, Том 2, Часть 2 (1914-1918), С. 426.
47 Radzinsky, *The Last Tsar*, pp. 286-287.
48 Buxhoeveden, *Left Behind*, p. 71.
49 Мироненко, *Дневники императора Николая II, 1894–1918*, Том 2, Часть 2 (1914-1918), С. 427.
50 Speranski, *La 'Maison à destination spéciale,'* p. 166.
51 Жук, *Исповедь цареубийц*, p. 475.
52 Massie, *The Last Diary of Tsaritsa Alexandra*, p. 138.

53 Strekotin is mistaken on two points: Alexis did not have black (or dark), but blue eyes, and his wound did not happen before the Revolution, but in Tobolsk, and he incurred a second trauma there in Ekaterinburg.

54 Воспоминания красногвардейца караульной команды дома Ипатьева А.А. Стрекотина о расстреле царской семьи [1934], ЦДООСО Ф. 221 Оп. 2. Д. 849. Л. 5-6.

55 Материалы следственного дела об убийстве императорской семьи в Екатеринбурге и Алапаевске, ГА РФ. Ф. 601. Оп. 2. Д. 51. Л. 18.

56 Жук, *Исповедь цареубийц*, p. 475.

57 The Typica [Russian: Обѣдница] are normally served between the services of the Sixth and the Ninth Hours, while during Great Lent it is served immediately after the end of the Ninth Hour. This service which is found in the Great Horologion [Book of Hours] is intended to be held only on days when there is not a Divine Liturgy. When the Divine Liturgy is held, the service of Typica is either omitted or incorporated into the Liturgy as the First, Second and Third Antiphons under the name of Typica and Beatitudes. In the text, the proper term of "Typica" will be used instead of "Obednitsa."

58 When Fr John saw the girls, only one year had passed since they had shaved their heads in Tsarskoe Selo on account of their infection with measles.

59 Testimony of Archpriest Ioann Storozhev, in Н. А. Соколов, *Дело об убийстве царской семьи в Екатеринбурге, 1918-1919*, pp. 71-82. *Agnes M. Diterichs Papers 1919-1922*, Box 1, Folder 6. Jordanville, New York: Holy Trinity Orthodox Seminary.

60 The Communist authorities closed the monastery in the 1920s. A long period of complete abandonment and ruin then followed. Finally, in 1994, the Holy Synod of the Russian Church granted approval for the renovation and reopening of the monastery. Today the monastery serves Liturgy regularly and is a great pilgrimage center to which hundreds of faithful come, especially to venerate the wonder-working icon of the Mother of God of Tikhvin.

61 Abbess Magdalena has been included in the Calendar of Saints of the Church as Venerable Abbess Magdalena the Confessor. Her memory is celebrated on 16 July Old Style, 29 July New Style.

62 In their depositions, the nuns reported the events giving dates in the Old Calendar. Here the New Calendar dates are given in square brackets for better chronological flow of the text.

63 Traditional Russian baked goods: пироги (pies), ватрушки (cheese breads).

64 Росс, *Гибель царской семьи*, p. 390-391.

65 *Ibid.*, p. 393.

66 Жук, *Исповедь цареубийц*, p. 472.

67 Запись беседы с И.И. Родзинским о расстреле царской семьи, сделанная в Радиокомитете по распоряжению ЦК КПСС, РГАСПИ. Ф. 588. Оп. 3. Д. 14. Л. 26.

68 Speranski, *La 'Maison à destination spéciale,'* p. 51.

69 Жук, *Исповедь цареубийц*, p. 477.

70 *Ibid.*

NOTES

71 Speranski, *La 'Maison à destination spéciale,'* pp. 49-50.
72 *Ibid.*, p. 52.
73 Жук, *Исповедь цареубийц*, р. 477.
74 Воспоминания красногвардейца караульной команды дома Ипатьева А.А. Стрекотина о расстреле царской семьи [1934], ЦДООСО Ф. 221 Оп. 2. Д. 849. Л. 5.
75 Radzinsky, *The Last Tsar*, p. 291.
76 Жук, *Исповедь цареубийц*, р. 477.
77 Speranski, *La 'Maison à destination spéciale,'* p. 55.
78 Жук, *Исповедь цареубийц*, р. 477.
79 Speranski, *La 'Maison à destination spéciale,'* pp. 55-56.
80 Жук, *Исповедь цареубийц*, р. 477.
81 Speranski, *La 'Maison à destination spéciale,'* p. 201.
82 *Ibid.*, p. 34.
83 *Ibid.*, 56-57.
84 Воспоминания красногвардейца караульной команды дома Ипатьева А.А. Стрекотина о расстреле царской семьи [1934], ЦДООСО Ф. 221 Оп. 2. Д. 849. Л. 6-7.
85 Speranski, *La 'Maison à destination spéciale,'* p. 50.
86 Соколов, *Предварительное следствие, 1919-1922 гг.*, Российский Архив. Вып. VIII, Док. 26. С. 90.
87 *Ibid.*, Док. 78. С. 292-293.
88 Speranski, *La 'Maison à destination spéciale,'* p. 57.
89 *Ibid.*, p. 58.
90 *Ibid.*, p. 57.
91 Right across the street from the Ipatiev House was the Church of the Ascension, which was celebrating on its feast day.
92 Мироненко, *Дневники императора Николая II, 1894–1918*, Том 2, Часть 2 (1914-1918), С. 430.
93 ГА РФ. Ф. 601. Оп. 2. Д. 27. Л. 25-26.
94 Мироненко, *Дневники императора Николая II, 1894–1918*, Том 2, Часть 2 (1914-1918), С. 431.
95 Kerensky, *The Crucifixion*, p. 172.
96 Steinberg and Khrustalev, *The Fall of the Romanovs*, p. 13.
97 Жук, *Исповедь цареубийц*, р. 478.
98 Росс, *Гибель царской семьи*, р. 392.
99 Мельник-Боткина, *Воспоминания о царской семье*, р. 130. [Tr. Note: This is a different edition of the same book from that cited in the previous quote]
100 Testimony of Archpriest Ioann Storozhev, in Н. А. Соколов, *Дело об убийстве царской семьи в Екатеринбурге, 1918-1919*, pp. 71-82. *Agnes M. Diterichs Papers 1919-1922*, Box 1, Folder 6. Jordanville, New York: Holy Trinity Orthodox Seminary.
101 Жук, *Исповедь цареубийц*, р. 474.
102 Testimony of Archpriest Ioann Storozhev, in Н. А. Соколов, *Дело об убийстве царской семьи в Екатеринбурге, 1918-1919*, pp. 71-82. *Agnes M. Diterichs*

Papers 1919-1922, Box 1, Folder 6. Jordanville, New York: Holy Trinity Orthodox Seminary.
103 Росс, *Гибель царской семьи*, p. 391.
104 Speranski, *La 'Maison à destination spéciale,'* pp. 117-124.
105 ГА РФ. Ф. 130. Оп. 2. Д. 653. Л. 12.
106 Жук, *Исповедь цареубийц*, p. 479.
107 Massie, *The Last Diary of Tsaritsa Alexandra*, p. 198.
108 Жук, *Исповедь цареубийц*, p. 478.
109 Massie, *The Last Diary of Tsaritsa Alexandra*, p. 198.
110 McCullagh, *A Prisoner of the Reds*, p. 129.
111 Протокол допроса бывшего охранника Ипатьевского дома П. С. Медведева, *Гибель царской семьи*, С. 231.
112 Воспоминания П.З. Ермакова, «Расстрел бывшего царя», ЦДООСО. Ф. 221. Оп. 2. Д. 774. Л. 7-12.
113 Из рассказа Я.М. Юровского о расстреле царской семьи на совещании старых большевиков в г. Свердловске [1 февраля 1934 г.], ЦДООСО. Ф. 41. Оп. 1. Д. 151. Л. 10-22.
114 Воспоминания коменданта дома Ипатьева Я.М. Юровского, «Последний царь нашел свое место», [Апрель-май 1922], АП РФ. Ф. 3. Оп. 58. Д. 280. Л. 12.
115 Из рассказа Я.М. Юровского о расстреле царской семьи на совещании старых большевиков в г. Свердловске [1 февраля 1934 г.], ЦДООСО. Ф. 41. Оп. 1. Д. 151. Л. 10-22.
116 Воспоминания коменданта дома Ипатьева Я.М. Юровского «Последний царь нашел свое место», [Апрель-май 1922], АП РФ. Ф. 3. Оп. 58. Д. 280. Л. 12.
117 The information for the following passages regarding the martyrdom of the Royal Martyrs and their servants are taken exclusively from the memoirs and depositions of the murderers and the Ipatiev guards, as well as from the forensic investigations and studies of the remains. The sources of the depositions and memoirs that are used here are the following (for the English translations of the sources' titles see Bibliography):
— Записка коменданта дома Ипатьева Я.М. Юровского о расстреле царской семьи и о попытках спрятать трупы [1920-е гг.], ЦДООСО Ф. 221 Оп. 2. Д. 497. 9-15.
— Воспоминания коменданта дома Ипатьева Я.М. Юровского, «Последний царь нашел свое место» [Апрель-май 1922], АП РФ. Ф. 3. Оп. 58. Д. 280. Л. 2-22.
— Из рассказа Я.М. Юровского о расстреле царской семьи на совещании старых большевиков в г. Свердловске [1 февраля 1934 г.], ЦДООСО. Ф. 41. Оп. 1. Д. 151. Л. 10-22.
— Медведев, М.А. (Кудрин), Расстрел царской семьи Романовых в Екатеринбурге в ночь на 17 июля 1918 г., [1963], РГАСПИ. Ф. 588. Оп. 3с. Д. 12. Л. 39-58; Воспоминания М.А. Медведева (Кудрина) о расстреле царской семьи [1957], РГАСПИ. Ф. 588. Оп. 3с. Д. 12. Л. 1-36.

— Протокол допроса бывшего охранника Ипатьевского дома П.С. Медведева членом Екатеринбургского окружного суда И. Сергеевым о гибели царской семьи [21 февраля 1919 г.], Историк и современник, Берлин: 1924, № 5, С. 207-212. Источник документа: Архив новейшей истории России. Серия «Публикации». Т. III. Скорбный путь Романовых (1917-1918 гг.). *Гибель царской семьи*. Сб. документов и материалов. М.: РОССПЭН, 2001.

— Воспоминания красногвардейца караульной команды дома Ипатьева А.А. Стрекотина о расстреле царской семьи [1934], ЦДООСО Ф. 221 Оп. 2. Д. 849. Л. 2-17.

— Кабанов, А.Г., «Последние дни Романовых» and «Последние дни династии Романовых в России» in Жук, *Исповедь цареубийц,* С. 125-151.

— Воспоминания В.Н. Нетребина, состоявшего во внутренней охране дома Ипатьева, о расстреле царской семьи, написанные для Уралистпарта [20 апреля 1925], ЦДООСО Ф. 41 Оп. 1 Д. 149 Л. 167-174 (с об.).

The archives and studies of forensic investigations that were taken in consideration in the description of the events of their martyrdom are:

— Попов, Проф. В.Л., «Исследование состояния зубо-челюстной системы черепов №№ 1-9», at http://purl.flvc.org/fgcu/fd/fgcu_wm_5253

— Nikitin, Dr. Sergey, "Grand Duchess Anastasia is buried in Saint Petersburg, 07/17/1998," Proceedings of the American Academy of Forensic Sciences (AAFS), Annual Meeting, Reno, Nevada, February 21-26, 2000. See also: http://www.searchfoundationinc.org/anastasia-1

— William R. Maples Collection, *DigitalFGVU: Florida Gulf Coast University's Digital Repository,* at https://fgcu.digital.flvc.org (analytic photographic material with forensic evidence).

118 Юровского, ЦДООСО Ф. 221 Оп. 2. Д. 497. 10; АП РФ. Ф. 3. Оп. 58. Д. 280. Л. 12.

119 Воспоминания красногвардейца караульной команды дома Ипатьева А.А. Стрекотина о расстреле царской семьи [1934], ЦДООСО Ф. 221 Оп. 2. Д. 849. Л. 9.

120 *Ibid.*

121 According to a widely known version of the events, Yurovsky asked the family and their companions at this point to take seats suitable for photographing, with a view to using the photograph as an assurance to their relatives that they were safe. However, there is no mention of this in any of the primary sources.

122 Юровского, ЦДООСО Ф. 221 Оп. 2. Д. 497. 10; АП РФ. Ф. 3. Оп. 58. Д. 280. Л. 13.

123 Медведев (Кудрин), Расстрел царской семьи Романовых в Екатеринбурге в ночь на 17 июля 1918 г., [1963], РГАСПИ. Ф. 588. Оп. 3с. Д. 12. Л. 50.

124 *Ibid.*, Л. 50.

125 Воспоминания коменданта дома Ипатьева Я.М. Юровского, «Последний царь нашел свое место», [Апрель-май 1922], АП РФ. Ф. 3. Оп. 58. Д. 280. Л. 13.

126 This poem was written by the poet Sergi Bekhteev in October of 1917 especially for the family that was then in exile in Tobolsk. Bekhteev sent the poem to

the family through Nastenka Hendrikova (See https://soulibre.ru/Сергей_Бехтеев). The English version given in our text is from Christine Benagh, *An Englishman in the Court of the Tsar, The spiritual Journey of Charles Sydney Gibbes*, Conciliar Press, CA, 2000, p. 250-251. Charles Gibbes "recalled the poetic prayer of Countess Hendrikova, herself a martyr, that the family had often read together as their days grew darker. Grand Duchess Olga undertook to translate it into English and had asked Syd to be sure her grammar was correct and her language appropriate, and he kept a copy among his papers," the one given here. This is not a literal translation. The Russian original, from Мельникъ, *Воспоминанiя о Царской Семьѣ и ея жизни до и послѣ революцiи*, Бѣлградъ, 1921, с. 77, is as follows (note the Old pre-revolutionary Orthography):

Пошли намъ, Господи, терпѣнье
Въ годину буйныхъ, мрачныхъ дней
Сносить народное гоненье
И пытки нашихъ палачей.

Дай крѣпость намъ, о Боже правый,
Злодѣйство ближняго прощать
И крестъ тяжелый и кровавый
Съ Твоею кротостью встрѣчать.

И въ дни мятежнаго волненья,
Когда ограбятъ насъ враги,
Терпѣть позоръ и оскорбленья,
Христосъ Спаситель, помоги.

Владыка мiра, Богъ вселенной,
Благослави молитвой насъ
И дай покой душѣ смиренной
Въ невыносимый, страшный часъ.

И у преддверiя могилы
Вдохни въ уста Твоихъ рабовъ
Нечеловѣческiя силы –
Молиться кротко за враговъ.

127 Rappaport, *The Last Days of the Romanovs*, p. 199.
128 Росс, *Гибель царской семьи*, pp. 393-394.
129 *Ibid.*, p. 392.
130 ГА РФ. Ф. 601. Оп. 2. Д. 27. Л. 8-9.
131 Шифрованная телеграмма А.Г. Белобородова секретарю Совнаркома Н.П. Горбунову об участи царской семьи. 17 июля 1918 г., Соколов, *Убийство царской семьи*, С. 310.

132 Ленин, *Биографическая хроника,* Vol. 5, pp. 648-649.
133 Halliburton, *Seven League Boots,* p. 143.
134 «Выписка из письма Великой княжны Ольги Николаевны из Тобольска», *Православная жизнь,* Vol. 7, July 1968. Jordanville, New York: Holy Trinity Monastery, pp. 3-4.
135 Gilliard, *Thirteen Years,* pp. 273-275.
136 In their letters Alexis and Kolya used to write their names backwards. Thus Алексей (Aleksey) was written Йескела (Yeskela).
137 Телекомпания НТВ, *Новые русские сенсации,* «Казнь российской империи», Москва, 2016.
138 Translation by Helen Azar, at http://www.theromanovfamily.com/alexei-romanov-letter-from-tobolsk/
139 This refers to the case of Anna Anderson which continued up to the end of her life in 1984, when it was ascertained by genetic (DNA) testing that Anna Anderson had no connection with the Romanovs.
140 See Coble, M.D., Loreille OM, Wadhams MJ, Edson SM, Maynard K, et al. (2009), Mystery Solved: The Identification of the Two Missing Romanov Children Using DNA Analysis. PLoS ONE 4(3): e4838. doi:10.1371/journal.pone.0004838; Coble, M.D., "The identification of the Romanovs: Can we (finally) put the controversies to rest?." *Investigative genetics* vol. 2,1 20. 26 Sep. 2011, doi:10.1186/2041-2223-2-20; Azar H. and Nelipa M., "Romanov Imperial Bones Revisited: why does doubt remain about who is buried in the St. Petersburg Fortress?," at https://www.academia.edu/7316355
141 See Nikitin, Dr. Sergey, "Grand Duchess Anastasia is buried in Saint Petersburg, 07/17/1998," Proceedings of the American Academy of Forensic Sciences (AAFS), Annual Meeting, Reno, Nevada, February 21-26, 2000, and http://www.searchfoundationinc.org/anastasia-1; Suggested studies on Forensic Facial Reconstruction and Photographic Superimposition: Norman J. Sauer, Amy R. Michael and Todd W. Fenton, "Human Identification Using Skull-Photo Superimposition and Forensic Image Comparison" in Dennis C. Dirkmaat (Ed.), *A Companion to Forensic Anthropology,* New Jersey: Blackwell Publishing Ltd, 2013, pp. 432-446; Gupta S, Gupta V, Vij H, Vij R, Tyagi N. Forensic Facial Reconstruction: The Final Frontier. *J Clin Diagn Res.* 2015;9(9):ZE26–ZE28. doi:10.7860/JCDR/2015/14621.6568
142 1 Samuel 2:30.
143 The Russian Orthodox Church Outside of Russia (Russian: Русская Православная Церковь Заграницей, РПЦЗ, usually known by its English acronym ROCOR), is an autonomous jurisdiction of the Patriarchate of Moscow. It was founded as an Orthodox jurisdiction at the beginning of the decade of the 1920s in response to Soviet policies regarding religion within the Soviet Union. Subsequently, it broke ties with the Moscow Patriarchate in 1927 when the Patriarch of Moscow, Sergius I, declared loyalty to the Soviet state. Finally, on 17 May, 2007, on the Feast of the Ascension of our Lord, the Russian Orthodox Church Outside of Russia signed an Act of Canonical Union with the Patriarchate of Moscow.

NOTES

IN THE WORDS OF THE SAINTS

1. "The Vision of our Holy Father John, Wonderworker of Kronstadt," Translated by Priestmonk Orestes, Christ the Saviour Orthodox Seminary, at http://orthochristian.com/104334.html
2. "The Life of Tsar-Martyr Nicholas II," *The Orthodox Word*, vol. 26, no. 4 (153), July-August, 1990; An online version can be found at https://www.fatheralexander.org/booklets/english/nicholas_ii_e.htm#n11
3. "Miracles of the Royal Martyrs," *The Orthodox Word*, #202. Platina, California: Saint Herman of Alaska Brotherhood, 1998, p. 215. The authors quote from Zhevakhov, N. D., *Recollections of the Assistant Ober-Procurator of the Holy Synod*, Vol. 1.
4. Kontzevitch, *Elder Nektary of Optina*, pp. 90-91.
5. John 16:21.
6. From a hymn in the Orthodox funeral service, composed by St John of Damascus (8th century).
7. Cf. Wisdom 7:1-6.
8. Cf. Sirach 10:4.
9. From the Canon of St Andrew of Crete.
10. Job 1:18.
11. Cf. *ibid.*, 6:12.
12. Cf. *ibid.*, 6:2-3.
13. *Ibid.*, 2:10.
14. *Ibid.*, 1:8.
15. *Ibid.*, 1:3.
16. The Russo-Japanese War, 1904-1905.
17. Ps. 35:1 (KJV).
18. Maximov and Ford, *St. Tikhon of Moscow*, pp. 179-182.
19. Новоспасский Монастырь, *Деяния Священного Собора Православной Российской Церкви 1917-1918 гг*, т. 9, Москва, 1994-2000 гг. pp. 182-183. The last quote in the sermon is from: Luke 11:28.
20. Maximov and Ford, *St. Tikhon of Moscow*, pp. 200-205. The sermon was originally printed in *Американский Православный Вестник*, 1905, #10, pp. 184-186.
21. See 1 Samuel 8:5, 19-20.
22. Ps. 72:1-2, 4, 12 (KJV).
23. Source unknown.
24. See Woolley, *Coronation Rites*, p. 154.
25. This is an old Russian proverb.
26. Note from source: "From an edict issued by Tsar Nicolas II to the Minister of the Interior A. G. Buligin in 1905. This edict laid the ground for the creation of the parliament or Duma in Russia."
27. According to the Old Calendar, the martyrdom of the Royal Family took place on 4 July, the day of commemoration of Saint Andrew of Crete.
28. His memory is celebrated on 17 October of the Church Calendar [which the Russian Church celebrates on 30 October of the Civil Calendar].

29 Tsar Alexis Mikhailovich Romanov the Meek (1645-1676), son and heir of the first Tsar of the Romanov dynasty, Michael Feodorovich Romanov.
30 See the section of this present work, "Portrait of a Tsar."
31 Saint John refers to the official cause of the mobilization of the Russian armies on the threshold of the First World War, which was the defense of the Serbian minority of the Austro-Hungarian Empire. See the section of this present work, "World War: The Great Heart of Russia Beats."
32 In 1915 the territory of ancient Kiev was recovered, which had been under Austro-Hungarian occupation for nearly a thousand years. The situation changed once more after the events of 1917.
33 Matthew 27:25.
34 John Maximovitch, Saint, "In Memory of the Royal Martyrs, Sermon given by His Eminence John, Bishop of Shanghai, during the memorial service for Tsar Nicholas II and those slain with him," *Orthodox Life,* Vol. 45/4, July – August 1995. Jordanville, New York: Holy Trinity Monastery. Primary source Церковная жизнь, #8, 1934. Republished in Православная Русь, #12, 1994.

EPILOGUE

1 Тройницкий, *Первая всеобщая перепись населенія Россійской Имперіи.* С.-Петербург: Изданіе центральнаго статистическаго комитета министерства внутреннихъ делъ, 1905.
2 Goulévitch, *Tsarisme et Révolution,* pp. 99-100.
3 Kennard, *The Russian Year Book 1911,* p. 59.
4 Pipes, *The Russian Revolution,* pp. 88-89.
5 Churchill, *The World Crisis 1916-1918,* Vol. 3, p. 224.

BIBLIOGRAPHY

Acton, Edward, Vladimir Iu. Cherniaev and William G. Rosenberg, (eds.), *Critical companion to the Russian Revolution, 1914-1921.* Bloomington: Indiana University Press, 1997.

Almedingen, Edith M., *An Unbroken Unity, A Memoir of Grand Duchess Serge of Russia 1864-1917.* London: The Bodley Head, 1964.

Angelis, Steven de, (transl. and ed.), *Empress Alexandra Feodorovna, Her Diaries: 1917&1918.* United States: Bookemon, 2016.

Azar, Helen, (transl. and ed.), *The Diary of Olga Romanov: Royal Witness to the Russian Revolution.* Pensylvania: Westholme, 2013.

– *Maria and Anastasia, The Youngest Romanov Grand Duchesses in Their Own Words: Letters, Diaries, Postcards.* United States: CreateSpace Independent Publishing Platform, 2015.

– *Journal of a Russian Grand Duchess: Complete Annotated 1913 Diary of Olga Romanov, Eldest Daughter of the Last Tsar.* United States: CreateSpace Independent Publishing Platform, 2015.

– *1913 Diary of Grand Duchess Maria Nikolaevna.* United States: CreateSpace Independent Publishing Platform, 2017.

– *In the Steps of the Romanovs: Final two years of the Russian Imperial Family 1916-1918.* United States: CreateSpace Independent Publishing Platform, 2018.

– and Eva & Dan McDonald, (transls. and eds.), *Russia's Last Romanovs: In Their Own Words.* United States: CreateSpace Independent Publishing Platform, 2013.

– and Nicholas B. A. Nicholson, (transls. and eds.), *Tatiana Romanov, Daughter of the Last Tsar: Diaries and Letters 1913-1918.* Pensylvania: Westholme, 2015.

Benagh, Christine, *An Englishman at the Court of the Tsar.* Ben Lomond, California: Conciliar Press, 2000.

Benckendorff, Count Paul, *Last Days at Tsarskoye Selo.* London: William Heinemann, 1927.

Bing, Edward J., (ed.), *The Letters of Tsar Nicholas and Empress Marie.* London: Nicholson and Watson, 1937.

Buxhoeveden, Baroness Sophie, *Left Behind: Fourteen Months in Siberia during the Revolution, December 1917-February 1919.* London: Longmans, Green and Co., 1919.

– *The Life and Tragedy of Alexandra Feodorovna*. London: Longmans, Green and Co., 1928.
Churchill, Winston S., *The World Crisis*, Vols. 1-5. London: Thornton Butterworth, 1923-1931.
Damascene (Orlovsky), Archimandrite, "Blessed Prascovia Ivanovna of Sarov", *New Confessors of Russia*, Vol. 1. Platina, California: Saint Herman of Alaska Brotherhood, 1998.
Dehn, Lili, *The Real Tsaritsa*. London: Thornton Butterworth, 1922.
Eagar, Margaretta, *Six Years at the Russian Court*. London: Hurst & Blackett, 1906.
Eugénie de Grèce, *Le tsarévitch: Enfant Martyr*. Paris: Perrin, 1990.
Fabrisky, Semyon S., *Of Bygone Days: The Memoirs of an Aide-de-Camp to the Emperor Nicholas II*. Ontario: Gilbert's Books, 2016.
Fischer, Louis, *The Life of Lenin*. New York: Harper Colophon Books, 1965.
Florinsky, Michael T., *The End of the Russian Empire*. New York: Collier Books, 1961.
– *Russia: A History and an Interpretation*, Vols. I-II. New York: Macmillan, 1964.
Fuhrmann, Joseph T., (ed.), *The Complete Wartime Correspondence of Tsar Nicholas II and the Empress Alexandra, April 1914-March 1917*. Westport, Connecticut: Greenwood, 1999.
Fülöp-Miller, René, *Rasputin: The Holy Devil*. New York: Garden City, 1928.
Gilliard, Pierre, *Thirteen Years at the Russian Court*. New York: George H. Doran, 1923.
Goar, Jacobus, Εὐχολόγιον *sive Rituale Græcorum*. Ex Typographia Bartholomæi Javarina: Venetiis, 1730.
Goulévitch, Arsène de, *Tsarisme et Révolution: du passé à l'avenir de la Russie*. Alexis Redier (Editeur), Paris, 1931.
Halliburton, Richard, *Seven League Boots*. London: Unwin, 1936.
Hanbury-Williams, Major General Sir John, *The Emperor Nicholas II as I Knew Him*. London: Arthur L. Humphreys, 1922.
Izvolsky, Alexander, *Recollections of a Foreign Minister*. Garden City, New York: Doubleday Page, 1921.
Kennard, Howard P., *The Russian Year Book 1911*. London: Eyre & Spottiswood Ltd, 1912.
Kenworthy, Scott M., *The Heart of Russia: Trinity-Sergius, Monasticism and Society after 1825*. New York: Oxford University Press, 2010.
Kerensky, Alexander, *The Catastrophe: Kerensky's Own Story of the Russian Revolution*. New York: D. Appleton & Co., 1927.
– *The Crucifixion of Liberty*. New York: Day, 1934.
– and Paul Bulygin, *The Murder of the Romanovs*. London: Hutchinson, 1935.
Kobylinsky, Colonel Eugene, "The Depositions of Colonel Kobylinski" in Robert Wilton, *The Last Days of the Romanovs*. London: Thornton Butterworth, 1920.
Kontzevitch, Helen, *Saint Seraphim Wonderworker of Sarov*. Wildwood: Saint Xenia Skete, 2004.

BIBLIOGRAPHY

Kontzevitch, Ivan, *Elder Nektary of Optina*. Platina, California: Saint Herman of Alaska Brotherhood, 1999.

Lieven, Dominic, *Nicholas II: Emperor of all the Russias*. London: John Murray, 1993.

– *Towards the Flame: Empire, War and the end of Tsarist Russia*. London: Penguin Books, 2015.

Ludendorff, Erich, *My War Memories*, 1914-1918, Vols. I-II. London: Hutchinson, 1919.

Mansergh, Nicholas, *The Coming of the First World War*. New York: Longmans, Green and Co., 1949.

Massie, Robert, *Nicholas and Alexandra*. New York: Random House, 2000.

– *The Final Chapter*. New York: Random House, 1995.

– (ed.), *The Last Diary of Tsaritsa Alexandra*. London: Yale University Press, 1997.

Maximov, Alex, and Dr David C. Ford, (transls. and eds.), *St. Tikhon of Moscow: Instructions and Teachings for the American Orthodox Faithful (1898-1907)*. Pensylvania: St Tikhon's Monastery Press, 2016.

Maylunas, Andrei, and Sergei Mironenko, (transls. and eds.), *A Lifelong Passion: Nicholas and Alexandra, Their Own Story*. London: Phoenix Giant, 1997.

Mazour, Anatole G., *Rise and Fall of the Romanovs*. Princeton: Van Nostrand, 1960.

McCullagh, Francis, *A Prisoner of the Reds: The Story of a British Officer Captured in Siberia*. London: John Murray, 1921.

Michailitschenko, Protodeacon Leonid, (transl.), *The Romanovs Under House Arrest: The Diary of Archpriest Afanasy I. Belyaev*. Jordanville, New York: Holy Trinity Publications, 2018.

Millar, Lyubov, *Grand Duchess Elizabeth of Russia: New Martyr of the Communist Yoke*. Redding, California: Nikodemos Orthodox Publication Society, 1991.

Mitrovic, Andrej, *Serbia's Great War: 1914-1918*. Indiana: Purdue University Press, 2007.

Mossolov, Alexander, *At the Court of the Last Tsar*. London: Metheun, 1935.

Nelipa, Margarita, *Killing Rasputin, The murder that ended the Russian Empire*. Denver, Colorado: Wild Blue Press, 2017.

Olsoufieff, Countess Alexandra, *H.I.H. The Grand Duchess Elisabeth Feodorovna of Russia*. London: John Murray, 1925.

Paleologue, Maurice, *An Ambassador's Memoirs*, Vols. I-III. New York: Doran, 1925.

Pares, Bernard, *A History of Russia*. London: Jonathan Cape, 1947.

– *The Fall of the Russian Monarchy*. New York: Vintage Books, 1961.

Payne, Robert, *The Life and Death of Lenin*. New York: Simon and Schuster, 1964.

Pipes, Richard, *The Russian Revolution*. New York: Knopf, 1990.

Polsky, Archpriest Michael, *The New Martyrs of Russia*. Wildwood, Alberta: Monastery Press, 2000.

Price, Kent de, (transl. and ed.), "Diary of Nicholas II, 1917-1918, an annotated translation", *Theses, Dissertations, Professional Papers,* Paper 2065. University of Montana, 1966.

Radzinsky, Edvard, *The Last Tsar: The Life and Death of Nicholas II.* New York: Doubleday, 1992.

Rappaport, Helen, *The Last Days of the Romanovs: Tragedy at Ekaterinburg.* New York: St. Martin's Griffin, 2008.

– *Four Sisters: The Lost Lives of the Romanov Grand Duchesses.* London: Macmillan, 2014.

– *The Race to Save the Romanovs: The Truth Behind the Secret Plans to Rescue Russia's Imperial Family.* London: Hutchinson, 2018.

Ruud, Charles A., and Sergei A. Stepanov, *Fontanka 16, The Tsar's secret police.* London: McGill-Queen's University Press, 1999.

Saint Herman of Alaska Brotherhood, *The Royal Passion-bearers of Russia: Their Life and Service.* Platina, California, 2014.

Shakespeare, William, *The Tragedy of King Richard II,* London: J. M. Dent and Co, 1895.

Smith, Douglas, *Former People: The Last Days of the Russian Aristocracy.* London: Macmillan, 2012.

Speranski, Valentin, *La 'Maison à destination spéciale'.* Paris: J. Ferenczi et Fils, 1929.

Spiridovitch, Général Alexandre, *Last Years of the Court at Tsarskoe Selo,* Vols. I-II. Ontario: Royal Russia, 2010-2017; *Les derniers années de la cour de Tsarskoe Selo,* Vols. I-II. Paris: Payot, 1928, unpublished English translation from French, by Robert Moshein, Texas, 2005.

– *Histoire du Terrorisme Russe 1886-1917* (traduit du russe par Vladimir Lazarevski). Paris: Payot, 1939.

Steinberg, Mark, and Vladimir Khrustalev, *The Fall of the Romanovs: Political Dreams and Personal Struggles in a Time of Revolution.* New Haven, Connecticut: Yale University Press, 1995.

Trewin, J. C., *The House of Special Purpose.* London: Macmillan, 1975.

Volkov, Alexei, *Memories of Alexei Volkov, Personal Valet to Tsarina Alexandra Feodorovna 1910-1918.* Translation from French by Robert Moshein, Texas, 2004. Retrieved March 19, 2018, from https://www.alexanderpalace.org/volkov

Vidal, Gore, *Palimpsest, A Memoir.* London: Abacus, 1996.

Vorres, Ian, *The Last Grand Duchess.* Toronto: Key Porter, 2001.

Vyrubova, Anna, *Memories of the Russian Court.* New York: Macmillan, 1923.

Wilton, Robert, *The Last Days of the Romanovs.* London: Thornton Butterworth, 1920.

Witte, Count Sergius, *Memoirs.* Translated and edited by Abraham Yarmolinsky. New York: Doubleday, Page & Company, 1921.

Woolley, Reginald Maxwell, *Coronation Rites.* Cambridge: University Press, 1915.

BIBLIOGRAPHY

RUSSIAN SOURCES

Авдонин А. Н., *Ганина яма: История поисков останков царской семьи.* Екатеринбург: Компания «Реал-Медиа», 2013.

Алферьев, Е. Е., *Император Николай II как человек сильной воли.* Нью-Йорк: Свято-Троицкий монастырь Джорданвилль, 1983.

Архив новейшей истории России, Серия «Публикации». Т. III. Скорбный путь Романовых (1917-1918 гг.) Гибель царской семьи: Сборник документов и материалов / Отв. ред. и сост. В. М. Хрусталёв, при участии М. Д. Стейнберга, *Москва:* РОССПЭН, 2001.

Архив Русской революции (АРР), 22 т., Берлин: Г. В. Гессеном, 1922.

Бескровный, Л. Г., *Армия и флот России в начале ХХ века.* Москва: Наука, 1986.

Бразоль, Б. Л., *Царствование Императора Николая II в цифрах и фактах. 1894-1917. Ответ клеветникам, расчленителям и русофобам.* Нью-Йорк, 1959.

Брачев, В. С., *Русское масонство XVIII-XX веков.* Санкт-Петербург: Стома, 2000.

Булыгин, П. П., *Убийство Романовых.* Москва: «Академия», 2001.

Воейков, В. Н., *С Царем и без Царя: Воспоминания последнего дворцового коменданта государя императора Николая II.* Москва: Воениздат, 1995.

Данилов, Ю., *Великий Князь Николай Николаевич.* Париж, 1930.

Деникин, А. И., *Очерки Русской смуты. Крушение власти и армии. Февраль-сентябрь 1917г.* Москва: Наука, 1991.

Ипатьев, В., *Работа химической промышленности на оборону во время мировой войны.* Петроград, 1920.

Кобылин, В., *Анатомия измены. Император Николай II и Генерал-адъютант М. В. Алексеев. Истоки антимонархического заговора.* Под редакцией Л. Е. Болотина. Санкт-Петербург, 1998.

Ленин, Владимир Ильич, *Биографическая хроника,* Том 5. Москва: Издательство политической литературы, 1974.

Жук, Ю. А. (Авт.- Сост.), *Исповедь цареубийц. Подлинная история великой трагедии. Убийство Царской Семьи в материалах предварительного следствия и воспоминаниях лиц, причастных к совершению этого преступления.* Москва: ООО «Издательский дом "Вече"», 2008.

Лемке, М. К., *250 дней в царской ставке: (25 сентября 1915 – 2 июля 1916 г.г.).* Петербург, 1920.

Лященко, П. И., *История народного хозяйства СССР,* Т. 2. Москва: ГИПЛ, 1956.

Марков, О. Д., *Русская армия 1914-1917.* Санкт-Петербург, 2001.

Мельгунов, С. П., *На путях к дворцовому перевороту (Заговоры перед революцией 1917 года).* Париж: Родина, 1931.

Международные Отношения в Эпоху Империализма: Документы из Архивов Царского и Временного Правительств 1878-1917 гг., Сер. 3: 1914-1917. Москва: Гос. соц.- экон. изд-во, 1938.

Мельник-Боткина, Татьяна, *Воспоминания о царской семьѣ и ея жизни до и послѣ революціи.* Бѣлградъ: Стефановичъ и ко., 1921.

– *Воспоминания о царской семье.* Москва: Захаров, 2009.

Милюков, П. Н., *Воспоминания.* Москва: Издательство Политической литературы, 1991.

Мироненко С. В. (отв. ред.), *Дневники императора Николая II 1894-1918,* 3 т. Серия «Бумаги дома Романовых». Москва: Российская политическая энциклопедия (РОССПЭН), 2011-2013.

Мультатули, П. В., *Господь да благословит решение мое: Император Николай II во главе действующей армии и заговор генералов.* Москва: НТЦ «Форум», 2007.

– *Император Николай II и заговор 17-го года: Как свергали монархию в России.* Москва: «Вече», 2013.

– *Дай Бог, только не втянуться в войну! Император Николай II и предвоенный кризис 1914 года: Факты против мифов.* Москва: Российский институт стратегических исследований, 2014.

– *Внешняя политика Императора Николая II: 1894-1917 гг. Этапы, достижения, итоги.* Москва: Изд-во М.Б. Смолина, 2019.

Начало войны 1914 г. Поденная запись б. Министерства Иностранных Дел "Красный архив", Т.4. изд. Центрархив, 1923.

Новоспасский Монастырь, *Деяния Священного Собора Православной Российской Церкви 1917-1918 гг.* Т. 9, Москва, 1994-2000 гг.

Ольденбург, С. С., *Царствование Императора Николая II,* 2 т. Белград: О-во распространения рус. нац. и патриот. лит., 1939.

Отречение Николая II: Воспоминания очевидцев, документы / Ред. П. Е. Щеголева; Вступ. ст. Л. Китаева и [М. Е. Кольцова]. - 2-е изд., доп. - Ленинград: Издательство "Красная газета", 1927.

Очерки истории Ленинграда, 6 т. Москва: Академия Наук СССР. 1955-1965.

Панкратов, В. С., *С царем в Тобольске: Из воспоминаний.* Москва: Слово, 1990.

Полное Собрание Законов Российской Империи, Собрание третье, Т. 25, Отд-ние 1: От № 25605 - 27172 и Дополнения, Санктпетербург, 1908.

Раппопорт С. А. (Ан-ский), *Моё знакомство с Г. Гапоном.* Собрание сочинений, С.-Петербург: Книгоиздательское Товарищество "Просвещение", 1913, Т. 5. Retrieved from http://www.az.lib.ru/a/anskij_s_a/text_1909_moyo_znakomstvo_s_gaponom.shtml

Росс, Н. Г. (Сост.), *Гибель царской семьи. Материалы следствия по делу об убийстве царской семьи (август 1918 – февраль 1920).* Франкфурт-на-Майне: Посев, 1987.

Смирнов, А. Ф., *Государственная Дума Российской империи, 1906-1917.* Москва: Книга и бизнес, 1998.

Соколов, Н. А., *Предварительное следствие, 1919-1922 гг.* Сост. Л. А. Лыкова. // Российский Архив: История Отечества в свидетельствах и документах XVIII-XX вв., РЦХИДНИ, Москва: Студия «Тритэ», 1998.

– *Дело об убийстве царской семьи в Екатеринбурге,* 1918-1919, in *Agnes M. Diterichs Papers 1919–1922.* Jordanville, New York: Holy Trinity Orthodox Seminary.

Сургучев, И. Д., "Детские годы Императора Николая II", *Бежин Луг,* № 1 (1992).

Тройницкий, Н. А. (Ред.), *Первая всеобщая перепись населенія Россійской Имперіи.* С.-Петербург: Изданіе центральнаго статистическаго комитета министерства внутреннихъ делъ, 1905.

Трусовой, Н. С., (Под. ред.), *Начало первой русской революции. январь – март 1905 г. (Революция 1905-1907 гг. в России. Документы и материалы).* Москва: Изд. Академии наук СССР, 1955.

Уткин, А. И., *Первая Мировая война.* Москва: Алгоритм, 2001.

Хрусталёв, В. М., *Романовы: Последние дни великой династии.* Москва: АСТ, 2013.

– *Великий Князь Михаил Александрович.* Москва: «Вече», 2008.

Царственные мученики в воспоминаниях верноподданных. Москва: Сретенский монастырь, Новая книга, Ковчег, 1999.

Шавельский, Г. И., *Воспоминания последнего протопресвитера русской армии и флота,* 2 т. Нью-Йорк: Издательство им. Чехова, 1954.

Шереметев, Д. С., *Изъ Воспоминаній о Государѣ Императорѣ Николаѣ II.* Брюссель, 1936.

Яковлев, Н. Н., *1 августа 1914.* Москва: Москвитянин 1993.

ARCHIVAL DOCUMENTS ON THE MURDER IN EKATERINBURG

Воспоминания В. В. Яковлева (Стоянович-Мячин, «Антон»), «Перевозка Николая Романова из Тобольска в Екатеринбург», ГА РФ. Ф. 601. Оп. 2. Д. 31. Л. 26-73, 75-81 об.

Воспоминания В. Н. Нетребина, состоявшего во внутренней охране дома Ипатьева, о расстреле царской семьи, написанные для Уралистпарта [20 апреля 1925], ЦДООСО Ф. 41 Оп. 1 Д. 149 Л. 167-174 (с об.).

Воспоминания коменданта дома Ипатьева Я. М. Юровского, «Последний царь нашел свое место», [Апрель-май 1922], АП РФ. Ф. 3. Оп. 58. Д. 280. Л. 2-22.

Воспоминания красногвардейца караульной команды дома Ипатьева А. А. Стрекотина о расстреле царской семьи [1934], ЦДООСО Ф. 221 Оп. 2. Д. 849. Л. 2-17.

Воспоминания М. А. Медведева (Кудрина) о расстреле царской семьи

[1957], РГАСПИ. Ф. 588. Оп. 3с. Д. 12. Л. 1-36.

Воспоминания П. З. Ермакова, «Расстрел бывшего царя», ЦДООСО. Ф. 221. Оп. 2. Д. 774. Л. 7-12.

Записка коменданта дома Ипатьева Я. М. Юровского о расстреле царской семьи и о попытках спрятать трупы [1920-е гг.], ЦДООСО Ф. 221 Оп. 2. Д. 497. 9-15.

Запись беседы с И. И. Родзинским о расстреле царской семьи, сделанная в Радиокомитете по распоряжению ЦК КПСС, РГАСПИ. Ф. 588. Оп. 3. Д. 14. Л. 26.

Из рассказа Я. М. Юровского о расстреле царской семьи на совещании старых большевиков в г. Свердловске [1 февраля 1934 г.], ЦДООСО. Ф. 41. Оп. 1. Д. 151. Л. 10-22.

Кабанов, А. Г., «Последние дни Романовых» and «Последние дни династии Романовых в России», в Жук, *Исповедь цареубийц*, С. 125-151.

Материалы следственного дела об убийстве императорской семьи в Екатеринбурге и Алапаевске, ГА РФ. Ф. 601. Оп. 2. Д. 51.

Медведев, М. А. (Кудрин), Расстрел царской семьи Романовых в Екатеринбурге в ночь на 17 июля 1918 г., [1963], РГАСПИ. Ф. 588. Оп. 3с. Д. 12. Л. 39-58.

Протокол допроса бывшего охранника Ипатьевского дома П. С. Медведева членом Екатеринбургского окружного суда И. Сергеевым о гибели царской семьи [21 февраля 1919 г.], Историк и современник, Берлин: 1924, № 5, С. 207-212.

ARTICLES

Ashton, Janet, "God in All Things: The Religious Beliefs of Russia's Last Empress and Their Personal and Political Context", *Electronic British Library* (2006), art. 4, https://www.bl.uk/eblj/2006articles/article4.html

"Bodies of Czar and Family Burned by Sulphuric Acid", *The Healdsburg Tribune,* March 4, 1920, p. 7.

Coudert, Amalia Kussner, "The Human Side of the Tsar", *Century Magazine,* Vol. LXXII. New York: The Century Co., 1906, pp. 845-855.

"Czar Rewards Father John", *New York Times,* August 27, 1904, p. 6.

"Czar to appeal for the remains of Russian saint to turn the fortunes of his Manchurian legions", *The San Francisco Call,* May 7, 1905, p. 1.

Dominick, Jesse, "In Memory of the Royal Martyrs, Through Personal Testimony". Retrieved July 30, 2017, from http://www.orthochristian.com/80716.html

Hapgood, Isabel F., "Russia's Czarina", *Harper's Bazaar,* Vol. XL, No. 2, New York: Hearst Corp., February 1906.

John Maximovitch, Saint, "In Memory of the Royal Martyrs, Sermon given by His Eminence John, Bishop of Shanghai, during the memorial service for Tsar Nicholas II and those slain with him", *Orthodox Life,* Vol. 45/4, July-August 1995. Jordanville, New York: Holy Trinity Monastery. Primary source Церковная жизнь, Вып. 8, 1934. Republished in Православная Русь, Вып. 12, 1994.

Kirill, Patriarch of Moscow and all Rus, "The Fates of Russians and Serbs Have Been Intertwined by Divine Providence". Retrieved January 20, 2019, from http://pravoslavie.ru/106399.html

Liebmann, R. Monk Zachariah, "Martyrology of the Communist Yoke: The Life of Tsar-Martyr Nicholas II", *The Orthodox Word,* #153. Platina, California: Saint Herman of Alaska Brotherhood, 1990.

"Miracles of the Royal Martyrs", *The Orthodox Word,* #202. Platina, California: Saint Herman of Alaska Brotherhood, 1998.

"President recalls WW1 retreat, thanks Greece, other allies", Radio Difuzno Preduzeće B92 Akcionarsko Društvo, Beograd (Zemun). Retrieved January 20, 2019, from https://www.b92.net/eng/news/politics.php?yyyy=2016&mm=04&dd=18&nav_id=97720

Sarandinaki, Peter, "Captain Peter Sarandinaki of SEARCH", an interview by Bob Atchison, Retrieved April 18, 2018, from http://forum.alexanderpalace.org/index.php?topic=1902.msg38192#msg38192

"St. Seraphim's Gift", *The Washington Post,* July 14, 1907, p. 13.

"The Vision of our Holy Father John, Wonderworker of Kronstadt". Retrieved October 15, 2017, from http://orthochristian.com/104334.html

"Tsar-Martyr Nicholas II And His Family", St Nicholas Russian Orthodox Church, McKinney, Texas. Retrieved August 15, 2017 from https://www.orthodox.net/russiannm/nicholas-ii-tsar-martyr-and-his-family.html

"Выписка из письма Великой княжны Ольги Николаевны из Тобольска", *Православная Жизнь,* Вып. 7. Jordanville, New York: Holy Trinity Russian Orthodox Monastery, July 1968.

Керенский, А. Ф., "Россия на историческом повороте", *Вопросы истории,* 1990, № 6. Москва: Наука.

Николаев, А. Б., "Кто профинансировал Февральскую революцию", *Национальные интересы,* № 2, 2007.

"Переписка Царственныхъ Мучениковъ съ Вел. Кн. Ксеніей Александровной", *Православная Жизнь,* Вып. 1. Jordanville, New York: Holy Trinity Russian Orthodox Monastery, July 1961.

Риазофор-Монах Анемподист, "Священномученик митрополит Владимир (Богоявленский) и борьба с революции," *Православная Жизнь,* 53, N 1 (636), Январь, 2003.

Седова, Яна, "В Плену Мифов и Стереотипов," *Наша Страна,* 17 July, 2010.

Холяев, С. В., "Три февраля 1917 года", *Вопросы истории,* 2003, №7, Москва: Наука.

Шумило, Светлана, & Виктор Сальник, "Нет больше той любви, как если кто положит душу свою за други своя". Retrieved January 20, 2019 from http://catacomb.org.ua/modules.php?name=Pages&go=page&pid=966

SCIENTIFIC STUDIES AND ARTICLES

Coble, MD., The identification of the Romanovs: Can we (finally) put the controversies to rest? *Investigative Genetics* 2011, 2:20.

Coble, MD., Loreille OM, Wadhams MJ, Edson SM, Maynard K, et al. (2009), Mystery Solved: The Identification of the Two Missing Romanov Children Using DNA Analysis. PLoS ONE 4(3): e4838. doi:10.1371/journal.pone.0004838.

Gupta S, Gupta V, Vij H, Vij R, Tyagi N. Forensic Facial Reconstruction: The Final Frontier. *J Clin Diagn Res.* 2015;9(9):ZE26–ZE28. doi:10.7860/JCDR/2015/14621.6568

Kolesnikov, Lev L. et al, Anatomical Appraisal of the Skulls and Teeth Associated with the Family of Tsar Nicolay Romanov, *The Anatomical Record* (New Anat.) 265:15-32, 2001.

Nikitin, Dr. Sergey, "Grand Duchess Anastasia is buried in Saint Petersburg, 07/17/1998", Proceedings of the American Academy of Forensic Sciences (AAFS), Annual Meeting, Reno, Nevada, February 21-26, 2000.

Norman J. Sauer, Amy R. Michael and Todd W. Fenton, "Human Identification Using Skull-Photo Superimposition and Forensic Image Comparison" in Dennis C. Dirkmaat (ed.), *A Companion to Forensic Anthropology.* New Jersey: Blackwell Publishing Ltd, 2013.

Попов, Профессор В.Л., "Исследование состояния зубо-челюстной системы черепов NoNo 1-9". Persistent link to this record: http://purl.flvc.org/fgcu/fd/fgcu_wm_5253

MULTIMEDIA SOURCES

Sarandinaki, Captain Peter (President of SEARCH Foundation, Inc.), and Dr Michael Coble (former Chief Scientist, US Armed Forces DNA Laboratory), *The search for the remains and identification of the two missing Romanov Children and Grand Duke Mikhail Romanov,* Washington, D.C.: Russian Orthodox Cathedral of St John the Baptist, 2016, @ http://www.searchfoundationinc.org/video-lecture

William R. Maples Collection, *DigitalFGVU: Florida Gulf Coast University's Digital Repository,* @ https://fgcu.digital.flvc.org

Star Media, *Первая мировая,* Сер. 1-8, Сценарий: М. Бандиленко, Режиссеры: А. Верещагин, А. Федосов. Художник-постановщик: А. Якимов. Продюсеры: В. Бабич, В. Ряшин, К. Эрнст, С. Титинков, Москва: 2014.

Телекомпания НТВ, Новые русские сенсации, "Казнь российской империи", Москва, 2016, @ www.youtube.com/watch?v=AJM4iM9PBCU

VISIT THE WEBSITE
OF THE ROMANOV ROYAL MARTYRS PROJECT

WWW.ROMANOVS.EU

VIDEOS
Watch our special Romanov video productions.

PHOTO GALLERY
Enjoy a selection of high-quality colored pictures and archival photo collections.

ARTICLES
Read our articles and discover historical and spiritual truths.

Original Theme Song. A soul-penetrating ballad featuring piano and violin. A song that will bring tears to your eyes.

WATCH, LISTEN & DOWNLOAD AT:
www.romanovs.eu/july-winter-tears

In the Path of Love & Blood

A special edition featuring 30 minutes of high-quality newsreel footage from the Russian State Documentary Film & Photo Archive (RGAKFD). The documentary features footage from the Stantart, the Crimea, the White Flower Day festival, Easter at Livadia, the Romanov Dynasty Tercentenary Celebrations, World War I, and much more.
Total runtime: 40 mins.

WATCH CLIPS AND ORDER AT:
www.romanovs.eu/path-of-love